The Green London Way

To Thomas, Matthew and Joel: and to all those who struggled to preserve the open spaces of London for their generation.

BOB GILBERT

The Green London Way

Bob Gilbert

Lawrence and Wishart London 2012

Lawrence and Wishart Limited
99a Wallis Road
London
E9 5LN

First published 1991 Reprinted 1994
New edition 2012
© Bob Gilbert 1991, 2012
Maps © Graham Scrivener 1991, 2012

British Library Cataloguing in Publication Data.
A catalogue record for this book is available from the British Library

ISBN 9781 907103 452

Contents

Acknowledgements

In preparing this new edition of *The Green London Way* I would like to thank all those who attempted sections of the walk alongside me: Gareth Harper, Ken Worpole, Joel Gilbert, Richard Juneman, Eileen Abbott, Rowan and Lara. Thanks also to my parents-in-law, David and Christine, for giving me somewhere quiet to escape to when I most needed it, and especial thanks, once again, to Graham Scrivener for his hand-drawn maps – and for remaining my friend all those years since we worked on the first edition together. And finally to Jane Hodges – for her love and support.

Bob Gilbert

My thanks go to Leslie Cackett, Master Typographer, late of the London College of Printing who taught me everything there was to know about Hand Lettering and Typography and to Flora Wilson, my wife, without whose support the maps would never have been completed.

Graham Scrivener

Sources

The following list covers some of the main London-wide books which have been invaluable sources of information. It does not include the many local texts referred to in individual chapters.

Brooks, J.A., *Ghosts of London* (2 volumes), Jarrold 1982
Clark, J., *In Our Grandmother's Footsteps*, Virago 1984
Crowe, A., *Parks and Woodlands of London*, Fourth Estate 1987
Fitter, R.S., *London's Natural History*, Collins 1945
Hudson, W.H., *Birds in London*, Longmans, Green and Co, 1898
Jones, E. and Woodward, C., *A Guide to the Architecture of London*, 3rd edition, Seven Dials 2000
Meller, Hugh, *London's Cemeteries*, Avebury 1983
Ordnance Survey and Taylor, P., *Old Ordnance Survey Maps (The London Sheets)*, Alan Godfrey Sexby, Lt-Col J., *The Municipal Parks, Gardens and Open Spaces of London; Their History and Associations*, Elliot Stock 1905
Weinreb, B., and Hibbert, C., *The London Encyclopedia*, Papermac

List of Maps

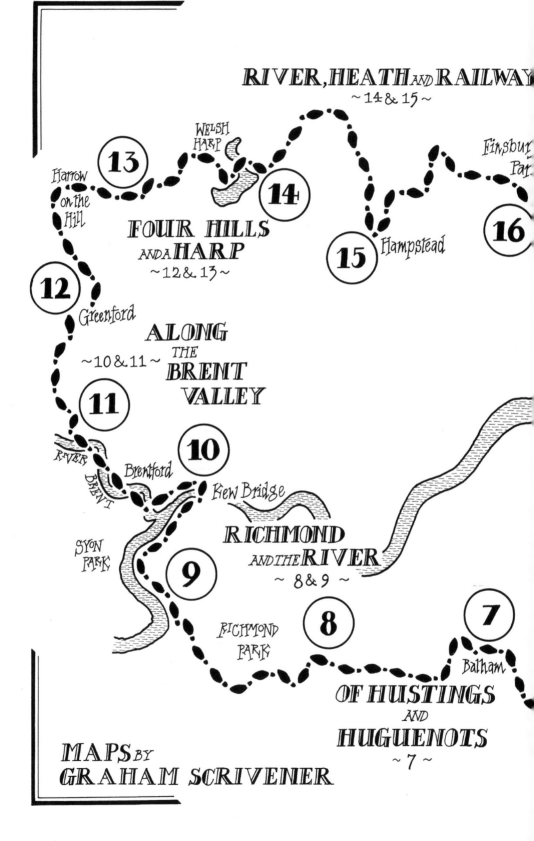

RIVER, HEATH AND RAILWAY
~ 14 & 15 ~

WELSH HARP

13

Finsbury Park

Harrow on the Hill

14

FOUR HILLS AND A HARP
~ 12 & 13 ~

16

15 Hampstead

12

Greenford

ALONG THE BRENT VALLEY
~ 10 & 11 ~

11

10

RIVER BRENT

Brentford

Kew Bridge

SYON PARK

9

RICHMOND AND THE RIVER
~ 8 & 9 ~

7

8

RICHMOND PARK

Balham

OF HUSTINGS AND HUGUENOTS
~ 7 ~

MAPS BY GRAHAM SCRIVENER

THE GREEN LONDON WAY

VICTORIAN PARKS AND MEDIEVAL MARSHES ~16 & 17~

17

RIVER LEA

START FINISH

FROM THE LEA TO THE LEVELS ~1~

18

VICTORIA PARK

Stratford

Beckton

AROUND THE BOW BACK RIVERS ~18~

2

4

Woolwich

THE PEASANTS HEATH AND THE COMMONERS HILL ~4~

OF PIG KEEPERS AND PALACES ~3~

SHOOTERS HILL

3

WOOLWICH AND THE WOODLANDS ~2~

5

THE COLLEGE, THE PALACE AND THE COMMONS ~5 & 6~

STREATHAM COMMON

Crystal Palace

6

N
W E
S

© SCRIY 2012

Introduction

CHANGING LONDON

Originally published in 1991, *The Green London Way* was the first long-distance footpath encircling London – and one of the first entirely urban long-distance footpaths in the country. In a dynamic city such as London – and London is one of the most dynamic capital cities in the world – it is inevitable that there have been considerable changes since then, and one of the most significant changes has been in our attitude to urban walking itself. What was once regarded as a rather cranky idea has now been enthusiastically embraced – including by some of those who rejected it at the time – and it even has its own celebrity adherents. This acceptance of the value of urban walking in its own right, and not just as a poor relation of a 'real' rural walk, can only be welcomed. It marks a change in attitude, an acceptance of a different sort of landscape, and a realisation of the richness that an urban exploration has to offer. It has led not just to an increase in the usage of London's paths, and therefore to a greater likelihood of their preservation, but also to the opening up of a number of new routes, including some through areas previously inaccessible. This new edition of *The Green London Way* has made full use of these – from the new route down the Wandle in west London through to the New River Path in the east. If there is an attendant danger in this otherwise welcome change, it could be said to reside in the plethora of signage that is now springing up around these routes, a version of the clutter that is now affecting our footpaths in the same way as it has long marred our streets. It is not uncommon for three or four different 'approved' routes to be signed along a single path, with the record so far held by a point on the Greenwich peninsula where no less than twelve pedestrian and cycle routes are signed at a single junction. The wary walker would be advised not to rely too heavily on any of them. The turning round of footpath signs to point in random wrong directions is a regular pastime in the capital, as though we were determined to slow the progress of any invader. There is an additional danger – as there is with our rural paths – that signed and 'major' routes may come to be seen as the 'approved' ones, with a consequent threat to the survival of the great network of minor and often uncelebrated paths that underpin them.

The route of *The Green London Way* is a journey around our social history. It is also intended, however, as a journey around the capital's natural history – and this is the second area of significant change since the first edition was published. In the twenty years that have intervened we have seen the decline of a number of species; the willow tit has disappeared as a London bird, the lesser spotted woodpecker is on its way out, and there have been worrying declines in many of our most familiar species: the house sparrow, song thrush, starling, house martin and swift. But there have been gains too; the great spotted woodpecker, the goldfinch and the long-tailed tit are now far more common. There are peregrine falcons nesting in locations right into the heart of London, an even greater number of inland cormorants, and some completely new arrivals – the lesser egret for example. It is in this last category that perhaps the most noticeable change has taken place. Twenty years ago the ring-necked parakeet was a curiosity found in a few isolated locations in west and south east London. Today it is almost everywhere, and for large sections of *The Green London Way* it is true to say that the commonest bird 'song' you will hear is the distinctive shriek of the parakeet.

There have been changes in the plant world too, and perhaps the most significant of these has been the increase in our urban fern population. It has taken decades for the impacts of the original Clean Air Acts to work through but today, with the air in the capital far less polluted, both lichens and ferns are far more abundant. Where once a single fern was a rare sight you can now see stretches of wall adorned with a male fern, wall rue, black spleenwort, hartstongue, polypody, maidenhair spleenwort and more. This is a welcome reminder that legislation can, where there is a will, genuinely reverse environmental degradation. Equally welcome has been the growth of a far more wildlife-friendly approach to the management of open spaces. This means more nature reserves and ecological parks and, even more significantly, a different approach to the management regimes of ordinary urban parks and cemeteries. Twenty years ago, when the greater part of London parkland could have been characterised as a 'green desert', an area of uncut grass in a park would generally have been the result of a failure in the mowing regime. Today, as is evidenced along *The Green London Way*, parks all over the city deliberately maintain uncut areas as 'meadow', thus simultaneously increasing biodiversity, adding visual interest and cutting costs.

There is also a danger in this change in attitude. It has been particularly manifest in the well-intentioned but largely indiscriminate sowing of 'wild flower' seed in order to create an 'instant' flora. This has become a lazy and completely misplaced practice. It involves plants that are not local to the area in which they are being sown, and indeed, in some cases plants that are not native to this country at all – witness the amount of Austrian chamomile that has been sown in place of the native version. It involves plants that are not right for the habitat in which they are being planted, and it totally ignores the fact that brownfield sites and other urban spaces have their own rich form of flora which would flourish if only we allowed it to. A striking example of this is to be found along the Greenway and around the Olympic site at Stratford, where artificially sown 'wild' flowers now compete with a rich, original flora – and where this form of management seems to be in total ignorance of the fact that in the danewort, or lesser elder, the site already hosted one of London's specialities. The idea, of course, whether conscious or not, is that wildlife is alright as long as we legitimise it; as long as it is managed and tidy and in the approved places. It is an idea that has led to such contradictions as the bulldozing of a brownfield site in order to create a 'nature reserve' or the damming of the tidal Lea accompanied by the creation of permitted 'wetland areas'.

But there is a third and final area of change which is perhaps the most significant. It is, of course, the continuing pressure of development, and at a pace which, in London, seems to belie the existence of any national or international recession. Change in a city is not just inevitable but healthy, and it has brought some improvements to *The Green London Way* – such as the opening up of the Royal Arsenal site in Woolwich, where we are now able to walk amongst some of its finest old buildings rather than peer at them through a rusting fence. But what is disturbing is the pace and the scale of the change, with whole new districts hastily thrown up, usually for the benefit of a very restricted section of our society. The result has been a new anonymity, a loss of neighbourhood and local identity and with it, the associated perils attached to the belief that 'community' can be created rather than having to grow organically. This scale of development, it has to be said, is more evident in the eastern half of London than in the west. The part of London that suffered most from poverty and deprivation, that endured the greatest concentration of heavy and often unhealthy industry, that was then most battered by wartime enemy bombardment, is now the part of London that is suffering most from dislocating and disruptive development, and from the destruction of existing communities. This is evident along *The Green London Way* in Stratford and around the 'Olympic fringes', in East Ham and Beckton and around the site of the old Royal docks, across the North Greenwich peninsula and all along the riverside from Woolwich to Greenwich. Here, in many cases, a sense of specific location has been lost in the creation of hasty placeless spaces that could be, literally, anywhere.

But London survives, as a wonderful mosaic of peoples and places and cultures, of history and natural history, and of an almost inexhaustible store of stories. In the preparation of this new edition, and in the light of all these changes – both for better and for worse – *The Green London Way* has been completely rewalked and revised. As a result of this, several sections of the route have been significantly improved and, to mark the Olympic site and the shift in the focus of London eastwards, the beginning and the end of the overall circuit have been relocated from Finsbury Park to Stratford. With these changes this new edition will, it is hoped, continue to provide a living commentary on London, one of the most splendid and fascinating cities in the world.

The Green London Way

The Green London Way is a long-distance footpath for London. It is a circular route of nearly 110 miles, not around London but through it. It brings the idea of the long-distance way right into the country's largest city. At the same time it is a route which divides into 18 separate and easily manageable walks, each one with its own distinctive character.

The Green London Way links river and canal, towpath and abandoned railway line, urban footpath and little-known alley, park and common, woodland and heath. It is an introduction to the best and most beautiful of London's open spaces. But it is not intended as an urban equivalent of the rural ramble; it is a mistake to approach even the city's largest and wildest open spaces – Bostall Wood, Wimbledon Common, Horsenden Hill – as a scaled-down version of the countryside. Urban walking is of a different order and requires a different sort of appreciation. Approached without preconceptions this exploration of London offers constant surprises and unexpected rewards, uncovering unsuspected routes and magnificent yet little-known buildings; but more than this, it reveals hidden facets of history and a surprising wealth of wildlife. And even in the most squalid of surroundings there can be a strange beauty that is completely unconventional. *The Green London Way* provides an overview of London's natural history, of its social history, and of the connections between the two. In particular it illustrates the struggles which have taken place, and which continue to take place, to preserve the city's open spaces.

Geologically London is a conveniently distinct unit. It is generally described as a basin, but in diagrammatic form more nearly resembles two soup bowls placed one inside the other. The outer, and higher, rim of these bowls is formed by chalk, which outcrops to the north of London as the Chilterns and to the south as the North Downs, both of which lie well outside the reaches of our route. The inner rim is formed by the well-known London clay, blue or orange, and heavy to work. At its highest points the clay is up to 300 feet thick and forms a ridge which constitutes sections of our route. In South London we follow it from Forest Hill to Streatham; in North London, from Haringey to Hampstead, where it is capped with sandy gravels, and then again when it outcrops at Harrow-on-the-Hill. From these high places London slopes down across the clay towards the river. The Thames today is only a fraction of its former size and during its fluctuations over previous millennia it has cut several much wider valleys which survive in the form of terraces to north and south of the existing river route. These terraces are particularly distinct to the south of the river and are capped with sandy and gravelly soils laid down by water action. These poor acidic soils made them less attractive for agriculture; they thus became common lands and to some extent this helped save them from development. This has given us the long line of heaths and Commons which we pick up on our walks at Blackheath and which stretches all the way from Plumstead to Lesnes Abbey Woods. It was the modern Thames which fashioned the city of London, however, and sections of our walk follow the Thames Path, as well as paths that follow its tributaries – the Wandle, the Lea, the Ravensbourne and the Brent.

Though concealed by so much concrete, the geology and the topography of London still have a striking impact upon its natural history. The oak woodlands of Oxleas or Horsenden are on the heavy clay. There are remnants of heathland flora on the sandy gravels of Hampstead, Bostall and even Blackheath. Walthamstow Marshes survives in the low valley of the Lea, and the wildlife of East London has an estuarine influence as the Thames valley broadens and flattens on its approach to the sea.

The impact of the human species upon this landscape is obvious and the growth of the city has brought with it development and destruction – and an enormous loss of life forms and their habitats. But there is another side to the picture, which is less often painted. The story of London's wildlife is an illustration of the tremendous recuperative power of nature. It is demonstrated in almost every street; by the lichen which grows on the pavement, the moss which grows on top of a wall and the wild plants which spring up at the bottom of a lamp-post. If humans built railways, it was foxes which travelled along the embankments. If we built and abandoned a gasworks, then partridge and little owl moved in to nest in the ruins. If old filter beds fell into disuse then in a few years they were colonised by willows, newts and herons. One of the most enduring images of *The Green London Way* is the sight of a skylark singing its heart out above a gas holder.

In addition to this 'recuperation', many developments in London actually brought new species with them. One hundred and fifty years ago some of our most familiar species, birds and plants which we take for granted, like the black-headed gull or the buddleia, could not have been seen in London. Reservoirs and waste tips brought the gulls, bomb-sites brought the rose-bay willow herb, power stations gave nest sites for the black redstart, and tower blocks and school belfries, homes for the kestrel. It is significant that the special conditions of London – which might be summarised as its walls and its warmth – facilitated the spread of a whole variety of species from many different parts of the globe. London's flora, like its human population, is international, and gives the lie to the conservationists' cliché that 'native' is good and 'alien' is doubtful.

London has its own selection of rare – or at least unusual – species and many of them are mentioned in these pages: dyers greenweed on Horsenden Hill, danewort along the Greenway, Essex skipper butterflies at Walthamstow Marshes, tropical grass on the Regents Canal. But the common confusion – that what is most unusual is therefore most interesting – should be avoided. *The Green London Way* should also help to increase our awareness and our appreciation of what is 'common'; of the plants, birds and animals which struggle for survival – and which succeed – all around us.

It is clear that the natural history of London is inextricably linked with its social history. The history of the people who have made, and make up, London is another main theme of *The Green London Way*. For the most part the 'famous names' approach, the focus on monarchs and their ministers, has been avoided. It has to be said, however, that this rule has been broken wherever a story has been too good not to tell, or where it has related to an unexpected local connection. The unexceptional Montacute Road near Catford, for example, is cue to the story of the murder of Edward II. The suburban Uxendon Crescent near Preston Road leads into the story of the Babington plot to spring Mary Stuart from prison. And of course the 'famous names' have always been admitted where they part of a struggle over rights of access or the ownership of a common. For the most part, however, the focus here has been the lost history of the ordinary people of London. Too often our approach to history, particularly as it is practised in guide books, turns ordinary people into the objects, even the victims, of history. Here they are seen as its makers. In

Newham, for example, the view of the tower blocks leads to an account of the struggles by their occupants: against local and national opposition, they were able to prove that these buildings were unfit to live in, and to bring about the decision to demolish them. Or, on Blackheath, we come across the story of not one but three different peasant uprisings that changed the course of British history. And these stories are not only about struggles but also about a city's ability to celebrate: the great anarchic displays of public exuberance which found expression in the Charlton Horn Fair or in the Garrat mock elections.

There is one particular way in which the lives and efforts of ordinary people have shaped the history of London and which is demonstrated time after time in this book. It is a remarkable fact, and one which cannot be repeated often enough, that almost every park, common, heath and wood of London has had to be fought for at some time in its history. The creation, and the preservation, of London's open spaces is a result of the struggles of the city's people. From Highgate Woods to Norwood Grove, from Wimbledon Common to the Lea Valley, almost every inch of open space has been lobbied over, campaigned about, and demonstrated for – sometimes with a physical battle. The stories of these struggles are some of the most exciting and inspiring of our journey. In Plumstead and in Forest Hill people marched in their thousands to save their commons. In Richmond it was a lone local brewer who took on the courts and the monarchy to re-establish the right of access to the park. In Hampstead fifteen different parliamentary bills had to be defeated in the struggle to preserve the heath. In Streatham local people turned out in secret to tear down gates and fences on the common as fast as the Lord of the Manor could put them up. And in scores of less dramatic cases, local residents set up committees, raised funds, pressurised Councils, challenged developers or contested Enquiries. The open spaces of London today are a monument to their efforts.

This tradition of struggle has been a long one. The earliest account along *The Green London Way* concerns the people of Norwood and Forest Hill, who, in the seventeenth century, marched behind the Reverend Colfe into the City to petition the king for the saving of West Wood. From then on, one account follows another, reaching an apogee in the nineteenth century, the period of London's most rapid expansion. The Victorians were great developers – but they were also passionate defenders of London's open spaces. It was Victorians who were prepared to break the law and to go to prison in defence of Plumstead Common and One Tree Hill, and the Victorians, too, who produced writers with a caustic wit that was frequently brought to bear in books and articles on the subject, and which are often quoted within these pages.

The struggle for London's open spaces is as intense today as it ever was. If, in 1990, the Department of Transport had accepted the recommendations of its own consultants, it would have ushered in the destruction of open spaces on such a scale as to make *The Green London Way* impossible. Walthamstow and Hackney Marshes, the three mile Parkland Walk, Horniman Gardens, Dulwich Park, most of the South London commons and even the leafy suburbs of Kew would all have been covered in tarmac or sliced through the middle for major new road schemes. It was the vociferous, passionate and often imaginative campaigning of dozens of groups, both local and London-wide, that led to the defeat of these proposals. Yet new road schemes, and new road widening schemes, continue to be put forward. The threat to London's open spaces continues, in the form of big development projects, but also in the more insidious but continuous nibbling away of small sites, with no account being taken of the cumulative impact of these losses. It is as a contribution to the continuing struggles to preserve London as a place fit to live in that this book has been written.

Using this Book

The Green London Way has been written for armchair as well as for active walkers. For this reason, and to maintain a narrative flow, it has been divided into chapters each dealing with a different part of London. The chapters describe one or two walks which are numbered in clockwise order around London, beginning and ending at Stratford in east London. The map which accompanies each walk is intended as an overview and for general context; for full route details the walker will need to refer to the written route instructions. It might also be useful to take on walks a London street map book. As well as being of assistance should any route-finding problems arise, it also allows for the fact that London is a living and therefore an ever-changing city. The street guide would help a walker negotiate a way around temporary closures or any other changes which might have occurred since the time of publication.

The London transport network has undergone further improvement since the last edition – most notably with the expansion of the Dockland Light Railway and the development of London Overground – and every walk now begins and ends at a station. The location of bus, train and underground stations are shown on the maps and set out in more detail in the text. Each walk begins with a section entitled 'Getting started'. This shows how to begin the walk from the nearest public transport facilities and how the walk connects with the previous walk in the circuit. The walk is then described in several stretches, the narrative for each section of the walk being preceded by an introduction, and information on the route, facilities and wildlife to look out for (though it should be noted that these can be subject to fairly rapid change). The 'Looking at Wildlife' section aims to summarise the main natural history features of each section of the walk, and points out particular species of trees, wild flowers, animals, birds or insects to look out for. There will often be further detail on this in the text. But there has been no attempt in this book to help with the identification of animals and plants: it would have been an impossible task, and the reader is referred to the many excellent field guides available for this purpose. Each section ends with information on 'getting home', detailing transport connections from the finishing point of the walk.

With the help of these instructions, and with the text that accompanies each section of *The Green London Way*, the walker and the reader will find themselves exploring new aspects of London and of its life. Savour it. And help to save it.

About the Walks

The 18 separate walks that make up *The Green London Way* vary from 3½ to 8 miles in length, beginning and ending at points well served by public transport. The one exception to this rule is the Woolwich and the Woodlands walk described in Chapter 2. At 9 ½ to 10 ½ miles, depending on which alternative you use, it is longer than most and is the only circular walk in the book.

It is easy to combine different walks together to make longer routes and instructions are always given to link a walk to the ones before and after it. It should be remembered however that urban walking can be more tiring, though in a different way, than country walking and that longer routes would remove the element of exploration which has been seen as an important part of this book. Although urban walking requires no special equipment, good footwear is important. Most routes cover rough ground and some can be muddy, especially in winter. Stretches of road, or even of tarmac path, can also be very demanding on the feet.

The walks in this book can be undertaken at any time of year. In the preparation of this book they have been walked at almost every time of day and throughout the seasons; in conditions varying from summer drought to deep snow. Like the countryside, London has different atmospheres in different weathers and there are even stretches that have been most enjoyed in the rain. The walks can be – and have been – easily adapted to suit children and to help with this details have been included of some additional attractions to keep them interested along the way.

For help in making a choice of routes, the 18 walks are summarised below.

WALK 1: STRATFORD TO NORTH WOOLWICH

Stratford town centre, Channelsea Path, the Greenway, Beckton and the District Park, the Royal Docks and Thames riverside, the Woolwich Ferry and foot tunnel.

Distance: 7½ miles

Terrain: Easy terrain with just a few ups and downs on the Mitchell Walk through Beckton. Very few stretches on roads.

Main features: An unusual walk which leads out of Stratford and along the top of Bazalgette's great embanked sewer, then down through Beckton to the riverside and the old Royal Docks. It includes such curious features as the Beckton Alps – an artificial hill built on gas works slag – and a footpath which runs across two sets of dock gates.

WALK 2: ABBEY WOODS AND SHOOTERS HILL

Woolwich riverside, the Royal Arsenal and Beresford Square market, Plumstead and Winn's Commons, Bostall Heath and Woods, Lesnes Abbey and Woods, Oxleas Wood, Castle Woods and Severndroog Castle, Eltham and Woolwich Commons.

Distance: 10½ miles

Terrain: Includes woodland paths and can be muddy at times. Little road walking, mostly at the beginning and end, though the closure of access to Woodlands Farm has added a short stretch of road walking in the middle of the walk.

Main features: A long circular walk – though it can be shortened at several points. After the initial climb up from the riverside it is almost entirely 'rural' and links commons, heaths, a beautiful ruined abbey, a folly and a string of ancient woodlands.

WALK 3: WOOLWICH TO GREENWICH

Woolwich Common, Charlton Park and Charlton Village, Maryon and Maryon Wilson Parks, Gilbert's Pit, the Thames Barrier, the Greenwich peninsula and the Thames Path to Greenwich.

Distance: 7 miles

Terrain: Easy terrain with a gentle initial ascent and minimal road walking.

Main features: A walk which is particularly rich in history and crosses relatively wild open spaces, attractive parks and an interesting stretch of river. It includes the fascinating but little-known Charlton House, one of best Jacobean houses in Britain, as well as a site of special geological interest, the Cutty Sark and the beautiful buildings of the Greenwich riverside – from a power station to a palace.

WALK 4: GREENWICH TO FOREST HILL

Greenwich and Greenwich Park, Blackheath and The Point, River Ravensbourne and the Waterlink Way, Hilly Fields, Brockley and Ladywell Cemeteries, Ladywell Fields, Blythe Hill Fields, One Tree Hill, Horniman Gardens.

Distance: 8 miles

Terrain: Easy terrain but with several ascents. A few stretches of road walking.

Main features: A varied walk primarily linked by a series of south London hills – with panoramic views over the city – with stretches of the River Ravensbourne in between. It includes Greenwich Park and the Observatory buildings, a corner of Blackheath, important in the Peasant's Revolt, and One Tree Hill, site of one of the most exciting battles to preserve our open spaces. The modern Ladywell Fields provide an excellent example of how an urban river can be 'renaturalised', and the route ends beside the Horniman Museum, well worth a visit in itself.

WALK 5: FOREST HILL TO CRYSTAL PALACE

Horniman Gardens, Dulwich Wood and Sydenham Hill Wood, Sydenham Wells Park, Crystal Palace Park.

Distance: 4 miles

Terrain: Includes woodland paths that can be muddy at times. Minimal road walking.

Main features: A short walk starting at the Horniman Museum and including both the beautiful woodlands at Dulwich and the large park built for the old Crystal Palace, best known for its 'prehistoric monsters'.

WALK 6: CRYSTAL PALACE TO BALHAM

Dulwich Upper Wood, Norwood Park, Norwood Grove, Streatham Common and The Rookery, Russell's Path and Tooting Common.

Distance: 5½ miles

Terrain: Easy terrain with two stretches of road walking and some mild ascent.

Main features: The high point of the walk is the complex of commons and public gardens around Streatham, including the very attractive Rookery. From here, Russell's Path, a surprisingly long stretch of urban footpath, leads on towards the wooded sections of Tooting Common.

WALK 7: BALHAM TO WIMBLEDON

Wandsworth Common and the Scope, Wandsworth Cemetery, the Wandle Valley, Wimbledon.

Distance: 5 miles

Terrain: Mostly easy though some stretches of the Wandle riverside can be muddy at times. Short stretches of road walking at the beginning and end.

Main features: Links Wandsworth Common with Wimbledon across the Wandle valley, taking in Wandsworth Cemetery and a long stretch of the newly opened up Wandle riverside. It also incorporates some rich historic connections – such as the story of the Garratt mock elections.

WALK 8: WIMBLEDON TO RICHMOND

Wimbledon, Cannizaro Park, Wimbledon Common, Richmond Park, Pembroke Lodge, Petersham Common, Richmond riverside.

Distance: 8 miles

Terrain: Varied terrain which could be muddy at times. Very little road walking.

Main features: A particularly beautiful walk and one which proves that it is possible to go for miles in some parts of London without ever reverting to a road. It includes the little known gem of Cannizaro Park, the wide – and surprisingly wild – open space of Wimbledon Common and Richmond Park, the beautiful Isabella Plantation, a 'secret' vista from the top of King Henry's Mound and a striking descent to the riverside.

WALK 9: RICHMOND TO KEW BRIDGE

Richmond, Richmond Palace, Thames Path, Old Deer Park and Kew Gardens.
Distance: 3½ miles

Terrain: Easy terrain with virtually no road walking.

Main features: Includes Richmond Green and the remains of the once-important palace of Richmond, followed by a walk along the Thames Path with views of Syon House and Isleworth on the opposite bank and of some of the Thames islands.

WALK 10: KEW BRIDGE TO HANWELL

Waterside Park, Brentford and The Butts, River Brent and the Grand Union Canal, Fitzherbert Walk, Wharncliffe Viaduct and Hanwell

Distance: 5 miles

Terrain: Some stretches can be muddy at times – especially along the Fitzherbert Walk. Little road walking.

Main features: Another particularly good walk which begins on the north bank of the Thames and then runs through the old part of Brentford, including 'The Butts'. It then follows the River Brent and the Grand Union Canal up as far as the famous Hanwell flight of locks and then back onto the River Brent as far as the dramatic Wharncliffe Viaduct.

WALK 11: HANWELL TO GREENFORD

Wharncliffe Viaduct and Church Fields, Brent Lodge Park, Bole's Meadows, Perivale Park.

Distance: 4 miles

Terrain: Easy riverside walking with minimal road walking.

Main features: A short walk which continues to follow the River Brent through a string of riverside parks and meadows – including a small free zoo and some surprisingly rural stretches.

WALK 12: GREENFORD TO SOUTH KENTON

Grand Union Canal, Horsenden Hill and Woods, Harrow-on-the-Hill and Northwick Park.

Distance: 6 miles

Terrain: Varied terrain including ascents and stretches which can be muddy. Includes one central section on roads.

Main features: A very attractive walk with some excellent views. Horsenden Hill ranks high amongst London's open spaces and Harrow-on-the-Hill, whatever you make of it, is unique.

WALK 13: SOUTH KENTON TO BRENT CROSS

Barn Hill and the Fryent Way Country Park, West Hendon Playing Fields and the Welsh Harp Reservoir, Brent Cross

Distance: 6 miles

Terrain: Can be very muddy in winter and includes ascents. Some stretches of road walking.

Main features: A walk which includes two more of the most valuable open spaces in London; the Fryent Way Country Park has the most extensive areas of ancient meadows along the route, while the Welsh Harp Reservoir and its wooded edges are rich in bird life. This is a walk of contrasts, from the quiet open heights of Barn Hill, and its views across to the new Wembley stadium, along little used paths around the reservoir and on to the busy bunker of Brent Cross.

WALK 14: BRENT CROSS TO HAMPSTEAD

Hendon Park, Brent Park, Brookside Walk, Hampstead Garden Suburb, Big Wood and Little Wood, Hampstead Heath and Hampstead.

Distance: 5½ miles

Terrain: Varied terrain some of which can be muddy at times. After two initial stretches, virtually no road walking.

Main features: An interesting and varied walk that begins at the hideous Brent Cross but soon follows the upper reaches of the River Brent and its tributary, the Mutton Brook, to reach Hampstead Garden Suburb, a fascinating experiment in social engineering. The final section crosses a corner of the heath to reach Hampstead and includes The Hill, perhaps the most beautiful public garden in London.

WALK 15: HAMPSTEAD TO FINSBURY PARK

Hampstead, Hampstead Heath and Kenwood, Highgate, Highgate Wood and Queens Wood, Parkland Walk.

Distance: 7 miles

Terrain: Varied and includes woodland and heathland paths that can be muddy at times. A small amount on roads but always interesting.

Main features: One of the best walks in the book with two famous urban 'villages', a slice of one of London's largest heaths, the restrained splendour of Kenwood House, two ancient woodlands and a final three mile stretch along an abandoned railway line.

WALK 16: FINSBURY PARK TO CLAPTON

Finsbury Park, New River Path, Stoke Newington Reservoirs, Clissold Park, Church Street and the 'village' area of Stoke Newington, Abney Park Cemetery, Walthamstow Marshes and the River Lea.

Distance: 6½ miles

Terrain: Easy terrain with some stretches of road walking but of significant interest in themselves.

Main features: A very varied walk including a stretch along the man-made 'New' River, bird-rich reservoirs, attractive parks, a historic urban village, an overgrown cemetery and the magnificent Walthamstow Marshes; a unique site in central London and the only extensive marshland on *The Green London Way*.

WALK 17: CLAPTON TO VICTORIA PARK

Millfields, Middlesex Filter Beds Nature Reserve, the 'Old Lea' and Hackney Marshes, Wick Woods, Mabley Green, Victoria Park, Regents Canal.

Distance: 5 miles

Terrain: Easy terrain. Little road walking.

Main features: An easy walk which includes a new nature reserve in abandoned filter beds, an attractive riverside stretch, some newly created woodland and East London's largest park, now being restored to something resembling its grand Victorian original.

WALK 18: VICTORIA PARK TO STRATFORD

Regents Canal and Hertford Union Canal, the Greenway and the Olympic Park, Bow Back Rivers, Three Mills, Mill Meads.

Distance: 4½ miles

Terrain: Easy terrain although the area around Mill Meads can be muddy and overgrown. Very little road walking.

Main features: A fascinating walk leading along east London canals onto a walkway with a panoramic view of the Olympic site. It also includes the Bow Back Rivers, with a particular atmosphere of their own, the fascinating Three Mills site and the Abbey Mills sewage pumping station – the 'cathedral of sewage' and one of the most beautiful buildings in London.

Keeping abreast of changes: *The Green London Way* website

London continues to change, and perhaps more rapidly than ever. To mark this new edition, Lawrence and Wishart plan to establish a *Green London Way* web-link where people can send in their comments or other information. To help keep the route up to date, walkers are invited to post any changes they come across, whether temporary or permanent. They are also welcome to point out any errors in the text, to post comments and suggestions, or stories of their walks – or to join in creating a record of all those who have walked the entire circuit.

For more information go to www.lwbooks.co.uk/books/archive/green_london.html

1. From the Lea to the Levels

STRATFORD, BECKTON AND NORTH WOOLWICH

The few villages of the Saxon manor of Hamme stood on a gravelly terrace stretching from the River Roding to the River Lea. Around them was a remarkably inhospitable area; the huge forest of Middlesex to the north, and to the south a great area of marshes or 'levels' running down to the Thames. The peculiar geography of the area left it unchanged in a wind-swept isolation for hundreds of years; but from the nineteenth century it helped to shape its particularly rapid and difficult development. From the industrial revolution onwards the two Hams, East and West, became an area of concentrated disadvantage.

When the City of London passed an ordinance expelling 'noxious industries', they came here instead: the chemical works, the 'oil boilers, gut spinners, varnish makers and printers' ink makers'. The availability of cheap, level and low-lying land, alongside the river and free of all legal restrictions, brought these, the docks, the iron-works and the ship-builders. With them came the mass of impoverished labourers, forced to build their shanty-towns upon the water-logged marshland. Living in a community without paved roads, drains or sewers, and afflicted with smallpox, cholera and typhoid, they did the work that kept the City wealthy.

The intervening years have not been much kinder. The Royal Docks brought a casual and precarious employment, and then took it away again. The largest gas works in the world have come and gone. The area lost two thirds of its housing and several thousand lives in the massive World War Two bombardment. And then the tower blocks were put up – and some of them fell down again. Today we see a fascinating and disturbing example of history repeating itself. The area that owed its original development to the fact that it was free of legal restrictions is now the largest development area in London – from the Olympic generated overspill in Stratford to the 'free enterprise zone' of the docklands. On both sites normal planning constraints and controls – and protections – were swept aside by special legislation in the interests of rapid and unrestrained 'growth'.

As the area faces yet another phase of disruption to the local community, the story of this chapter remains one of survival: the survival of a people whose character has become a part of popular mythology. And survival too of wildlife in amazing abundance: angelica on an old lock-gate, danewort colonising the sewer banks, sea wormwood on scraps of wasteland, dabchicks and shelduck in empty docks and teal and foxes on the muddy banks of the Thames.

24

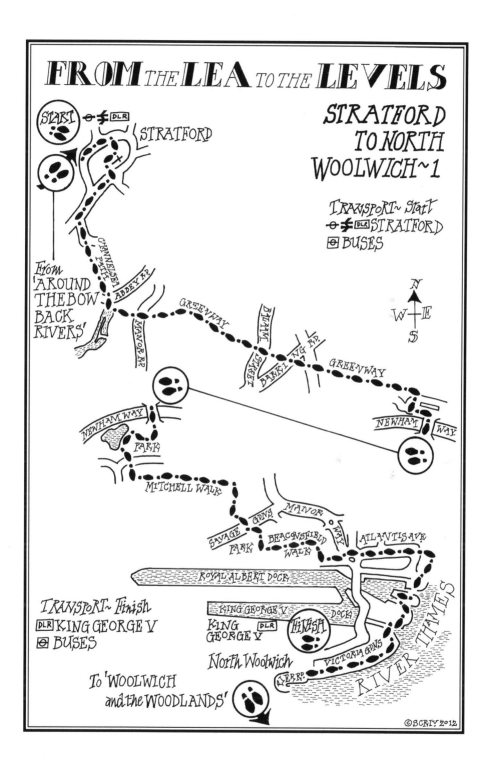

FROM THE LEA TO THE LEVELS

STRATFORD TO NORTH WOOLWICH ~ 1

START ⊕ ⚡ DLR STRATFORD

TRANSPORT ~ Start
⊕ ⚡ DLR STRATFORD
⊡ BUSES

From 'AROUND THE BOW BACK RIVERS'

CHANNELSEA PATH

ABBEY RD.

MANOR RD.

GREENWAY

HIGH STREET

BANKING RD.

GREENWAY

N
W · E
S

NEWHAM WAY

PARK

NEWHAM WAY

MITCHELL WALK

SAVAGE GDNS

PARK

BEACONSFIELD WALK

MANOR WAY

ATLANTIS AVE

ROYAL ALBERT DOCK

KING GEORGE V DOCK

TRANSPORT ~ Finish
DLR KING GEORGE V
⊡ BUSES

KING GEORGE V DLR

FINISH

North Woolwich

ALBERT RD.

VICTORIA GDNS

RIVER THAMES

To 'WOOLWICH and the WOODLANDS'

©SCRIY 2012

This chapter covers a single walk of 7½ miles from Stratford to the Thames crossing at North Woolwich.

■ WALK 1: STRATFORD TO NORTH WOOLWICH

Getting started

From Stratford Station:

(Network Rail (Liverpool Street), Underground (Central line, Jubilee line), DLR, London Overground)

From Stratford Bus Station:

(25, 69, 86, 97, 104, 108, 158, 238, 241, 257, 262, 276, 308, 339, 425, 473)

The walk starts from the bottom of the steps, leading up to the Westfield Shopping Centre, outside the main station entrance.

From Walk 18:

Walk 1 continues directly from the end of Walk 18.

Stratford City: Porcelain and the People's Theatre

ROUTE:

- With your back to the station, turn left through Meridian Square and along Great Eastern Road.
- On reaching the end of Angel Lane, turn right across Great Eastern Road to reach Theatre Square. Cross the square towards the Theatre Royal.
- In front of the theatre turn left along the pedestrian walk until you reach Salway Place on the right. Continue across the square, following the path at its end to reach Broadway.
- Turn right along Broadway and take the second and main entrance into the churchyard on your left.
- Walk through the churchyard, between the front of the church and the martyr's memorial, emerging onto the main road (also called Broadway). Turn right along the road to reach the pedestrian crossing.
- Cross the main road and turn right along Broadway, passing the old Town Hall and continuing into High Street.
- Continue past Stratford High Street DLR station to reach Cam Road on the left, beside traffic lights.

FACILITIES: Bar at Theatre Royal, pubs and cafés along Broadway. Toilets in the Stratford Centre.

LOOKING AT WILDLIFE: Just beyond Meridian Square there is a rather surprising group of large and attractive crack willow trees; a lone reminder that this was once marshland.

The new Stratford is a sudden eruption of massive shopping centres, high rise office blocks and residential towers, dwarfing the grand Victorian buildings that line the Broadway and concealing the character of this one-time Essex town beneath the anonymity of a commercial 'anyplace'. It is an essential outgrowth of the London Olympics, set on what was once Stratford Marsh immediately adjacent to the town, and something of a comment on the values of the modern Olympic movement. As the Jesuit poet Gerard Manley Hopkins, born here in Stratford in 1876, put it in characteristic verse, 'all is seared with trade; bleared, smeared with toil'. To what extent the existing inhabitants of this corner of London have benefited from this rapid and massive development, spreading from here across Hackney Wick and Bow, and to what extent they have been displaced or supplanted by it, is a matter that is open to debate. It was, after all, the proud slogan of the development that 'Stratford is giving itself a new identity'.

There is however one element of continuity. Stratford always was, and still remains, an important transport hub. It begins with the name itself, first recorded in the late tenth century, and which means 'the street of the ford'. The first proper bridge across the sprawling Lea came later – round about 1110 when Queen Maud, wife of Henry I, built, along the line of the current High Street, a causeway which crossed five water-courses in the space of 600 yards. Later the town was to become an important railway junction too. The first station, built in 1839, became a hub for the eastern rail region, and here too, for nearly a hundred and thirty years, the Eastern Counties Railway operated their locomotive and rolling stock works. Today Stratford has grown into a major interchange; the meeting point of main roads, bus routes, railways, tube lines, London Overground and the Dockland Light Railway. Together they now occupy a large part of central Stratford.

This was always something of an industrial centre. Like all of the eastern suburbs, it had a concentration of those 'noxious industries' banned from within the City itself, butchers and slaughterhouses, oil and timber mills, calico and silk printing works, distilleries and manufactories of gunpowder. They were, however, to have some interesting by-products. The rendered fat from the slaughterhouses, for example, was used in making soap and the site of the early Yardley's factory on High Street is marked with a mural, rather decorously showing maidens in mop caps gathering lavender. Even more significantly it was here in Stratford that bone china – or at least its precursor- was invented. The Bow porcelain factory, known as 'New Canton' was established here by Thomas Frye in 1747 and from 1748 used a soft-paste porcelain with the inclusion of 45% bone ash, giving the resultant china a warm creamy appearance. At its height the porcelain produced here – which included the first English full-length portrait figure – was said to rival the best of European or Chinese art, though it was also notoriously variable in output and never achieved great commercial success. Though it was closed by 1776, it left a lasting mark on the history of porcelain and china.

Our route through Stratford begins with the new Westfield Centre behind us and the older Stratford Centre in front. Stratford in other words has been subject to two major regeneration initiatives within forty years – a statement perhaps on the impact of the economic imperative of growth on architectural life-spans. Opened in 1971, the Stratford Centre was part of an initiative known as 'New Stratford', but it is now dwarfed, and its future threatened, by the Westfield Centre, the 'largest indoor shopping centre in Western Europe', with its 300 shops, 70 restaurants and seven miles of shop windows. The fact that it also has a massive car park is something of an irony: the lauding of the London Olympics as the greenest ever necessitated the closure of the Westfield car park for the duration of the Games. But since the planned closure was solely for the duration of the games, part of their legacy remains the creation of 5,000 new car parking spaces.

A short distance along the Great Eastern Road we reach Theatre Square and the Royal Theatre. The theatre has a long and distinguished history, commencing in 1884, but its most famous era was between 1953 and 1979, the years of Joan Littlewood and Gerry Raffles and their Theatre Workshop Company. It had been founded in the north of England in 1945 as a 'people's theatre', a new approach that sought to involve both artists and audiences in a 'living event'. After eight years of touring the company were ready to take on a permanent venue, and, having failed to find one in Glasgow, it was to Stratford that they came. The Royal Theatre was at that time in a state of severe dilapidation, so in between rehearsals the company cleaned, painted and repaired, whilst living as a commune in the theatre's changing rooms. Their policy was to revive and preserve the best of traditional British and European drama whilst also presenting modern plays on contemporary themes. Recognition came internationally before they were properly celebrated at home but their long list of eventual and successful productions included two that were made into films – *A Taste Of Honey* and *O What A Lovely War*. Despite its very significant reputation, the theatre was still threatened by the 'regeneration' of the late 1960s. The entire surrounding area was demolished and, despite its Grade II* listed status, the theatre would almost certainly have gone too, were it not for the efforts of Gerry Raffles, who maintained an almost permanent watch, tearing down barriers erected by the builders next to the theatre and making sure that the bulldozers didn't 'accidentally' demolish one of its walls. Meanwhile, Joan and a band of volunteers cleared rubble to establish an adventure playground on an adjacent site. The theatre was saved, and some five years later was at the height of its success when, at the age of 51, Gerry Raffles died suddenly. Joan Littlewood retired in grief and never returned to theatre again. It is perhaps ironic that the square next to the theatre buildings, part of the development which he so bitterly opposed, is today named Gerry Raffles Square in his honour.

Emerging onto Broadway we pass the Parish Church of St John's – large but rather drab in its yellow stock bridge. The church may be understated – but not the monument in front of it. Six-sided, with ornamental pillars and canopies, and topped with an outsized tapering cone, it is a memorial to eighteen protestant martyrs burnt at the stake on Stratford Green during the Maryan persecutions of 1555-56. Each face of the monument commemorates a different group, the largest of them eleven men and two women who were 'brought pinioned from Newgate and suffered death here … in the presence of 20,000 people for their firm adherence to the word of God … They were all burnt in one fire with such love to one another and constancy to our saviour Christ that it made all the lookers-on to marvel'. The exact nature of the differences between them and the temporarily ascendant Catholics is enumerated in the inscription to the Reverend Tom Rose, Vicar of West Ham, tortured for opposing Catholic teaching on 'auricular confession, transubstantiation, purgatory and images'.

There is a further monument just beyond the apex of the churchyard, a plainer pinnacle facing the old Town Hall across the road – a relic of the time when Stratford was the administrative centre for the Borough of West Ham. It is in memory of Samuel Gurney, a Quaker banker who lived at Ham House. Gurney was a leader of the anti-slavery movement, a campaigner for penal reform and a patron for the infant colony of Liberia, as well as a local philanthropist, establishing among other things the Poplar Hospital for Accidents. One of his many siblings was the more famous Elizabeth Fry, whilst his brother-in-law was Samuel Hoare, who led the fight against the development of Hampstead Heath – and whom we shall get to know better in Chapter 10 of *The Green London Way*.

Along the Channelsea Path

ROUTE:

- From High Street turn left into Cam Road. Where the road curves to the left, continue on the footpath running straight ahead (Channelsea Path).
- Continue for just under ½ mile until the tarmac path ends at Abbey Road. Do not exit onto the road here but continue straight ahead on a grassy path through the Channelsea Wildlife Area to emerge onto the road a little further along.
- Cross the road here (taking care of the blind bend) to reach the Greenway gate a little to the left.
- Follow the path alongside the stub end of the Channelsea River to reach the steps onto the Greenway embankment.

LOOKING AT WILDLIFE: The Channelsea Wildlife Area is a small area of restored meadow supporting a variety of grassland species, including vetches and wild carrot.

Among the several navigable channels of the tidal River Lea was the Channelsea River, which carried craft into the heart of industrial Stratford and served simultaneously as a drinking supply and a means of sewage disposal for the surrounding inhabitants. It survives today as a northern fragment on the Olympic Park site and a southern section linked to the main river below Three Mills. The longest, central section was, however, infilled in the 1970s, and today forms the route of the Channelsea Path with remnants of the old riverside retaining walls visible here and there along it. It remains a pleasant path despite being overlooked for at least part of its route by fearsome security fencing. Honeysuckle and clematis are scrambling up the chain link fencing and will no doubt eventually soften these high and severe surrounds, deemed necessary to protect the adjacent Jubilee Line depot – another indication of Stratford's importance as a transport hub. When these sheds – and the adjacent Jubilee line – were being built in the 1970s, archaeological excavations uncovered 674 burials from a Cistercian cemetery, for this was the site of the once great abbey of Stratford Langthorne.

In the days when the River Lea divided the area much more significantly than it does in the twenty-first century, there were, in effect, two Stratfords. To the west of the river was Stratford-atte-Bow, whilst to the east was Stratford Langthorne, a name denoting the presence of a tall hawthorn. The Abbey, dedicated to St Mary, was founded here by William de Montfichet in 1135. It was one of the largest Cistercian abbeys in England, with control of 20 manors throughout Essex and 1,500 acres of its own land. Much of its wealth came from its control of the mills along the Lea, which ground wheat for local bakers to supply bread to the City of London, a practice which was later to lead to disputes with the Guild of Bakers.

The Abbey has a place in the development of English democracy, for it was here in 1266 that Henry III finally made peace with the barons after the Baronial Wars –during which he had been briefly displaced by Simon de Montfort – and agreed a settlement that went under the name of the Dictum of Kenilworth. In 1381, however, the abbey was sacked in the course of the Peasants' Revolt, its goods removed and its charter burnt. Having been subsequently rebuilt, it met its final end in 1583: under Henry VIII's dissolution of the monasteries it disappeared almost completely from the landscape – local landowners unsentimentally removing most its stone for their own purposes. It survives today only in the names of several small parks and two streets – including Abbey Road which we cross at the end of this section of our walk.

The Greenway

ROUTE:

- On reaching the Greenway embankment turn left to cross the Channelsea River and follow the embankment for a little over 2 miles, crossing several roads en route.
- After crossing Prince Regent Lane and then Boundary Lane, the embankment runs alongside a large (and rather forbidding) group of school buildings on the right before reaching a point where it is crossed by a fenced path.
- Take the steps on the right and the short path leading onto Stokes Road.

LOOKING AT WILDLIFE: Although the short grass of the central part of the embankment contains little variety, there are interesting plant species to be found along the edges and on the embankment slopes. These include fennel and wild hop, oxeye daisy, vervain, white melilot and viper's bugloss. While some of these are self established, others are most likely the result of the managed sowing of 'wild' flower mixes. The self-sown plants include narrow-leaved ragwort, a recently arrived South African alien, and some unexpected patches of gorse. Kestrel can also occasionally be seen hovering over the flanking slopes.

In 1858 as June temperatures reached 95°F, the smell of raw sewage in the vicinity of the Houses of Parliament became so intense that sheets soaked in disinfectant had to be hung at all the windows. It became the 'Year of the Great Stink', brought about by the growth of the population of London, by the increasing amounts of industrial effluent and, paradoxically, by the invention of the water closet or 'flush' lavatory.

Before 1850 human waste went into cesspools which were emptied from time to time by 'nightmen'. After this date all new houses were required by law to have WCs, and the contents of London's lavatories were flushed direct and untreated via storm drains into the Thames. The banks of the river were deep in sewage solids, and people were said to flee in panic whenever a paddle steamer approached for fear of the stench it would produce as it stirred up the putrefying water. This was the situation when Joseph Bazalgette, engineer to the Metropolitan Board of Works, came up with his plans for the redesign of the whole system. He proposed a scheme of intercepting sewers picking up the contents of the existing storm drains and conveying them away to the east of London to a huge disposal works at Beckton, East Ham. Through two miles of roof tops and terraced housing, our route now follows that of the sewage, along the North London Outfall Sewer, now euphemistically renamed the Greenway.

West Ham, where this journey starts, was originally a hamlet in the countryside beyond London. But between 1841 and 1911 it saw its population grow from 13,000 to 289,000 becoming in the process the eighth largest town in the whole of England and Wales. The greatest impetus for the development of industry in the area was the 1844 Metropolitan Buildings Act, which had placed severe restrictions upon 'noxious trades' within London. West Ham was just outside the jurisdiction of the Act, so the noxious trades came flocking here instead, further encouraged by the cheap price of land and the availability of water transport.

By the end of the nineteenth century 335 firms in chemicals, gas, engineering, shipbuilding, sugar refining, metalwork and confectionery had established themselves in a belt along the Thames from the Lea to North Woolwich. The first waves of residential development to house the increasing numbers of workers were the small townships of south West Ham – Canning Town, Hallsville, Silvertown, North Woolwich. Each one was tied to a particular industry or even to an individual works. The development of the northern part of the Borough came when the building of the railways made commuting possible – to and from the City or the industries alongside the Thames. The arrival of a slightly better-off class of skilled workman encouraged the building of terraced housing in this part of the Borough, and with this came the break-up of the last rural estates.

The line of the sewer embankment is a line right through West Ham's social history. To the south was the concentration of industry and the earlier, poorer, shabbier shanty-towns. To the north were the slightly later, slightly better off working-class communities such as Plaistow, West Ham and Forest Gate. But being outside the City boundaries, none of the borough was connected to the great sewer line which had cut it in half, and 'bubbling and seething cesspools' remained a feature of the area. The construction of the West Ham Pumping Station, to lift the local sewage into the Northern Outfall system, marks the eventual rectification of this injustice. Unpretentious but quietly handsome, it can be seen on our left immediately after we have joined the embankment.

Beyond this, we soon pass two adjacent areas of open space – the Memorial Recreation Ground and the East London Cemetery. The flat expanse of playing fields here was originally laid out on a site known as Pigswell Fields by Arnold Mills, the last President of the Thames Ironworks. This great shipyard below Canning Town, which closed in 1912, once supported several football teams, one of which was to evolve into West Ham United, who played the first four years of their professional life here, before moving to Upton Park in 1904. The site was taken over by West Ham Council in 1924.

The East London Cemetery, except for the fairly wild strip alongside the sewer embankment is one of the more scenically dull of London's cemeteries; however, it must have been more attractive financially. It was developed by the East London Cemetery Company in 1872. 'The population of the surrounding neighbourhood', they pointed out with some relish in their share prospectus, 'is 150,000, and the death returns for the year 1868 was over 3,000'.

Particularly good for business was the Princess Alice disaster, one of the worst civilian disasters in British history. On 3 September 1878 the Princess Alice, a pleasure steamer, was returning along the Thames from a day trip to Tilbury, laden with holiday-makers. At 7.40pm it rounded Tripcock Point into Gallions Reach, and turned directly under the bows of the Bywell Castle, a collier. The Princess Alice was cut in two and sank within five minutes. The full number of dead was never ascertained, but it exceeded 650. The official monument to the incident is in the Woolwich Cemetery, but the graves of many of the victims are here at West Ham.

There is a monument in the Cemetery to the victims of another of the many disasters that have afflicted the working people of East and West Ham. Opposite the main entrance is a large slab bearing a ship's anchor, which commemorates the events at the Thames Ironworks in June 1898, when thousands gathered to watch the launch of the battleship HMS Albion. As the ship hit the water, the ten-foot wave it threw up swept away part of the staging erected around the slip. Two hundred women and children, the families of the men who had built the ship, were swept with it into the water with it.

There is yet another, and even more central, chapter in Newham history for which this graveyard is significant. During World War Two, 3221 'devices' were dropped on West Ham alone. It was almost the first target for enemy bombers flying in from the Channel, attempting to smash both London's industrial base and its civilian morale. The docks burnt for days on end. The shipyards and gasworks were ablaze. Even the sewer line was hit and spilt out its contents onto Manor Road. In all, and 27 per cent of West Ham's housing was destroyed and among the acres of simple slabs erected here are many for the victims of that period.

Looking out across Newham from the elevation of the embankment a later generation of slabs reveals itself beyond, echoing those in the cemetery. They are the tower blocks, themselves a secondary consequence of the blitz. The post-war councils were faced with an enormous problem of rehousing. The answer, to some, seemed to be to build high. This idea was opposed by residents and by sections of the Council but by the early 1950s the first ten-storey blocks were going up. In 1952 the Housing committee of West Ham had written to Harold Macmillan, then Minister for Housing, enquiring whether government subsidies 'could not operate to favour low rise rather than high rise housing'. Macmillan replied: 'there is an unwarrantable prejudice against flats so that excessive amounts of land are being consumed in the provision of low densities of ordinary housing. The national interest demands that this should be curbed.' By the 1960s the Council, encouraged by government subsidies and a new Borough Architect, was espousing the idea with enthusiasm and building blocks of up to 22 storeys. In 1965 the process was speeded up still further with the introduction of prefabrication and the new Lars-Nielsen system of factory production. Eventually 21,000 people were living in the area, in 110 tower blocks making this the densest concentration of such homes in London.

One of these tenants was Mrs Ivy Hodge. On 16 May 1968 she got up at 5.50am on the eighteenth floor of Ronan Point and lit her gas-cooker. The explosion which followed blew out the load-bearing wall. Like a collapsing house of cards the corner rooms of Ronan Point, from floor 22 downwards, flipped down, one on top of the other. Five people died and seventeen were injured.

Amazingly, tenants were later moved back into a repaired Ronan Point and it took many more years of campaigning by the Tower Blocks Tenants Campaign and their consultant architect Sam Webb to bring an end to this breed of high-rise housing. In 1984 cracks began to appear in the load-bearing walls of the blocks and walls began to part company with floors. In order to put tenants' minds at rest the Council used an empty flat to carry out what they called a 'controlled fire test'. After twenty minutes the fire brigade were called in to bring the test to a premature close. Within a few weeks the tenants had been moved out again, and this time it was for good.

On our final stretch along the embankment another grand civic project becomes visible in the distance. Still some three miles away, it looks like a giant guillotine but is in fact the flood barrier at the mouth of Barking Creek, where the River Roding joins the Thames. Built in 1982 it is a companion piece to the Thames Barrier and part of the overall flood defence system for London.

Beckton

ROUTE:

- Follow Stokes Road to its end and turn left onto Roman Road.
- From Roman Road take the first turning on the right, leading to a footbridge, and cross this over the main A13 road.
- From the bottom of the footbridge steps turn left immediately off the

main road and follow a short stretch of road leading to the entrance to Beckton District Park.

- On entering the park follow the main path and cycle-way straight ahead and soon curving to the right. Take the first branch to the right and remain on it until it curves first right then left to run alongside the lake.
- The path continues between the lake and a children's playground then reaches a cross paths. Turn left then take the path that forks off left again just past the ball games area, to reach a gate onto the road.
- Cross the road (Tollgate Road) and continue into the park on the far side. Just beyond the primary school buildings, take the branch to the left which runs downhill and crosses a road (Dove Approach).
- Climb the steps on the far side of the road and continue along a pleasant tree-lined path (Mitchell Walk), climbing up and down over a number of road junctions.
- The route eventually becomes a tarmac path running past houses, a school building and the Beckton Globe Leisure Centre.
- Just beyond the Globe, at a crossing of paths, turn right, following the path onto Triumph Road.
- At the T-junction with Frobisher Road continue on the path straight ahead, crossing Newling Close to reach Porter Road.
- Follow Porter Road to emerge on Savage Gardens opposite another large grassed area (New Beckton Park).
- Cross the road and turn left for approximately twenty yards to reach a tarmac path on the right between the pitches and a fenced area.
- Follow this path and on reaching a row of houses follow the path to the left between fencing and houses to emerge on East Ham Manor Way beside a zebra crossing.
- Go straight across the zebra and continue ahead down Beaconsfield Walk.
- At the end of the Walk turn right onto the road (Ferndale Street). Where the road takes a sharp right turn to become Cyprus Place, take the path that runs across the grass diagonally to your left, just beyond the entrance to Yeoman Close.
- Follow the path as it runs behind houses to reach the main road by a large roundabout.

FACILITIES: Toilets and a seasonal refreshment kiosk in Beckton District Park.

LOOKING AT WILDLIFE: There is an interesting collection of trees in Beckton Park which have been helpfully labelled. They include Cedar of Lebanon, cider gum, Algerian ash, Algerian fir, Hungarian oak, Wellingtonia and tulip tree. There are also wilder sections planted with native tree species. The park lake supports common wildfowl and heron, with great crested grebe and pochard in the winter.

From the Greenway to the docks we are crossing Beckton. Its name comes from Simon Adams Beck, who founded here the largest gas-works in the world; one of the mightiest industrial undertakings of its time, occupying a space larger than the City of London. In 1860 Beck was appointed governor of the Gas, Light and Coke Co, and used the powers made available by the newly passed Metropolitan Gas Act to buy up numerous small gas companies and establish a local monopoly. Beginning with four retort houses adjacent to Gallions Reach, where collier ships unloaded direct from the Thames, it grew to the point where one million tons of coal was being imported annually to supply fourteen retort houses producing 63 million cubic feet of gas a day.

For the workers there was a model village, a 'busy if not altogether lovely colony', according to an 1870 *Illustrated London News*, 'often enveloped in its own private fog'. This was the fog of the retort-house furnaces, where temperatures reached 2000 to 3000°F. The work of the stokers at their doors was described in *Pearsons Magazine* in 1896:

It is terrible work this incessant stoking at the furnace doors ... simultaneously three retort doors are thrown open. A wave of tremendous heat rushes forth and with long rakes the silent strenuous figures of the men draw forth the glowing coke. The fiery shower at once falls onto the floor beneath, the furnace being instantaneously refilled with coal, shovelful after shovelful being hurled inside, to be apparently at once consumed, so terrific is the heat.

One of these young gas stokers was Will Thorne, who went on to become an outstanding working-class leader. Thorne had little formal education and was reputedly taught to read by Eleanor Marx, the daughter of Karl. He was a founder of the National Union of Gas Workers and General Labourers, which had 30,000 members within six months of its inaugural meeting in West Ham. He led the unsuccessful gas workers strike of 1889 – a forerunner by only a few months of the national dock strike – and was elected to West Ham Council in 1894. In 1906 he became Labour MP for South West Ham by which time West Ham had become the first ever socialist-controlled local authority in the country.

The waste product from the furnaces fuelled by Thorne and his fellow stokers went to form a giant slag heap. At 246 feet high it was considered the highest man-made hill in London and earned itself the ironic local nickname of the 'Beckton Alps'.

Eventually, competition from electricity and the introduction of North Sea gas spelt the end for Beckton Gas Works and the last of the retort houses was closed in 1967, but Beckton Alps remained. It can be viewed off to the east, as we cross the footbridge over the busy A13, one of the few surviving remnants of this once mighty enterprise. In 1983 the London Docklands Development Corporation spent £2.4 million on landscaping it and installing a ski run, opened by the then Princess of Wales. But it never quite lived up to expectations and by 2001 had been closed. The 'Alps', which for a time provided panoramic views over east London, have today become a sad site, semi-derelict, strewn with waste and now only partially accessible. They constitute an ironic comment on the London Dockland Development Corporation's website boast that 'there can be no more appropriate symbol of how Beckton has changed for the better than Beckton Alps'.

The Development Corporation – or LDDC – had been charged by Michael

Heseltine with the remaking of Beckton, an area of post-industrial desolation set in the bleak marshlands of the Thames and the floodplain of Barking Creek. Most of the area was in the ownership of the Port of London Authority, which had ear-marked it for the development of a fourth major dock complex, the 'North Albert dock'. But by 1982 it was apparent that this was never going to happen and the LDDC took over. Their aim was not just to redevelop the area but to do so by attracting private capital and to increase levels of home ownership – unlike the local authority master plan for the area that had envisaged a giant Council estate. Beckton was to consist, therefore, almost entirely of private housing and to be seen as the golden opportunity for east enders who wanted to 'better themselves'. Between 1981 and 1995 the population here grew from 5,000 to 18,000 and it has all the hallmarks of the totally designed development; an ordered pattern of streets set with 'district' parks, pedestrian 'corridors', transport 'interchanges' and retail centres –rather than corner shops. It is perhaps largely because of the totally inorganic nature of its growth –and the fact that it is just as hard to create a 'social ecology' as it is to replicate a natural one- that Beckton has never really fulfilled its dream.

The Royal Docks

ROUTE:

- Follow the roundabout to the left, crossing Woolwich Manor Way and Royal Docks Road to reach and walk beneath Gallions Reach DLR station.
- Continue ahead into Atlantis Avenue, crossing the junction with Armada way and continuing straight ahead to reach the river beside a large radio mast.
- Turn right to follow the riverside path. The path follows the river then turns right around the end of a concrete ramp to reach the lock gates of the Royal Albert Dock.
- Cross the lock gates then turn right on the access road beyond. Where the road bears sharp right, take the rather overgrown path on the left.
- The path continues along the riverside before reaching a set of steps and a gate leading to a second set of lock gates.
- Cross the lock gates and follow the path through another gate and over steps to go through the gap in the iron railings on your left.

LOOKING AT WILDLIFE: Around Gallions Reach Station and along Atlantis Avenue there are fragmentary 'brownfield' sites, with plants including both the Oxford and the narrow-leaved ragwort, weld, white melilot, common toadflax, wild carrot, and, most significantly, sea wormwood. There are more interesting plants to be seen along the riverside path, with brownfield species on one side and waterside species on the other. Plants to be found here include greater knapweed, corn chamomile, vetches, everlasting pea, pellitory-of-the-wall, sea aster and sea beet. Waders, wildfowl, grebes, gulls, heron and cormorant can be seen along the river and sometimes in the dock basins.

The docks of the 'Royal' group belong to a second great period of dock-building in London. The first, up-river, docks were built in the age of sail by sea-faring or city men. The new docks were built by a new generation of tycoons, who were exploiting the possibilities of steam, railways and telegraph. Among them was George Parker Bidder, who had been the engineer for the scheme which brought the railway from the City to North Woolwich. In the course of this project he and his contractor-associates had acquired large areas of marshland from Barking Road down to the Thames.

In 1850 work began on this land for the Royal Victoria Dock, and by 1855 it was already a flourishing concern. By 1870, however, even this new dock was proving too small for the newest vessels. Furthermore, it was on the west side of a broad peninsula and by building to the east, four miles could be cut from the journey into London. Bidder's original intention was to link the Victoria Dock to Gallions Reach by canal but, the original contractors having gone bankrupt, it was not until the 1870s that the London and St Katherine Dock Co took up the scheme again. At this point the idea of the canal expanded to become the Royal Albert Dock, which opened in 1880 and was, in its day, the finest and largest in the world. It was the first dock to be supplied with electricity, had its own direct rail link to the City, and made the dock basin accessible to ships of up to 12,000 tons.

The earliest docks had been built of stone and were intended to be durable; however, under the new doctrine of 'progress', implying rapid change, the Royal docks were built with a definite and limited life-span in mind. The emphasis was to be on a fast 'turn around'. Instead of the multi-storeyed warehouses which provided the storage facilities of the traditional Port of London, these docks were lined with single-storey transit-sheds, through which goods were to pass for immediate dispatch. The Royal Docks group was completed by the building of the King George V Dock in 1921. One of the first works of the newly established Port of London Authority, it could accommodate ships of over 30,000 tons. Together the group constituted ten miles of quays and 250 acres of water, one of the largest areas of impounded water in the world.

Our route across the docks crosses the entrance basins to both the Royal Albert and the King George V docks. Somehow, the development going on all around them fails to bring these long grey sheets of water to life. From the Albert gates it is the University of East London campus that we can see off to the west, with the circular, butterfly-roofed blocks of the student accommodation looking like someone's attempt to jazz up a group of Martello Towers. The paths that we follow along the riverside are now rather neglected and overgrown, but they would once have been busy pedestrian routes carrying hundreds of workers on their daily journey to and from the docks or the adjacent Harland and Wolff shipyards. This stretch of the river is known as Gallions Reach, named either after the Gallyons, a land-owning family in the fourteenth century, or, according to the more romantic version, after the Venetian galleys which once sailed up the river here. From the foreshore you can see across to the little light which marks Tripcock Point where the Princess Alice went down. Behind it are the old testing grounds of the Royal Arsenal, until recently largely abandoned and littered with unexploded ammunition. You can still make out the grassed shape of the Twin Tumps, where ammunition would once have been stored, and which is now a nature reserve.

There are good opportunities for watching nature on this side of the river, too, with an ever-increasing variety of gulls, waders and wildfowl using the river right up to the City. Heron sometimes stand reflectively on the mudflats, whilst shoveller, teal, wigeon, pochard, tufted duck and shelduck are all present at times. The ubiquitous mallard and coot are there too, their numbers sometimes reaching the thousands. Among the waders, redshank, spotted redshank, greenshank, common sandpiper, ringed plover and little ringed plover occur, as do all the commoner species of gull, Canada geese, great crested grebes and mute swans. With the dock trade gone, the river at dusk, with the tide on the turn, can be quiet as a pond and sparkling with reflected lights. Small brown waders run about like automatons on the mud-banks, gradually becoming indistinct, while little groups of duck gather nervously about the lock gates. The occasional greater black-backed gull looms large and dramatic overhead and cormorants fly purposefully up-river, keeping low over the water and making for their roosts on the reservoirs.

North Woolwich

ROUTE

- Turn left beyond the railings, walk over the concrete ramp and follow the grassy path that runs along the riverside next to the Galleons estate.
- Cross the second set of steps back across the river wall and continue along the riverside path through the estate.
- Leave the estate through the button operated gate and turn left to regain the riverside.
- Continue along the riverside walk and through a gate into the Royal Victoria Gardens.
- Cross the park and climb the ramp at the far end to continue along the riverside.
- Climb a set of steps on the right hand side emerging onto Pier Road opposite the old North Woolwich station building.

To join Walk 1:
Turn left to reach the entrance to the Woolwich Foot Tunnel and follow the tunnel to the far side of the river.

To complete this walk:
For DLR, turn right up Pier Road, crossing Albert Road and continuing ahead to reach King George V DLR station.

For buses, turn left along Pier Road.

LOOKING AT WILDLIFE: There are more views of Thames wildlife from the riverside path, which is flanked with a blackthorn hedge through the Galleons Estate. Trees in Royal Victoria Gardens include willow leaved pear, umbrella pine and Himalayan tree cotoneaster.

North Woolwich is a strange and isolated area of industry and housing, cut off from the rest of London by the river and by the huge expanse of the docks. For hundreds of years it was also a geographical anomaly. In 1086, Hamon, a Norman noble, became Sheriff of Kent. He happened to own two properties on the opposite side of the river, in what was then Essex, and succeeded in redrawing the county boundaries to add these two detached segments of his manorial estate into the county over which he had control. Thus they became North Woolwich, and remained administratively part of Kent, and then of Woolwich Borough Council, until 1965, the year of the major reorganisation of the London boroughs. Only then was North Woolwich put back properly onto the north bank and incorporated with East Ham and West Ham into the new borough of Newham.

The area was in fact nothing but marshland providing cattle grazing until Bidder brought the Stratford and Thames Junction Railway here in 1847. By connecting his railway to the steam ferry he planned to provide the fastest route from South London into the city, but in 1849 the opening of the Greenwich and Woolwich Railway took away much of his trade, and he proposed instead the residential development of the area. In 1850 he came up with another idea and opened the Royal Pavilion Gardens as an inducement to visitors to use his railway. The railway itself survived until 2006 as the terminus of the North London Line from Richmond. Although its service has been replaced by the Dockland Light Railway, a short distance to the north, its quietly grand station building still stands, where we leave the riverside for Pier Road, shortly after crossing the gardens.

The gardens were once a major entertainment site for working-class Londoners. The Royal Pavilion Hotel provided a music hall and supper-club, whilst in the adjacent grounds as many as 17,000 people would arrive by train or steamboat in a single day to see such events as 'Henry Coxwell's balloon ascents', 'Jean Price and Gevani' on trapeze, the Volunteer Band on the esplanade or the ballet 'Le Demon de Paradis'.

By the 1880s the gardens were in decline, and they were put up for sale in 1885. A movement arose to save them as a 'breathing space for the occupants of these very dreary localities', and they were eventually purchased on the proceeds of the City of London's coal and wine duties, and with donations from a variety of charities and private individuals including £50 from Queen Victoria herself. They were re-opened by the London County Council as the Royal Victoria Gardens in 1890, and still provide a quietly pleasant conclusion to this stretch of the walk – though not the climactic one we might have expected in the days when this was the site of splashing fountains, flashing illuminations, a rifle gallery, a ballroom, a marquee, several stages, refreshment rooms, an Italian garden, and a dancing platform complete with its own full orchestra.

Getting home

King George V Station: DLR lines

Buses: 473, 474

2. Woolwich and the Woodlands

WOOLWICH, PLUMSTEAD AND ABBEY WOOD

It was the Thames that shaped Woolwich: a little fishing village set below a bend in the river and surrounded by marshes. In prehistoric times it had been a bigger, shallower river, set in its own huge flood-plain. Gradually, as the river aged, it cut deeper and straighter, down to its present course and level, leaving a line of steep terrace slopes behind it. They remain a distinctive part of the topography today, running up from the river levels, through Greenwich, Charlton, Woolwich and Plumstead, to plateaux topped with estuarine sands and gravels. It is the soils of these terrace tops which have given rise to the line of commons running from Blackheath to Bostall Woods.

If the first great influence was geography, the second and more recent was the military. It was war and the threat of war which turned Woolwich from a village into a town and gave it a period of prosperity. It began with the navy. In 1512 Henry VIII chose this site for his royal dockyard, and within two years this previously insignificant village had become the launching place of the greatest ship in the world, *Henry Grace a Dieu* or *Great Harry*. For three hundred years thereafter Woolwich was our great naval dockyard, until sail and oak gave way to steam and iron and Woolwich gave way to Tyne and Clyde. By 1869, and with great consequent unemployment, Woolwich was finished as a shipyard. But by this time the army had arrived in the borough.

Throughout the eighteenth century the Royal Arsenal at Woolwich grew to become the largest munitions works in the country. The whole economy of Woolwich became dependent upon it. The Royal Artillery Company moved here, the Royal Military Academy and the military hospitals were sited here, the marshes were taken over for testing and storing munitions, and the commons for drilling and exercising the troops. Even the coat of arms of Woolwich was military: a shield with three cannons.

There is a less-well known story which runs alongside this, a story which turns the Woolwich and the Woodlands history of Woolwich into something more than a set of regimental memoirs. It is the story of the people whose lives and work were dependent upon the Arsenal, of the 'dust hole' and the 'smoke hole', of the 'peace Arsenal' and of the formation of one of the country's most successful co-operative organisations. For these people the commons were their countryside. Yet this unique area of heathland, a treasure of London's open space and one of its most important wildlife sites, was only saved for the

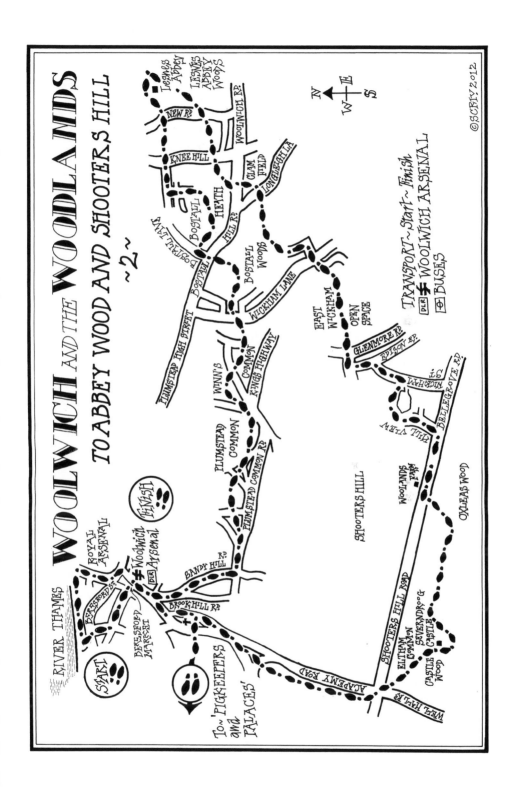

WOOLWICH AND THE WOODLANDS
TO ABBEY WOOD AND SHOOTERS HILL
~2~

©SCRIV 2012

TRANSPORT ~ Start ~ Finish
DLR ⚊ WOOLWICH ARSENAL
🚌 BUSES

RIVER THAMES

START

ROYAL ARSENAL

BERESFORD ST

⚊ Woolwich DLR Arsenal

BERESFORD MARSH

FINISH

⚊ Woolwich Arsenal

To ~ PIGKEEPERS and PALACES'

BROOKHILL RD

SANDY HILL RD

PLUMSTEAD HIGH STREET

PLUMSTEAD COMMON RD

PLUMSTEAD COMMON

WINN'S COMMON

KING'S HIGHWAY

BOSTALL LANE

BOSTALL HILL RD

HEATH

BOSTALL

KNEE HILL

NEW RD

Iesnes Abbey

LESNES ABBEY WOODS

WOOLWICH RD

CLAM FIELD

LONGLEIGH LA

BOSTALL WOODS

WICKHAM LANE

EAST WICKHAM OPEN SPACE

GLENMORE RD

EPSON RD

WICKHAM ST

BELLEGROVE RD

HILL VIEW

SHOOTERS HILL

WOODLANDS FARM

OXLEAS WOOD

SHOOTERS HILL ROAD

ELTHAM COMMON

SEVERNDROOG CASTLE

CASTLE WOOD

ACADEMY ROAD

WELL HALL RD

N
E
W
S

public after a long-running battle with the War Office. It was a battle which culminated in riots, arrest and imprisonment.

Nor was this the last battle to be fought over the beautiful open spaces of these London Thames terraces. For over twenty years the ancient woodlands, sandy heaths and public parks of south east London were under threat from the proposed East London River Crossing, a threat that was at its height when the first edition of the *Green London Way* was published. Upheld by two public inquiries but opposed all the way by People Against the River Crossing and other campaigners, it was finally scrapped by the Department for Transport in 1993, only to be replaced by the proposal for a six-lane Thames Gateway Bridge. Many suspected that the proposed bridge, linking Thamesmead with Beckton, would lead inevitably to the development of precisely the same sort of massive road network that was contained in the earlier proposals, not just destroying ecological sites on the south side of the river but cutting through – and further fragmenting – the poorest communities of east London. A further public inquiry received nearly 5,000 objections and rejected the scheme, but it continued to receive support from the Labour government until it was finally ditched by the new Mayor of London in 2008. The question of an eastern London river crossing remains, however, unresolved – and aggravated by proposals to build over 100,000 new homes as part of the Thames Gateway Project, surely one of the most environmentally inappropriate schemes of modern times. It will, it seems, be necessary to remain vigilant for some time to come if this unique corner of the capital is to continue to be protected.

This chapter covers a single walk, the longest in the book, beginning and ending at Woolwich. From Woolwich Ferry it covers 9½ miles to link directly with the next chapter at Woolwich Common. Alternatively, it can be treated as a single circular walk, 10½ miles long beginning and ending in Woolwich Town Centre. Either way, there are some steep ascents and descents and sections of the walk can be muddy.

■ WALK 2: ABBEY WOOD AND SHOOTERS HILL

Getting started

From Woolwich Arsenal DLR (DLR lines):

Take exit marked 'Town Centre' and follow Powis Street immediately opposite.

Turn right at the junction with Hare Street and continue across Woolwich High Street at end.

Turn left in front of the Leisure Centre then right down Glass Yard to reach the foot tunnel entrance and the riverside.

From Woolwich Arsenal Network Rail (Cannon Street/Charing Cross):

Cross Woolwich New Road to follow General Gordon Place, along the side of the square and immediately opposite.

Turn right into Green's End then left into Powis Street.

Turn right at the junction with Hare Street and continue across Woolwich High Street at end.

Turn left in front of the Leisure Centre then right down Glass Yard to reach the foot tunnel entrance and the riverside.

From Buses (51, 99, 161, 177, 180, 386, 472)

Alight Woolwich High Street/Woolwich Ferry:

Follow Woolwich High Street towards the Leisure Centre then turn down Glass Yard to reach the foot tunnel entrance and the riverside.

From Walk 1:

Take the foot tunnel under the river.

From the Dust Hole

ROUTE:

- From the foot tunnel follow the riverside path then cross steps to reach the Royal Arsenal site.
- Turn right up the main avenue (No.1 Street) then follow the path to the left of the Brass Foundry building to reach the main road (Beresford Street).
- Cross Beresford Street to enter Beresford Square beside the old Arsenal gateway.

FACILITIES: Toilets, pubs and cafes in Beresford Square.

LOOKING AT WILDLIFE: Ducks and waders can sometimes be seen on the Thames whilst cormorants are now particularly common. Terns, particularly common tern, can also be seen, often following the Woolwich Ferry. The new riverside park includes a sown wildflower meadow, although the introduced plants are rapidly being replaced by more hardy 'brownfield' species.

'The dirtiest, filthiest, and most thoroughly mismanaged town of its size in the kingdom'. This was Woolwich in 1847 and it's dirtiest, filthiest, and most notorious quarter was the maze of little streets squeezed into the space between Woolwich High Street and the river. Here in a jumble of dilapidated homes, pubs and low lodging houses, up to five families were living in a single room, using blankets as partitions for their only shred of privacy. This was the 'Dusthole', where soldiers were forbidden and police afraid to enter. The only solution the authorities could come up with was demolition, and by 1912 it had all gone, making way for Ferry Approach and a new power station. Today the site is a neat riverside path and leisure complex – the stock in trade of twentieth-century planning replacing the chaos of unplanned streets. One or two of their names, like Bell Water Gate and Rope Yard Rails are all that remains.

From the new riverside park we enter the Arsenal site close to what would have been the Warren Lane Gate. The Warren was the original name for this area of marshes, which, being only half a mile from the Royal Dockyards, was convenient as a site for military stores. During the reign of Charles II, when the Dutch fleet was penetrating the Thames Estuary, the site was fortified, and from then it was to grow in both size and importance. The Royal Laboratory for the 'manufacture of fireworks and gunpowder', established earlier in the century, moved here in 1695, and by 1717 the government had established a brass foundry and was also manufacturing its own guns. From this time the character, if not yet the name, of the Royal Arsenal was established.

There were major extensions to the Arsenal throughout the nineteenth century and many of the new buildings erected during this period were the work of convicts housed in hulks on the river. These men and women, who lived and died on the hulks, and whose graves dotted the adjacent marshes, gave their name to a flower. The little purple dead-nettle grows abundantly on disturbed ground, and from its frequency on the prisoners' graves it earned the local name of 'convict's flower'.

The growth of the Arsenal mirrored the growth in the size and scale of warfare. It reached its greatest size during the Great War. By 1918 it covered 1,200 acres, with a multitude of buildings, its own canal and railway and a workforce of 75,000. The ups and downs of the industry had a profound effect upon the economy of Woolwich. During the Napoleonic Wars the local population grew by 73 per cent; during the Crimean Wars nearby Plumstead tripled in size; and during the Boer War the grand Town Hall was erected. Conversely, the end of the First World War was to lead to unemployment, poverty and recession. Dismissals at this time were so rapid that the Superintendent of Women Workers shook farewell with 30,000 hands in a week. For a fortnight afterwards he had to wear his arm in a sling.

It was amidst the turmoil of this time, with columns of the newly unemployed women workers marching on Whitehall, that the Peace Arsenal campaign was launched. It was based, as workers testified to a government committee, on the wish to change from 'the manufacture of the instruments of death to the repairing of the colossal wastage caused by the greatest tragedy of all time'. The campaign had some success and for a time alternative work was undertaken. Railway wagons and lorries were repaired; GPO equipment, milk churns and dairy appliances, penny blanks and medals, and most importantly 100 locomotives, were built here. But it was not enough, and the government's commitment to the scheme proved to have been superficial, its purpose having been to reduce the threat of public unrest. Within a few years workers were being laid off again, including the disabled ex-servicemen who had been promised employment. The total number of workers dropped to 20,000, and by 1922 the brave experiment was discontinued.

The workers made other and more lasting contributions to peacetime pursuits. The engineers, for example, ran their own professional football team. By 1912, it had become too expensive for them to support, and moved as an independent club to Islington. There, as the Arsenal, it became one of the great clubs of British soccer. The workforce also founded its own co-operative trading organisation, with the name of the Royal Arsenal Co-operative Society. This society wielded an influence over the whole of south east London and its story recurs several times in the course of this chapter.

There are 23 listed buildings surviving from the old Arsenal. The finest of them, the work of such celebrated architects as John Vanbrugh and Nicholas Hawksmoor, lie on its western fringes. Concealed until recently behind high walls and locked gates, they survive today as part of, and almost swamped by, the recent 'rediscovery' of the riverside. The restored buildings of the brass foundry, the Royal Laboratory, Dial Square and the original military academy now form the heart of a massive development that will eventually include nearly 2,800 homes in a fashionably titled 'heritage quarter'. These old industrial buildings at least save it from the historical anonymity that has swamped much of the riverside. Iain Sinclair, in *Ghost Milk*, describes it as 'the furthest point at which the cultural outflow from the Millennium Dome ... [is] manifest': its public artworks, obligatory in modern development, including the 16 cast iron figures that constitute Peter Burke's 'Assembly' – 'rusting sub-Gormley artworks in a defensive circle ... waiting for the word of command, ready to storm the converted storehouse where James Wyatt was once Surveyor of Ordnance'. Incongruously, not far away, is the matronly Deus Lunas, a late Roman sculpture in beautifully textured stone.

This area was the administrative hub of the Arsenal, but from here the site stretched far to the east onto the Thames-side marshes. In twenty 'Danger Huts', built of light iron sheeting lined with matchwood, workers stuffed shells with gunpowder. This was high-risk work and in the worst incident in 1903 sixteen workers were killed when one of the huts exploded. Beyond these were the moated 'tumps' where the munitions were stored. From this area, 500 acres were handed over to the Greater London Council in 1967 and became the site of Thamesmead New Town. 'Tump 53' survives and has been transformed into a nature reserve administered by the London Wildlife Trust.

The Master General of Ordnance under George IV was the Marquis of Beresford and both Beresford Road and Beresford Square are named after him. The fine, and now restored, archway leading into the square was once the Arsenal's main gateway and thousands of workers poured out from here every evening into the market. The original Woolwich market was sited in the old town and the Beresford Square market grew up as a popular unofficial alternative. The local Board made various attempts over the years to crush it, but it was their own market which eventually disappeared, while the unofficial version prospered. Its heyday was in the years before the First World War, and in his book *The Woolwich Story*, E. Jefferson gives a brilliant and detailed account of an evening in the market at that time. Among the hundreds of stalls lit by swaying oil lamps there was, for example, old Ebenezer Gunter:

> ... a man whose life ambition was apparently to eliminate the hacking cough and eradicate pimples on the face. Short and bearded, he was a wily old bird who really enjoyed his weekly swindle. He had a humour which suffered him to be the butt of witty hecklers in the audience because he knew that in the end he would sell them cough sweets or ointment at a price out of all proportion to their costs ... His ointment compounded of petroleum jelly with a little almond oil and a lot of beguiling speech met

with an equally good reception and while doing nobody any harm did Mr. Gunter a lot of good. That is why we do not see him this evening – he now spends his days in comfortable retirement at the seaside.

From the smoke hole

ROUTE:

- Cross Beresford Square diagonally to your left to leave through the ornamental arch and turn right onto Woolwich New Road.
- Continue straight ahead passing Gordon Square and a short distance beyond it turn left into Anglesea Road then immediately right into Brookhill Road.
- At the next junction bear left again into Sandy Hill Road. At the junction at the top of the hill continue straight ahead until you reach the major junction of Plumstead Common Road and Edge Hill.
- Turn left onto Plumstead Common Road and continue to St Margaret's Grove. Turn left then almost immediately right onto the common.
- Follow the path, keeping straight ahead, as far as the first road across the common beside the Green Chain Walk signs.
- Cross the road and continue on the footpath through a second section of common and a recreational area.
- Cross a second road and a small section of common ahead to reach the apex of two roads and the stump of the windmill above a pub.
- Cross towards the windmill and continue along Old Mill Road following the side of the common. At the junction with Chestnut Rise, cross Old Mill Road and then take the path heading off diagonally left towards the hollow.
- Follow the path down into the Slade and up the other side. Cross the road ahead and turn left following the Green Chain Walk posts parallel to the children's play area.
- Bear right around the top of the children's play area and continue across the grass ahead towards the right hand side of a little copse with a path leading down into a second, smaller hollow.
- Follow parallel to the road that crosses this part of the common (Winn's Common Road) and at its end turn right along Grosmont Road.
- Carry on past the terrace of houses to reach a signposted path on the left heading down through the trees and leading to Wickham Lane.

FACILITIES: Pubs and toilets on Plumstead Common.

LOOKING AT WILDLIFE: There is a rich variety of trees on the common, including sessile oak and several species of poplar. Bird life includes warblers, tits, finches, kestrels and jays. There are many indications of the gravelly Blackheath beds, and 'fairy rings' of field mushrooms on Winn's Common.

The enlarged Gordon Square, fronting the solid and worthy offices of the Woolwich Equitable Building Society, was for many years not so much a square as a hole in the ground. It was an open-topped railway cutting, through which steam trains ran into Woolwich Arsenal Station. It was named the 'smoke hole' by the surrounding traders whose wares were constantly being coated with soot. Eventually tailor Thomas Brown organised a protest petition which was signed by 20,000 people. By 1928 the campaign had been won, the 'smoke hole' was covered over and the newly created square named after General Gordon, who had been born in Woolwich.

From the square the streets take us up to the steep slopes of the Thames terraces. The lower parts of the slopes are chiefly composed of Thanet sands, a fine loamy sand, pale grey to buff in colour, which was dug for the manufacture of bottle glass. It gave its name to Sandy Hill Road and the water, which sank through the sand to emerge as a spring at the bottom, to Brookhill Road. These steep river-cut slopes of London are always attractive, airy places with fine views. What is unusual about this one is, as Charles Booth noted in 1902, 'it is one of the few districts in London where the workman has made the sides and crests of the steep hills his own.' Elsewhere they were all colonised by the city's wealthier inhabitants.

The beds of Thanet sands are topped by the stonier Woolwich and Reading beds and these in turn by the Blackheath beds, a mixture of sands and shingle. They gave rise to stony, acid soils which were unsuitable for cultivation and remained instead as heathland covered with gorse and broom and tough wiry grasses. Their status as common lands was unchallenged for hundreds of years. Until, in fact, the 1870s.

This was the era of the Franco-Prussian War and a time therefore of further military expansion. The War Office had already acquired Woolwich Common for drilling and exercising the Royal Artillery Company and was now on the lookout for more land.

The rights to the Plumstead Commons were held by Queens College, Oxford, who, having already failed once that year to enclose the land, now entered into a private deal with the War Office. The commons were fenced off, the public excluded and the boots of marching feet turned the grassy tracts into a waste land. All protests to the War Office and the Metropolitan Board of Works were ignored, and on 1 July 1876, 10,000 Woolwich citizens assembled in Beresford Square and marched under the leadership of John de Morgan up to the common. The new fences and gates were torn down and thrown onto a bonfire. The Fire Brigade arrived to put it out, were greeted with a hail of stones and retreated. John de Morgan was arrested and taken away to Maidstone Jail. Seventeen days later his sentence was revoked and he was out again. Within a few weeks he was at the head of another march onto the common and this time it was effigies of public officials which were burnt. Within eighteen months Parliament was passing the Plumstead Common Act, and the common lands were saved.

There are actually two areas of common here, separated from each other by a hollow known as the Slade. To the west is Plumstead Common proper, the most interesting feature of which today, apart from the views, is the sail-less stump of one of London's few windmills. The first mill here was built in 1636 but in 1763, during a violent storm, it was tailwinded and toppled over. The miller narrowly escaped with his life but a visiting customer was blown from a ladder and subsequently died. When James Groom opened the present mill in

1764 he also obtained a licence to sell ale from his house, part of which he converted into a drinking parlour. The mill closed in 1847 and the turret was removed in 1853, but the ale-house remains more or less intact today and is still open for business. Beyond it the common falls away into the Slade where the River Wogebourne cut a deep coomb on its way from Shooters Hill down to the Thames. Only the somewhat neglected pond now testifies to its existence.

The second common is Winns Common, named after a one-time tenant of the Old Workhouse. Here there are dark green circles in the grass created by the 'fairy rings' of the champignon mushroom, and a prehistoric tumulus incongruously surrounded by rugby pitches. Beyond, the path dips down the attractively wooded slope of Bleak Hill, which is not bleak at all, and into the valley which separates the commons from the long stretches of Bostall and Lesnes Abbey Woods.

From the dene hole

ROUTE:

- Cross Wickham Lane into Rutherglen Road and take the path immediately on the left, leading round the back of the houses and then up a green corridor towards the woods.
- On entering the woods turn left at the first crossing (leaving the Green Chain Walk signs).
- Follow the broad track which climbs then descends towards a road. Immediately before reaching the road, take the path that climbs up on the right through trees.
- On reaching the first crossing of paths turn left down a flight of steps to the road (Bostall Hill).
- Cross the road to follow Bostall Lane opposite. Shortly after passing Bevan Road, look for a rather indistinct trodden path up the grassy bank on the right beside a traffic hump. It soon becomes a clear path winding up steeply through trees to reach a distinct grassy plateau.
- Cross the plateau diagonally to the left to a gravelly path, then drop down on the far side.
- Bear immediately left on a path that follows first the bottom then the right hand side of a wooded valley.
- Bear left at the junction of paths beside a Bostall Heath Zone Map and follow the concrete path to reach a road (Commonwealth Way).
- Cross the road to take the alleyway ahead (Shornell's Way) and follow it to its end, crossing another road on the way.
- At the end of the alleyway turn right onto Federation Road. Pass the entrance to the campsite to reach Knee Hill.

FACILITIES: Co-operative Woods Camp and Caravan Site is on Federation Road, Abbey Wood, SE2 OLS (01310 2233). It is open for camping from Easter to the end of October.

LOOKING AT WILDLIFE: There is a good selection of native tree species, though with disappointingly little understorey. Despite this there is some interesting relic heathland flora including such species as lesser chickweed, subterranean clover and some surviving patches of heather. There is a population of both slow worm and common lizard and an interesting variety of bird species. There is also a good selection of fungi in the early autumn.

Wickham Lane runs down the deep valley once formed by the Plumstead River which cut down through the clay, gravel and sands to reach the chalk, the bottom layer of the geological soup-bowl that makes up London. Chalk was a valuable commodity, and the valley was once dotted with the pits and quarries from which it was extracted before being burnt in kilns excavated from the valley sides. The resulting lime was sold for a variety of purposes – for building, for agriculture and for the chemical industry. But there is a more surprising side to this story: the chalk was not only quarried, it was also mined. The land below Wickham Lane and its surrounding streets is riddled with more than two miles of lost passages and chambers.

Mining here was a feature of the 1800s and lasted into the beginning of the twentieth century. According to annual returns filed with the Secretary of State, 49 men were employed in 1905, 35 of them working below ground. The chalk thus extracted was mixed with the overlying brick earth for the manufacture of London stock bricks. By 1920 the industry had collapsed, the mine entrances were sealed, and maintenance work ceased on the passageways. Consequently it was not long before the mines began to collapse as well. In 1937 a crater suddenly opened in a children's playground in Rockcliffe Gardens, and the swings disappeared into a pit thirty feet deep and eighty foot across.

In the following year a garden collapsed in Alliance Road and the council decided to call in a company to drill bores to locate the exact line of the passages beneath. On 2 June 1938, Samuel Morgan, while working on filling in the boreholes now that their function had been fulfilled, was standing ten foot from a bore when the ground disappeared beneath him. Two of his colleagues scrabbled in the newly opened pit in an attempt to save his life – they were later to receive awards for bravery – but their efforts were to no avail. The sides of the pit caved in and Samuel's head disappeared underground. His body was recovered next day from under thirty foot of soil.

There were so many collapses after this that during the 1940s and 1950s the area was described as looking like a battlefield, with craters in the roads and cracks in walls and buildings. Residents were given no advice except to leave their homes, and were eventually forced to form an association to secure rehousing or compensation. After a furore which reached as far as the prime minister's office, action was finally taken. The mine entrances were opened and fly ash blown into them. As water naturally percolated through the chalk, the ash set hard, forming a solid plug in the shafts and chambers.

The mines are only one set of the underground holes riddling the rock of this region. An even more puzzling phenomenon is the dene holes. These are vertical shafts penetrating from twenty to forty foot into the ground and ending in a domed chamber with side passages leading off to sets of smaller chambers. These are found in various parts of south east England, always on chalk, and no-one knows their origin. Theories abound however: they are places of religious ritual or 'oubliettes' for captured Danes, prehistoric flint mines or pits dug by the Romano-British for the storage of grain. None of the explanations is completely convincing, though some support for a Roman connection was lent by the thirty foot dene hole to be found off Wickham Lane. Remains found here included seven Roman vases, a knife, a bell and a tile. Dene holes were found in the whole of the region from here through to Bostall Woods and Lesnes Abbey. Whatever their origin, they have all now been filled in – and their secret has been buried with them.

Bostall Heath and Woods remain, as they were described by E. Cecil in 1907, 'one of the most thoroughly rural spots within the London area'. They have a sense of isolation which at times is almost menacing. Steep slopes lead up to a plateau of former heathland, where birch, beech and oak surround quiet, almost secret, grassy clearings. There are sessile oaks and a few conifers, both of them trees of lighter, sandier soils and therefore comparatively uncommon in London. In 1906 the pines were ravaged by a species of beetle but a few still stand, alongside holly and sweet chestnut in the woods and sorrel, heather, gorse, and bracken on the grasslands. Altogether, it is an area as outstanding as Hampstead Heath, but far less frequented. At dusk, when rabbits come out to graze and darkness settles amongst the trees it could be a hundred miles from anywhere.

The eastern half of Bostall Heath now goes under the separate name of Co-operative Woods. The members of the Royal Arsenal Co-operative Society were keen to follow the ideals of the Rochdale Pioneers and to extend the concept of mutual aid for the working classes as far as they could; hence the RACS developed into an organisation including shops, a pig farm, a dairy, a bakery, an abattoir, a jam factory, a funeral service, a motor coach service, a convalescent club, an educational service and a variety of loan and savings clubs. With a support network reaching into every aspect of their members' lives, it was not surprising that they turned their minds to one of their members' greatest needs: housing. In 1899 they purchased the Bostall Farm and building began in 1900, the laying of the first stone being an occasion of great rejoicing. A procession of the Society's vehicles with accompanying bands paraded the principle streets of Woolwich and Plumstead and finished at the Bostall Estate for an official ceremony. Workers on the project were paid ½d an hour above the union rate and 1052 houses had been completed by 1915. They are arranged in streets bearing the characteristic names of the movement: Rochdale Street, Owenite Street, Congress Road and Commonwealth Way. Twenty-six acres were maintained as improved woodland and in the early days these were on hire for outings at 7s 6d per day. In the summer of 1907 the London County Council organised the first open-air school in England in Co-operative Woods. The land was eventually rented out and in 1968 became the most attractively sited campsite close to central London.

From the Abbey to East Wickham

ROUTE:

- From Federation Road cross Knee Hill and take the narrow gap in the railings to follow the path ahead.
- Follow the grassy track passing the Lesnes Abbey sign and then running

between groups of trees to reach, at the far side, some green gates on the right.
- Go through the gates and down the track to reach a road (New Road).
- Cross the road to reach the path leading up to Lesnes Abbey.
- On leaving the Abbey take the path marked with Green Chain Walk posts which leads through the formal gardens then through a hedge into the woods.
- Follow the path ahead, following the Green Chain Walk signpost to Bostall and Oxleas Woods.
- Continue to follow the frequent Green Chain Walk marker posts. The path crosses two roads and then a small estate, followed by a third road and a corner of Bostall Heath, before emerging opposite the football pitches of Clam Field.
- Turn right, then, just after the line of trees, left across the field, to pick up the line of Green Chain Walk marker posts again.
- Turn right on the road on the far side to reach a bowling green then turn left along the signed path, being sure to take the fork to the left, signposted to East Wickham Open Space.
- Follow the posts through Bostall Woods and then alongside Plumstead Cemetery to reach Wickham Lane. Some posts can be partially concealed by foliage during summer and at one unmarked junction, with an oak tree in a triangle of grass, continue straight ahead.
- Turn left on Wickham Lane and right onto Highbank Close to follow the markers onto East Wickham Open Space.

FACILITIES: Toilets beside the abbey.

LOOKING AT WILDLIFE: Lesnes Abbey Woods are primarily known for the spring display of wild daffodils. There is a large stand of sessile oak with some mature sweet chestnuts, and a better variety of shrubs and wild flowers than in Bostall Wood. The smaller pond supports waterside plants and dragonflies. There is a good range of woodland bird species including woodpeckers and warblers and this is a good site for bats including the common and soprano pipistrelles and the noctule, a species elsewhere in decline in London. The stones of Lesnes Abbey support an excellent collection of ferns.

When Henry II cried out in his calculated rage, 'Will no-one rid me of this turbulent priest', it was probably Richard de Luci who took him at his word. Richard was the Chief Justiciar of England, the man who acted as Regent when Henry was travelling abroad. He had been excommunicated for his support of Henry in the dispute with Thomas Becket, and was definitely implicated in the plot to murder Thomas in Canterbury Cathedral. Thereafter he seems to have lived in fear of his immortal soul. In 1178, two years before his death, he undertook an act of penance by donating land and money for the building of an abbey and church. He dedicated them to the Virgin Mary – and to St Thomas Becket. He then retired from active life to live at the abbey.

This was an Augustinian abbey, built just above the flood plain of the

Thames. One of its responsibilities was the maintenance of the dykes and river walls on the Plumstead marshes, and after it was suppressed by Cardinal Wolsey in 1524, both the abbey and the river walls fell into decay. In 1537 the banks burst and 2000 acres of marsh were flooded. They were to remain under water for another seventy years. For a time ownership of the abbey changed hands with monotonous regularity, one of the less lucky owners being William Brereton, whose association with Anne Boleyn was to cost him his life. In 1633 it became the property of Christ's Hospital and remained with them until it was purchased by the London County Council in 1936.

What remains of the abbey today is a neat and well-maintained ground plan surrounded by attractively organised flower beds, lawns and a mulberry tree. It reveals the foundations of the chapter house and cloisters, the dormitory, refectory and kitchen and above all the abbey church with its 132 foot nave. The stones which held up the abbey buildings now support a rich and attractive variety of wild plants. There is thyme-leaved sandwort, black medick and wall barley, and a particularly good assortment of ferns, including harts tongue, black spleenwort, maidenhair spleenwort, polypody, and male fern.

Perhaps the plants rather than the ruins provide the best sense of continuity with the days when this was a busy working community. In 1506 William Bayse, sub-prior of the abbey, compiled a notebook which listed plants with healing properties to be found in the vicinity of the abbey. There are references to 'sharpburrs, daffodyll, fumytory, endyvs, dragen' and to 'celyndyn [which] is good to drink for the jaundy', especially, apparently, 'if yt be gathered on Lammes day, fastyng'. Beyond the abbey gardens and beneath the woodland trees, at least one of these species is still flourishing. Abbey Woods have probably the finest display of wild daffodils in London. The fenced areas of woodland are carpeted with them in early April. No sooner are they over than the floor of the woods is white with the massed star-like flowers of wood anemone. Later still, as spring gives way to early summer, it is the massed ranks of bluebell which cover the ground, like a blue haze, a mist of flowers rising from the woodland floor. In addition to all this contemporary wildlife, and with its location on the Blackheath beds, Lesnes is also particularly rich in fossils, a situation that was first noticed in 1872, when William Whittaker observed that rabbits were repeatedly bringing fossils to the surface when digging their burrows. The remains of over 26 species of mammal have now been found here, as well as those of early birds, crocodiles, sting rays and sand sharks. The area even has a fossil species named after it – the early grazing herbivore Lessnessina packmani.

The oddly named Clam Field leads back to another corner of Bostall Woods. This time we follow the boundary marked by Goldie Leigh Lodge and the Plumstead Cemetery. This part of the estate was acquired by the Woolwich Poor Law Guardians, who opened an orphanage here in 1902. It was a Dickensian institution in the prevailing 'barrack' style and was rapidly rebuilt after a damning government report of the same year decried the conditions in such homes. Today the Goldie Leigh hospital is a home for children with very severe handicaps, many of whom attend their own school on the site.

The Green Chain Walk which we have been following for much of our route is part of a pioneering project created by four London boroughs – Bexley, Bromley, Greenwich and Lewisham – in response to development pressures in London. Beginning in 1977 they jointly designated 4,500 acres of open space as the 'Green Chain' and set about linking them with signposted Green Chain Walks. The network now covers some 40 miles, linking places as far apart as Crystal Palace, Chislehurst Common, the Thames Barrier and Erith.

Over Shooters Hill

ROUTE:

- Follow the Green Chain Walk posts across East Wickham Open Space to reach the exit onto the road.
- Turn left onto Glenmore Road then immediately right onto Dryden Road.
- Take the first left turning off Dryden Road (Edison Road) and the next right into Chaucer Road.
- Follow Chaucer Road to reach a signposted footpath (FP245) on the right, opposite the end of Wickham Street.
- Follow the path until it eventually joins Hill View Drive. Walk down the Drive to reach the main road (Bellegrove Road).

FACILITIES: Pub on Chaucer Road.

LOOKING AT WILDLIFE: Following the improvements to the East Wickham Open Space there are now at least forty bird species and twenty different species of butterfly, amidst a good selection of native shrubs and trees.

The 90 acres of East Wickham Open Space began life as a Council tip. They were later grassed over to become one of those dull and biologically bereft expanses of municipal mown grassland once so typical of our public open spaces. Today this once sterile site has been brought back to life and is an excellent example of a changing approach to the management of our public open spaces. It began, here, in 1988, with the launch of the East Wickham Conservation Project. Since then, approximately half the site has been left unmown, complemented by the large scale planting of native trees and shrubs. Now, on a sunny day you can walk here between hedgerows of dog rose and spindle, hear a whitethroat sing and watch common blue and Essex skipper butterflies on the wing.

Beyond it, after a short stretch of road, a footpath leads us between a cemetery on one side, and on the other, a sudden view of open fields dipping down to a pleasant wooded brook. This is Woodlands Farm and, originally, the Green London Way ran right across it on a path the status of which is now in dispute, with the gates firmly locked against walkers. Our route however still skirts the side of the farm, now an educational trust but previously the closest working farm to central London. Set up by the RACS in the 1920s, it is another example of the expansion of co-operative services in the area. Its main function was to supply pork and bacon to the co-op's butchers and it contained its own 'model' pig unit and abattoir, with the fields supplying barley for feed and straw for bedding. Here is preserved an isolated piece of the Kentish countryside with wych elm, elder, oak, hawthorn, osier, crack willow and crab apple in the hedgerows, and flocks of finches flighting from tree to tree. London has continued its relentless march outwards and surrounded rather than swallowed this site. It creates a strange sense of displacement to walk from the streets and estates of urban south London to come across grazing cattle on these rolling fields stretching up to the summit of Shooters Hill.

The Hill is 432 feet high and has for several thousand years carried over its crest one of the main routes into London. Here the Romans built their Watling Street on the site of an ancient trackway and by the thirteenth century it had become part of the Pilgrim's Way to Canterbury. This important route ran up the steep slopes of a hill surrounded by dense woodland, the remnants of which survive today. Not surprisingly it was also the notorious haunt of footpads and highwaymen who held up travellers and took collections for what they called the 'highwayman's benevolent fund'. During Elizabethan times it became known as the Hill of Blood and the vestry book of Eltham Parish Church shows several entries like that of 1616: 'Paid to a poore man that was robbed at shouters-hille of all that he had a 100 mile (from) home ... 6d.'

As a warning to the highwaymen a gibbet was erected at the summit; however the bodies, left to rot where they hung, failed to deter the highwaymen while putting the fear of god into everyone else. 'A filthy sight it was to see', wrote Samuel Pepys in his diary, 'how his flesh is shrunk to his bones'. Dominating the skyline today instead is the 1910 water tower, an octagonal building in multi-coloured brick and stone. Shooters Hill once had a considerable reputation as a spa, with waters containing magnesium sulphate, and during the 1760s grandiose and fanciful plans were being put forward to develop a whole new spa town here. The first few houses of the scheme were erected and remain today, but the complexities of land ownership ensured its eventual collapse.

Another scheme, floated in 1847, was that of turning the hill into a huge terraced cemetery with accommodation for 10,000 catacombs. This too came to nothing. Threats of one sort or another to the survival of these last fragments of the ancient forest have continued to the present day, with the most recent being the proposals for an East London River Crossing – six miles of highway sweeping through Falconwood Field, Shepherdleas Wood, Oxleas Wood, Shooters Hill Golf Course, Woodlands Farm, Plumstead Common and Bostall Woods. Though both this and the subsequent proposals for a Thames Gateway Bridge have now been withdrawn, the incessant noise of traffic can still be heard throughout Oxleas Wood, the background rumble of the tens of thousands of cars and lorries passing daily down the A2 in its canyon to the south. They are a reminder of the ever-present threat posed by the imperative of road expansion to the future of even our most magnificent open spaces.

Oxleas Wood to Eltham Common

ROUTE:

- Turn right along the main road (Bellgrove Road) to reach and cross the pedestrian crossing. Continue in the same direction for a couple of hundred yards then turn left into the woods.
- Follow the Green Chain Walk signs on a path which leads initially parallel to the main road and then turns into the woodland.
- Follow the broad ride to the second crosspaths and a Green Chain Walk signpost. Turn right here following the route for the Thames Barrier.
- Follow the marker posts through the woods until emerging onto Oxleas Meadow. Walk straight across the front of the cafe and ahead to pick up the markers on the Woolwich Common branch of the Green Chain Walk.
- After passing some formal terraces on your right, turn left at the next junction. Continue ahead through the trees until the path curves sharply right to reach a junction.
- Turn left at the junction and continue downhill. At the next junction turn right to reach a gap in a wall.
- Continue though the gap, passing alongside formal gardens. On reaching the main flight of steps, turn right up them and continue through the gardens to climb two more flights of steps on the far side.
- Continue ahead to reach Severndroog Castle.
- Continue beyond the castle to join another path and carry on ahead. Ignore the tarmac path to the left to take the shady path on the left beyond it, beside the little car park.
- Fork immediately right and continue to reach Eltham Common. On emerging from the trees continue diagonally across the grass to reach the road by the corner of the buildings on the far side.
- At the road junction ahead of you, cross to the diagonally opposite corner and bear right onto Academy Road.

FACILITIES: Café and toilets on Oxleas Meadow.

LOOKING AT WILDLIFE: There is a wealth of wildlife in the woodland complex of this section. Specialities include guelder rose, wild cherry, wild service tree and butcher's broom. As well as a wide range of woodland flowers there is a good quantity of fungi, including many edible species. Bird species include woodpeckers, nuthatch, tree creeper, spotted flycatcher, the wood warbler, and on occasions the woodcock. Butterfly species include small tortoiseshell, comma, peacock, speckled wood, meadow brown, holly blue and orange tip.

Oxleas Wood, Shepherdleas Wood, Jack Wood and Castle Wood together constitute one of the most extensive areas of long established woodland in London. Such is their significance that they have been declared a Site of Special Scientific Interest. Unlike the woodlands we have already passed through they are on the London clay rather than the sand and gravel, and for this reason the sessile oak is replaced here by the pedunculate oak, the oak more usual in southern England.

Among the thirty species of tree and shrub to be found here, the wild cherry and the wild service tree are particularly interesting, as indicators of ancient woodland. Wild service was once used in the brewing of an alcoholic drink known as chequers, and it is from this that many country pubs – and the prime minister's country residence – get their name. The drink was supposed to be an effective cure for colic or 'the torments' – hence its scientific name of *sorbus tormenalis*.

The trees of Oxleas Wood were coppiced up to the Second World War and were returned to this form of management by the former Greater London Council. This eminently sensible arrangement keeps the trees in good condition, setting back the process of ageing, while at the same time providing wood for baulking timber, benches and fencing. Coppicing also has the effect of exposing the woodland floor to more light and thus increasing the range of wild flowers that can grow there. Oxleas boasts a long list of such species, including bluebell, yellow pimpernel, wood sage, hedge woundwort, wood anemone, wood violet, yellow archangel, and common cow-wheat. One of the specialities is butcher's broom. This strange prickly plant with tiny greenish-white flowers is another indicator of long-established woodland. It derives its name from the fact that switches from it were cut and used to clean butcher's chopping blocks. The many fungi species so far identified include the famous fly agaric or 'magic mushroom', *amanita muscaria*. Its red cap with white spots is the familiar illustration of fairy stories and it has a long association with folklore, religion and mythology.

The discovery in July 1987, by spider expert Edward Milner, of a rare green hunting spider *Micrommata virescens*, caused considerable excitement in the area. This was the first time the spider had been found in London for two hundred and fifty years, and the event made the headlines of the local paper. The *Bexley and Eltham Leader* raised the hope that where all else had failed a 2½ inch spider might hold up the East London River Crossing.

Jack Wood and Castle Wood to the west of the complex are a strange mix of wild wood with council flower beds and formal planting. There are terraces and parterres, with grand views of South London out as far as the North Downs, the remnants of disappeared villas and their grounds. One strange folly which remains, though now sadly dilapidated, is Severndroog Castle. This eccentric triangular tower was erected in 1784 by his widow as a monument to Eltham resident Sir William James. As a castle it seems rather a sad affair, and has to be approached up the steps from the west for its grandeur to be appreciated. James himself was a romantic figure. Born the son of a tenant miller in Pembrokeshire in 1721he was at sea by the age of 12. The various tales told about his early days include his escape from a prison in Havana and his survival for twenty days in an open boat by drinking from a snuff box. In 1747 he joined the East India Company, his job being to patrol the Malabar coast between Bombay and Goa, protecting company convoys from Arab pirates, most of whom were based on the island fortress of Severndroog. In 1755, exceeding his orders, James led a direct attack on Severndroog. The fortress was bombarded and laid waste and one thousand fleeing pirates were captured after the main magazine had blown up. In later days James became an MP and a wealthy man. He bought the Park Farm Estate in Eltham, and is buried in Eltham churchyard.

Woolwich Common

ROUTE:

- Continue on Academy Road, taking the first path onto the common on the left, just beyond the bus stop.
- Follow the path which bears right and runs gently downhill, parallel to Academy Road.
- Continue on the path as far as you can until it joins the road at the junction of Circular Way and Woolwich Common.
- Turn briefly left along Circular Way alongside the hedge that fronts the children's play centre and then right at its end. The lay-out of the paths immediately in front of you may be affected by the erection of the temporary Olympic site. Head across the grass, keeping the main road off to your right, and aiming towards the needle-shaped monument at the apex of the common.
- At the road junction beyond the column, cross to the diagonally opposite corner and continue ahead along Woolwich New Road, forking right and downhill at its junction with Grand Depository Road.

To join Walk 3

Turn left to climb the flight of steps just beside the garrison church.

To complete this walk

Continue along Woolwich New Road to reach Woolwich town centre and the stations.

LOOKING AT WILDLIFE: There is a rich and varied flora on Woolwich Common. The covered reservoir area supports a small reed bed with a variety of horsetail and sedge species, including the uncommon slender sedge, whilst the northern section includes dense areas of shrub including species such as spindle and blackthorn. Whilst this area is good for warblers in summer, the grasslands to the south contain a very rich range of vetches, including several scarce species such as yellow vetchling, and a good range of grassland butterflies. Kestrels can commonly be seen hunting over the common, as can the occasional sparrow hawk.

'**Far away down the avenues of time** we discern the beginning of our ancient common. A wild heathland under the wooded slopes of Shooters Hill, from whose recesses the skin-clad savage emerges to survey the desolation of the marshes and the heights of Hampstead Heath …' So began *The Story of Woolwich Common*, jointly published in 1928 by the Chamber of Commerce, the Regional Town Planning Committee, the Council of Social Services, the

Rotary Club and the Kent County Playing Fields Association. What had drawn all these bodies together was the fight to save the common.

Until the nineteenth century this was open land, with gorse growing between ponds and alongside a running stream. Then, in 1802, the Board of Ordnance purchased the areas now known as Barracks Field and Repository Ground, and rights over the rest of Charlton and Woolwich Commons. The landowners received £57,000, Woolwich Vestry received £3,000 and Charlton Vestry, which objected to the whole scheme, received nothing. As for the commoners, their rights were 'extinguished'.

The Board of Ordnance wanted to use the Common for a drill ground for the troops of the Royal Artillery Regiment – whose barracks had just been built on the edge of the common. Very soon, however, the open grassland was being put to a different use; the barracks were not big enough and many soldiers began to build their own shanty town on the common. It soon became rife with cholera, and remained a public scandal until 1804.

The War Office having done nothing, it was left to Lady Maryon-Wilson, whose family name is commemorated in two local parks, to knock down the hovels at her own expense and have them replaced with new huts. These remained on the common till 1875. Meanwhile, other military buildings were rapidly eroding the rest of the open land. In 1806 the Royal Academy buildings went up and these were followed by the two military hospitals, one of which destroyed Charlton Common altogether. It was the proposal to build a nurses' home, again on common ground, which finally proved too much. The Woolwich Common Joint Committee was formed, published the history of Woolwich Common, and launched a public appeal. Battle, albeit in a gentlemanly sort of way, was joined. The outcome was an uneasy compromise. The 'common' remains the property of the Ministry of Defence, but it has agreed so far to refrain from any further erosion or development.

Woolwich Common, like many others, is largely a flat expanse of grassland. Yet unlike others, it retains considerable wildlife interest. One of the richest areas is the site of an old covered reservoir, now hidden by trees, just where we enter the Common on Academy Road. The Reservoir was dug by convict labour in 1848, but it was never really needed since water was plentiful locally. Today the sloping sides constitute an artificial wetland with their own little reed bed, watered, presumably, by the leaking reservoir. The top of the reservoir is a bright display of pink and white flowered goats rue, deep red everlasting pea, and bright yellow hawkweeds. Meadow browns, blues and other butterflies feed from flower to flower, grasshoppers sing and a large colony of well-fed diadem spiders sit on webs stretched between the high stalks of the hawkweeds.

Half-way down the length of the common there is a sudden dip. We are confronted with a five foot drop and a marked transition in the flora. Looking south over the higher ground, the grassland is lush and green; looking north it is lower and thinner and has a purplish haze. The southern part of the common is on the London clay, rich in nutrients and supporting a wide variety of grasses and of vetches. The north section, by complete contrast, is on the Blackheath beds. The soil is sandy and hence acidic and low in nutrients. The pebbles which constitute the Blackheath gravels can easily be seen in the bare patches on the surface. Such a soil creates a truly heath-like section of the common, where common bent makes up 85 per cent of the ground cover, and where sorrel, broom, gorse and birch add to the typical heathland flora. The transition between the two parts of the common marks a return from the slopes of Shooters Hill onto the level of the old river terrace which we followed through Plumstead Common and Bostall Heath. Ahead of us the terrace dips down again to the Thames and to Woolwich town centre where our walk began.

Getting home

Woolwich Arsenal DLR: DLR lines

Woolwich Arsenal Network Rail: Cannon Street/Charing Cross

Buses (from Gordon Square): 51, 53, 54, 96, 99, 122, 161, 177, 178, 180, 244, 291, 380, 386, 422, 469, 472.

3. Of Pig Keepers and Palaces

FROM WOOLWICH TO GREENWICH

When the Saxons settled around London they gave us our 'tons' – Brixton, Kennington, Islington and Paddington. Charlton, or Cerletone, was where the cerls or free churls lived, raising their pigs along the riverside and owing allegiance to no-one. From this community arose the village on the hill above the river: a cluster of houses surrounding the inn, a manor house, the parish church of St Luke's, and its adjacent village green, home of the gloriously anarchic 'Horn Fair'. Nineteenth-century rationalism and the demands of 'public order' swept away the Horn Fair, but despite this, and all the other changes of the centuries, Charlton has managed to retain a distinct identity and a definite village atmosphere.

But the Village is really one of two Charltons – and the second Charlton has largely been lost. Below the hill was Lower Charlton or Charlton Riverside, where the fishermen and barge dwellers and river people lived. Always a race apart, their homesteads in the marshes developed after the 1850s into a tight-knit working-class community separate from, and somewhat suspicious of, the world beyond its boundaries. This was the area of the 'Four Streets', fringed by wharves, barge-works, rope-walks, cable-layers and all the paraphernalia of the riverside.

Two miles, as the fish swims, from these two communities is a portion of London which stands at the completely opposite end of the social and political spectrum: Greenwich, one-time centre of the 'known' world, of imperial ambition, naval adventure and merchant expedition. It was here that monarchs from Henry VIII to James II built their palaces and conducted their courts, dynasties were made or broken, and the fate of thousands decided.

The link between Greenwich, with its pomp and its palaces, and the two Charltons, home of the working class and the free churls, is the link between all the diverse elements of London's history – its river. And along the river here – which incorporates the site of the Dome and the North Greenwich peninsula – there has been more recent change than in any other stretch of the Green London Way. This massive change represents a further era in the city's complex relationship with its river, which was the original reason for London's existence. As Dockers' leader John Burns put it, 'every drop is liquid history'. It was alongside the river that the Celtic settlement of Llyn-din was established, which rose to prominence under the Romans as Londinium, the first fordable point on the river between Dover and the capital at St Albans. By 1594 the river gave

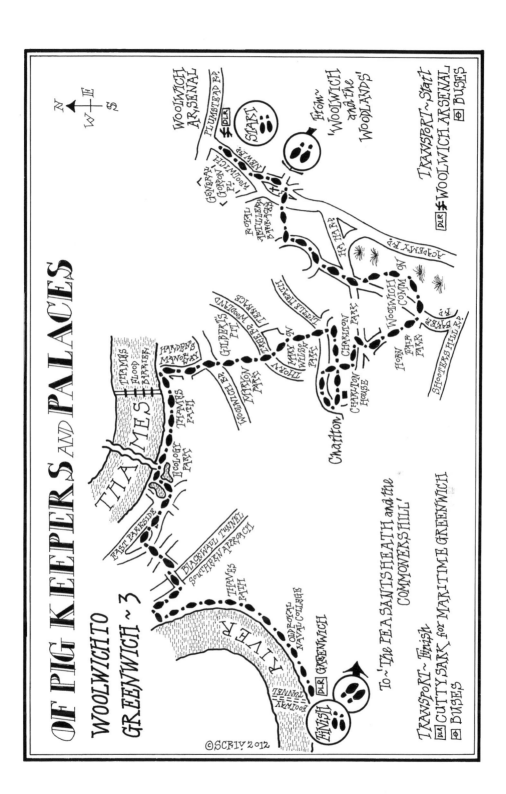

OF PIG KEEPERS AND PALACES

WOOLWICH TO GREENWICH ~ 3

©SCRIV 2012

employment to at least 40,000 people, and by the 1870s 2,000 vessels might be gathered at any one time in the four miles of reaches between London Bridge and Deptford. By the beginning of the twentieth century it was the location of the largest dock complex in the world.

Yet within a few decades of the ending of World War II, all this was over. The docks had closed, the big ships had gone and with them the trade of the lighterman, the waterman, the docker, the stevedore, the coal heaver and the pilot. The busiest port in the world was now miles of abandoned quays and empty, echoing warehouses and acres of industrial dereliction. There followed an amazing discovery – that these cramped areas where the tightly packed homes of the poorest communities jostled against the dock walls, were actually highly desirable residential zones. An era of massive development has turned this London riverside into office towers, shopping malls, yachting marinas and miles of fashionable homes and town houses for wealthier Londoners. Not only has any working connection between the city and its river been lost, but so has the distinctiveness of its individual communities. Under the ahistoric pastiche of post-modern housing styles, it is hard to say any more whether you are in East Greenwich, Rotherhithe, Shadwell or Silvertown. For the new docklanders the river is no longer a central part of their lives and their livelihoods, no longer the link between their past, present and future. It is simply a 'feature' defining a desirable property.

Meanwhile, the old riverside community of the Four Streets has disappeared under the works for the Thames Barrier, which was planned to save London from flooding for at least a hundred years. In fact, by the latest calculations it will be ineffective in fifty and the area most under threat will be the low-lying areas of the new docklands development. It seems that the river may, after all, have the last word.

This chapter covers a single 7 mile walk from Woolwich town centre to the Cutty Sark at Greenwich. There is substantial redevelopment along parts of the route and this may lead to temporary path diversions.

■ WALK 3: WOOLWICH TO GREENWICH

Getting started

From Woolwich Arsenal DLR (DLR lines)

Woolwich Arsenal Network Rail (Cannon Street/Charing Cross)

and from Buses (51, 53, 54, 96, 99, 122, 161, 177, 178, 180, 244, 291, 380, 386, 422, 469, 472) – alight in Gordon Square:

With your back to the front of the stations turn left onto Woolwich New Road. Keep straight ahead, continuing beyond the square until reaching a fork just beyond the church. Keep left here.

Follow the road alongside a long brick wall and shortly after passing Connaught Mews, look for a narrow flight of steps in the bank on the right.

From Walk 2:

Turn left from Woolwich New Road onto the steps beside the ruined church.

The Garrison Town

ROUTE:

- At the top of the steps continue alongside the ruined church to reach the main road. Cross the road and go through the gate opposite to follow the path between the parade ground and the rugby pitches.
- Leave through the gate at the far side and turn left along Repository Road, following as far as the junction with Ha Ha Road and Charlton Park Lane.
- Cross the junction to Stadium Road straight ahead and walk across the grass alongside the perimeter fence slightly to the left.
- Where the fence reaches a corner, with a car park off to your right, continue ahead on a trodden path towards the left hand corner of another perimeter fence (around a covered reservoir) ahead of you.
- Join the tarmac path here running straight ahead and gently uphill with the reservoir fence on your right.
- On reaching the first cross-paths turn right and almost immediately fork left following a mown grass path to reach Baker Road.

FACILITIES: Toilets, pubs and cafes on Beresford Square.

LOOKING AT WILDLIFE: There is an interesting flora growing on the walls along Woolwich New Road, including wall rue and harts tongue ferns. On Repository Road, beyond the barracks, look for the two huge-leaved Japanese horse chestnut trees at the top of the attractive grassed slade. There is an interesting and varied flora on Woolwich Common; from bare-ground species like buck's-horn plantain and red spurrey through to meadow plants like goat's beard, scabious, wild carrot and a particularly rich variety of vetches. These support a good range of grassland butterflies. Kestrels can commonly be seen hunting over the common as can the occasional sparrow hawk. There is, in addition, a variety of interesting trees, including a very fine line of mature hybrid black poplars on Stadium Road.

Whilst the naval and military heritage of Greenwich is world-renowned, the distinctive – and distinguished – military history of Woolwich, just a couple of miles along the riverside, remains largely overlooked. Woolwich is not only downstream but down market, retaining the atmosphere of a gritty, working-class town, even though it too can boast a remarkable collection of buildings by some of the country's best-known architects.

Walking north from the town centre up the Woolwich New Road –'new' since 1790 – you still have the sense of the old garrison town, its severe flanking walls reminiscent of the one-time dingy barracks that spread out across this area. Time has softened them somewhat with a rich growth of wall-plants, but not sufficiently to prepare you for the contrasting grandeur of the buildings to come. Climbing the steep steps of the embankment you find yourself, first, alongside the old garrison church of St George. Designed by T.H. Wyatt, it is distinctly Italianate in character, with a Romanesque basilica and Corinthian columns. It was commissioned by Sir Sidney Herbert, then Secretary of State for War, with the express instruction that it be modelled on a huge church built by his uncle, the Earl of Pembroke, in Wiltshire. Impressive it would have been, but no doubt baroquely over-bearing, for its interior walls were clad with marble, its windows filled with stained-glass depictions of famous artillery officers, and its ceilings draped with over three hundred memorial banners. It is probably, therefore, one of those buildings that appeals more in its ruin than in its original. It suffered a direct hit from a V1 in 1944, and, still remaining consecrated, serves as a walled memorial garden. Exposed to full view – and the open air – are the dazzlingly colourful mosaics – with St George rearing on his white horse above the high altar as a memorial to members of those members of the Royal Artillery Regiment to have received the Victoria Cross. Perhaps the most poignant elements of this memorial chapel, however, are the shrapnel marks still clearly visible on its external walls.

Across the main road, in a display of even greater grandeur, stands the elegant extended frontage of the Royal Artillery Barracks. This, according to which source you read, is the longest continuous building frontage in London, in Britain, in Europe or the world – though some texts use the qualifying word 'Georgian', which rather shortens the field. But it is long – over 1,000 feet in fact – with an impressive white triumphal arch in the centre, decorated with Doric columns and rampant lions and flanked by six stock-brick barracks linked by pillared porticoes. Behind this façade the buildings were originally laid out in a grid-iron pattern to recreate a Roman town, but little of this now survives. The main occupants were the Royal Artillery Regiment, which started life, unsurprisingly, in the nearby Arsenal. When their quarters there became overcrowded, they moved to what became known locally as the 'red barracks' in 1776. It must have been a dramatic improvement, for here, alongside accommodation for up to four thousand men and stabling for horses, were a library, reading rooms, a large riding school, a chapel for over a thousand people – and a large hall for balls. Perhaps the most surprising element, however, was the conversion of one of the arcaded areas into a public theatre in 1863. With a capacity in excess of one thousand, the theatre survived war-time bomb damage and continued to 1956, hosting professional repertory companies as well as staging productions by the RA Officers Dramatic Club – including productions such as *Orders are Orders*, with the regimental band playing in the interval, which received a favourable review in *The Times* in March 1938.

For many years the future of this site was in question, but a wider review of barracks across the capital, and the closure of sites such as the Royal Horse Artillery in St John's Wood, has secured its future – and that of a military tradition in Woolwich that stretches back over several hundred years. Given this tradition, it is perhaps appropriate that Barracks Field, and the northernmost part of the common adjacent to it, were chosen for the Olympic shooting events, although this decision was hotly contested by the Bisley Shooting Grounds. The facilities of this temporary site – four indoor ranges with seating for over 7,000 people, as well as a number of outdoor ranges, providing a home for rifle and pistol events as well as for the paralympic archery – were designed for reassembly elsewhere after the event, in the spirit of a more 'sustainable' Olympics. However, at the time of writing it is unclear where that might be, and for what purpose – or what long-term damage the resultant compaction and other effects will have on this part of the common.

Perhaps the most intriguing of the structures we pass is not so much a building as a hole in the ground. A 'ha ha' is a boundary ditch containing some sort of fence – or, as in this case, a retaining wall – that restricts the movement of livestock whilst not actually spoiling the view with any form of visible barrier. As might be expected, they were usually a feature of the large country estate, introduced to the West by Charles Bridgeman but most commonly associated with Capability Brown. According to Walpole, they derive their unusual name from the expression that you might come up with when stumbling across one.

The one that we cross, at the junction of Ha Ha and Repository Roads, is unusually long. Now a listed 'building', it was dug in 1774 to prevent the sheep and cattle that were grazed on the common on their way into the London meat markets from wandering into the gunnery range. An odd feature is that the mostly hidden brick wall emerges above ground for the last seventy metres or so, as the land falls away along Charlton Park Lane to our right, and becomes the boundary wall of the gatehouse.

Glimpsed over the trees as we climb the common are the four jaunty cupolas atop the central block of the Royal Military Academy. Designed by James Wyatt – like T.H. Wyatt, the product of a large dynasty of architectural Wyatts – it is apparently based on the Tower of London's central White Tower, but, in this more miniature form, manages to look rather out of keeping and almost oriental. Not unfairly it has been criticised as 'a rather silly contrast to the classicism of the Barracks'.

It was built here in 1806, another move from an original Arsenal site, and intended as 'a new campus for sons of military men and the more respectable classes'. Accordingly, its curriculum included English, maths, swordsmanship and dancing. There was even a parliamentary debate in 1873 over objections to the inclusion of *Romeo and Juliet* in the syllabus, due to its unsuitability for young men studying for the army. Despite this emasculating influence, its alumni include Kitchener, Gordon, Napoleon IV and Sir George Everest – after whom the mountain was named. But perhaps its most notable legacies are its contributions to the English language. The very first site for the Academy was in a converted workshop and the new Academy remained affectionately nick-named 'the shop'. It is from this that we get the expression to 'talk shop', meaning to talk in technical jargon. Meanwhile, first year students at 'the shop' were commonly known as 'snookers', a term which, via a journey to India, became the name for the now familiar military variant of billiards.

The Academy was closed in 1937 and its facilities later merged with

Sandhurst. Today the site has become yet another executive housing development. It is good to think therefore that its legacy lives on, if in slightly insidious ways.

The Horn Fair

ROUTE:

- Turn left along Baker Road and after a short distance find the path on the right beginning immediately beyond the car parking area.
- Follow the path through a gate and turn right to follow the perimeter of the BMX track (Green Chain Walk signs) to reach a gate at the far side emerging onto a road.
- Walk straight ahead up Inigo Jones Road. At the end turn right, and on reaching the junction with Canberra Road, go straight across to reach a gate into Charlton Park.

While out hunting one day from his palace at Eltham, King John crossed Shooters Hill and came across a mill. He decided to stop there for refreshment. The miller was out and the king, finding the miller's wife alone, set out to seduce her. The seduction was still in process when the miller returned. He drew his knife rushed at the king, before recognising who he was and falling to his knees. The king led the miller to the door and in recompense granted him all the land he could see between there and the river – together with all the revenues from an annual fair. The conditions were that he forgave his wife and, on each anniversary of that day, made a pilgrimage to the river boundary wearing a pair of horns. His neighbours mockingly christened the place 'Cuckold's Point' and the annual fair became the 'Horn Fair', horns being the symbol of a cuckold.

Like many of the best stories, this account of the origin of the Horn Fair is apocryphal. It was held each year on the green outside St Luke's, the parish church of Charlton, on 18 October, St Luke's Day. The saint is traditionally depicted composing his gospel beside a cow and an ox with large horns, which has led to the suggestion that the fair was held in honour of St Luke. However, Christianity has a well-tested habit of taking over older legends and festivals and turning them to new account. Herne, the horned god of the woods, was a very important pagan deity and, given the ribald nature of the Horn Fair festivities, it is very likely that they are of much older origin.

The 'horns' were always a central part of the fair, which began with a procession from the riverside, led by a mock king and queen, in which horns would be worn on hats and men would dress as women. On reaching the parish church they would walk round it three times then take to the adjacent village green where they 'fell to lecherie and songs, daunces, harping, piping and also to glotony and sinne and so turned holiness to cursydnesse'. A 1711 report describes the 'Ancient Guild of Fumblers' who assembled at the Fair to sing popular songs and to hit each other with ladles. Perhaps the ladles were made from horn, for there was always a large number of stalls and pedlars selling a wide variety of articles made from this material. The Fair was notorious for licentious and unbridled behaviour and was described as 'the rudest fair in England'. It lasted for three days and was attended by upwards of 15,000 people, who, according to an eighteenth century newspaper account, were 'so fond of spirituous liquor that it is sold publicly at Hornfair by people with wheelbarrows'.

In 1819, in an effort to disassociate the celebrations from the church, the fair was moved away from the village green and onto a site known as Fairfields. By the 1870s the development of the rail network brought East Enders to the Fair in ever larger numbers, and eventually the authorities decided to suppress it. It was banned by a parliamentary Order in Council of 1872.

Hornfair Park, where our walk begins, was originally part of the Maryon-Wilson estate. It was purchased by the London County Council and opened as a public park in 1936. When the LCC acquired the adjacent Blue Cross Kennels for a new housing development in 1958, the animal cemetery from the kennels was designed into a small enclosure and included in the park. Prince Henry Road and Inigo Jones Road, which link Hornfair Park and Charlton Park, both bear names recalling aspects of the history of the area. Inigo Jones is said to have lived for a time at Cherry Orchard in Charlton and was traditionally, though erroneously, credited with the design of Charlton House. Prince Henry, son of James I, was regarded as the model prince, but he died at 18. By this age he had already gathered around himself a brilliant circle, among whom Inigo Jones was a leading figure. It was for his personal tutor, Adam Newton, that Charlton House was built.

Charlton House and Park

ROUTE:

- Turn left inside the park, following parallel to the park perimeter until you reach the main tarmac path.
- Turn right along the path and on the far side of the park turn left on another tarmac path to reach the front of Charlton House.
- On leaving the house bear right along the curving entrance drive then turn right along The Village, which soon becomes Charlton Park Road.
- Opposite Charlton Lane take the gate on the right back into the park.
- Turn left in the park, following the path which curves round to meet another path. Turn left again and after passing the changing rooms turn left to reach an exit gate back onto the road.

FACILITIES: Toilets and café in Charlton House. Toilets and refreshment kiosk in Charlton Park. Pubs and cafés in The Village. There is a historical exhibition in Charlton House.

LOOKING AT WILDLIFE: The park has some fine old trees including an ancient mulberry, large horse chestnuts, and avenues of holm oak and yew. There is a resident population of squirrels, tits, finches and jays.

The palaces and royal buildings of Greenwich receive millions of visitors every year. A short distance away Charlton House must be one of the most determinedly overlooked buildings in London. Yet it is one of the finest Jacobean houses in the country, rising red and massive above Charlton Park and the surrounding suburbs. It is built in the shape of a shallow E, with an impressive tower on either flank topped with a cupola and spire. Its rooves carry a collection of chimneys like twisted candy, and its soft red brickwork is complemented by white ashlar blocks on every cornice, mullion and frame. There is an especial exuberance, however, about its main entrance – a slightly projecting porch extending for the whole height of the building. It carries elaborate workmanship in a mixture of styles, bearing columns, scrolls, human and animal masks, coats of arms and the bust of an unidentified woman. This, together with its interior detail, is described in *Nairn's London* as 'sinister poetry ... the most undisciplined ornament in all England'.

The site was completed for Adam Newton in 1612, though the architect is unknown. John Evelyn suggests in his diary that it was built for Prince Henry himself, and not for his tutor, but if this was the case, his early death prevented his occupancy. Newton died around 1630 and is buried in Charlton Church. He was succeeded by Sir Henry Newton, who lost most of the family fortune as a result of backing the wrong side in the civil war. He was forced to move from here to Warwickshire and later sold the house to Sir William Ducie. Ducie, according to the records, paid £8,500 for it in 1658 and sold it for £5,468 in 1680 – an early reminder that house prices do not always rise, but also part of a continuing story of ill-luck for those connected with the house. This was to continue under the next owner, Sir William Langhorn, a retired East India merchant. He was twice married but was never able to beget an heir, something he bitterly regretted. After his death in 1714 his ghost continued to inhabit the house, and is still reported to appear, either pursuing women visitors about the building or as an unspecific 'presence' in the bedrooms. Even unluckier was one of the subsequent and most famous tenants, Spencer Percival, who became prime minister in 1809. Four years later, while still in post, he was assassinated in the lobby of the House of Commons. Like Adam Newton, he is buried in Charlton Church.

The feeling of ill-omen surrounding Charlton House can only be heightened by the strange detail of its decoration. The grand entrance porch and much of the interior bear a grotesque ornamentation unique in English houses. There are representations of the devil, horned heads, grimacing wolves, leering faces with lolling tongues and a menagerie of outlandish half-human, half-animal creatures. Adam Newton himself had a somewhat mysterious history and when this is put together with the suspicious death of the Prince, who died of an unidentified fever, and the proximity of the house to the pagan Horn Fair, all the ingredients exist for some fascinating speculation. In *Charlton House: A Hidden History*, local historian Ron Pepper traces a link between Newton and the powerful, occult, European-wide, secret society of the day, the Prieure de Sion. Newton, he suggests, may have been a member of the Society, uniquely placed to bring the future King of England under its influence. Pepper speculates that the Prince may have been less malleable than the Society expected and that they accordingly disposed of him.

Charlton House passed eventually into the ownership of the Maryon-Wilson family, whose name occupies a central place in the history of Charlton and will figure again in the story of Hampstead Heath. The last member of the family to occupy the house was one Sir Spencer Pocklington Maryon Maryon-Wilson, 11th Baronet. He sold the house with 108 acres of land to Greenwich Borough Council, who opened it as a public library.

During World War Two the building was fitted out with a gas chamber for testing gas masks, and also with a model living room to demonstrate how a room could be made gas-proof. It suffered severe bomb damage in this period and during rebuilding workmen discovered the body of a baby boy in one of the chimneys. This leant credence to another of Charlton's complement of spectres – the ghost of a servant girl who wanders through the grounds with a baby in her arms. Today, as a public library, cafe and community centre, it must be one of the most spectacularly located such facilities in the country. There are more attractive buildings set around it; a range of Dutch-gabled buildings to the left and, to the right, what was once a summer house and dining room. Built only 20 years later than the main buildings its Palladian style –and curious keel-shaped roof- present an interesting contrast to the Jacobean house. Its attribution to the famous Inigo Jones did not protect it from the ultimate indignity of being turned into a public lavatory in the 1930s, a use which has now, fortunately, discontinued.

At one time Charlton Park was unique in holding two of the designated 'Great Trees of London'. The Nettle tree that bore this title lost its top half in a storm of April 2002 when it crashed down on top of a lamp-post and a car. The rest of it, being found to be rotting, was speedily demolished. The second 'great' tree is happily still standing, here by the summer house; a black mulberry reputedly dating to 1608, a date which, if it could be confirmed, would make it the oldest in the country. James I had a peculiar relationship with this species of tree. He had a well-known dislike of smoking, describing it as 'a custom loathsome to the eye, hateful to the nose, harmful to the brain, dangerous to the lungs'. In an attempt to crowd out the tobacco plantations he ordered that thousands of mulberry trees be planted in the crown colony of Virginia. His other planting effort was even less successful. Keen to establish a silk industry in England he imported the tree to England and established a number of plantations, including one of two hundred trees here in Charlton Park. In this, however, he made a serious error. The larvae of the silk moth feed entirely on the leaves of the white mulberry. James had mistakenly introduced the inedible black mulberry. It seems that even the king had bad luck at Charlton.

Hanging Wood and Happy Valley

ROUTE:

- Cross the road (Charlton Park Road) and enter Maryon Wilson Park to the right. Follow the path until it splits in three and take the main central path to reach the animal enclosures.

- Continue past the paddocks to reach Thorntree Road. Turn right and after a few yards find the path on the left leading to Gilbert's Pit.
- Follow the path where it heads right across a clearing and continue, keeping the fenced ridge to your right.
- On reaching the railway follow the path across it to reach and descend the steps.
- Ignore the first gate on your left and continue on through the park. Leave at the next gate and take the crossing over the main road (Woolwich Road).
- Continue on the path straight ahead, passing between the factory buildings and the gardens to reach the riverside beside the Thames Barrier.

FACILITIES: Toilets in Maryon Wilson Park.

LOOKING AT WILDLIFE: There is a wide variety of trees and of commoner woodland and garden birds in the two parks and around Gilbert's Pit. Maryon Wilson Park has animal enclosures with ponies, sheep, pigs, fallow deer, waterfowl, bantams, and peafowl. The Thames Barrier Gardens have sown wildflower meadows which support a good invertebrate population in summer.

Beyond the walls of Charlton Park, and flanking the village to the north, was the dense Hanging Wood, notorious retreat of robbers and home of the highwaymen who roamed Shooters Hill. It was 32 acres of this site which Sir Spencer Maryon-Wilson donated to the London County Council in 1924, and on which the Maryon-Wilson Park was opened. Once a cheery looking park, it now has the appearance of one that can't make up its mind whether it wants to be a park at all, or to return to the wildness of Hanging Wood. It currently maintains something of an uneasy compromise between the two, with brambles, nettles and knotweed shooting up between some fine old trees.

Maryon Park on the other side of Thorntree Road – previously Hanging Wood Road – has a different atmosphere. It is one of the most beautiful of London's small parks and spans the slopes of the steep Thames terraces. The heavily wooded banks wrap around it to north and west giving a sense of seclusion and perhaps of some rather disturbing mystery. Perhaps this is why Antonioni chose it for some of the most haunting scenes in his film *Blow-Up*.

This park was also a gift from Sir Spencer Maryon-Wilson to the LCC and was opened in 1891, with several subsequent additions of land, including acres of disused sand pit. The last of these to survive is Gilbert's Pit, now a celebrated geological site, and our route follows the ridge around it. The sand pits remained a feature of Charlton life into the twentieth century, the sand being dug for ballast, for scouring, for the glass industry – in particular the local bottle factory – and as moulding sand at the nearby Royal Arsenal. It was also used for spreading across parlour floors in the days before carpets were in widespread use. Gilbert's Pit is today a Site of Special Scientific Interest, its exposed strata revealing a complete sequence of rocks covering a period of 60 million years.

Many of these strata now bear the names of the south London areas where they have been studied; the Blackheath beds, the Woolwich formations, the Lewisham leaf beds and the Lambeth sediments. Not surprisingly, the site has been a magnet for geologists for nearly two hundred years.

The view from the top of the terraces must have contributed to the choice of this site for early settlement. The famous Egyptologist, William Flinders Petrie, who was born in Maryon Road, was the first to survey the site in 1891. Then in 1915, major excavations revealed a Romano-British settlement covering a large area from the present Thorntree Road entrance northwards. Comprised of a double bank and ditch surrounding a group of hut dwellings, it was in occupation for a period of four hundred years ending in the fourth century AD. Sadly, from 1915 onwards, the site was progressively destroyed by quarrying.

The Maryon-Wilsons were lords of the manor of Charlton for over two hundred years, their land mainly in Upper Charlton. Beyond, in Lower Charlton and along the riverside, their place was taken by the Roupels, and these two families owned 60 per cent of all the land and properties in the area. Conrad Rupell arrived in the country in 1689 as Captain to the bodyguard of William of Orange. His descendants obtained prominent positions as salt-tax collectors, customs officers, lawyers and masters in Chancery. By the nineteenth century they had acquired the chalk and sand hill slopes between Victoria Way and Charlton Lane and much of the marshland fronting the river; they then set about the major industrial development of riverside Charlton, aided by the arrival of the railway. From 1850 the marshes were infilled for factory sites and housing. Farmer Samuel Harden's market – which gave its name to Hardens Manor Way – gave way to factories such as Siemens, the electrical and telegraph engineers and cable layers, which once employed 17,000 people.

Many of them would have lived in the adjoining community known locally as 'the Four Streets'. Jo Anderson, whose family came from the area, describes it beautifully in her book *Anchor and Hope*, published by Hodder and Stoughton in 1980. 'The Woolwich Road,' her uncle had told her, 'might have been the Brandenburg Gate.' On one side lived the city clerks and other white collar workers, on the other the riverside people: 'My wife, as is now, lived over on the other side, and was never allowed to cross the road to the Waterman's Arms area. All the boys over her side wore school uniforms and neat little caps. They never walked past us, they sped past.'

The Four Streets was a tight-packed huddle of 'two up and two downers', with little corner shops 'sweet with the smell of barrelled beans and new baked bread, home-made toffee and fresh herring'. The small back gardens, with their roses and cabbage patches, were a cacophony of chickens and ducks, and housed rabbit hutches, pigeon coops and kennels for the greyhounds. Within the area was the East Street Mission, which in 1903 initiated a weekly football match on the meadow near Siemens. The team which played here became known as the Charlton Reds and after several changes of venue found itself a home on the fields just off Hanging Wood Lane, where Benson the Butcher fattened his cattle. By now they were Charlton Athletic, top of what was then the second division, and their ground was 'Happy Valley'.

Most of the area disappeared under the works for the Thames Barrier, and one of those new and sterile industrial estates regarded as 'urban renewal'. Almost the only remaining building is the Lads of the Village pub. Surrounded for a hundred years by small terraced streets, it now stands in unsplendid isolation. Having lost the population who once packed it, it struggled on for a while under the more prosaic name of the Thames Barrier Arms and is now no longer a pub at all.

From the Barrier to the Peninsular

ROUTE:

- At the Thames Barrier turn left along the riverside passing through a tunnel under the Barrier buildings and then along the riverside walk.
- Follow the Riverside Walk signs along the riverside path, including several short sections of roadway, until passing the Greenwich Yacht Club and reaching the Greenwich Ecology Park.

FACILITIES: The Thames Barrier has a souvenir shop, café, toilets and disabled toilets and an Information Centre (admission fee). There are some attractive riverside pubs along the route.

LOOKING AT WILDLIFE: The variety of bird life along the tidal Thames has been increasing. Cormorant are common and a variety of ducks, swans, gulls, terns and waders may all be seen at the right time of year. Linnets and wagtail species can sometimes be seen on the riverside path. There are some interesting wild flowers, including species such as toadflax, pepper saxifrage, St John's wort and wood sedge along the footpath, with stonecrop and pellitory-of-the-wall growing on structures. There is also a rich variety of marginal plants on the river banks, including scurvy grass and hemlock water dropwort.

When surge and storm conditions hit south east England in 1953, they brought tides which were 18 foot higher than normal sea level at London Bridge. Sea defences all along the east coast and the Thames estuary were overcome. In the ensuing floods 309 people drowned.

Forty-five square miles of Central London lie below the level of those 1953 tides and the threat of flooding since then has been steadily increasing. There are a number of causes. Climate change is melting the polar ice caps and inexorably raising the level of the world's oceans. Britain itself is slowly tilting to the south east at the rate of about 30cms every hundred years, whilst London, resting on a bed of clay, is sinking. If – or when – surge conditions combine with high tides and strong winds, the city could be inundated. Over 1¼ million people would be affected, tens of thousands of homes lost, gas and electricity cut off, the underground flooded, the water supply contaminated, and the work of the capital brought to a halt. It was to avoid such a scenario that the Thames Barrier was planned.

The barrier straddles the river with a series of curving hooded piers, each thirteen stories high and containing the operating machinery. The piers resemble nothing so much as a solemn procession of silver-cowled monks making their way between one bank and the other. Between these piers are slung the gates, the central ones over 200 feet long and 70 feet high. When they are in the open position they are not visible, being embedded in the river bottom, but when flood conditions threaten they swivel upwards, presenting their rounded fronts to the surge. They are known as 'rising sector' gates, and the idea is said to have occurred to engineer Charles Draper while he was at home, and turning on the tap of his gas fire. The Thames Barrier was opened on 8 May 1984, having taken 4000 men and women eight years to build at a cost of nearly £500 million. Their work was nearly undone again when the dredger *Sand Kite* collided with one of the piers during thick fog in October 1997. As the ship went down she dumped her 3,300 tonne load of aggregate, before sinking by the bow on top of one of the barrier's gates. The estimate for potential flood damage during the time the barrier was out of operation was put at £13 billion.

The longer term problem, however, is that sea levels continue to rise – and London to sink. There seem to be various sets of figures in circulation indicating just how many times the barrier has had to be raised, but the most reliable should be those given by the Environment Agency in response to a parliamentary question in 2007. According to this, the barrier was raised eight times between 1982 and 1990, compared with 31 times in the next decade, and a further 56 times between 2000 and 2007. With current projections showing that the barrier will cope with conditions only up to 2060/2070, London will soon have to come up with another, larger, and even more expensive, solution.

From the barrier we follow the riverside path as far as Greenwich, with a brief excursion inland cutting off the great loop of Blackwall Reach. This is now part of the Thames Path, a 180-mile walking route linking London with the source of the Thames near Kemble in Gloucestershire.

We soon reach the end of the old Four Streets area, marked by the Anchor and Hope pub. This attractive pub, with its lantern roof, is reputedly the place where Hogarth, that chronicler of English dissipation, printed his *Idle Apprentice*. There has been a beer-house on this site for centuries and alongside it sailing barges and brigs would moor to load ballast before heading out to sea. If conditions turned nasty, the skipper might be forced to 'anchor and hope', waiting sometimes several days for the weather to change. Today, however, there are few, if any, brigs or barges along the Charlton Roads. As recently as the early 1960s the riverside here would have provided a fascinating scene of noisy, busy and diverse Thames industry, with sugar boats, cable-laying ships, small tankers, jute, flax and hemp carriers, rafts of floating logs and a whole flotilla of barges moored along the riverside. On-shore would have been the bottle works, the brick company, the coal carriers, the rope works, the barge builders and the large ships' fittings yard of Stone Manganese. The loss of all this industry led to a loss of the employment that went with it, and of the communities that depended on it. Now they have been almost entirely displaced for development, the riverside of today becoming a location but no longer a locality. It is a transformation into anonymity, exemplified perhaps by the North Greenwich peninsular which we reach at the end of the Charlton Roads.

Across the Greenwich Peninsular

ROUTE:

- Continue along the path between the river and the Greenwich Ecology Park. Towards the end of the park you reach a wooden reception building on your left. Turn left up the ramp that leads to the building but instead of going into it, take the gate to its right leading onto a boardwalk.
- Follow the boardwalk between the Ecology Park and housing until you reach another gate at the far end.
- Go through the gate and turn right on a park avenue that leads across a wooden bridge and between two housing blocks.
- Continue ahead with a row of shops on your right and a road on your left to reach a pedestrian crossing over John Harrison Way. Cross this and follow the path slightly to your left that runs ahead through Central Park.
- The path descends a few steps and runs past the end of a row of cottages (River Way). Continue beyond this, climbing a few steps and continuing for about a hundred yards to reach a cross paths.
- Turn left here, crossing the park to reach West Parkside. Cross the road to pick up the path that continues ahead on the other side.
- The path emerges onto Millennium Way. Cross this and continue ahead on the road immediately opposite (Boord Street), which bends right to reach the main Blackwall Tunnel Southern Approach.
- Cross the footbridge over the main road. On descending the ramp on the far side continue ahead, in the direction of the tunnel entrance. After about a hundred and fifty yards turn left onto a footpath leading to the riverside.

FACILITIES: There is an attractive pub on River Way.

LOOKING AT WILDLIFE: The boardwalk alongside the Ecology Park crosses open water, reed beds and alder carr. Plants include hemp agrimony, betony, grass vetchling, marsh marigold and yellow loosestrife. Dragonflies seen here include the blue-tailed damselfly and common darter. The adjacent Ecology Park is open Wednesdays to Sundays from 10am to 5pm. Beyond the boardwalk, Southern Park Meadows have been sown with wild flowers, including oxeye daisy, greater knapweed, yellow rattle, cowslip and perforate St John's wort.

Beyond the Charlton Roads, Bugsby's Reach and Blackwall Reach frame the sides of the narrow peninsular that culminates in Blackwall Point. This tight little ribbon of land was as isolated in its day as the better known Isle of Dogs on the opposite shore. Squeezed between the river and the waterlogged land to the south, it was known as 'The Marsh'. It became the site of sugar refineries, gas works, power stations and a whole concentration of unhealthy industry, afflicting the residents with one of the highest incidences of industrial diseases in the country; it was at one stage officially declared 'the unhealthiest place in

London'. It was also, in its years of industrial decline, a scene of moving hoppers, of pipe lines hissing steam, of ragwort blooming on scruffy waste land, of huge gas holders and of a stark and blackened London School Board building. Across it all was the ceaseless dull roar of traffic, the heady smell of gas, and the thick sweet odour of malt and grain. It was the decision to locate the 'Millennium Dome' at the very apex of the peninsular that began its regeneration and also set the tone for the reinvention of the area as a whole, with its Greenwich Millennium Village, its car parks and pedestrian plazas, its parks and pavilions, and its office blocks the colours of a deranged bathroom tiling. With its brave new world promotion as the 'Greenwich peninsula, a place where you can', it offered the perfect lifestyle to the correct demographic. Like the 1990s wave of town centres it also became the sort of designer town that could be anywhere in the country – and where a post–industrial desolation is replaced by one both planned and post-modern.

Our route across the peninsula starts pleasantly enough, on a boardwalk across reed beds and lakes adjacent to the Ecology Park, and leading on to the Southern Park Meadows. Central Park, which runs from here up the spine of the peninsula, contains two isolated reminders of the area's earlier history. A granite memorial to employees of the South Metropolitan Gas Company killed in the First World War reminds us of what was once the area's main employer; whilst, not far beyond it, River Place is a reminder of where the employees lived. Here an isolated row of nineteenth-century two-storey gasworkers' cottages stands in the incongruous surroundings of the park, with, at their end, the attractive, bow-fronted, eighteenth-century Pilot Inn. On a wall near one end of the terrace, its older, more exotic name of 'Ceylon Place' is still visible in fading white paint.

Crossing the park beyond here we have what is perhaps our best view of the Dome, its silvery tent-like shape surmounted and suspended by high yellow pylons. Built to mark the beginning of the new millennium, its design was intended to reflect the passage of time; its diameter of 365 metres, its highest point of 52 metres and its twelve pylons representing the days, weeks and months of the year. Since this idea is more theoretical than apparent, it is perhaps another aspect of passing time that is more poignantly represented here. Intentionally or not, the leaning pylons bear a striking resemblance to the now vanished cranes that once lined the riverside in their thousands.

The Millennium Dome, as it was originally known, was always a contentious project, and came eventually to represent something of the overweening political ambition of its time. Opened on 31 December 1999, it was in financial difficulties within its very first year. The problem was not a lack of visitors – it was the county's biggest tourist attraction in 2000 – but the fact that its planners had grossly overestimated them. By 2001 it was already a white elephant, empty and costing the country £1 million a month to maintain. Various attempts to resuscitate it failed, until in 2005 it was renamed the O2 as part of a £6-million-a-year deal, and reinvented as an 'entertainment district', with a cinema, restaurants and bars surrounding a central arena and exhibition space. It was this space that was chosen to become the Olympic venue for gymnastics, trampolining and the basketball finals. Such is the corporate nature of the modern Olympics, however, that a temporary name change, to 'Greenwich Pavilion', was ordered for the duration of the Games, since the tele-communications company O2 was not one of the official sponsors.

Shortly after leaving Central Park we cross the busy and fume-laden approach to the Blackwall Tunnel. Blackwall itself is on the north bank of the river, and was once home to the great Blackwall Shipyards, where wooden sailing ships, navy frigates, and the tea and cotton clippers were built. As the Isle of Dogs docklands developed on the north bank, schemes were drawn up to dig a linking tunnel under the Thames. The first of these was by Joseph Bazalgette, whom we have met elsewhere as the designer of the great new sewage system for London. But, despite his earlier successes, some experts, most notably Alexander Binnie, Chief Engineer of the Metropolitan Board of Works, had serious doubts about the soundness of his scheme. The Board of Works was about to be dissolved to make way for the new London County Council, and – largely to prevent the outgoing Board from placing a contract for Bazalgette's scheme – Parliament agreed to the LCC taking over its powers ten days before the appointed date of 1 April 1889.

Binnie became the chief engineer for the LCC and re-designed the tunnel. Its construction marked a major advance in tunnelling techniques for it was driven below the river using the combination of a tunnelling shield and compressed air. The 800 people who built it advanced at the rate of only 100 feet a month along the total length of 6,200 feet. Since it was designed for use primarily by horse-drawn carts and wagons, it was essential to avoid steep gradients, and the tunnel roof had to be taken as close as possible to the bed of the river – at one point they are separated by only five feet. The tunnel was opened in 1897 and had justified its construction within a year: during its first year 335,425 vehicles and over 4 million pedestrians passed through. By the 1950s it was almost permanently congested and to relieve the flow the Greater London Council built what is now the southbound tunnel, between 1960 and 1967.

To Ballast Quay and the Trafalgar Tavern

ROUTE:

- On reaching the riverside, turn left and follow the path for approximately half a mile until you reach Ballast Quay.
- Continue on the riverside route through Ballast Quay and Crane Street to reach the Trafalgar Tavern.

FACILITIES: Several attractive riverside pubs.

LOOKING AT WILDLIFE: More opportunities to see the bird life of the river, though much of the riverside plant life has been lost to development.

From the Blackwall Tunnel entrance we are following the river back to the south along Blackwall Reach. As with the North Greenwich peninsula, we are walking here through one of the most radically, and recently, changed areas of

London. Looking across to the opposite shore, there are good views of the Isle of Dogs. During the nineteenth century this was another thriving docklands area, but by the 1960s it was in the terminal stages of decline. The abandoned acres of dockland here became an experiment in 'enterprise culture' – the Isle of Dogs Free Enterprise Zone, which gave rise to Canary Wharf and its associated developments, an area patrolled and protected by its own private security force. The beautiful and expensive new homes of the 'Zone', some with their own beaches, can be seen lining the river all the way from Compass Point to Island Gardens. The remnants of the old dockland community, meanwhile, were displaced, or else surrounded by the ensuing developers' free-for-all. The surviving houses of Millwall and Cubitt Town sit inland, hidden behind these often gated riverside developments, and in a relationship of some tension with them. Similarly, on this south bank, the whole stretch has become a single continuous development zone, rising immodestly between the river and the old streets and attractive terraces of East Greenwich. With this new wave of building, the once eccentric path has become sanitised. Where once it ran through the middle of working yards, sometimes under the heaving and clanking of overhead machinery, or into a tunnel through the heart of a factory, it now follows a tidily paved route, devoid of cultural associations, between anonymous housing blocks and artificial beaches.

It is only at Ballast Quay that we reconnect with some semblance of history. The Quay takes its name from the Blackheath gravel which was loaded here onto departing ships, and which fetched a very good price on the continent. The work was supervised from a Harbour Master's Office which still stands, alongside the Cutty Sark public house and a pretty row of late seventeenth century houses. Further along, the great and blank-walled bulk of Greenwich Power Station, built in 1906, sits astride the riverside path. In its shadow, in one of the strangest juxtapositions of architecture in London, is the little seventeenth-century Trinity Hospital. The two buildings create a fascinating combination, the power station looking like a big brother to the hospital, towering above it with a glowering protectiveness, as if daring anyone to disturb the tranquility of the hospital precincts. It has even allowed the ivy from the hospital gardens to cover expanses of its huge west wall.

The Trinity Hospital, or Norfolk College, was founded in 1613 by Henry Howard, Earl of Northampton, as a home for twenty pensioners, eight of whom were to come from Norfolk, where Howard had been born. Its white castellated walls are topped by a clock tower and weather vane and if the wooden gates are open you can see through to the tiny courtyard, where a fountain tinkles into a central pool. It has a sense of inviolable peacefulness and would be suggestive, were this not a Christian foundation, of the outer courtyard of an Islamic heaven.

In front of the hospital is a short stretch of road known as High Quay. Its name comes from the quay which was specially constructed here in the fifteenth century to facilitate unloading from the high Venetian galleys. The plaque set into the wall, however, commemorates not high galleys but a high tide. The last major inundation of central London came on 7 January 1928. Seventy-five foot of this wall was demolished by the water which swept through the Hospital and into Greenwich.

The last stretch of road before the path reaches Greenwich itself is Crane Street. On the corner here, with a balcony over the river, is the Trafalgar Tavern. Wilkie Collins, Captain Marryat, Thackeray and Dickens all dined here, and Dickens used it for the setting of Bella Wilfer's wedding breakfast in *Our Mutual Friend*. Despite its illustrious place in literary history, the tavern closed in 1915, but it has the unusual distinction of having been saved rather than destroyed by the Second World War, for it was the onset of war which scotched the planned redevelopment of the site. It is now open for business again.

The Woolwich and Blackwall reaches of the river were regularly worked by whitebait fishers, whose catch was off-loaded at waterside inns, and the Trafalgar was the scene for several special whitebait events. One was an annual ministerial whitebait dinner, held at the end of each parliamentary session throughout the reign of Queen Victoria. Another was an annual whitebait festival, when decorated barges would ply between Swan Stairs and Greenwich Pier and unload their catch straight from net to pot.

Whitebait was probably the last fish to be caught commercially in the river. Long gone were the days when oysters were sold at 1d a dozen, and London apprentices petitioned that 'they be not fed salmon so often'. Throughout the nineteenth century the level of pollution was continually increasing, to the detriment of Londoners, who died of regular outbreaks of cholera and typhoid. In the twentieth century, the cocktail of human sewage, domestic waste and the effluvium from fish markets, tanneries and slaughter houses was compounded with a growing quantity of industrial pollutants. By the end of the Second World War it was said that the hydrogen sulphide released by the river was tarnishing the silver in ship's saloons, the buttons on uniformed jackets and the brass on ships' fittings. Suicides died of poisoning rather than drowning, and the stomach pump became a standard part of rescue equipment. Nothing could live in these poisonous waters. In 1957 investigators found the forty-three miles of the Thames between Kew Bridge and Gravesend to be completely devoid of fish, bird or any other 'significant aquatic organism'.

The recovery of the tidal Thames between 1950 and the 1980s is one of the most often-told success stories of London. Improvements in sewage treatment plant, greater regulation, improvement in industrial processes and the determination of organisations like the GLC, the Thames Water Authority and the Port of London Authority reduced pollution in the Thames by 90 per cent in thirty years. And this led to a return of the wildlife. In 1967 the riverside power stations of the Central Electricity Generating Board combined in a scheme to monitor the return of fish to the Thames. By 1974 their list of species had grown to 91, and included salmon and a sea-horse. This was followed by the return of the birds, beginning with large flocks of wildfowl during the cold winters of the early 1960s. Ducks, swans, geese, waders and heron all use the river today and one of the commonest sights is of cormorant, perched on buoys, or the masts of boats, or skimming low over the water in their evening flight upstream.

This great improvement of the river is not, however, an irreversible phenomenon. In October 2007 Thames Water topped an Environment Agency 'league table' for worst polluters in the country, being fined £128,000 for a series of incidents including sewage discharges into the Thames. The development of the dockland sites has already had a considerable negative impact on bird species, and with regular changes taking place within the water industry and in the regulation of rivers, Londoners will have to keep close watch to ensure that the Thames remains a living river.

Into Greenwich

ROUTE:

To join Walk 4 or to complete this walk:
Continue along the riverside route in front of the Old Royal Naval College buildings to reach the Cutty Sark and Greenwich Town Centre.

FACILITIES: Greenwich has toilets, cafés and pubs. There is a particularly wide choice in the market area. The Cutty Sark, the Painted Hall and the College Chapel are open to the public (entrance fee for Cutty Sark).

In 1427 Humphrey, Duke of Gloucester, brother of Henry V and Regent to the infant Henry VI, built Bella Court, a palatial residence on the riverside. But when the new king eventually came to power, his court was riven with internal divisions, and Gloucester became a possible focus for public opposition. His enemies moved against him. He was arrested in 1447, and murdered one week later in his prison cell. Margaret of Anjou, Henry's queen, became owner of Bella Court.

For four hundred years this site remained the home of monarchs. As the Palace of Pleasaunce, and later the Palace of Placentia, it was the birthplace of both Henry VIII and Elizabeth I, both of whom ran their courts from here. James I came to live here too, and it was he who first enclosed the neighbouring hunting grounds of Greenwich Park. James I also began to build a new summer palace for his wife, Anne of Denmark. Queen Anne died before it was completed, but its construction was continued under the instruction of Charles I for his own wife Henrietta Maria. Designed by Inigo Jones – another link between Charlton and Greenwich – the Queen's House was the first house in the country to be built in the new classical style. A cool white villa, restrained and elegant, it can be seen set back across the main road, between the blocks of the Royal Naval College. The building inspired many others, including the White House in Washington, and even the generals of the Commonwealth seem to have respected it. While they despoiled the great Palace of Placentia, stripping it of all its treasures, stabling horses in its halls and quartering troops about its buildings, the officers had their quarters in the Queens House, and Oliver Cromwell himself was brought here to lie in state after his death.

By the time of the restoration, the main palace was in ruins. Charles II planned to build a new palace on the site, but only one block was ever completed. It was around this block, and the ruins of the great Palace of Placentia, that the Old Royal Naval College buildings arose.

They were not originally built as a Naval College. After the British fleet had defeated the French at the Battle of the Bay of La Hogue, Queen Mary, wife of William of Orange, came down to Greenwich to greet the victorious returning sailors. What she saw of the sick and wounded disembarking shocked her profoundly and she decided to build a Royal Hospital for Seamen, appointing Christopher Wren as architect. He waived all his fees, wishing 'to have some share in this great work of mercy'. The Queen rejected the initial designs on the grounds that they blocked the view of the river from the Queens House. Wren had to come up with new plans that divided the buildings into separate blocks, leaving a clear view down the middle. To this caprice of Queen Mary we owe the continuity of a magnificent vista, clear from the top of Greenwich Park through to the Isle of Dogs on the opposite bank of the river.

The hospital was finally completed in 1750 and became the home of several hundred naval pensioners. By 1814, after Nelson's death at Trafalgar and the end of the Napoleonic Wars, it had reached its capacity of 2710 inmates. After this it went into decline, until eventually the hospital was closed in 1869 – the same year in which, on the banks of the Clyde in Dumbarton, the Cutty Sark was launched.

The listed 'buildings' of London include sewage works, gas-holders, underground stations, twenty-two concrete prehistoric monsters and a ship. The ship is the Cutty Sark, and it was a showpiece in its own day. Built to a revolutionary new design from America, it was sleeker and sharper than anything that went before. Its innovatory raked masts give it an air of jaunty self confidence, and there is something unmistakeably sensuous in its lines. As soon as it was launched the Cutty Sark was racing the other clippers on the long run to and from China. With its streamlined shape and its 30,000 square feet of sail, the Cutty Sark could reach maximum speeds of 17½ knots – 360 miles in a day. But despite all these advantages, the shipyard which built it went bust from the expense and the Cutty Sark itself was overtaken by another, and more significant revolution – the coming of steam. The first steam ships were no faster than the clippers, but they could use the new Suez Canal, whilst the sailing ships had to travel the whole length of Africa and round the Cape.

The Cutty Sark was transferred to the Australian wool run and held her own there for another twenty-five years, but this was putting off the inevitable. With their deeper holds and more regular services, the steam ships came to supplant the clipper even there.

Getting home

Cutty Sark for Maritime Greenwich: DLR lines

Buses (from town centre): 129, 177, 180, 188, 199, 286, 386.

4. The Peasants' Heath and the Commoners' Hill

FROM GREENWICH TO FOREST HILL

The southward sweep of the London suburbs has inundated farms and fields, woods and hills and rural riversides. The huge area of housing which now covers so many square miles of what was once Kent and Surrey developed over a comparatively short period of time, the product of a Victorian building boom made possible by a transport revolution. The great nineteenth century period of railway building gave South London the busiest and most complex suburban network in the world, and it made it possible for the ever-growing army of clerks and scribblers who served the City to live further and further from their places of work, thus producing the dormitory suburbs of London.

Some of these railway routes have already come and gone, and along this walk we pass several remnants – in Brenchley Gardens and alongside Horniman Park for example – of long abandoned branch lines. These and others fell victim to the great contraction of our railway services that culminated in the 1960s. One of the most encouraging aspects of recent development in London, however, has been a rediscovery of the value of railways, with this area benefiting particularly from the new route expansion of the London Overground and the Dockland Light Railway.

South of the Thames, the DLR extension to Lewisham follows closely the route of the River Ravensbourne, with the river even being shifted in one place to make way for it. It is this same river valley that we follow for much of our walk from Greenwich to Forest Hill. The Ravensbourne runs a mere eleven miles from Keston and the Kent and Surrey borders, picking up along the way tributaries such as the Poole River, the Quaggy and the Kyd Brook. Here, shortly before it joins the Thames as the Deptford Creek, it has scoured a surprisingly deep valley – and had an equally significant impact upon the history of the area. It brought jobs and industry through its corn and silk mills, and even a fascinating connection to the Royal Armoury and the armour worn by Henry VIII himself. It was also a vital supply of drinking water, with the Ravensbourne Water Company drilling artesian wells along its course and building the Deptford – and later the Kent – Waterworks on Brookmill Road. But this relationship was a tempestuous one and the narrow river in its deep but densely populated valley was also prone to flooding, with sometimes disastrous

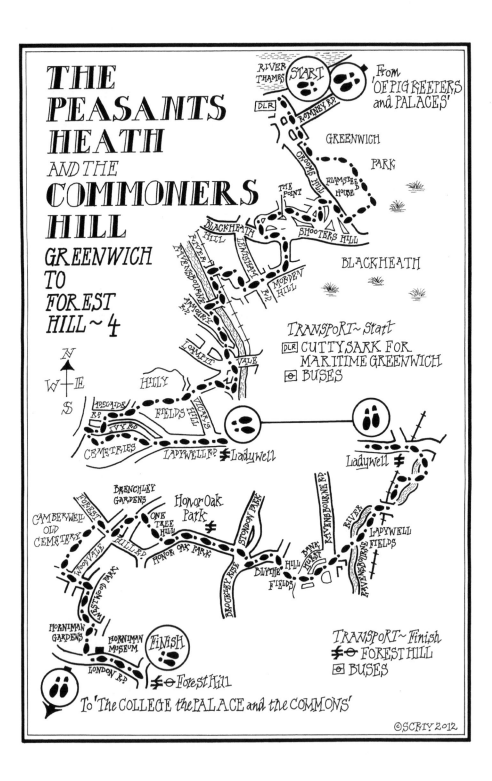

THE
PEASANTS
HEATH
AND THE
COMMONERS
HILL

GREENWICH
TO
FOREST
HILL ~ 4

RIVER
THAMES
START
From
'OF PIG KEEPERS
and PALACES'
DLR
ROMNEY RD.

GREENWICH
PARK

CROOMS HILL
FLAMSTEED
HOUSE
THE
POINT
SHOOTERS HILL

BLACKHEATH
HILL
LEWISHAM HILL
RIVER RAVENSBOURNE
MORDEN HILL

LEWISHAM RD.
ARMOURY RD.
LOAMPIT VALE

BLACKHEATH

TRANSPORT ~ Start
DLR CUTTY SARK FOR
MARITIME GREENWICH
⊡ BUSES

N
W ✦ E
S

HILLY
ADELAIDE RD.
IVY RD.
CEMETRIES
FIELDS
VICAR'S HILL
LADYWELL RD.
✠ Ladywell

Ladywell ✠
RIVER RAVENSBOURNE RD.

BRENCHLEY
GARDENS
Honor Oak
Park ✠
STONDON PARK
RIVER LADYWELL
FIELDS
CAMBERWELL
OLD
CEMETERY
FOREST HILL RD.
ONE
TREE
HILL
HONOR OAK PARK
BANK HURST
RAVENSBOURNE
WOODVALE
EASTWOOD PARK
BROCKLEY RISE
BLYTHE HILL
FIELDS

HORNIMAN
GARDENS
HORNIMAN
MUSEUM
FINISH
LONDON RD.
✠⊖ Forest Hill

TRANSPORT ~ Finish
✠⊖ FOREST HILL
⊡ BUSES

To 'The COLLEGE the PALACE and the COMMONS'

©SCRIV 2012

82

consequences. Our route along today's river illustrates different approaches to the containment of this ever-present threat; from the channel's encasement in severe and sterile concrete through to the more recent naturalisation of sections of the river banks, restoring the ecology and providing areas of natural containment and absorption. Projects such as those in Cornmill Gardens and Ladywell Fields are another tremendous improvement to this area, and should be exemplars for similar approaches across the capital.

But this is not just a valley walk. It also links a string of high places – high, at least, in London terms – that lie alongside the Ravensbourne, and which somehow survived the tide of development that otherwise engulfed the area. Between them they provide not just a sequence of magnificent viewpoints but also the opportunity to rediscover elements of the area's rural history – in street name, in story and in the surviving fragments of heath, wood and field. Blackheath, transformed from a wild, undulating heath into a flat plain for footballers, still has its precious corners. There are reminders of lost farmlands at Hilly Fields and Ladywell Fields and Blythe Hill Fields, and best of all there is that fragment of the Great North Wood that remains today as One Tree Hill. What all of these places have in common is that people have had to fight for them – sometimes quite literally. Contained in this chapter, and in this corner of London, are stories of struggle from the first recorded fight for commoners' rights anywhere in Britain, through to the 1897 'Battle for One Tree Hill'. Included along the way are the great peasant gatherings at Blackheath and Octavia Hill's campaign to save Hilly Fields. These stories proved an inspiration during all those times when unfettered development threatened the open spaces and the unique character of London and when, sometimes on the very same sites, ordinary people had to struggle again and again to preserve all that is best in their environment.

This chapter covers a single 8 mile walk from the Cutty Sark at Greenwich to Horniman Park at Forest Hill. It can however be split into two walks, of approximately 4 miles each, from Greenwich to Ladywell and from Ladywell to Forest Hill.

■ WALK 4: GREENWICH TO FOREST HILL

Getting started

From Cutty Sark for Maritime Greenwich (DLR lines):

From the station entrance, turn left along the arcade then left along Greenwich Church Street to reach the Cutty Sark and the riverside.

From Greenwich Station (Charing Cross/Cannon Street):

Turn left onto Greenwich High Road and continue onto Greenwich Church Street to reach the Cutty Sark and the riverside.

From Buses (129, 177, 180, 188, 199, 286, 386):

Alight in town centre

Follow King William Walk or Greenwich Church Street and signposts to Cutty Sark and the riverside.

From Walk 3:

Continue from end of previous walk.

Greenwich Park

ROUTE:

- From the riverside, walk up the left hand side of the Cutty Sark to reach King William Walk. Follow this straight ahead, crossing the main road (Nelson Road) and continuing, to reach the park gates.
- On entering the park take the right hand path of the two which fork to the left, bearing right again in a short distance and continuing uphill to reach the prominent Observatory buildings.
- From the top of the hill follow the main park avenue alongside the Observatory buildings. At the junction of roads cross to the right and pick up the path which leads off between rows of ancient trees and then beside a covered reservoir.
- Leave the park by the little gate beside Macartney House.

FACILITIES: Greenwich has numerous pubs and cafés. There is a particularly wide choice in the market area. There are toilets beside the Cutty Sark, in King William Walk and at the Observatories, where there is also another café. The Cutty Sark is open to the public (entrance fee) and there are free exhibitions at the Observatories.

LOOKING AT WILDLIFE: There are over ninety species of bird recorded for Greenwich Park, and breeding species include stock dove, woodpeckers, coal tit, jackdaw and spotted flycatcher. The high ground around the Wolfe statue is also a good observation point for autumn migrants. There is an excellent collection of trees, including ancient oaks and sweet chestnuts and exotic species such as prickly castor oil, Pride of India, Chinese yellow-wood, foxglove tree, paper birch, Lebanese and Deodar cedars. There is a wildfowl collection in the formal gardens and, next to these, the Wilderness has herds of red and fallow deer.

When the Duke of Gloucester built Bella Court by the riverside in 1427 (see Chapter 3), he also obtained a Royal Licence to enclose two hundred acres of Blackheath for hunting. This area of rough pasture, woodland and heath forms the basis of the Greenwich Park of today, but not without a major transformation in its appearance. Whilst in exile in France, Charles had become familiar with the work of the great landscape artist Le Notre, which he would have seen at Versailles and elsewhere. In 1661, shortly after the restoration, he decided on a similar grand geometric design for the grounds of the palace at Greenwich. Although his exact involvement is uncertain, Le

Notre was certainly consulted on the plans. The particular problem for the designers was the split nature of the site, the sudden drop in levels constituted by the Thames river terraces. It was solved by the layout of a system of avenues and vistas culminating at the highest point, where the Wolfe statue now stands; below this a series of earthworks, known as the Giant Steps, led down the steep slope to the river level. These steps remain in only a degraded form and the slope has become a favourite site for tobogganing in winter, or for dizzy children to roll down in summer. This was the first place in England where a complex network of avenues was used as the main feature in a park design, and it was a direct forerunner of the development of landscape gardens during the eighteenth century.

Blackheath Avenue, the centrepiece of the design, provides a strong and historic central axis which subsequent developments have served to emphasise. From the spire of All Saints Church on the other side of Blackheath, the vista runs along the avenue to the 1930 statue of General Wolfe, the work of Tait Mackenzie. From here it continues down the slope to the Queens House, between the blocks of the Royal Hospital and across the river to Island Gardens and the Isle of Dogs. It previously continued to the spire of another church, St Anne's Limehouse; today it terminates in the phallic monstrosity of 1 Canada Square, the centrepiece of Canary Wharf. This huge monument to money, at the centre of the development of the docklands, has thrown everything else in London out of scale. Not only have the Greenwich buildings lost much of their former grandeur, but the whole of London has had its focal point pushed several miles to the east. The view from the park demonstrates clearly how the skyline of London no longer centres on its churches or cathedrals but on the banks and office blocks which have come to dwarf them.

The 1660 planting plans for the park included 1000 elms and a large number of sweet chestnuts. Many of the chestnuts survive, ancient rugged trees with deeply ridged bark sweeping in great curves round the broad boles. A mature sweet chestnut is one of the most beautiful of trees and these specimens represent the oldest surviving ornamentally planted trees in England. They predate the first of the Observatory buildings by fifteen years. In 1675 Charles II commissioned Wren to design a building 'for the Observators' habitation and a little for Pompe'. Charles, however, wanted his 'pompe' on the cheap; he cut the budget for the building and decreed that it be paid for from the sale of old gunpowder. In Flamsteed House Wren nonetheless produced a beautiful building, an octagonal red-brick tower rising directly from the top of the hill. Closer examination reveals one of the economies forced upon the builder; some of the 'stone' facings are actually made of wood.

The Rev John Flamsteed, after whom the building is named, lived and worked here as the first Astronomer Royal. He continued to experience problems with the king's stinginess. He received an 'incompetent allowance' of £100 a year for himself and his staff and was obliged to take up private tutoring to make ends meet. The king failed even in his commitment to provide instruments for his 'Royal' Observatory. Flamsteed's main work was in the detailed plotting of stars, from which he was attempting to make a perfect computation of longitude. Isaac Newton, one of the people who depended on these observations for his own work, seems to have abused his relationship with Flamsteed by publishing, under the title of *Historia Celestis*, a pirated version of Flamsteed's work. Flamsteed was understandably bitter. 'How unworthily, nay treacherously, I am dealt with by sir Isaac Newton', he wrote; and three years later he managed to obtain all 300 copies of the book and burnt them as 'a sacrifice to Heavenly Truth'.

When Airey's Meridian was finally accepted as longitude zero for the world in 1884, it was only sixteen yards from the location fixed for it by Flamsteed 200 years earlier. In the same year an international conference in Washington accepted Greenwich Mean Time as the basis of the world's time-keeping system. The atmospheric pollution around London, especially the output from the Greenwich and Deptford power stations, eventually made the area unsuitable for astronomic observation, and the Observatory moved from here in 1948.

The Park was first opened to the public in the eighteenth century and became a firm favourite on the London tourist itinerary. It now receives over two million visitors a year and this, combined with the earlier effects of pollution, has caused extensive damage and a serious erosion problem. Wild flowers have decreased in numbers, though birds have staged a more recent recovery, foxes are common and the ubiquitous grey squirrels were feeding from the hand here long before they were such a familiar sight elsewhere. The animals most closely connected with the history of the park are no longer wild at all: deer were first introduced here in 1510 and for many years they ranged freely. Now they are enclosed in 'The Wilderness', a fenced area adjacent to the formal gardens. Here, no longer the 'monarchs of the glen' or the prey of kings, they doze in the dappled shade of trees or try to beg food from visitors, despite the signs forbidding it. They have become, said Henry James, describing a visit to the park, as 'tame as sleepy children'.

It remains to be seen what effect the decision to stage the Olympic equestrian events and the modern pentathlon in the park will have on its long-term ecology. This was the most controversial of all the locations for the 2012 games, because it involved putting onto this relatively small site of just 300 acres, an arena with seating for 23,000, a 6-kilometre riding course and a 1-kilometre running course, together with all the necessary supporting infrastructure – and at a cost of £42 million. It was described in his blog by journalist Andrew Gilligan as 'a bonkers idea'; the planning application attracted 2,000 objections; and a protest petition was signed by a further 13,500 people – among them such local luminaries as historian Richard Starkey and singer Willard White. All this was hardly surprising given that the construction of this temporary site involved an estimated 6,420 lorry movements in the park, and a further 36,000 vehicle movements during the games, for competitors, officials and visitors – across a site that is literally packed with ancient monuments. The main argument of LOCOG, the Olympic organising committee, seemed to be that Greenwich Park, which is within easy reach of Stratford, would maintain the 'compactness' of the games. Since Badminton, one of the other potential sites for the equestrian events, was specifically established for horse trials as a result of the 1948 London Olympics, the decision is tinged with historical irony.

Blackheath and the Point

ROUTE:

- From the park gate cross the road (Crooms Hill), and walk across the grassy triangle ahead to take the gravel path leading down the slope to the right.
- Turn left at the first joining of paths and after a few yards descend the steps on the right to reach Hyde Vale.
- Turn left along Hyde Vale and towards the top take the path on the right running alongside houses, which soon joins West Grove.
- Continue ahead to turn right into West Grove Lane, descending to Point Hill.
- Cross Point Hill and follow the path opposite. Passing a set of steps on the left you come to a junction of paths. Continue downhill to the right to reach Maidenstone Hill.
- Follow Maidenstone Hill downhill then turn right into Dutton Street and left into Trinity Grove. Walk down Trinity Grove to reach Dabin Crescent at the bottom.
- Turn left to rejoin Maidenstone Hill, then right to emerge on the main road (Blackheath Hill).

LOOKING AT WILDLIFE: Blackheath – historically an important botanical site on the outskirts of London – has been denuded of much of its wildlife except in its wilder corners, such as that above Hyde Vale. A number of bird species, including summer visitors, such as the chiffchaff, still occur; butterflies include meadow brown and speckled wood, and the stag beetle is said to be endemic. A variety of grasshoppers can be found in the longer grass, including the lesser marsh grasshopper, a coastal species which has spread from the Thames marshes. Buckshorn plantain is often a maritime plant species, but this can also be found, in trampled areas, especially around benches.

In 1381 the peasantry of South East England occupied London. It was the culmination of the Peasants' Revolt, which saw uprisings in no less than twenty-eight counties. After years in which landless labourers had struggled against subsistence wages, and half-freed villeins against manorial oppression, had come the final provocation – the first attempt in this country to impose a poll tax. In order to pay for its French wars, the government of the boy-king Richard II had levied a charge of three groats per person on everyone over the age of fifteen.

From Kent and Essex huge contingents of peasants marched on the capital. They were inspired by the popular Christianity of hedge preachers and itinerant friars such as John Ball, who preached the revolutionary doctrine of the equality of all in the eyes of God. Their largest contingent marched from Kent onto Blackheath. Led by Wat Tyler, a blacksmith from Dartford, they arrived here 10,000 strong on 12 June. Using the heath as their camp they sortied into London, where they found the gates opened before them by the London poor and a sympathetic party amongst the aldermen. As they streamed through London, the 'impregnable' Tower was surrendered, the Fleet and Marshalsea prisons opened, the Monastery of St John of Jerusalem burnt and the Temple library destroyed, together with all the hated lawyers' rolls.

King Richard, still only fourteen years old, went to meet the rebel force at Smithfield.

During this meeting William Walworth, Lord Mayor of London, pulled Tyler from his horse and stabbed him to death. The rebels dispersed, most of them returning to their lands, where they were met with revengeful punishment by their 'lords'. The leaders of the revolt were executed and the uprising seemed to have been defeated. But it was to leave an indelible mark on history. In the short term, the hated poll tax was abolished. In the longer term, the peasantry had shown what a potent force it could be when roused; and it was six hundred years before anyone attempted to levy a poll tax again.

Only seventy years later Blackheath was once again the focus of rebellion. Almost bankrupted by its years of wasteful war, the government of Henry VI attempted to make good its deficit by imposing higher taxes on a country already simmering with discontent. In 1450 Jack Cade led 20,000 Kent and Essex yeomen onto the heath, where they set up camp. They laid the 'Blackheath Petition' before the Royal Council, calling on the king 'to punish evil ministers and procure a redress of grievance'. The state pretended to consider the demands whilst sending Sir Humphrey Stafford with a force to crush the rebels. But it was Stafford who was defeated and killed, and the rebels entered London in triumph. After occupying the capital for three days the rebels received an offer from the government to consider their demands and began to disperse to their homes. Promises however were not enough for Jack Cade who continued to demand real concessions. But his support had melted away. He was forced to flee into hiding in Sussex, where the king's forces eventually caught up with and murdered him. His name is commemorated in Cade Road on the heath.

By 1497 the rebels were back, in what was to be the last and most tragic of the great peasant rallyings on the heath. This time they had marched all the way from Cornwall, 6,000 of them led by Thomas Flannock and Michael Joseph, in protest against taxes levied to pay for the Scottish wars. This time there was to be no treating or negotiating. Henry VII dispatched his army and in the 'Battle of Blackheath' up to 2,000 of the rebels were killed, their bodies being unceremoniously dumped in mass graves. The survivors surrendered and their leaders were taken for execution.

Whitfield Mount, behind the Whitfield pond on Goffers Road, is the remains of one of these burying places.

For thousands of years Blackheath was a wild tract of heathland covered with gorse and heather. In the eighteenth century the great Swedish scientist Linnaeus arrived here on a visit, and is said to have been so struck by the masses of yellow gorse blossom that he fell to his knees in wonder and offered up thanksgiving to the 'great Creator of Nature'. It was Linnaeus who devised the scientific binomial system which remains the basis of taxonomy. Should he turn up on the heath today he would find very little wildlife left to label. As late as 1859, its fauna was listed as including weasel, stoat, polecat, hare, harvest mouse and even the rare natterjack toad. At one time there were more species of grass to be found on Blackheath than anywhere else in Southern England. But its animals are gone; and its grass is now the tough imported strains of football pitches. Blackheath is, for the most part, a tired and barren green waste.

Even its one-time undulations were infilled with rubble from the blitz. Litter floats in its remaining ponds and the whole plateau has been reduced to a dreary uniformity, a flat expanse of football and rugby pitches sliced up by an excessive network of roads. The main interest of the heath now lies in its history, in the architecture of its surrounding houses, and in the one or two surviving corners that have escaped over-regulation. These include the old gravel pits around Vanbrugh Park and the slopes of Hyde Vale. It is at this latter point that our own route emerges from Greenwich Park.

The rambling red-brick range beside the Croomshill Gate is Macartney House, built around 1676, and from 1751 to 1758 the home of General James Wolfe. Further up Chesterfield Walk is the stylish villa known as the Rangers House. Lord Chesterfield, who inherited it in 1748, wrote here the book which became famous as *Letters to his Son*. The letters are full of pompous homilies: 'There is nothing so illiberal and so ill-bred as audible laughter' wrote Chesterfield; and 'women ... are only children of a larger growth'. The recipient of such wisdom was Phillip Stanhope, Chesterfield's natural son. Perhaps the most revealing feature of their relationship is that Stanhope married and raised a family – and kept it a life-long secret from his father. Rangers House, later the official residence of the royal sinecure post, the Greenwich Park Ranger, is today a museum housing the Wernher collection of paintings, porcelain and jewellery.

Across Hyde Vale we reach The Point, a small westward extension of the Blackheath plateau, in an area of elegant eighteenth-century housing. From here there is an uninterrupted panorama of London, taking in Greenwich, Deptford and the City. The Point is in fact a hollow hill: in 1780 a local builder chanced across a vertical shaft which led down into three caverns, the largest of which was 58 foot long, 30 foot wide and 12 foot high. The origin of the caverns is unknown but it is likely they were chalk excavations of some kind, for here layers of chalk are nearer to the surface than anywhere else around Blackheath. The entrepreneurial Victorians subsequently put the caverns to use. The public were admitted for viewings at 4d a time, and once a bar had been fitted they became a regular venue for drinking parties, balls and dances. No doubt the local residents were continually disturbed by the revellers attracted to their neighbourhood and in 1853 came the final outrage: a practical 'joker' doused all the lights in the course of a masked ball, panic ensued and there was a stampede for the exits. The outcry about this led to the closure of the caverns and the entrance passage was filled in so effectively that it became impossible to re-locate. In 1938, when the local authorities commissioned a report on the possible use of the caverns as air-raid shelters, they were unable to find the entrance, and were forced to sink a new shaft down. Their conclusions were that the caverns were unsuitable for shelters but a passage in their report describes the main chamber, still with half-burnt candles standing on the abandoned bar. The site has become a sort of sealed time capsule, remaining just as it was left late one night by the revellers of 1853.

The Valley of the Ravensbourne

ROUTE:

- Cross Blackheath Hill and walk up it to the left. On reaching a fork by a group of attractive old houses, bear right into Dartmouth Hill and then almost immediately right onto a path beside Montague House.
- Follow the path as it broadens into a lane and ends at a junction with Morden Hill.
- Turn right down Morden Hill. Where it meets Lewisham Road, cross the road and continue on the far side. After passing the last block of an estate on the right, you reach the entrance to an alleyway lined with lamp posts. Follow the alley (Silk Mills Passage) to its end, continuing straight ahead along a short stretch of road to reach the junction with Elverson Road/Nectarine Way.
- Turn left to cross Coldbath Street and reach the DLR station. Cross the footbridge over the railway.
- On the far side of the footbridge turn left to join a path ahead of you running alongside the river.
- After a short distance, cross the small footbridge on your right then turn immediately left to continue to follow the river along Armoury Road and through a small estate.
- A few hundred yards along look for a paved path coming off to the right that runs between a housing block and a hedge, heading towards a grey metal fence and a tunnel under the railway.
- Go through the tunnel to emerge onto Thurston Road opposite Jerrard Street.
- Turn left along Thurston Road to reach the junction with the main road (Loampit Vale).
- Cross the main road and turn left. Just before the railway arches join the path on the right that runs alongside the arches to rejoin the riverside.
- Follow the riverside through Cornmill Gardens and beyond the gardens continue ahead on Waterway Avenue.
- At the end of the avenue turn right onto Smead Way. At the end of Smead Way turn left under the railway arch onto Ellerdale Street.

FACILITIES: Pub at the junction of Morden Hill and Lewisham Road.

LOOKING AT WILDLIFE: Alkanet, salad burnet and giant hogweed all grow along Morden Lane. The Ravensbourne has conventional concrete banks in many places but in others natural, gravelly banks where natural banks have been re-introduced. These support a wetland flora including hairy willow herb and hemlock water dropwort. Grey wagtail and even the occasional kingfisher can be seen here.

The smart houses of Dartmouth Hill and its surrounding streets began as an illegal encroachment on common land. Building began on the Heath in 1690 and continued in a piecemeal way until 1866, when those already living there decided to prevent anybody else doing what they had already done by founding a preservation society. Within a year they had already managed to get an Act through parliament preventing any further development on Blackheath. It was part of the first national legislation giving protection to common land.

On Morden Hill – named after one of the major landowners in the area – we make a descent which is perhaps as much social as it is geographic, taking us from the beautiful old houses of Blackheath down to the housing estates of Lewisham, set in the flood plain of the River Ravensbourne. What looks today a tame and restricted little stream has, over thousands of years, cut down through forty foot of sands and gravels and into the underlying chalk. The steep slopes here were the site of Loats Pit, where chalk was quarried and burnt in kilns. According to Duncan's 1908 *History of Lewisham*, they provided much of the lime required for the rebuilding of London after the Great Fire.

According to legend, Julius Caesar was campaigning in Southern England when his forces ran out of water. They were forced to encamp whilst sending out detachments in search of a supply. They were unsuccessful but Caesar himself had noted ravens regularly flying to and from a spot not far from the camp. He sent out more men to investigate and they came upon the small spring on Keston Heath still known as Caesar's or Raven's Well. Legend does not relate how everyone else had missed so obvious a source. From this spring arises our river, the Ravens Bourne, flowing eleven miles to reach the Thames at Deptford. Its industrial potential was recognised early and by the time of the Domesday Book there were already eleven mills in the Lewisham area, one of which was purchased in 1688 by the famous diarist John Evelyn for grinding colour. The names of several others are still commemorated in the local street names: Brookmill Road, Cornmill Lane, Silk Mills Path and Armoury Road. All of the uses indicated here came into play in the history of the most important of the mills. It sat on the north bank of the river, served by Silk Mills Path, though it began life as a corn mill. In 1371 it was converted to the function of grinding steel. When Henry VIII came to the throne in 1509, England was still importing most of its armour from workshops in Germany or Flanders. Henry therefore decided it would be strategic to set up his own armoury at his palace in Greenwich, and recruited armourers from across Europe for this purpose. The old Ravensbourne corn mill was now the much grander Royal Armoury Mill, grinding steel for the palace workshops. Thus it is that this little corner of London was involved in the production of the armour worn by the king. In particular, it was charged with the production of the armour to be worn by the king and his team of champions at the great contest of the Field of the Cloth of Gold. According to contemporary accounts, it had to be put together at very short notice, owing to a late change in the complex regulations governing the composition of what could be worn – a sort of early equivalent of the technicalities today governing Formula One racing. The last royal suit of armour produced here was for Charles II, by which time the nature of warfare had changed significantly. The mills struggled on and by 1807 had become a small arms factory. That was not, however, to be their final incarnation for in 1824 they were converted to the production of silk thread and forty years later were specialising in gold and silver trimmings – and the production of the first ever tinsel. The mill buildings were finally demolished in 1937 and this historic site is today covered by a Tesco's car park.

Despite attempts to contain its confined and tortuous channel, the Ravensbourne was always particularly liable to flooding. In September 1968, after a week of heavy rain, the river burst its banks from Loampit Vale through Lewisham and all the way upstream to Beckenham. The tributaries of the river were overflowing too, the Poole River up as far as Bell Green, while the Quaggy inundated Kidbrooke. The normally insignificant Quaggy rose in a few hours from six inches to fourteen foot in depth. There was another fourteen foot of water filling the Odeon Cinema in Lewisham. The High Street became a river four foot deep, whilst basement flats in the area were inundated almost to their ceilings. Hundreds of people were evacuated to emergency centres, 40,000 phones were cut off, firemen took to boats and the Mayor toured the area, not in his Mayoral limousine, but in a dinghy. Walking this stretch of the river today you are able to see both the old fashioned concrete defences but also the new and more enlightened approach to riverine management – the recreation of natural river banks and softer margins that are, at one and the same time, ecologically richer, more pleasant to walk and more effective at flood containment. It is an approach we are to see at its finest when our route reaches Ladywell Fields.

From Hilly Fields to Ladywell Fields

ROUTE:

- Continue to the top of Ellerdale Road then turn left into Vicar's Hill. Take the first gate on the right into Hilly Fields.
- Follow the path as it curves to the left and runs across the top of the Fields. Continue ahead across crosspaths, passing a stone circle and a brick pavilion to reach the tennis courts.
- Turn left just beyond the tennis courts, between the courts and the children's playground, ignore the first turning on the right that runs through the playground and take the second one just beyond it.
- Follow this path as it runs downhill beside the meadow area and reaches the apex of two roads, with Adelaide Avenue running straight ahead.
- Cross to the other side of Adelaide Avenue and continue along it, passing the attractive St Margaret's Square on your left.
- Just beyond the Square go down the steps on your left and along the estate road to reach Ivy Road, opposite the brick wall of the cemetery.
- Turn right along Ivy Road to reach the gates of Brockley Cemetery at the junction of Ivy Road and Brockley Road.
  NOTE: The cemetery is open between 10am and 3.30pm from November to February and between 10am and 4.30 the rest of the year.

- On entering the cemetery take the path immediately to the left. Follow it parallel to the cemetery perimeter until it curves sharply away to the right. Carry straight ahead here following the trodden short cut over the grass to join another tarmac path.
- Turn left along this path, continuing to follow the cemetery perimeter.
- When this path too bears to the right, follow it to pass a small green 'roundabout' and continue on the tarmac path running ahead and then to the left, passing a walled war memorial to your left and the chapel buildings off to your right.
- Continue ahead to reach the exit gates to Ladywell Cemetery beyond a second War Memorial cross.
- On leaving the gates cross the end of Ivy Road into Ladywell Road. Cross to the other side of Ladywell Road and continue ahead for just under half a mile, passing the junction with Adelaide Avenue and reaching a bridge over the railway.
  NOTE: Ladywell Station (Charing Cross/Cannon Street) is beside the bridge and can be used to break this chapter into two shorter walks.

FACILITIES: Cafés in Brockley, close to the cemetery entrance.

LOOKING AT WILDLIFE: There is a restored meadow area on Hilly Fields supporting a variety of plant and butterfly species. Ladywell and Brockley cemeteries have a collection of planted tree species (including weeping ash, Turkey oaks and yews) as well as naturalised nature conservation areas.

Octavia Hill was one of the many remarkable women of the Victorian era. Born in 1838 she originally trained as an artist and became a protégé, and later a close friend, of John Ruskin. In early adulthood she developed a passionate interest in the housing conditions of the London working classes; her idea was to buy up areas of housing herself and then to improve them for the tenants. She made her first purchases through Ruskin in 1865, and by 1874 had the plan on a firm business footing, raising funds through friends and devoting her time to housing reform. In 1884 the Ecclesiastical Commissioners, one of the largest property owners in London, began to put her in charge of some of their own areas of housing and it was in this way that she assumed responsibility for 133 homes in Deptford and began her connection with the area. 'Poor Deptford, our black sheep' she called it, finding it an area particularly resistant to her brand of reforms. In a poorly furnished room in one of the Deptford houses she one day noticed a vase of freshly picked wild flowers. She was told they had been picked on Hilly Fields, and set off the same day to locate the place.

Octavia was concerned not only with the housing conditions of the London poor but with the quality of the environment in which they had to live. In 1875 she had campaigned unsuccessfully to save her beloved Swiss Cottage Fields from development, and thereafter became an executive member of the Commons Preservation Society. Time and again she found herself campaigning against the building developments that were devouring the open spaces enjoyed by Londoners, especially those for whom the opportunity to walk across common or field was one of the few reliefs from atrocious living conditions. 'The thousands of rich people', she said in 1883, 'who owe their wealth to London, or who avail themselves of its advantages, have not, as far as I know, given one single acre of ground, that could have been sold for building over, to Londoners for recreation ground or Park, if we except Leicester Square.'

The Hilly Fields discovered by Octavia Hill was a London clay outcrop above the Thanet sands, a beautiful hilly prominence rising to 175 feet, with extensive views over London. Somehow it had so far escaped the development which was swallowing up Brockley all around it. The area then was mostly farmland, with an area of game shooting common to the south. This latter part had already been leased to developers for building, and Octavia realised that none of the site would be spared for long. She helped establish a committee to save the Fields and set about raising funds for its purchase. The recently formed London County Council soon lent its support, but it was not without a difficult and protracted campaign that the fields were finally secured for the public. They were 'opened' on 16 May 1896, by which time Octavia Hill had moved on to other campaigns, among them that abiding monument to her work, the National Trust, which she co-founded in 1885.

From Hilly Fields we descend again to reach the gates to the cemetery. These 37 acres were in fact once two separate cemeteries, being Brockley Cemetery where you enter and Ladywell Cemetery by the time you leave. Under the original names of Lewisham and Deptford Cemeteries, they opened in 1858, within a few months of each other. They were part of the first wave of Victorian cemeteries enabled by an 1854 Act of Parliament, which allowed for the building of burial grounds that were no longer attached to churches, a response to the unhealthy overcrowding afflicting church graveyards. The 'short cut' across the grass that we follow marks the grassy ridge that once separated them and there are still few direct routes running from one to the other.

The 131,000 people buried here include a number of interesting figures – among them Sir George Grove, author of the famous musical dictionary, Fernando Tarrida del Murmol, a Cuban anarchist, and the poet and painter David Jones. Jones is not the only poet to be buried here for the cemetery also contains the grave of Ernest Dowson. His was a short and unhappy life. His father died of consumption, his mother committed suicide, he was unsuccessful in love and the two collaborative novels he worked on were a failure. He died of alcoholism at the young age of 32. Few can even claim to have read his poetry, yet he left us with some memorable additions to the English language. The phrase 'days of wine and roses' comes from one of his poems, whilst Margaret Mitchell took the title of Gone With the Wind from another. Even Cole Porter used one of his lines in a song title. Most surprisingly, he was the first person to use the word soccer in written language – though he spelt it socca. It is good to report therefore that his derelict and badly vandalised grave was restored and commemorated by a memorial service in August 2010 – some 110 years after his untimely death.

Beyond the cemeteries we enter Ladywell itself. It is named after not one well but two. The 'lady' in question was probably the Virgin Mary, to whom the wells were dedicated, though some accounts suggest it was the attendant who dispensed the healing water. These were chalybeate springs with a high mineral content and particularly recommended at the time for the treatment of eye complaints. One of the springs was beside the river just beyond the Ladywell Bridge, and the site was later taken over by the swimming baths. This building, now a community centre, remains one of the most interesting and attractive in the area. It is of red brick with granite window dressings and string courses. Best of all, though, is the round water tower with pierced surrounds and pointed windows. The walls of the Baths have a strange adornment; they are pitted with hundreds of vertical grooves where children queuing impatiently for admittance ground their threepenny bits into the brickwork.

From Ladywell Fields to Blythe Hill Fields

ROUTE:

- On crossing the railway bridge take the second footpath on the right. A short detour straight ahead leads to the Church. For the main route fork right at the first junction of paths to cross the footbridge.
- Turn left in Ladywell Park. Follow the riverside to the end of this section of park then cross a footbridge over the river, followed by a footbridge over the railway to the right.
- Carry on along the riverside through the next section of the Fields until you reach a footbridge. Cross it and turn left to continue along the river on its opposite side. (A short detour straight ahead at the footbridge leads to one of the Great Trees of London.)
- After passing beneath a railway bridge take the second of the paths leading off to the right and running uphill to meet the road (Ravensbourne Park).
- Turn left along the road. Take the first right (Ravensbourne Park Crescent) and the first right again (Montacute Road). On reaching the T-junction the passage immediately opposite leads onto Blythe Hill Fields.

FACILITIES: Café on Ladywell Fields.

LOOKING AT WILDLIFE: The restoration of the Ravensbourne through Ladywell Fields has transformed the natural diversity of the site. As well as the returning waterside plants there are newly created wildflower meadows sown with cornfield annuals such as chamomile, cornflower, corn cockle, poppies and oxeye daisy. This in turn attracts a good variety of invertebrates and an increasing bat population, including Leisler's bat and both common and soprano pipistrelle. Stag beetles, a London speciality, have also been found on the site. There is a good selection of trees, with yew and turkey oak in St Mary's churchyard and a wide variety within the park itself, including walnut, mature black poplars, balsam poplar and a weeping wych elm. One of the designated 'Great Trees of London' is to be found on the Middle Fields, between the footpath and the riverside. Known as the 'Lewisham Dutch Elm', it is a probably natural hybrid between the English and the wych elm, sometimes known as the Flanders elm.

From Ladywell Road our route follows the winding course of the river for over a mile through Ladywell Park and the Fields. In the nineteenth century the rich water meadows were glebe land attached to the parish of St Mary's. In 1889 they were purchased by the London County Council and the Lewisham Board of Works. The meadows were drained and landscaped, the river straightened, its bends cut off to form islands, and the whole opened as the new Ladywell Recreation Grounds. In a mistaken approach to flood relief – and perhaps to health and safety – the river was controlled and contained, encased in concrete and hidden behind fencing, its islands planted with sickly bushes of aucuba and box. The broad and shallow river, shown in a photo of 1900 with children still paddling along its banks and sheep grazing in the background, had become a municipal embarrassment. The restoration of the river today is one of the finest achievements to be seen along the length of the entire Green London Way, and a credit to Lewisham Council. With a grant from the London Development Agency, and as part of the longer Waterlinks Way project, a meandering brook – siphoned off from the main channel – once again runs through Ladywell Park. Waterside plants have colonised its banks, bats feed above it in the evening, and adjacent areas have been sown with wildflower meadows. It has achieved, simultaneously, habitat restoration, improved biodiversity and more effective flood relief – as well as making this one of the most pleasant smaller parks along the Green London Way.

At the northern end of the Fields, close to where we enter them, is the Parish Church of St Mary's, a classical, aristocratic structure belonging to a time when Lewisham and Ladywell were much wealthier places. Parts of the tower date back to the fifteenth century, but most of the church belongs to the eighteenth and nineteenth centuries. Its most striking feature is the unusual Grecian porch, four columns supporting a large and rather out-of-scale pediment. The attractive little churchyard between the path and the river contains the grave of the Irish poet Thomas Dermody.

The few short streets which link Ladywell Fields to Blythe Hill Fields are unremarkable but for the name of one of them. Montacute Road leads a short distance from Bankhurst Road to Blythe Hill. It also leads into a story of intrigue, torture and regicide.

Edward II came to the throne of England in 1307. He was not a man who would enjoy or excel at the martial activities – war and the tournament – which would have earned him the respect of the troublesome barons of England. Nor were they impressed by his homosexual relationships. He was defeated at the Battle of Bannockburn in 1314, and this seriously weakened his already shaky standing. He married Isabella, daughter of Philip the Fair of France, but as their relationship worsened she spent more time back in France. The story goes that there she met Roger Mortimer, one of the great Marcher Lords, in exile after an unsuccessful revolt, and that the two became lovers and began to plot a take-over of the English throne. They landed in 1326 and Edward was usurped with hardly a hand raised in his defence. He was imprisoned eventually in Berkeley Castle, where legend has it that, on the night of 21 September 1327, they sent murderers into his cell, who killed him by pushing a red hot poker into his bowels.

The new king Edward III, son of Isabella and Edward II, was still a boy. For four years Roger and Isabella were able to rule in his stead, but when Edward III reached his majority the situation suddenly and unexpectedly changed. One night a group of Edward's closest associates entered Nottingham Castle by a secret passage and seized Mortimer. The leader of the band was William Montague, also known as Montacute. Sir Roger Mortimer was arraigned before parliament and hung at Tyburn. Isabella was placed under house arrest at Castle Rising, and remained there in isolation for the rest of her life. Montacute was rewarded with the Manor of Catford, and Montacute Road, within the bounds of the old Manor, now bears his name.

The Battle for One Tree Hill

ROUTE:

- Cross Blythe Hill Fields ignoring paths running downhill to right and left and continue ahead to reach the exit onto Brockley View.
- Turn right down Brockley View and left at the bottom into Codrington Hill.
- Follow Codrington Hill to the main road (Stondon Park) and cross it to continue ahead into Gabriel Street.
- Continue to the end of Gabriel Street and then turn right into Grierson Road, reaching Honor Oak Park almost opposite the station.
- Cross Honor Oak Park and turn left along it.
- Continue past the entrance to the sports ground and then the allotments. Just beyond them take the gate on the right which leads up steps onto a woodland path past the church.
- At the summit of One Tree Hill carry on straight ahead to descend on the other side.
- Follow the path all the way downhill to reach the road (Brenchley Gardens). Cross the road and enter the gardens by the gate opposite.

FACILITIES: Cafés on Honor Oak Park.

LOOKING AT WILDLIFE: Like many other parks, Blythe Hill now includes uncut areas supporting an increased variety of grassland plant species. One Tree Hill supports both areas of acid grassland and mixed secondary woodland, with oak and ash and introduced species like plane and robinia. There is a good variety of woodland birds including jays, tits and warblers, with speckled wood butterflies along the paths and clearings. Its speciality plants include heath grass and compact rush.

Blythe Hill is another in the succession of prominences which we follow across South London. Its modest 200 feet is sufficient to provide another excellent viewpoint, especially to the east and over the Isle of Dogs. It also saved it from development and the hill was 'opened' as a public park in 1935. It is now surrounded by the rather amorphous but pleasant suburb of Brockley.

The name comes from two Anglo-Saxon words, broc meaning brook and leah, meaning a clearing or glade. Until the eighteenth century Brockley was a village set in a clearing in the huge expanse of the Great North Wood, which stretched for miles over much of what is now South London. The wood survives in names such as Norwood, Forest Wood, Forest Hill and Westwood, and in this remaining fragment at Honor Oak. The 'honour' oak itself stands at the top of One Tree Hill. It is said to derive its name from Elizabeth I, who picnicked here in 1662 whilst out 'a-maying' with Sir Richard Buckley, but the real origin is undoubtedly much older; a large oak tree at the top of a hill has a pre-Christian religious significance. This importance continued into comparatively recent times, for the beating of the Parish bounds, which took place once every three years, always ended under the branches of the honour oak. Traditionally the ceremony would finish with the singing of Psalm 104; it is no doubt a comment on the decline of organised religion that when the ceremony last took place in 1899, the assembled dignitaries could not remember the words of Psalm 104 and were forced to sing the much shorter Psalm 100 instead.

The woodland which now clothes One Tree Hill is secondary woodland, much changed since the days of the great forest. The native oaks and ashes which grow there are mixed with introduced and exotic species from many other parts of the world – flowering cherries, false acacia, sycamore and plane. Similarly the honourable oak surrounded by palings at the summit is not the original ancient tree but a more recent replacement, planted in 1905 in a ceremony which marked the outcome of the 'Battle for One Tree Hill'.

For generations the residents of Honor Oak had regarded One Tree Hill as common land. Then, one morning in 1896, they awoke to find the hill surrounded by a six-foot fence. It had been erected by the local golf club, which now claimed to have a legitimate lease on the land. Within a few days an 'Enclosure of Honor Oak Hill Protest Committee' was holding its first meeting in the Samuel Bowley Coffee Tavern on Peckham Rye. With the support of the Commons Preservation Society it began the laborious business of researching the legal status of the land. This constitutional mode of procedure was too slow for most local people and public anger boiled over when two local boys faced criminal proceedings from the golf club for alleged damage to the fence.

On the next Sunday, 15,000 people gathered on the slopes of the hill. Directing their attacks from Honor Oak Park and Honor Oak Rise, they tore down the fence and swarmed across the Hill in what the authorities described as 'a disorderly multitude'. The groundkeeper's cottage was attacked and seriously damaged and the crowds dispersed only as police reinforcements arrived.

The following Saturday three disaffected members of the Protest Committee, which had dissociated itself from the demonstration, cut down a section of the fence and, having notified the press, the police and the golf club in advance, invited the authorities to arrest them. The next day, crowds estimated variously as between 50,000 and 100,000 again massed around the hill. This time they were met by large contingents of foot and mounted police. As the crowd stormed the fences the police made a mounted charge. Missiles were thrown, furze bushes set ablaze and a police inspector injured. Nine people were arrested, of whom five were sent to prison for their part in the battle to liberate the hill.

In spite of these activities, it was not until 1902 and the establishment of the

London County Council that the land was saved for the public. Using its new compulsory purchase powers it took the golf club to court and completed its acquisition two years later. In 1905, in the presence of 30,000 spectators, One Tree Hill was officially re-opened to the public and the latest of the 'oaks of honour' planted on its summit.

At the bottom of the hill stands Brenchley Gardens, built partly on the line of the old Crystal Palace railway. The main part of this attractive but slightly ramshackle park, with its rose pergola, its fragrant cypresses and its shrubberies, was opened in 1928. The Camberwell Borough Council decided to name the gardens after William Brenchley, one time Mayor of Camberwell and the first Freeman of the Borough.

The LCC had a policy that sites should not be named after people who were still alive and therefore refused to endorse the name. In an imaginative counter-stroke the Borough Council announced that it was still calling them Brenchley Gardens – after the village of Brenchley in Kent.

The Battle for Westwood

ROUTE:

- Bear left in Brenchley Gardens and continue through the gardens and the woodland area to exit at the far end onto Forest Hill Road opposite Wood Vale.
- Cross Forest Hill Road and turn right, crossing the end of Wood Vale to reach the entrance to Camberwell Old Cemetery.
- Go through the gates of the cemetery and continue straight ahead. Bear left at the first fork to reach a crossing of paths between hedged rose gardens, where you continue ahead and slightly to the left.
- Where this path begins to loop back round on itself, take a path on the left that leads to the exit gate in the far left hand corner of the cemetery.
- Beyond the gate, turn left to cross Wood Vale and enter Langton Park opposite. Turn right at the top into Westwood Park.
- Follow Westwood Park until it bends sharply to the left. Just beyond the bend take the footpath on the right running between the houses.

To join Walk 5:

On reaching a junction of paths, turn right to follow alongside the railway nature reserve.

To complete this walk:

On reaching a junction of paths, turn left and follow the path till it reaches a gate into the park.

Go through the gate and turn left inside the park. Follow this path as it curves to the right below the bandstand.

Climb the steps beside the bandstand and turn right to join the main avenue ahead running down beside the Horniman Museum.

Turn left along the front of the museum to leave by the last gate onto London Road. There are buses on London Road, or turn left along London Road to reach Forest Hill Station at its junction with Devonshire Road.

FACILITIES: Toilets in Horniman Gardens. Ladies toilets in Camberwell Old Cemetery. Pub in Wood Vale. Cafés in Horniman Museum and in Forest Hill.

LOOKING AT WILDLIFE: The woodland in Camberwell Cemetery has a population of woodland birds, flowers and butterflies. Horniman Gardens has animal enclosures with bantam, guinea fowl, cranes, wallabies and rabbits. There is a very fine collection of exotic trees, including western hemlock, deodar, mop headed acacia, red maple, snake bark maple, corkscrew willow and red oak. The fine formal gardens include a very attractive water garden and a conservatory. The Museum's new extension also includes an impressive green roof.

Camberwell Old Cemetery, unusually for a cemetery designed for 'the middle, artisan and poorer classes', was laid out in great style. Founded in 1856, it covered nearly thirty acres and was equipped with chapels designed by the great George Gilbert Scott. Following these promising beginnings, however, it soon fell into a state of disrepair. Today, by contrast, it is one of the most attractive of the still 'active' cemeteries in London. There is a 'semi-maintained' condition here, which avoids that stultifying and sterile conformity of so many of our modern cemeteries, where the headstones stand in unrelieved rows, as boring, and as mundane, as a supermarket queue. Here jays and finches and speckled wood butterflies fly among ashes, chestnuts, sycamores and thorn trees, and away in the south west corner a large unused area has returned to woodland.

The cemetery runs alongside Wood Vale, once the boundary between Kent and Surrey, and which we cross to reach Westwood Park. The names recall stretches of the Great North Wood, and Westwood is honourable amongst them. It was the site of the first recorded fight for commoners' rights in Britain. The Westwood once extended over five hundred acres and was part of the Manor of Lewisham. The poorer inhabitants of the area had for generations used it for pasturage and for furze cutting, and regarded it as common land; but in 1605 it was granted by the king to Henry Newport, a local member of the gentry and a 'yeoman of ye boiling house to James I'. The commoners immediately made complaint and the case came to trial in 1606.

The Commissioners attempted the impossible by coming down on both sides and saying it was both the 'Kings waste' to dispose of as he pleased, and a common. Naturally this satisfied nobody and the case went on to the Court of Exchequer in 1607. The commoners won their case but Newport and two associates immediately, and despite the ruling, took possession of 347 acres of the common.

The case was brought to court a third time, this time with a jury from the County of Kent, which decided in Newport's favour. He immediately began to make ditches and enclose the common, driving the commoners off and killing their cattle. The commoners responded by demolishing the fences and filling the ditches. As the crisis came to a head the local vicar, Abraham Colfe, led one hundred parishioners to London to make a direct appeal to the king, who referred the case to the Lords of Privy Council. A retrial was ordered. On 16 October 1615 it came before the Barons of the Exchequer; the rest of the story is told by the Reverend Colfe:

> The Lord's holy name for ever for his great tender mercies be blessed a verdict passed in the behalfe of the poore inhabitants and on the 18th of November following judgement was also granted and a copy of both of the order and of ye judgement taken out under the seale of the Exchequer Chamber which is kept by us.

It was a great victory for the commoners and lasted for two hundred years. In 1810 an Act of Parliament was passed authorising the enclosure of the whole of the common. Westwood, except as a street name, disappeared.

The footpaths from Westwood lead us to the Horniman Gardens and the Horniman Museum, a free gift from Frederick Horniman 'to the people for ever'. Frederick was the son of John Horniman who had founded a tea business and became the first person to sell tea in sealed packets. He had been a keen collector since childhood and was able to indulge his passion with a vengeance in his work for the tea company. He travelled at least twice round the world, taking in Egypt, India, Sri Lanka, Burma, China, Japan, Canada and the USA. From each of these countries he made a point of bringing back artefacts illustrating either their natural history or their arts and handicrafts.

In 1868 he moved into Surrey House at the top of Forest Hill, where eventually his 'artefacts' filled so much space that there was no longer room for both his family and his collection. It was the family which had to move – and they took up residence in the adjacent Surrey Mount, which stood on the highest point of what is now Horniman Gardens. Its name, though eroding rapidly, can still be seen on the stone pillars of the main gate. In 1890 Frederick, who was by now both Chairman of the tea firm and MP for Falmouth, opened his collection to the public as a free museum.

Within seven years it was receiving over 90,000 visitors a year, with 3,270 people crowding into Surrey House on a single Bank Holiday. It was obvious that a brand new building was necessary.

Frederick Horniman, and the architect C. Harrison Townsend, have given us one of the most interesting and individual buildings in London. Completed in 1901 in Art Nouveau style, it cleverly makes use of the steep slope into which it is set. The arched frontage of the South Hall faces the road, and set slightly apart from it is a tower in beautifully grained and honey-coloured stone, with rounded corners from which four little subsidiary towers emerge as naturally as buds. The hall frontage bears a large mosaic panel by Anning Bell, its 117,000 pieces depicting a rather obscure allegory on the course of human life. From the museum, the Gardens, which were originally the grounds of Surrey Mount, slope up through lawns and shrubberies, a sunken formal garden and a water garden, to a summit at 300 foot, the same height as One Tree Hill. In the autumn there is a stunning display of autumn colour as the great variety of exotic trees across the grounds turn red, brown, yellow, ochre and golden.

There is a miniature zoo, a genuine Dutch Barn and no less than three nature trails.

One of these trails follows the comparatively wild railway embankment adjacent to the park, another remnant of the Crystal Palace Branch line. Another crosses a terrace on the eastern side of the park, with extensive views over Kent and London. Here on summer evenings the ghosts of an Edwardian couple are said to appear, dancing arm in arm. There can be no more agreeable way to conduct a haunting.

Getting home

Forest Hill Station: Network Rail (London Bridge), London Overground

Buses: (from London Road) 185, 176, 197, 356; (from Forest Hill Station) 122

5. The College, the Palace and the Commons

FROM FOREST HILL TO BALHAM

Excepting some of the most 'desirable' riverside areas, a general rule could be formulated for the residential districts of London – that income increases with altitude.

The inner layer of the geological phenomenon known as the London basin is comprised of a layer of clay: blue, grey or orange; heavy, sticky and sodden, the London gardener's curse. It is thinnest down by the river but reaches up to 300 feet thick towards its rim. And it is along this rim that many of the most sought-after residential districts in London are to be found: Highgate, Hampstead, and Harrow-on-the Hill in the north, and in the south the suburbs that we follow on this section of the walk: Forest Hill, Dulwich, Sydenham Hill, Crystal Palace, and Streatham Common – where the air was said to come 'straight from Brighton'.

Dulwich owes much of its present shape, and its considerable beauty, to ex-actor Edward Alleyn, who settled here in the seventeenth century and bestowed upon the village most of his wealth. During the same century Sydenham was becoming fashionable; its 'wells' had been discovered, and even the king came here to sample the waters. Streatham, which had its own wells, reached its apogee a hundred years later, when Hester Thrale was entertaining most of the great names of the day on her estate at Streatham Park. But for this part of London as a whole, the greatest era of development, the highpoint of the high places, came after the arrival of the Crystal Palace in 1852.

The Palace was a place for all classes. The Victorians came in their thousands to see the exhibitions, to listen to the huge organ and the enormous choirs, to gape at the incredible building, to walk in the grounds, to watch the extravagant water displays, to gasp at the fireworks or to wonder at the concrete dinosaurs. They came, but this being the intensely class-conscious society that it was, they did not mix. From the High Level Station through to the Palace, the upper classes had their own separate platforms, tunnels and entrances. And these wealthy Victorians made the high and healthy eminences around the Palace site their home. Today the surrounding suburbs are still full of their beautiful villas, with tall belvederes, granite porches and grand, stained-glass windows.

In the great fire of 1936 the Palace disappeared overnight. Following this the suburb itself declined, with many of its villas entering multi-occupation or

THE COLLEGE, THE PALACE AND THE COMMONS

FOREST HILL TO CRYSTAL PALACE ~ 5

From 'THE PEASANTS HEATH and the COMMONERS HILL'

HORNIMAN GARDENS

HORNIMAN MUSEUM

LONDON ROAD

Forest Hill

START

GOLF COURSE

SYDENHAM HILL WOOD

DULWICH

WOOD

LOW CROSS WOOD LANE

SYDENHAM HILL

WELLS PARK RD

SYDENHAM WELLS PARK

WESTWOOD HILL

To 'CRYSTAL PALACE to BALHAM'

SYDENHAM

CRYSTAL PALACE PDE

CRYSTAL PALACE PARK

CRYSTAL PALACE PARK RD

FINISH

Crystal Palace

ANERLEY HILL

THICKET ROAD

TRANSPORT ~ Finish
⚡⊖ CRYSTAL PALACE
🚌 BUSES

TRANSPORT ~ Start
⚡⊖ FOREST HILL
🚌 BUSES

©SCRIY 2012

becoming part of bed-sit land. But all classes meet again in this chapter, from the Whig minister who drafted the Reform Bill in Streatham, to socialist activists like John Burns and Annie Besant; from Hester Thrale, 'queen' of her own Streatham Park court to Margaret Finch, the 'queen' of the gypsies; from Ned Allen of the London stage, Lord of the Manor of Dulwich, to the proud and penniless gardener who lived as a hermit in its woods.

This chapter covers 9½ miles from Forest Hill to Balham. It can be taken as two shorter walks:

WALK 5: Forest Hill to Crystal Palace Parade (4 miles).

WALK 6: Crystal Palace Parade to Balham High Street (5½ miles).

▓ WALK 5: FOREST HILL TO CRYSTAL PALACE

Getting started

From Forest Hill Station (Network Rail (London Bridge), London Overground, 122 bus):

From the main station exit, adjacent to Platform 1, cross the road to reach London Road opposite.

Follow this for about one third of a mile to reach Horniman Museum.

Buses (185, 176, 197, 356):

Alight at Horniman Museum on London Road

The walk begins at the main gate of Horniman Museum

From Walk 4:

Following the footpath from Westwood Park, turn right at the junction of paths to reach the entrance to the nature reserve alongside Horniman Gardens.

The Dulwich Woods

ROUTE:

- Go through the main gate of Horniman Gardens and follow the main drive running alongside the Museum until you reach the bandstand.
- Go down the steps beside the bandstand and turn right. The path curves to the left to reach the park perimeter. Take the gate on the right leading onto a footpath.
- Turn left along the footpath until reaching a junction of paths.
- Follow the path which bears to the left to reach the entrance to the railway embankment nature reserve. Enter the nature reserve and turn

left, following it to the end to rejoin the main path just before the road. NOTE: If the reserve is not open continue along the main path until the two routes join again just before London Road.

- Cross the main road (London Road/Lordship Lane) at the pedestrian crossing and just to the right, take the path leading off between houses near the junction of Sydenham Hill and Lordship Lane.
- Follow the path as it leads off to the right following a line of lamp-posts and then running alongside the perimeter of the woods to reach a gate into the wood.
- Go through the gate and turn right, descending the slope to reach and cross a footbridge.
- Beyond the footbridge turn immediately left through a gate into Dulwich Wood and follow the main path that runs downhill to the right.
- Continue on this path keeping first a golf course and later, allotments, to your right.
- The path curves round to the right at the top of the allotments. Follow the broad track straight ahead, keeping the chain link fence off to your right.
- Continue ahead through the woods, ignoring cross paths and keeping straight ahead at a clearing where five paths meet, to eventually reach a gate in an iron fence. Turn left along the tarmac lane.
- Follow the lane until it ends on Crescent Wood Lane, opposite the Dulwich Wood House.

FACILITIES: Toilets and cafés in Forest Hill. Toilets and café in the Horniman Museum. Toilets in Horniman Gardens.

LOOKING AT WILDLIFE: Along the nature reserve there is secondary woodland including sessile oak and some fine grey poplars. Beneath these there are some interesting woodland plants, including butcher's broom and large colonies of the parasitical ivy-leaved broomrape, a plant which seems to have been increasing in London in the last few years. This is also one of the locations for that London speciality, the stag beetle. Dulwich and Sydenham Woods are relict ancient woodland of sessile oak and hornbeam, containing a large variety of tree, flower, bird and butterfly species. Birds include stock dove and all three woodpeckers, and a plant to look out for is the shade-loving Solomon's seal.

In 1605 Francis Calton sold the Manor of Dulwich to Edward Alleyn for the sum of £5,000, and that, according to Alleyn, was £1,000 more than any other man would have given for it. Alleyn was born in 1566, the son of an innkeeper of Bishopsgate, but, as Ned Allen, he was to become famous as both an actor and a theatre proprietor. Described as 'the Roscius of his age', he even had a sonnet composed in his honour by his friend Ben Jonson. According to a popular story, Ned Allen's life was transformed as the result of a theatrical apparition. The cast of a play in which he was performing contained twelve demons, but one night he found himself somehow confronting thirteen of them, and decided it was time to re-assess his life. He left the theatre and devoted the rest of his time on earth to good works.

This wonderful story has latterly been discounted, but the fact remains that Alleyn retired from his theatrical career a rich man and spent the rest of his life in a combination of philanthropy and the pursuit of preferment. In 1519 he became Lord of the Manor of Thirle, and in 1604 Lord of the Manor of Kensington. In this same year he bought for himself the title of 'Chief Master, Ruler and Overseer of All and Singular of His Majesty's Games, of Bears, Bulls and Mastive Dogs'. It was in the next year that he bought the Manor of Dulwich, where he moved in 1613.

This move was to shape the whole future development of the area: he founded almshouses and schools, including the famous Dulwich College, and endowed the 1200 acre 'Estate of Alleyn's College of Gods Gift'. Dulwich Village remains today one of the most attractive and select of the London suburbs, and much of the village, together with the Dulwich woodlands, remains under the control of the Estate.

Alleyn's original bequest ordered that a portion of his estates should remain a woodland divided into ten equal portions, which would be lopped in rotation to supply the college with fuel. The names of many of these portions still survive in one form or another: Lapse Wood, Low Cross Wood, Sydenham Hill Wood, Kingswood and Peckarmans Wood. Today the 27 acre Sydenham Hill Wood belongs to the London Borough of Southwark and is managed by the London Wildlife Trust; the rest belong to the College Estates and have, until recently, been kept strictly private.

Both of these owners have attempted at different times to build in the woods. In 1985 Southwark Council applied to build 125 flats on Lapsewood but was defeated after a public enquiry, although development was allowed in one small part of the site. In 1988 the same Council turned down the third application from the Dulwich College Estates to build flats in the woods. The Dulwich Village Preservation Society threatened to take the Estate Governors to the Charity Commissioners if they should appeal against this decision. The Governors, they said, were acting like feudal landlords and were contradicting the terms of Alleyn's will. Nonetheless the Estate Governors did take their application to appeal and at a public enquiry in 1989 they were turned down for the fourth time.

Our route begins through Horniman Gardens, described in Chapter 4, and the nature reserve that runs along its perimeter. Described as 'the oldest nature reserve in London', this now wooded embankment once constituted part of the Crystal Palace and South London Junction Railway on its approach to what was the Lordship Lane Station. We cross Lordship Lane where it abruptly changes its name, a change which is no doubt to do with the fact that this was also once the boundary between the Manors – or Lordships – of Dulwich and Friern. We soon pick up the railway route again, however, crossing it in Sydenham Hill Wood over a footbridge with rustic wooden arches, which give it a vaguely Japanese appearance. The brick piers carry the bridge across a cutting through which the railway ran en route to its final destination at the Crystal Palace High Level Station. In 1871 the impressionist painter Pissarro sat on this bridge painting a view of a steam train puffing towards him out of Lordship Lane Station, through a landscape comprised largely of fields. The painting hangs today in the Courtauld Galleries in the Strand.

From the footbridge we cut across the thickest, stillest, richest part of Dulwich Woods to reach Low Cross Lane, the cross referred to here being the cut made in a tree or on the ground to mark out the Parish boundary. It was walking in these woodlands that Browning composed his famous lines:

> The lark's on the wing, the snail's on the thorn
> God's in his heaven – all's right with the world.

It was also in this section of the woodland that the 'Dulwich hermit', Samuel Matthews, is said to have had his home. Matthews came from Wales to serve as a gardener in Dulwich College, but after the death of his wife in 1796 he retired into seclusion. Here in the woods he dug himself a cave in the mud and roofed it with fern, furze and brambles, remaining there until friends heard about his condition and took him back to Wales. He managed to escape their ministrations, however, and made his way back to Dulwich and his home in the woods, where on 28 December 1802, he was found murdered. The rumour had arisen that he was a miser guarding a stash of treasure – why else should anyone want to live in solitude in the wild? Samuel was found with a hook in his throat with which the killers had tried to drag his body from the low-entranced cave. The crime remained unsolved until 1809, when, on his death-bed in Lewisham Workhouse, Isaac Evans confessed to being the perpetrator of the 'Dulwich Woods tragedy'.

From the Woods to the Wells

ROUTE:

- On reaching Crescent Wood Lane turn right to reach the junction with Sydenham Hill. Go straight across to enter Wells Park Road, opposite.
- Continue ahead on Wells Park Road to reach Sydenham Wells Park on the right just beyond the junction with Longton Avenue.
- Take the first entrance to the park and bear right to walk downhill. After passing a second entrance gate on your right, go straight ahead at the crossing of paths and continue along the broad tarmac path to reach the ornamental lakes.
- Turn sharp right immediately after the lakes to reach the gate onto Longton Avenue. Go straight across into Ormanton Road.
- Continue ahead to cross Westwood Hill into Charleville Circus.
- Go round either side of the Circus to reach Crystal Palace Park Road. Cross the road and turn left to reach the Fisherman's Gate entrance to Crystal Palace Park on the right.

FACILITIES: Dulwich Wood House is a pub with garden. Disabled toilets and children's playground in Sydenham Wells Park.

LOOKING AT WILDLIFE: The lakes have a variety of wildfowl and visiting herons, and are surrounded by waterside plants and other wild flowers.

There is a good selection of trees including swamp cypress. The park, like much of South London, supports a large and noisy population of ring-necked parakeets.

The Dulwich Wood House, cream-painted with a white belvedere, was built around 1840 and is a local listed building – more deservedly so than the modern building next door. 'Six Pillars', a Grade II Historical Building, dates from 1935 and is in the 'International Style', so-called presumably because of its blandness and lack of any cultural references whatsoever.

John Logie Baird, inventor of television, lived at 3 Crescent Wood Road from 1934 to 1936. His TV laboratories were situated in the nearby Crystal Palace, and were entirely destroyed in the fire of 1936. Here, at the height of Sydenham Hill, once the boundary between Kent and Surrey, is a clear view of Baird's 'memorial', the BBC TV aerial atop the Crystal Palace Hill. Sydenham Hill, originally part of the Westwood Common, was an area of weather-boarded cottages surrounded by market gardens and orchards until it became increasingly fashionable following the success of the Crystal Palace. Its high location made it healthy too, so that Upper Sydenham came to consist of large, wealthy, family villas, whilst the working people lived in Lower Sydenham below.

In 1640 the discovery was made on the Sydenham portion of the Westwood Common of wells whose water was of 'a mild cathartic quality, nearly resembling those of Epsom'. As their fashionable use developed they were said to have 'performed great cures in scrofulous, scorbutic, paralytic and other stubborn diseases', and even, by one contemporary commentator, to be 'a certain cure for every ill to which humanity is heir'. The wells were covered over in the mid-nineteenth century, but a scientific analysis of the waters was made many years later during a temporary re-emergence of a spring near Crystal Palace. They were found to contain large quantities of magnesium sulphate – more commonly known as Epsom salts.

The 17½ acres of undulating slopes which today constitute Sydenham Wells Park were purchased by the Metropolitan Board of Works and laid out with broad pathways, ornamental plantations and a succession of small lakes and rivulets. The main speech at the opening ceremony in 1901 was made by the trade unionist and socialist John Burns, an appropriate choice for a number of reasons. Earlier in his life Burns had for six months driven the first electric tram in England, one of the 'features' in the Crystal Palace Park. Burns also had a particular concern for the right of public meeting in parks and commons. As a leader of the Dock Strike in 1889 he was an associate of Ben Tillett and Tom Mann and by 1892 he had become MP for Battersea, sitting as one of the first Independent Labour Party members in the House. Walter Greening heard him give his opening speech and commented that, although the 'stentorian-voiced orator, the doughty John Burns' did not make him a convert to radicalism, he was nevertheless 'forcedly impressed with the manliness of his utterances and practical common-sense remarks arising from the circumstances appertaining to the proceedings in which he was taking part'.

From Festival to Fire: the career of a Crystal Palace

ROUTE:

- Turn left on entering Fisherman's Gate.
- Where the main path heads down into the sports centre bear left again onto a broad path earthen path beside three stone blocks.
- Keep straight ahead, keeping the park perimeter to your left until reaching a second exit gate (Penge Gate) beside the café and Information Centre.
- Take the path immediately to the left of the café, upwards towards the apex of the lake.
- Turn right alongside the lake, then left past the family of Irish elks.
- Bear right over the ornamental bridge, then left beside the lake to cross another footbridge on your left.
- Beyond the footbridge bear left along the waterside, passing more dinosaurs.
- At the top end of the lake take the path on the right leading up the bank.
- Continue past the Capel Manor Centre, along a path with the sports centre and its access road on your right, until you reach Crystal Palace Station.

To join Walk 6 and for buses (Crystal Palace Parade)

Continue beyond the station, cross a small road and then the main access road to the Sports Centre to reach another gate into the park on your right where the access road has its junction with Anerley Hill.

Enter the park and take the second of the two paths on your left.

Passing the sphinxes, walk a short distance along the terrace then climb the grassy bank to your left to reach a tarmac roadway beside the white cast iron fragment of the Crystal Palace.

Follow the roadway to reach the bus station on Crystal Palace Parade.

For Crystal Palace Station and buses (Anerley Hill):

Turn left on passing the station to reach the entrance.

FACILITIES: Crystal Palace Park has toilets, a children's playground and two cafés. There is also a Children's Farm (closed Wednesdays) at the Capel Manor Centre with pigs, llamas, horses and ponies. The Crystal Palace Museum is near the top of Anerley Hill (check opening times, which may vary) and there are toilets, pubs and cafés on Crystal Palace Parade.

LOOKING AT WILDLIFE: Crystal Palace Park has a good collection of exotic trees, including contorted willow, Monterey pine and Indian bean tree, with a fine display of autumn colour. The lakes support a variety of waterfowl, especially in winter, when birds such as shoveller and great crested grebe can be seen alongside heron and cormorant. The lake also has a surrounding of wild plants, including St John's wort, gypsywort, figwort and purple loosestrife.

It was Prince Albert's idea: a Great Exhibition displaying the power and scope of British imperialism, a monument to Victorian self-confidence and its cultural domination of the world. The design of the building, which would itself reflect these achievements, came about almost by accident. A member of the organising committee, whilst reading a copy of the *Illustrated London News*, noticed a picture of the green-houses at Chatsworth, built for the Duke of Devonshire by Joseph Paxton. The idea for the 'Crystal Palace' was born.

The Palace was erected by Paxton in Hyde Park in 1851 but its popularity led the organisers to look for a permanent home for the building once the exhibition was over. In 1852 road and rail wagons carried 9,642 tons of iron, 500 tons of glass, 30 miles of guttering and 200 miles of wooden sash out to the top of Sydenham Hill. The 1,608 foot long palace was re-erected on a site which overlooked London, Kent and Surrey.

The extravagant grandeur of the palace had now to be matched in the lay-out of its 200 acres of grounds. In a brilliant imaginative stroke the shimmering glass surfaces of the Palace, with their ever-changing play of light, were recreated in the grounds in the shimmering and shifting surfaces of a water park. The whole design of the grounds was to meet this end – 11,788 separate jets and fountains, ten miles of underground piping and a complex system of reservoirs fed from their own artesian well. On its grandest nights the park could put on a display consuming as much as 6 million gallons of water, with its highest jets reaching 250 foot into the air.

Palace and grounds were opened by Queen Victoria on 10 June 1854 before a crowd of 40,000 people. It became a pleasure garden for the nation, a forerunner of the theme park, with exhibitions, choral festivals, funfairs, balloon ascents, aeronautical shows, a pneumatic railway, an electric tram ride, spectacular firework displays and a wide range of theatrical and sporting events. Even the FA Cup Final was staged here from 1894 to 1924.

Victorian architecture, for all its pretensions, is amongst the most exuberant and exciting in the country. But its extravagance was unsustainable by a later age: by the early twentieth century the grand Crystal Palace had become a liability. It must have been a sad and shabby site in its decline, its acres of windows cracked and grubby, its miles of iron girders rusting, its fountains no longer functioning and its grand paths weeding over. The end was sudden. It came on the night of 30 November 1936. The fire which destroyed the Crystal Palace was attended by 90 fire engines and could be seen from as far away as Brighton. A sea of molten glass flowed down Anerley Hill and the great organ could be heard eerily playing itself as fire-heated draughts of air rushed upwards through the pipes. By the morning nothing but two flanking water towers remained. The circumstances surrounding the fire remain a mystery. An official account blames it on a workman's blow-torch igniting a paint store but popular accounts take note of the fact that an 'accidental' fire had conveniently disposed of a loss-making liability.

All that remains today is the arcaded terrace at the top of the park, on which the foundation of the glass edifice once rested, together with a few half-ruined sphinxes and statues. They reinforce the melancholy that pervades the site and which the grandeur of the view fails to dissipate. The ghost of what once was, of the lost splendour of a more certain age, hangs heavy here and it is almost a relief to move on again. Even the park feels like somewhere with more of a past than a present, for it has been cruelly handled, losing its coherence to insensitive piecemeal development. Much of this is related to the presence of the National Sports Centre, plumped down in the very centre of the park in 1964, with athletics stadium, Olympic pool, tower-block accommodation for competitors and all the associated paraphernalia. It has taken the heart out of the site, marred the view from the terrace and deprived it of any sense of unity or landscape coherence, turning it instead into an untidy mish-mash of scattered features – an ambling periphery with no core.

Plans are once again under discussion for the complete refurbishment of the park, with planning permission granted in 2010 for a new scheme drawn up by the London Development Agency. Even this has been mired in controversy, however, for it involves selling off part of the site by the Sydenham Gate, for the development of new housing, in order to fund the rest of the scheme.

The most interesting remaining feature is undoubtedly the area around the Lower Lake. The lake is so divided by bridges, paths and islands that it actually looks like several lakes. It was the main reservoir for the park and its water levels fluctuated so greatly when the water displays were in operation that it became known as the Tidal Lake.

The largest of the islands contained, from 1953, a Children's Zoo hopefully to be one day restored to the site. The other two carry creatures more ancient – the famous prehistoric monsters which form one of the strangest listed buildings in London. From the incongruously mown grass – for a neurotic municipal tidiness intervenes even here – amidst a backdrop of cypresses, juniper, pines and monkey puzzle, they stick their heads up over rocks, grimace in their green and concrete way and fail to frighten the waterfowl, whose only real concern is to get the next handout of white bread from the Sunday afternoon strollers. There is a pterodactyl about to take off, eyes glaring, one paw raised; there are Irish elk with their young among the aucuba; prehistoric crocodiles under the weeping willows, with long and narrow snouts whose bulbous ends look like eye-droppers; tortoises with fangs; amphibious dinosaurs with corkscrew necks; and the mighty iguanodon, with skin as rough as a lychee, snarling to keep up appearances whilst obviously wondering what the hell is going on.

The display as a whole was intended to illustrate the course of evolution, working from west to east across the park. It was designed by the delightfully named Waterhouse Hawkins, with scientific advice provided by Professor Richard Owen, the man who gave the world the word 'dinosaur'. On New Year's Eve 1854, when the work was just completed, they gave a dinner party in the open belly of the iguanodon, its top half being cemented in place later.

Getting home

Crystal Palace Station: Network Rail (London Bridge/Victoria), London Overground

Buses: (from Anerley Hill) 157, 249, 410, 432; (from Crystal Palace Parade) 3, 122, 202, 227, 363, 450

■ WALK 6: CRYSTAL PALACE TO BALHAM

Getting started

From Crystal Palace Station (Network Rail (London Bridge/Victoria), London Overground, Buses (157, 249, 410, 432)):

Turn right from the station exit to enter the park.

Turn immediately left in the park, cross a small road and then the main access road to the Sports Centre, to reach another gate into the park on your right where the access road has its junction with Anerley Hill.

Enter the park and take the second of the two paths on your left.

Passing the sphinxes, walk a short distance along the terrace then climb the grassy bank on your left to reach a tarmac roadway beside the white, cast iron fragment of the Crystal Palace.

Follow the roadway to reach the bus station on Crystal Palace Parade.

From Walk 5 and Crystal Palace Parade Bus Station (3, 122, 202, 227, 363, 450):

Cross Crystal Palace Parade to join Farquhar Road.

The Vicar's Oak and the Vicar's Wife

ROUTE:

- Follow Farquhar Road and cross Bowley Close to take the second turning on the right (Bowley Lane). After a short distance take the gate on the left into the woods, opposite Spinney Gardens.
- Follow the path, keeping to the right at junctions until you reach a small fenced pond.
- After passing the pond and crossing a small plank bridge, bear left at a junction next to a flight of steps.
- Follow the main path downhill now bearing left at junctions until reaching the Woodland Centre. Turn right alongside it to reach a gate back on to Farquhar Road.
- Cross the road and walk straight ahead up Dulwich Wood Avenue, opposite.
- On reaching Colby Road on the right, a very short detour along it leads to Annie Besant's house. The main route crosses Colby Road to continue along Dulwich Wood Avenue until reaching a gate into Long Meadow on your left.

FACILITIES: Cafés, pubs and toilets on Crystal Palace Parade.

LOOKING AT WILDLIFE: Dulwich Upper Wood has five acres of deciduous woodland with a variety of woodland birds. Wild flowers include common spotted orchid and large amounts of the parasitic ivy broomrape. Fungi include the wood agaric and a variety of boletes.

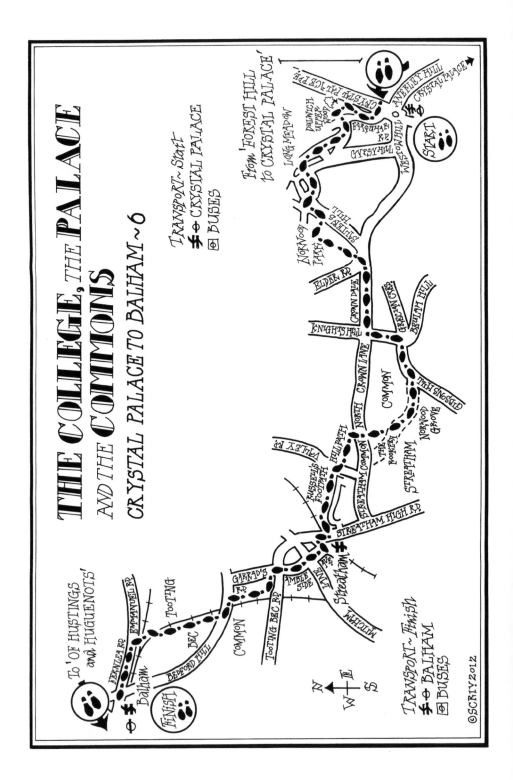

THE COLLEGE, THE PALACE AND THE COMMONS

CRYSTAL PALACE TO BALHAM ~6

The Crystal Palace Parade, though a mere 110 foot above sea level, is the highest point on Sydenham Hill. Here, on the 'summit', stood the great Vicar's Oak which at one time gave its name to the area. There are numerous places throughout England named after oak trees and in London alone we have Burnt Oak, Gospel Oak, Royal Oak and Honor Oak (see Chapter Four). Though these places are often given a Christian or a monarchical connection, the special significance of the oak predates both our religion and our royalty. Here, the Vicar's Oak was such a significant feature that the boundaries of five parishes met beneath it. Even today the London boroughs of Bromley, Croydon, Lambeth and Southwark meet at the roundabout at the south end of the Parade, whilst a fifth, Lewisham, abuts the opposite end.

Farquhar Road, leading off the Parade, gets its name from Sir George Farquhar, the first Secretary of the Crystal Palace Company. From the top of the road we look down on new housing that occupies the site of the old Crystal Palace High Level Station, the terminus for the line which we have come across repeatedly in our walk. Here, at the Crystal Palace, it arrived in style. Like the great central London termini it was completely arched over and its separate first, second and third class platforms stretched the whole length of the Parade. At its peak it handled 10 to 12,000 passengers an hour, who made their way in subways – a separate one for each class of passenger – under the Parade, direct to the Palace turnstiles. The 24 bays of these passageways, with their brick built fan-vaulted ceilings, are just about all that survives of the High Level Station. The planners concerned with improving the Crystal Palace area will not have completed their job until they find a way of re-opening them to public inspection. The station, built in 1865, fell into decrepitude after the 1936 fire. It was closed in 1954 and demolished in 1961.

Of the Great North Wood which once covered this area, one small fragment survives. Dulwich Upper Wood is five acres of mixed deciduous woodland, owned by the Dulwich College Estates and managed by the Trust for Urban Ecology as a nature reserve. As well as some of the ancient woodland, the site covers the basement and garden areas of several Victorian villas, bomb casualties of the Second World War. There is therefore an odd mix of species; of native oaks alongside garden robinias, horse chestnut, damson and bay. In this small but beautiful fragment of woodland blackcap and chiffchaff sing on spring mornings, the foraging nuthatch gives its long, loud piping call, foxgloves bloom in the shade of oaks, and the speckled wood butterfly glides along the woodland edges. The Trust has established a tree nursery on the site and is gradually carrying out coppicing and other management work to increase the diversity of the wildlife. They should also be applauded for opening the woods to complete public access rather than treating them as a 'reserve' with restricted visiting hours.

Where Dulwich Wood Avenue crosses Colby Road, a detour of just a few yards down it leads to number 39, where, a plaque records, Annie Besant lived in 1874. After a disastrous marriage to her local vicar, Frank Besant, she left him and moved to Colby Road in 1873. Besant was an astonishing and versatile woman, a writer, free-thinker, socialist and great orator, with a particular concern for the living and working conditions of women and children in London. She was an active supporter of the striking Bryant and May match girls and founded the socialist paper *The Link*. In 1889 she joined the Theosophists, and eventually moved to India, where she became a supporter of Home Rule. Her contribution to the struggle was recognised when she was elected President of the Indian National Congress. She died in Madras in 1933.

Gipsy Hill and Norwood Park

ROUTE:

- Cross Long Meadow to reach the gate opposite, and slightly to the right, and exit onto Gipsy Hill.
- Cross Gipsy Hill and turn briefly right to take Oaks Avenue, the first turning on the left.
- At the end of Oaks Avenue, turn left and left again into Salter's Hill. Walk beneath the rail bridge to find the first entrance into the park on the right.
- Follow the tarmac path uphill and, at the junction of paths, continue straight ahead, passing the viewpoint to reach the fenced paddling pool.
- Turn left and follow the pool perimeter as it curves round to the right, passing a children's play area.
- Take the first turning to the left beyond the play area and half way along this path take the turning on the right, running downhill to exit the park at the junction of Crown Dale and Central Hill.
- Cross Central Hill and turn right up the main road (Crown Dale). Follow Central Hill for just under ½ mile to reach the major road junction at the top of the hill.
- Turn left into Beulah Hill and then take the first right into Gibsons Hill.

FACILITIES: Cafés at junction of Crown Dale and Beulah Hill.

LOOKING AT WILDLIFE: Long Meadow has been planted with a native hedgerow and with a variety of trees, especially willows. The upper part of the meadow is left uncut for most of the year to encourage wild flowers. There are more interesting trees in Norwood Park, including a number of oak species, as well as congregations of winter gulls.

Long Meadow seems to have undergone a regular series of name changes. It was once Bell Meadow, being one of a group of fields located at the back of the old Bell Inn, but an even earlier name was Frenchman's Field. This does not refer to a nationality but to the local dairyman, Thomas French. In fact cows were pastured here until relatively recent times, and herded daily up the hill to reach Thomas French and Co's Dairy, a building which still stands, although much converted. No doubt it was the quantity of water running freely down from the hill that provided such good quality pasturage and which explains the brilliant display of buttercups in the uncut portions of the field today – though it has frustrated some of the tree planting efforts of the local Dulwich Society.

Gipsy Hill itself is entered on the far side of the meadow. The windmill which once stood at the top of the hill functioned until 1853. It was proposed at one time to build a second windmill, but the idea, apparently, was opposed by the locals, who felt that 'there wasn't enough wind to work two at once'. The hill gets its name from the gipsies who were encamped in this corner of the Great North Wood from at least the seventeenth century and probably much earlier. They lived for the most part in poverty, collecting wood and making it into pegs, baskets and butcher's hooks for itinerant sale. Their most famous 'Queen' was Margaret Finch, who died in 1740 at the age of 108. It was said that towards the end of her life she remained squatting in one position for so long that when she died her limbs could not be straightened and she had to be buried in a square box. Her funeral was paid for by local publicans in recognition of the custom she had brought them. One of these customers was the wife of Samuel Pepys and her visit is recorded in an entry in his diary in 1668. By 1777 the gipsies' reputation had spread so wide that a Covent Garden pantomime, 'The Norwood Gipsies' was based upon them.

Despite this entertainment value and the income they had seemingly generated for the area, the gipsies had by the end of the eighteenth century been deemed a public nuisance. They suffered continual harassment from the local constabulary after the passing of the Vagrancy Act in 1797 and when in the early nineteenth century this harassment was compounded by the effects of enclosure, the gipsies were driven off altogether, leaving only their name behind.

The enclosures of the 1800s ensured that, by the end of the century, the whole of that part of the Great North Wood which gave its name to Norwood, had been clear-felled and developed. By 1903 the only area of any size left was that now forming Norwood Park. As Great Elderhall Coppice it had been part of the Manor of Lambeth and therefore in the ownership of the See of Canterbury. The Ecclesiastical Commissioners, amongst the most ardent in pushing through Acts of Enclosure, sold off this last remaining piece of land to the London County Council in 1903. It opened as a public park in 1911.

Once it was a coppiced common land surrounded by strawberry fields. Along one side ran the now lost River Effra, a row of thatched and white-washed cottages standing along its bank. Today we have instead a rather featureless expanse of grass, a gathering ground for winter gulls, with dotted here and there an older oak or poplar. The most interesting feature is the viewpoint from the top of the hill, although the explanatory GLC plaque has already been made out of date by the Canary Wharf development, which impedes the view to the east. Nevertheless Alexandra Park and Epping Forest stand out as distant high ground, and the city stretches out below them from Millbank to the Isle of Dogs. In the foreground to the right is the green-capped spire of Dulwich College and looming above that the wooded crest of Sydenham Hill, crowned with the Crystal Palace TV mast.

Off to the left as we descend towards Crown Dale is the massive and forbidding pile of the Fidelis Convent, the sort of building that could have inspired Mervyn Peake's *Gormenghast*. There is a more attractive nineteenth-century building at the top of Crown Hill, requiring a short detour along Crown Lane before following our route down Beulah Hill. Like Tower Bridge or St Pancras Station, it is one of those Victorian buildings which, although poaching styles from all over the place, gets away with it because of a supreme self confidence. Here are columned porticos, a stone-faced front porch which runs the whole height of the building, roof finials, a mass of chimneys, roundels at the gable ends and an orange-red brick that glows in the evening light. Built in 1894 as the British Home and Hospital for Incurables, it was one of the very first such establishments in Britain. Beulah Hill has its own grandiose Victorian pile in St Joseph's College, with the apse of its chapel abutting the road to display the relief of St Joseph de Salle clutching books and surrounded by children whom, presumably, he is instructing.

Streatham Common and Russell's Path

ROUTE:

- Descend Gibsons Hill and at the second junction take the gate on the left into Norwood Grove. Turn right up the path which runs parallel to the lane, to reach The Mansion.
- Follow the path around the outside of the perimeter fence of The Mansion until reaching a small gate on your right at a junction of paths.
- Go through the gate into the formal gardens and bear immediately left, continuing through the rose arbour and passing to the left of The Mansion to reach a lane.
- Turn left along the lane (Copgate Path) and follow it onto Streatham Common.
- On passing the entrance to The Rookery at the top of the hill (worth a detour to the left), take the small path off to the right which crosses the end of the car park.
- Keep straight ahead across the grass to reach the main road beside an iron bollard.
- Cross the road to find the opening into Hill Path. At the end of the path turn right onto Valley Road to find the entrance to Russell's Path leading off to the left.
- Follow to the end of Russell's Path, crossing another road en route, and emerging eventually up steps onto Streatham High Road.

FACILITIES: Toilets in the formal gardens beside The Mansion. Café on Streatham Common near the Rookery. Cafés and pubs on Streatham High Road.

LOOKING AT WILDLIFE: Mature parkland trees in Norwood Grove, including oak and cedar and an ancient mulberry. Open woodland and heathland flora on the Common, including gorse and Scots pine, and a good variety of woodland birds. Holly, holm oak and yew overhang Hill Path.

From the southern tip of the very urban borough of Lambeth, Gibsons Hill leads down into what looks like the rural fringes of Surrey. At a turn in the road we come into parklands and open fields, and a view which stretches out over Mitcham – and the dark bulk of the Beddington Power Station – as far as the

Surrey heaths. Gibsons Hill was the home of Stenton Covington, who played a large part in the preservation of this South London countryside.

The sinuous slope of Norwood Grove, dotted with mature trees like an old English estate, leads up to The Mansion, a fine white house with a bow in the middle of the facade and a long conservatory all along one side, topped with little glass cupolas which look like copies from the Brighton pavilion. The house was clearly designed as the family seat of a weighty Victorian 'captain of industry'. Its fine plaster-work ceilings can still be glimpsed through the upper windows and the house was set about with formal features – a trefoil garden, a rose pergola, ponderous cedars and a gnarled old mulberry on a perfectly level lawn. It was built in the early nineteenth century, the home of Arthur Anderson, founder of the P&O steamship company.

Norwood Grove is just one of several delights contained in this little north east corner of Streatham Common. Here the path runs alongside the only remaining woodlands of the common; a dappled light falls through trees onto hazel, bramble and gorse, and the local population of grey squirrels has become cocky enough to steal a picnicker's sandwiches. And beside this is a 'secret' garden, The Rookery, one of the finest municipal gardens in London.

Streatham's common lands were unchallenged for centuries, until in 1794 the Duke of Bedford, the freeholder, illegally sold off the fuel rights to a private buyer. The commoners immediately gathered in protest and prevented the sale by the drastic measure of setting fire to all the gorse. The Duke responded by enclosing the grazing areas but the *Gentleman's Magazine* reported that on the very same evening a hackney coach drove to the spot, and six men, draped in black and with crapes over their faces, got out of the carriage, cut down the paled enclosure, got back into the coach, and drove off.

By this date the Common was already fashionable for its three wells. The most important of these had been discovered in 1659, when, according to story, the ground gave way beneath a horse and plough. The waters rose here at a temperature of 52°F, and were described as having a slight smell of sulphur and a sparkling taste. They were held to be particularly good for the eyes and for 'the expulsion of worms'. By 1701 hundreds of people were arriving to take the waters and to attend the concerts at Streatham Wells House, which, says Colonel Sexby, 'made the crowds of visitors as gay and frivolous as their ailments would allow'. But by the end of the nineteenth century the wells had long since fallen into disuse.

In 1888 the major part of the common was sold by the Ecclesiastical Commissioners to the Metropolitan Board of Works for the nominal sum of £5. The Wells House however, now known as The Rookery, was in private hands and went on the market in 1912. It was then that Stenton Covington came on the scene, founding a preservation society that campaigned for the public purchase of the estate. The committee succeeded in raising half the purchase price, the rest was met by the London County Council and the Borough of Wandsworth, and the Rookery was opened to the public in 1913.

Eleven years later Mr Covington was back in action when the adjacent Norwood Grove was threatened with development. The committee was re-activated and the LCC, this time with the Croydon Corporation, was persuaded to buy the site for the public. Once again the preservation committee raised a substantial portion of the purchase price.

One of the old medicinal wells can still be seen in the Rookery, in the beautiful setting of the Old English Garden. There is also a White Garden, rock and water gardens and a picnic area in the 'Orchard', all remnants of the days when Councils could afford to invest in the provision of a beautiful environment.

An unusual sequence of footpaths leads from the common into central Streatham. The first of these is Hill Path, which begins next to St Michael's Convent, where mature hollies, yew trees and dark evergreen oaks overhang the first part of the way. The convent was previously Park Hill, residence of the Tate family, whose sugar fortune endowed the Tate Gallery. The second of the Streatham wells was to be found in the grounds here, whilst the third is on Valley Road, where we make the connection between Hill Path and Russell's Footpath. This third well was in the grounds of the old United Dairy Depot and the water, at 1d for three pails, was delivered by the dairymen along with the milk. With the sales of bottled water as high as they are, perhaps there will one day be door-to-door deliveries again.

Russell's Footpath runs in a long straight line between rows of back gardens. Several generations of Lord Russell lived in Streatham – presumably one of them made this his route to the common, thus giving the path its name. During the nineteenth century the Reverend Wriothesley Russell was the tenant of the rectory, and one of his regular visitors was Lord John Russell, the Whig Cabinet Minister. Lord John is said to have used a stay at the Rectory to draft the Great Reform Bill which was passed in 1832, greatly extending the right to vote and abolishing the old 'rotten boroughs'. The initial defeat of the Bill precipitated a general election, and Russell campaigned throughout the country, often attended by huge and agitated crowds. In the course of one journey to Devon hundreds turned out to see him pass and Sidney Smith wrote to Lady Holland that:

the people along the way were very much disappointed by his smallness. I told them he was very much larger before the bill was thrown out, but was reduced by excessive anxiety about the people. This brought tears to their eyes.

From the Bec to Balham

ROUTE:

- Turn right onto Streatham High Road then left onto Gleneagle Road, just after Station Approach.
- Cross the road and turn right into Ambleside Avenue.
- Follow Ambleside Avenue across Mitcham Lane and continue ahead to reach Tooting Bec Road and the common.
- Turn left along the edge of the common and just before the railway bridge take the path on the right. Keep parallel to the railway line through the woods to reach Bedford Hill.

- At Bedford Hill turn left and cross the railway bridge. Turn right onto the common again and walk through the woods, parallel to the other side of the railway.
- At the far side of the common join the path ahead, going under two railway bridges to reach Fernlea Road.

To join Walk 7 and to complete this walk:

Turn left and follow Fernlea Road and then Balham Station Road to reach Balham High Road and the stations.

FACILITIES: Pubs and cafés in Streatham and again in Balham, especially around the stations. There is a café on Tooting Common near the corner of Hillbury Road and Bedford Hill.

LOOKING AT WILDLIFE: The two areas of woodland on Tooting Common support a surprising variety of birds, including goldcrest, spotted flycatcher, long-tailed tit and nuthatch. There is also a good variety of autumn fungi, including fly agaric, death cap, puffballs, boletus and parasol mushroom.

Tooting has two commons, Tooting Bec and Tooting Graveney. The larger of the two, and the one we cross, is the Bec, which draws its name from the Abbey of St Mary de Bec-Hellouin in Normandy, which held the Manor of Upper Tooting in the Middle Ages. This one-time wild stretch of woodland had the usual sad history of incursions, until in 1861 the Duke of Bedford put both the manor and the common up for sale.

The commoners immediately met together to discuss the possibility of a joint purchase. They learnt, however, that Mr W.J. Thompson, a City of London broker who had lived in Tooting for eighteen years, had decided to bid for it himself. Since Mr Thompson was known to be opposed to enclosure, it was unanimously decided not to put in any bid against him. However, the commoners were to be disappointed. Henry Warwick Cole takes up the tale in *Fraser's Magazine*:

> Mr Thompson ... as carefully avoided giving any pledge that would bind him on the subject, as he did giving any hint that might disabuse the minds of his neighbours from the conclusion so favourable to himself which they had too hastily arrived at ... his prudence was so effective that he was suffered, at the sale, to become the purchaser of the manor and the houses and cottages for £3,285 only ...
>
> The premises were conveyed to Mr Thompson in December 1862, when a new light instantaneously, and as if by magic, broke in upon his mind as to the extensive nature of the rights of lords and the limited nature of the rights of commoners ... perhaps the circumstance that some of the common was established by himself as worth £1000 an acre for building, may have induced him to study the merits of the legal question with more individualism than impartiality. Under the influence of his new impressions he vigorously set to work to inclose the whole common, and convert it to building-land for his own benefit.

But not without opposition. Every time Mr Thompson put up fences the local people pulled them down again, and the battle continued until 1870, when Mr Betts, the local butcher, obtained a court injunction forbidding further enclosure. Five years later the Metropolitan Board of Works came to the rescue and purchased the commons as public open space for the sum of £17,771, a profit to Mr Thompson of £14,000.

Tooting Bec has two remaining areas of woodland, one on either side of Bedford Hill, and in season they support an interesting variety of fungi. Among them is the sinisterly named Death Cap, *Amanita phalloides*. Fungi in this country are held in an inordinate and undue dread, but in this case at least it is justified. This one species is responsible for 90 per cent of fatal poisonings. Its cap is olive-green, the colour of someone already sickening, and its toxins are unaffected by cooking. One cap is more than enough to cause death.

One of the early incursions made upon the common, with the Duke of Bedford's express permission, was for the large house and grounds of Streatham Park. The estate was built by Mr Thrale, the founder of Thrales Brewery. His wife Hester was an astute, ambitious and intelligent woman, and their home became the centre of an impressive social circle. Frequent visitors included Goldsmith, Burke, Chambers, Garrick and Fanny Burney, all of whom had their portraits painted by another of the regular house guests, Sir Joshua Reynolds. Most regular of them all, however, was Samuel Johnson, who, after his second visit, took up more or less permanent residence for almost fifteen years. He wrote *Lives of the Poets* here and had a favourite walk up to the top of Streatham Common and back.

Mr Thrale died in 1781, from eating 'too much quail liver paté'. Johnson, despite his well-known misogyny, had been in love with Hester Thrale for many years, but perhaps it took the death of Mr Thrale for this to become apparent. Hester, for her part, became noticeably cooler towards Johnson and very soon announced her engagement to her children's music teacher, Mr Piozzi. When he received her letter containing the news the 72 year-old Johnson wrote back instantly:

> I who have loved you, reverenced you and served you, I who long thought you the first of human kind, entreat that before your fate is irrevocable, I may once more see you.

Hester went ahead with the marriage. Johnson burnt all her letters and never saw her again, dying two years later. The new Mrs Piozzi went on to successfully publish his biography, *The Anecdotes of the Late Dr Samuel Johnson*.

Getting home

Balham Station: Network Rail (Victoria)

Balham Underground Station: Northern line.

Buses: (Balham High Road) 155, 249, 355

6. Of Hustings and Huguenots

FROM WANDSWORTH COMMON TO WIMBLEDON

Wandsworth and Wimbledon – and their respective commons – frame the walk in this chapter. They sit on either side of the Wandle valley, linked by the geological forces that formed them – and by the human ones that almost unmade them again. Between them runs the River Wandle, a small and now rather undistinguished river, but one with a great history. It was this fast flowing tributary that cut down through the steep Thames terraces exposing the river-borne gravels. And it was the relatively poor and acid soils of these gravels that helped form the south London heaths and commons –and which, subsequently, helped save them from agricultural development.

Between these commons, the gentle slopes of the valley cut down to more fertile soils. The alluvial deposits that coated the London clay provided the banks of the river with a rich horticultural past, a past that survives now only in place names like Plough Lane or Haydon's Road, after the farmer whose fields it crossed. This value of the riverside for cultivation was soon overtaken by the value of the River Wandle, and its banks, for trades dependent on water and on water power. This beautiful chalk stream, famous for its trout fishing, became one of the most industrialised stretches of river in the world. In particular it became a centre for Huguenot immigrants, who arrived here with their special skills, built their mills and played a central part in the industrial development of Wandsworth.

But there is a historical link as well as a geological one between the two ends of our walk. From their grand house on Wimbledon Hill and all the way to Wandsworth, most of the area was in the ownership of the Spencer family. And, having established themselves in the area, they set out to exploit it as much as they could. Trees which had been carefully managed on the commons for centuries were felled and sold off for firewood. Gravel was scoured from the terraces, and a brickyard built, producing over 20,000 tiles a week. And when the values from these began to decline it was the commons themselves that the family began, illegally, to sell off, a process of constant encroachments that has led today to Wandsworth Common becoming one of the most dissected pieces of open space in London. It was a side of family history that remained unmentioned when Princess Diana was being married off to Prince Charles.

As well, therefore, as the story of the river, which runs like a thread through the middle of the walk, this chapter is the story of the common people of the area, from their struggles against successive Earls Spencer to preserve the

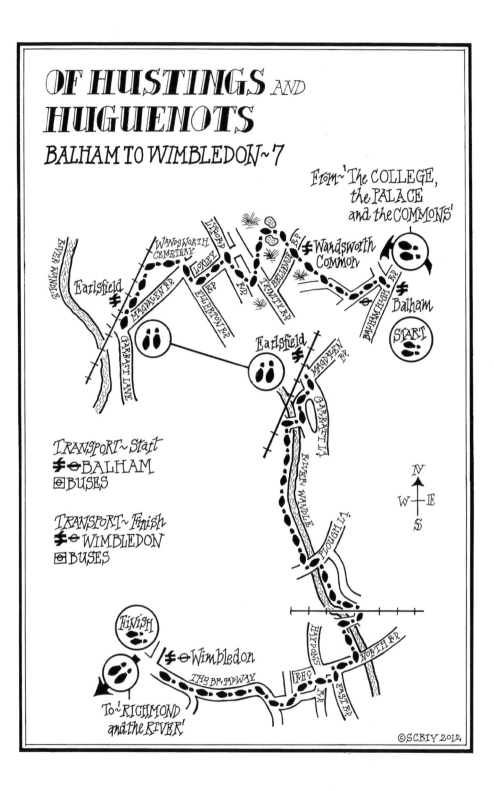

OF HUSTINGS AND HUGUENOTS

BALHAM TO WIMBLEDON ~ 7

commons, through to the stories, recorded in Wandsworth Cemetery, of their sacrifices in the two World Wars. And among these stories is the amazing account of the 'Garratt elections' – huge and ribald celebrations that took place around the election of a mock 'mayor' for an insignificant hamlet – and which became in turn a sort of long-running satire on the state of national politics.

This chapter covers a single walk of 5 miles from Balham Station to Wimbledon Station.

▨ WALK 7: Balham to Wimbledon

Getting started

From Balham Station (Network Rail (Victoria)):
From the end of Balham Station Road cross the main road (Balham High Road) to enter Chestnut Grove immediately opposite.

From Balham Underground Station (Northern line):
Follow the exit signs into Chestnut Grove and turn left.

From buses (155, 249, 355):
Alight at Balham Underground Station on Balham High Road
From Balham High Road turn into Chestnut Grove just beside the Underground Station.

From Walk 6:
From the end of Balham Station Road cross the main road (Balham High Road) to enter Chestnut Grove immediately opposite.

Wandsworth Common and the Scope

ROUTE:

- On entering Chestnut Grove turn immediately left into Boundaries Road.
- Take the first turning on the right into Balham Park Road.
- Where the road bends left take the footpath on the right onto Wandsworth Common. Follow alongside the railway to reach Wandsworth Common Station.
- Follow the footpath though the station and continue on the path that runs alongside the railway to reach the main road. Cross the road and follow the tarmac path which continues alongside the railway across the common.
- On reaching the lakes, follow along the right hand side of the first lake and, towards its end, take the board walk on the left, crossing it to the far side.
- Bear right on the far side to reach the tarmac path and turn left along it.

- Just after a crosspaths, leave the tarmac path as it curves right alongside the backs of houses and instead keep straight ahead along an avenue of trees.
- On reaching the main road go straight across to follow the trodden path opposite. Follow this to the first junction, by a lamp-post.
- Turn right and carry on to reach Lyford Road. Turn right up Lyford Road and then left onto Loxley Road.
- Follow Loxley Road to its end then turn right onto Ellerton Road.
- At the end of Ellerton Road cross Magdalen Road to enter Wandsworth Cemetery.

FACILITIES: Cafés and pubs around Balham Station and a pub close to Wandsworth Common Station.

LOOKING AT WILDLIFE: Wandsworth Common has over fifty species of tree, among which the sweet smelling balsam poplar is particularly evident on the path to Wandsworth Common Station. The ponds have a variety of common wild fowl, with some less usual species sometimes turning up in winter. The Scope is an area of semi-natural grassland dominated by purple moor grass. Among the interesting plants to be found here, strawberry clover is of particular interest.

The 175-acre **Wandsworth Common** has suffered more from encroachment and is more cut up by roads and railways than any other of the metropolitan commons of London. This poor, emaciated, ill-used open space is now in no less than ten separate sections. From the eighteenth century onwards Wandsworth and Wimbledon Commons and all the area between them were in the hands of the Spencer family, and the Spencers, according to Robert Hunter writing in the *English Illustrated Magazine* in 1886, appear to have regarded the common 'as a means of being generous at other people's expense'. Henry Warwick Cole writing in *Fraser's Magazine* in May of the same year, is just as scathing:

Wandsworth Common which was once from its great beauty a very jewel of the metropolis, has fared cruelly under the Spencer family. It now comprises about 150 acres only; but the present lord and his predecessor have sold, within the last 13 years, upwards of 140 acres for sums which have realised £15,336 ... The consequences of the want of spirit displayed by the commoners of Wandsworth have been most calamitous. Not only has half the common been illegally enclosed but the remaining half has been subject to the vilest treatment. The green turf has been stripped off its surface, the trees have been injured or destroyed, enormous quantities of gravel have been extracted without regard to any considerations but the convenience of those who dig it and large pits have been formed, filled to the depth of several feet with water from which one morning there was pulled out the body of a drowned man, who had vainly sought health and recreation there and had lost his life in the attempt. Mr Rose

... gave his personal assistance in fishing for the dead body, but found that the personal excitement it gave him before breakfast was, after all, only a poor competitor for the former amenities of the place.

Between 1794 and 1866 there were 53 enclosures carried out on the Common, varying in size from a quarter of an acre to 96 acres. Some were illegal, but all of them were approved by the successive Earls Spencer. In the 1850s the situation was compounded by the railway companies, with the London and South Western and the London and Brighton Railways both driving across the common major routes which splintered it into fragments.

Finally, in 1870, Henry Peek, an active campaigner in the protection of commons, got together a committee to save what was left. The situation at Wandsworth between the commoners, the local community and the landowners was only settled after agreement had been reached in a long-running dispute over the larger Wimbledon Common. But in 1871 the Wandsworth Common Act was passed and the common assigned to Conservators elected by the Parish ratepayers. In a settlement very similar to that reached in Wimbledon, Earl Spencer received an annuity of £250, calculated as his average earnings from the sale of gravel from the common. By 1887 the Parish ratepayers were fed up with bearing the cost locally and Wandsworth Common, more of a nuisance than a place of recreation according to Cecil, passed under the management of the Metropolitan Board of Works.

Despite this sad history, the common still has a few interesting attributes. The local authorities, for example, have planted a wide variety of trees: alder, aspen, swamp cypress, Turkey oak, red oak, balsam poplar, elm, silver maple, manna ash, scarlet hawthorn and many more. There are also the lakes, remnants of the era of gravel digging. They have reed-beds and bracken-covered islands, with rhododendrons, crack willow, giant hogweed and some storm-beaten birches. There is the usual collection of town park water birds: mallard and feral duck and an assortment of odd shaped hybrids, with coot, moorhen, black-headed gulls and the ubiquitous Canada geese. It is when these are supplemented by winter visitors such as pochard or even barnacle or white-fronted geese that the ponds become particularly interesting.

But both the exotic tree species and the rather tame park-type pond are clearly the usual municipal additions, attempting to revive an otherwise desecrated space. They lack the vigour, diversity, excitement and restorative power of genuine wildness. And there is just one corner of Wandsworth Common where this can still be found. It is tucked away in the south west corner, where our route lies and where, in 1852, the Reverend John Craig built an 85 foot long telescope. It was slung from towers 64-foot high and rested on a support running on a circular railway. It was a very imperfect instrument, but was the largest telescope ever built up to its time, and it gave its name to this part of the common – 'the Scope'.

The Scope today is an area of semi-natural grassland almost unique in inner London. It supports twenty species of grass, including large tussocks of the purple-moor grass so reminiscent of soggy Pennine walks. This flourishes in the damper areas and, with hairy sedge, surrounds the little pond dug here by the

British Trust for Conservation Volunteers in 1980. It is an attractive place at any time of year, even in winter when the moor-grass tussocks turn from green to pale yellow, the last bristly leaves of comfrey stand alongside the browning spires of weld, polypore fungi project from the bare birch trees, and robins sing their characteristic thin and melancholic trill.

Wandsworth Cemetery and the Somme

ROUTE:

- On entering the cemetery follow the main path ahead until reaching the third path on the left, opposite The Cottage.
- Follow this path until reaching a group of war memorials at a crossing of paths. Turn right here.
- Follow the path to reach and climb the embankment at its far end and turn left along its top.
- Follow the embankment as far as you can. The path narrows and finally descends a set of wooden steps back into the main part of the cemetery.
- Bear right at the bottom of the steps and head for the gate at the far end of the cemetery that leads back onto Magdalen Road.

LOOKING AT WILDLIFE: Part of the cemetery site is now managed for nature conservation, with the embankment slopes left uncut till early summer to encourage wild flowers such as common toadflax, lady's bedstraw and St John's wort. The cemetery headstones support a variety of lichen species, and there are some fine specimen trees, including avenues of horse chestnut, Lombardy poplar and balsam poplar.

The gates which lead into Wandsworth Cemetery are a Grade II listed building. The rest of this 1878 cemetery site seems, at first sight, undistinguished. It contains however some fascinating features, not least among them its large number of war memorials. There are no less than eight in all, to the civilian casualties of Wandsworth but also to the combatants from a surprisingly wide range of nations. In fact the War Graves Commission lists 592 military burials at this site – 477 of them from World War I – with special plots devoted to soldiers from as far afield as Australia, New Zealand, South Africa and Newfoundland. That they are all gathered together in this small corner of south west London may seem, at first, a conundrum. The answer lies in the conversion, at the start of World War I, of the Royal Victoria Patriotic School on Trinity Road, just on the edge of Wandsworth Common, into the Third London General Hospital (Territorial Forces). The hospital housed, at any one time, over 1000 injured soldiers and adopted what, according to its own Gazette, was the benign and enlightened policy of mixing the nationalities together rather than housing them on separate wards. And many of those who, having travelled from all over the world to serve the 'mother country', died of their wounds in these wards, are buried in Wandsworth Cemetery.

Our route through the cemetery takes us past a column commemorating James Carmichael, 1858-1934, Director General of Housing for England and Wales, early photographs of whom are housed in the National Portrait Gallery. From here, down one of the several parallel paths that run the length of the site, we come to a central crossing around which are grouped a whole number of World War I memorials. Here, in a beautifully tended plot, a collection of simple white slabs, all dating from 1916 and 1917, bear the symbol of a caribou head, surrounded by a wreath of laurels. It identifies them all, the very oldest among them just 25 years of age, as members of the Royal Newfoundland Regiment.

At the outbreak of the First World War, Newfoundland was still a Dominion of the British Empire and not yet a part of Canada. Despite being a rural area remote from the homeland, and with no military organisation of its own since 1870, it nonetheless raised a regiment of over 1000 men, nicknamed the 'blue puttees'. Having served with distinction in the terrible conditions of Gallipoli – where they were chosen to provide the rearguard during the eventual retreat from the peninsula – they moved on to the Western Front in March 1916. Here they were stationed at the hamlet of Beaumont-Hamel at the northern end of a 28-mile front that was very soon to become infamous as the battlefield of the Somme. Early on the morning of 1 July 1916, British sappers exploded a large mine in the 'Hawthorn tunnel' under the German lines. It was intended to soften up the German defences, and did indeed knock out a particular strongpoint. But it also served to alert them to the fact that an attack was imminent. When it did come, just ten minutes later, their well-fortified lines were ready and the first British assault was quickly halted.

The Newfoundlanders were not part of that assault but were being held in reserve in a trench known as St John's Road, some 250 yards back. At 8.45 am they received the order to go forward but by then the communications trenches leading to the front were blocked with dead and wounded. It was decided to send them over the top where they were, giving them not just the enemy defences but the British barbed wire to navigate. As they appeared over the crest they were by now the only figures moving in the landscape. And not for long. Within 15 to 20 minutes of leaving the St John's Road trench the majority of them were dead or dying – and most of them without ever leaving the British lines. All 22 officers and 658 other ranks were casualties, and of the 780 men who took part in the attack only 68 were available for roll-call the next morning. The regiment – and the young men who composed it – had been wiped out in less than half an hour.

Diagonally opposite the Newfoundland plot stands a line of graves from the opposite end of the world, young men from the South African Infantry, the impala of their regimental crest forming an interesting contrast with the Newfoundlander's caribou. Here too is their regimental motto in both Afrikaans and English: Eendracht maakt macht. In translation it seems strangely ironic for the South Africa of their time: Unity Makes Strength.

The path which we follow from here leads to an embankment close to the railway lines, which looks as though it must once have been a railway siding itself. Its banks are now left uncut for part of the year to encourage wildlife, and its crest is lined with tall, thin Lombardy poplars – giving it both an Italianate and an appropriately funereal air. It is an impression that is heightened by the heavy sweet scent of balsam poplars hanging in the air, as though it were some oil used in embalming. This 'lane of the dead' leads us to yet another war memorial. It is, as it says; 'To the citizens of Wandsworth who are laid to rest here having lost their lives to enemy action in World War II and whose names are perpetuated on this memorial'. But in fact there are only four names here – the remaining 24 burials are of those whose remains were never identified. Above them, the Wandsworth crest inscribed on the memorial includes the droplets said to represent the tears of the Huguenot refugees. They seem particularly appropriate here.

Earlsfield and the Mayors of Garratt

ROUTE:

- Exit the cemetery to turn right onto Magdalen Road and continue to the main road (Garratt Lane), close to Earlsfield station.
- Turn left onto Garratt Lane taking the turning almost immediately on the right (Summerley Street).

FACILITIES: Pubs and cafés on Garratt Lane.

The hamlet of Garratt, once described as 'an insignificant dirt village in the parish of Wandsworth' became, in the eighteenth century, the scene of one of the strangest, and most popular street celebrations in London – the fantastical elections of a completely fictitious mayor.

Although several different versions are given of the origins of these proceedings, it seems most probable that they stem from one of the earlier attempts of Wandsworth commoners to protect their rights. In the early 1700s a group of them formed a society and their chairperson became known, with mock dignity, as the 'Mayor of Garratt'. The elections for this post became, in time, a burlesque of national politics, and were held to coincide with general elections.

The first recorded elections were in 1747, and by the 1760s the event was attended by up to 100,000 people, whose carriages, carts and horses were said to have blocked every road around Wandsworth for over a mile. The candidates were generally working-class London characters, whose chief requirement, according to Colonel Sexby, was 'an unlimited capacity for talking', preferably combined 'with some physical deformity or peculiarity'. On election day they would gather in fantastic costume, each with their own retinue, and process in decorated carts and carriages –often provided or even driven by the aristocracy – from Wandsworth to Garratt Green. Here it was that 'Squire Blow-me-down', 'Lord Twankum', 'Sir Trincalo Boreas', 'Admiral Sir Christopher Dashwood', and many other characters over the years, took 'The Oath of Qualification for the ancient Borough of Garrat, according, and as it stands on the old record, handed down to us by the grand Volgee, by order of the great Chin Kaw Chipo, first Emperor of the Moon. Anno Mundi 68'. After this, to much heckling, ribald comment or raucous support, the candidates made their election speeches. Finally the successful candidate was chosen by popular acclaim and the crowds got down to the serious business of drinking the local pubs dry.

Like the Horn Fair, the Middlesex elections and many other good English festivities, the elections were a scene of bawdy and almost riotous behaviour. The candidates' speeches were a mix of sexual innuendo and political satire. Some of the speeches were written by leading political and theatrical figures of the day, including Samuel Foote, David Garrick and John Wilkes. And from the 1760s the Garratt election became particularly associated with radical politics.

One of the most successful of the Garratt mayors was 'Sir Jeffrey Dunstan', a strong supporter of John Wilkes, who was returned to 'office' three times and was described as 'the most popular candidate that ever appeared on the Garratt hustings'. Dunstan was a foundling who took his name from the parish where he had been abandoned as a baby. He was only four foot high, with a large head and knock knees, a vagrant wig-seller by trade and a man of outspoken wit. According to Hone's 1826 *Everyday Book*, he was no respecter of persons and was so severe in his jokes on the corruptions and compromises of power that this street-jester was prosecuted for using what were then called seditious expressions; and, as a caricature of the times, which ought never to be forgotten, he was in 1793 tried, convicted and imprisoned. Dunstan died in 1797, after a bout of heavy drinking. One year before this the Garratt elections had been finally suppressed by an establishment which the French revolution had made increasingly nervous of the 'mob' and all its manifestations. Despite several attempts to revive it since, the Garratt Elections have joined the Charlton Horn Fair as one of the great, anarchic expressions of exuberance that have disappeared from the streets of London.

Garratt too has disappeared, swallowed up in the expansion of urban Wandsworth. Its name survives in Garratt Lane and in Garratt Green, now an uninspiring grass triangle on nearby Burntwood Road. The area has had its very name appropriated by the Victorian developers. The last Lord of this, the Manor of All Farthing, covered the surrounding fields with housing in the late nineteenth century, and proceeded to rename the area after his wife, Earl. Hence Earlsfield – a name with about as much historical or social significance as Hillview, Sunnyside or The Cedars.

Along the Valley of the Wandle

ROUTE:

- Where Summerley Street reaches its junction with Trewint Street, turn right to cross the river.
- On the far side of the bridge take the path on the left that runs alongside the river bank.
- Continue along the river path, ignoring any side turnings, until it emerges on a main road (Plough Lane).

- Join the road and turn left to cross the river, joining the riverside walk again which now continues on the opposite bank.
- Continue ahead, again ignoring all side paths, until the path reaches a railway line and bridge crossing the river ahead of you and beside a little viewing platform.
- Follow the path as it curves left to follow the railway embankment and then right to run beneath it.
- On the far side of the railway turn immediately right into the Wandle Nature Park. Continue ahead along the main path, which runs roughly parallel to the opposite side of the railway, back towards the riverside and passing a small pond on the way.
- Cross the footbridge ahead of you then turn immediately left to follow the opposite bank of the river.
- Follow this path, ignoring an exit on the right, until the path emerges onto a road (North Road).

LOOKING AT WILDLIFE: The thin strip of riverside land supports a variety of common bird species and of wasteland wild flowers. Shortly after crossing Plough Lane the route passes several rather incongruous groups of Monterey pines, set among the more appropriate crack willows and white poplars. Goldcrests may occasionally be seen here.

The clear waters of the English chalk streams were once one of the country's ecological treasures. Loaded now with agricultural effluent and fertiliser run-off and suffering from excessive extraction, they are in serious decline, but the Wandle was once among the finest of them. This quiet country stream with its watercress beds was famous for its trout, described by Izaak Walton as 'marked with marble spots like a tortoise'. An even more famous angler here, though perhaps less accomplished at it, was Horatio Nelson. The river flowed behind the house of Lady Hamilton at Merton Place, and it was in her garden that he taught himself to fish again, using his one good arm. Having diverted a part of the river for his benefit she nicknamed it the 'Nile' in his honour.

This same idyllic stream was destined to become the hardest working and most industrialised river in Europe. Fed by springs around Carshalton, it runs eleven miles to join the Thames at Wandsworth. In that short distance it drops 100 feet, and this rapid flow, combined with the proximity to London and to the great highway of the Thames, meant that by the mid eighteenth century it was driving 94 water mills. Neither were these the peaceful grinders of rural grain, but – more akin to Blake's 'satanic mills' – there were calico works, snuff mills, oil mills, bleaching grounds, log and paper mills, dye-works, copper mills, skinning mills and breweries.

The very beginnings of this development came with the arrival of the Huguenots. In 1685 the French King, Louis XIV, revoked the Edict of Nantes, under which the nation's protestants had been given a measure of toleration. This led to an exodus of 'huguenots' to protestant European countries. Of those who came to England many settled in Wandsworth, Streatham and Tooting. They brought with them energy, determination and a knowledge of industrial processes, in particular of the harnessing of water power. The mildly alkaline waters of the Wandle were ideal for their industries: silk weaving, copper engraving, hat making, bleaching, dyeing and colouring. Ironically their customers came to include the Roman Catholic cardinals, who turned to the Huguenots for their red robes and hats. In recognition of their contribution to the borough, the presence of the Huguenots was represented on the coat of arms. Against a background of the chequers of Surrey is incorporated a pattern of small droplets – the tears of the refugees.

The arrival of steam led to further development and further decline in water quality. As late as the 1970s local residents would notice that the river was running red, pink or blue, depending on the dye they were using in the up-stream tanneries. But by now many of the factories had converted to new uses, including the production of paints, solvents and chemicals. Finally, in the 1990s the river was officially declared a sewer.

Today the Wandle is being rediscovered. In 2007 Thames Water and the Wandle Trust launched a five year plan to revive and revitalise the river – though the plan got off to an unfortunate start when Thames Water accidentally spilt huge quantities of cleaning chemicals into the river during routine maintenance of the sewage treatment works at Beddington. Campaigning by the Wandle Trust has also led to the opening of the Wandle Trail along its once hidden banks. It has been a long time coming, since Octavia Hill first suggested the idea of a walking route linking the green spaces along the Wandle over 120 years ago.

Nonetheless this stretch of the Wandle represents yet another era in our industrial history and in the history of the river – one which in fact may best be described as 'post-industrial'. Here, beside the brown and rapid river, we walk through a weedy wasteland flanked with bus garages, Council depots, container sites, storage yards, allotments and post-war housing estates. It is a landscape of pylons, weirs and pipelines and, for those attuned to urban walking it has an appeal – and a peculiar fascination – of its own. The gentle humming of electricity generating stations and the more raucous drilling and thumping that marks the arrival of new development is accompanied by a surprising amount of bird song, and here and there a line of pollarded willows, despite its setting alongside industrial estates, gives a strange echo of the Wandle's long-lost rural past.

From the Wandle to Wimbledon

ROUTE:

- On reaching North Road leave the riverside and turn right. Continue as far as the first turning on the left (East Road) just opposite the leisure centre.
- Turn left down East Road and after a few yards find an alleyway between houses through a barrier on the right.
- Keep straight ahead, crossing an estate road and passing through two more barriers until the path curves round to the left to reach a crossing of paths beside a lamp post.

- Turn right here to reach the main road (Haydon Road).
- Go straight across Haydon Road and into Packham Road to reach the recreation ground.
- Take the perimeter path to the left or cut diagonally left across the grass to reach the gate at the far left hand corner of the recreation ground.
- Exit onto the road (Quicks Road) and turn right.
- Turn right onto Merton Road at the end. It soon curves round to the left to become The Broadway.

To join Walk 8 or to complete this walk:

Follow The Broadway ahead for just under ½ mile to reach Wimbledon town centre.

FACILITIES: Cafés, pubs and disabled toilets in Wimbledon town centre.

Wimbledon, according to Ed Glinert in his *Literary Guide to London*, is 'expensive, snooty and culturally moribund'. That may be a trifle harsh – and it certainly doesn't take account of the excellence of Nigel Williams' satires on his native SW19. It is however something of an upstart place, a Johnny-come-lately of a suburb, built largely around the fortunes of three rich families: the Cecils, the Spencers and the Churchills. The Cecils came first, Sir Edward Cecil building Wimbledon House at the top of the hill, to the north of the present station. Strangely, it burnt again down in 1628, the day after his country house had been accidentally blown up by gunpowder. Following this excess of carelessness, misfortune seems to have followed the estate, for by 1712 it was sold to Theodore Janssen, one of the directors of the South Sea Company, who was then bankrupted by the company's spectacular collapse – the famous South Sea Bubble. He was forced to put the entire Manor of Wimbledon onto the market, and it was purchased by Sarah Churchill, Duchess of Marlborough. She soon put up another new house on the site and, in 1744, bequeathed it to her favourite grandson, John Spencer. John had done well to ingratiate himself with the Duchess, for he had a notorious reputation, was known as 'Bad Jack', and, as his contribution to the run of bad luck, had drunk himself to death by the age of 38. But it was his ownership that began the long association of this area with the Spencer family – who have retained the manor ever since.

Bad Jack's son, also John Spencer, became the first Earl Spencer and used Lancelot 'Capability' Brown to landscape the grounds around his manor house – including the site of the current Wimbledon Park. Both John Spencers were, however, forbidden by a clause in the Duchess of Marlborough's will from playing any active part in politics. No such injunction lay upon the second Earl, George John Spencer. He began as MP for Northampton in 1780, and by 1794 had risen to be First Lord of the Admiralty. He was the person instrumental in Nelson's advancement to Admiral, and a staunch supporter of the Whigs. When the manor house burnt down yet again in 1785, the new one he built became a social centre for the party, and for all those in society with whig leanings. The most popular events organised by him and his wife Lavinia were grand whig 'breakfasts', which in fact went on well into the afternoon. One of the practical effects of his entertaining was that the estate was almost bankrupted. Thus began the numerous attempts to enclose both Wandsworth and Wimbledon Commons.

It was in the 1880s that housing came to much of the rest of Wimbledon, enabled by the arrival of the railway in 1838, one of the earliest routes to be built in London. To avoid the high ground of the village it was situated in open country some half a mile away, in what was soon to become 'Lower Wimbledon', and it is towards Lower Wimbledon that the final part of our route takes us; across Haydon Road, built through Farmer Haydon's fields, across the recreation ground, and up the Broadway, passing the theatre, where Gracie Fields, Marlene Dietrich and Danny La Rue all once performed.

Getting home

Wimbledon Station: London Bridge/Waterloo

Wimbledon Underground Station: District Line

Trams: Towards Croydon

Buses: 57, 93, 131, 156, 163, 164, 200, 219, 493

7. Richmond and the River

WIMBLEDON, RICHMOND AND KEW

Between Wimbledon and Kew Bridge, *The Green London Way* offers the unforgettable experience of nearly ten miles of uninterrupted, urban off-road walking. From the high plateau of Wimbledon Common and the rolling parkland of Richmond, down the steep slope of Richmond Hill, through the sheep-grazed meadows of the riverside and alongside Old Deer Park and Kew Gardens on the Thames tow-path, this route may lead us across the occasional road, but after our initial section through Wimbledon town centre, not once do we have to follow one. In this one chapter we have London's largest park and London's largest common – and this being Richmond even the humble village green has to be one of the largest in the country. There is some beautiful walking here, but more than this, when put into the context of the whole route, there is a striking insight into the social layout of London.

From London's leafy south west, travel to the diametrically opposite side of London and you have a diametrically opposite picture. London traditionally, and like many other British cities, concentrated its rich in the west and its poor in the east. Patterns of development are now shifting across the capital, with the poor being driven increasingly to the outer fringes, but the legacy of this pattern can still be seen in the distribution of open spaces. In the London Borough of Richmond there are 13 hectares of open space for every thousand residents. Over in the north east, in the London Borough of Islington, there is the dramatic contrast of one thousand people sharing 0.4 hectares of public open space. And in the adjacent east end boroughs of Hackney and Tower Hamlets, the pace of new residential development remains intense, with an increasing emphasis on multi-storey blocks, and insufficient regard for the provision of additional public open space or even of private gardens.

The story of Richmond and the riverside, meanwhile, has been very much the story of the aristocracy and the royalty who lived here; at Pembroke Lodge, Cannizaro House, Richmond Palace, Zion House, Kew Palace, or at one of a large number of other fabulous and fashionable villas. And between them they would have made the whole walk impossible had it not been for the struggles of the more humble inhabitants of Richmond. Without these people, Wimbledon Common, Richmond Park and Petersham Common would all now be lost to public access. This section of the walk illustrates the greatness of ordinary people and the ordinariness of great ones. For in this chapter Lords are defeated and Kings are beheaded, and George III meets the tragic fate of a growing and

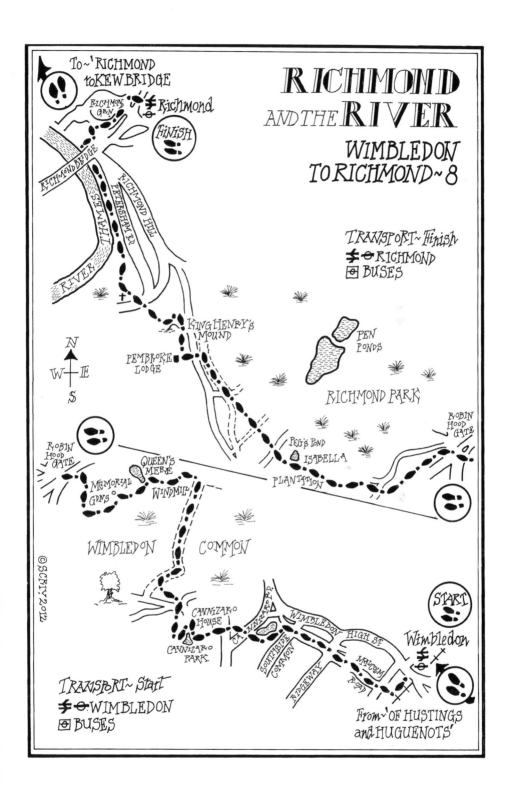

RICHMOND AND THE RIVER

WIMBLEDON TO RICHMOND ~ 8

To ~ 'RICHMOND to KEW BRIDGE

RICHMOND GRN

Richmond

FINISH

RICHMOND BRIDGE

RIVER THAMES

PETERSHAM RD

RICHMOND HILL

TRANSPORT ~ Finish
RICHMOND
BUSES

KING HENRY'S MOUND

PEN PONDS

PEMBROKE LODGE

N
W · E
S

RICHMOND PARK

ROBIN HOOD GATE

PEG'S POND
ISABELLA
PLANTATION

ROBIN HOOD GATE

QUEEN'S MERE

MEMORIAL GDNS

WINDMILL

WIMBLEDON   COMMON

CANNIZARO HOUSE

CANNIZARO PARK

CANNIZARO RD

WIMBLEDON HIGH ST

SOUTHSIDE COMMON

RIDGEWAY

MALCOLM ROAD

START

Wimbledon

© SCRIV 2012

TRANSPORT ~ Start
WIMBLEDON
BUSES

From ~ 'OF HUSTINGS and HUGUENOTS'

incurable insanity. On the other hand, we have very ordinary people like the brewer John Lewis of Richmond who, almost single-handed, took on the courts and the King's daughter and kept Richmond Park open for our enjoyment today.

This chapter covers 11 miles from Wimbledon Station to Kew Bridge. It can be taken as two separate walks:

WALK 8: Wimbledon to Richmond (8 miles)

WALK 9: Richmond to Kew Bridge (3½ miles)

■ WALK 8: WIMBLEDON TO RICHMOND

Getting started

From Balham Station (Network Rail (Victoria)), **Balham Underground Station** (Northern line), **and buses** (155, 249, 355 to Balham High Road) **and from Walk 7:**
The walk begins outside the stations in Wimbledon town centre

Tennis, Trams and a Transformer

ROUTE:

- From the main rail and underground station cross the road (Wimbledon Bridge) to find the path that starts between the multi-storey car park and the red brick shopping centre.
- Follow the path alongside the railway until reaching a footbridge on your left. Do not cross the bridge but turn right along the short stub of Alt Grove.
- Turn left at the T-junction and cross the road to pick up the signposted path a few yards further along on the right, running behind houses.
- Cross Worple Road at the end of the path and continue straight ahead up Malcolm Road.
- At the end of Malcolm Road take the path (Sunnyside Path) which begins on the right hand side.
- Ignore a branch to the right and continue uphill along the path to reach Sunnyside Road. Continue straight ahead up the road.
- At the end of Sunnyside Road turn right on the main road (Ridgway) and after a few yards turn left onto Lingfield Road.
- Follow Lingfield Road to its end to emerge at the apex of Wimbledon Common.

FACILITIES: Pubs and cafés in Wimbledon town centre.

LOOKING AT WILDLIFE: Some fine Scots Pines along Sunnyside Path.

The story of the growth of Wimbledon is also the story of England's successive transport revolutions. It was the building of a road by Thomas Cecil in 1588 that transformed the village from a cultural backwater to one of the social centres of Elizabethan and Stuart England. And it was the subsequent opening of the railway in 1838 that attracted the professional classes to build their large houses and gardens here – with the attached development of smaller homes for the servants, shopkeepers, gardeners and everyone else who serviced them. Interestingly, however, it was the coming of the trams to Wimbledon that was to have one of the biggest impacts. So significant was their arrival that on the opening of the line in May 1907, children were given the day off school to go and watch. This display of civic confidence proved well-placed, since the arrival of the trams heralded a new era of development, with rows of streets being laid out over the next few years to provide smaller and cheaper housing for the working classes.

It is a welcome fact that trams have now returned to Wimbledon, but it is alongside the railway that our walk begins, following the lines as they head south west towards Basingstoke and Southampton. Turning right after a short distance, however, we leave the rail side to reach Worple Road – and another significant site in the history of Wimbledon. It was on Worple Road in 1877 that the All England Croquet Club gave over one of its lawns for the first ever world tennis championship. Grandiose though this may sound, the aim of the event was to raise the funds for a pony-drawn roller for the lawns – and to this end seats for the final were charged at a shilling each. The winner, out of the original 22 all male contestants, was one Spencer Gore, who then uttered the immortal words 'Lawn tennis will never rank among our great games'.

Despite his prediction, lawn tennis went on to overshadow croquet, and the tennis 'world' championship became an annual event – though it was another twenty-eight years before there was a non-British winner. The England headquarters of this rapidly growing sport left Worple Road in 1922 for a site on Church Road, to the north of Wimbledon. Today, with 26 courts and a spectator capacity of 30,000, it has become the venue for the world's most famous championship, with seats at the final now charged at £110 each, as well as the venue for the 2012 Olympic tennis. It is good to know, therefore, that some element of that early tradition survives. Wimbledon remains the only grand slam tournament still played on grass, a testament to its origins on a croquet lawn on Worple Road.

The roads that we follow through Wimbledon en route to the Common reveal an interesting variety of housing: Victorian terraces, workmen's cottages, a Tudor house on Ridgway, and grand Victorian residencies along Lingfield Road in the most amazing diversity of styles. Perhaps the most interesting building of all, however, is far more modest. At the end of Sunnyside Path stands a circular wrought iron structure with decorative panels. Just over six feet high, it is topped with a conical roof and an ornate tapering pinnacle. It has something of a jaunty Parisian air but successfully does its best to conceal its true identity. It is in fact a Victorian electricity transformer station and, as such, one of the oddest listed buildings in London.

Rushmere and Cannizaro Park

ROUTE:

- From the corner of the common a number of paths radiate across the grass. Take the path forking left that runs to the immediate left-hand side of the pond.
- Continue on the path beyond the pond and ignore cross paths to reach the road.
- Cross the road and after a few yards fork left over the apex of the green. You are heading towards the ornamental gates of Cannizaro Park, set in the red brick wall.
- Go through the imposing park gates and follow the drive towards the house.
- Follow the path that runs to the side and then around the back of the house, until you reach the terrace. Then take the path that bears off to the right, away from the terrace and sloping downhill.
- The path descends steps and then bears right between a pond and a walled garden. Stay on this path, ignoring side paths, as it curves to the left round the back of the walled garden then loops back to the right to reach a gate.
- Leave the park through the gate and follow the stony track ahead to arrive on a tarmac road beside the common.

LOOKING AT WILDLIFE: There is soft rush and yellow flag around Rushmere, although the invasive New Zealand pygmy-weed is also present. Parsley-piert grows in the surrounding grass. Cannizaro Park has a magnificent collection of trees, including cork oaks, Japanese maples, mulberries and such exotic trees as sassafras, Chilean flame tree, kowhai and pomegranate. The interesting parasitic plant, purple toothwort, has been found in the gardens, and feral mandarin duck can be seen on the pond.

FACILITIES: There is a café and toilets in Cannizaro Park.

Rushmere pond is the oldest of the nine ponds on Wimbledon Common, dating back at least to Tudor times. Its name derives from the rushes which once fringed its banks and which provided thatch for the local cottages. The rushes are all but gone now, as are the ducks which the cottagers once kept here, and even the shoal of koi carp which was somehow established here for a few years.

Through the wrought iron gates of Cannizaro House, their brick pillars topped with imposing stone balls, you pass beyond the world of the commoners, and their reedy duck pond, and into the cool elegance of one of the great estates. Here, a tree-lined avenue leads to fountains and the grand, cream-coloured house. Beyond this is the rolling six-acre lawn and a view across the gardens to what still seems a rural scene of distant hills and the Richmond church spire. Though the present house is not much more than a hundred years old, replacing the original that was destroyed by fire, it aspires to look much older. With its soft red brick wings set within a larger whitewashed range, its central projecting

RICHMOND AND THE RIVER

bay flanked by Grecian vases in arched alcoves, its balustraded portico and its steeply raked slate roof, it seems to mix styles from across European architectural history. The estate itself dates back to the first part of the eighteenth century; and one of the early tenants was a Sicilian nobleman, Francisco Platamone, Count St Antonio, later duke of Cannizaro. He lived here for a few years in the early nineteenth century, having married a Miss Johnstone, the wealthy daughter of the British Governor of West Florida. Despite the fact that he seems to have spent most of his time living with a lover in Milan, she hung on to his name – as did the site.

Acquired by the London Borough of Merton in 1949, the park is one of the hidden treasures of London. Were these beautiful gardens almost anywhere else in London they would be far more celebrated, but here they seem slightly lost besides the adjacent, wide open spaces of Wimbledon and Richmond and remain pretty much a secret even to the inhabitants of south west London. Yet there is here the finest display of camellias, rhododendrons and azaleas in London, together with a collection of over 400 species of tree and shrub. There is a sunken garden, a walled garden, a water garden, a Mediterranean garden and, appropriately, an Italian garden. There is colour at almost every time of year and the site almost demands to be visited at different seasons. As our path turns to reach the back of house, it passes a rather elaborate octagonal structure, currently the home of a number of cockatiel and designed, apparently, in the style of Pisa Cathedral. Even the aviary is grand at Cannizaro.

Wimbledon Common and the Windmill

ROUTE:

- On reaching the tarmac road at the end of the track (Camp Road), turn right. After a few yards a second road joins it opposite the West Common Golf Club, running in sharply from the left. Cross this road to find the track that runs alongside it on its opposite side.
- Follow this track running almost back on yourself and parallel to the road, until it is crossed by a broad unmade road. Turn right along this and go through a white gate.
- Ignoring a branch to the left, continue along the unmade road as it heads towards trees, with the houses of North View away to your right. The track loops to the left and then becomes a broad, straight route (Windmill Road) running up through the heart of the common for over half a mile. Ignore all side paths to eventually reach a green gate close to a group of buildings.
- Go through the gate onto the tarmac road. Ignore the initial short turning to the left and follow the second one that curves around the far end of the group of buildings to reach the entrance to the windmill.
- Continue around the buildings to the left passing the cafe and the toilet block to emerge onto a grassed area with the London Scottish Golf Club on your left and a car park on your right.

- Bear right alongside the far perimeter of the car park and after a few yards turn left along a well trodden path that leads downhill between trees to reach the apex of Queensmere.
- Facing the tip of the lake, take the path that runs uphill through trees to your immediate left.
- Carry on straight ahead across a golf course green and then through another group of trees to reach a second green.
- Continue ahead, ignoring forks to left and right, following the main track along the edge of the green and then downhill through woodland hollies.
- On reaching the T-junction at the bottom of the hill, turn right then almost immediately left to reach the War Memorial through a gap in the surrounding hedge.
- On leaving the War Memorial, turn back to face the way you have come and walk half-right to reach the gap in the hedge to the right of the one you came through.
- Cross a track and then a small ditch to reach the main track through the woods and turn right along it.
- At the first fork bear right and then right again where it joins another track and heads down towards Beverley Brook.
- Do not cross the brook but follow the track to the right as it runs between the brook on your left and sports pitches on your right.
- On reaching the Pavilion buildings, turn left across the footbridge just before them and follow the path ahead that leads towards the main road.

FACILITIES: Windmill Tea Rooms (daily 9-5). Toilets at the windmill. Windmill Museum (usually opens April-October, check hours. Entrance fee)

LOOKING AT WILDLIFE: Wimbledon Common constitutes 50 per cent of all the heathland in London and is a Site of Special Scientific Interest. Its plants include gorse, creeping willow, brown sedge, purple moor grass and three species of heather, with the white-flowered climbing corydalis a speciality. The rich variety of birds includes all three woodpeckers, woodcock, hobby, cuckoo, skylark, spotted flycatcher, redpoll, yellowhammer, tree pipit, tree creeper, stonechat, a variety of warblers and much more. There are heron and a variety of wildfowl on Queensmere, where specialist waterside plants include marsh pennywort and marsh willow herb. The oaks around Queensmere support a population of purple hairstreak butterflies. Other special insects on the common include the black darter dragonfly, rare bees and solitary wasps, the green tiger beetle and the mounded nests of the yellow meadow ant – an indicator of ancient meadow. There is a good variety of autumn fungi, especially in the woodland, including impressive displays of the bright red fly agaric around stands of birch.

At the highest point of a high plateau, set in a crook of the Thames, stands a common without rival in London. Across 1,412 acres of heathland, scrub, grassland and wood, Wimbledon Common and Putney Heath run into one another and jointly cover an area more than three times the size of north

London's Hampstead Heath. Hudson described this common as 'wider and more refreshing to the spirit than any other in the metropolis', and it remains true today, despite the intrusion of both traffic noise and golf across large tracts of its otherwise unspoilt acres.

Roughly speaking the common can be considered in two parts. The eastern section is higher, with areas of scrub and rough grassland dominating its glacial gravels. Westwards it slopes away into the vale cut by the Beverley Brook and it is here, on the London clay, that the main areas of woodland are found. Oak, beech, hornbeam, sweet chestnut, rowan and maple all grow here, while right down in the vale itself, and alongside the brook, aspens and dogwood are found on the alluvial soils. There are even areas of sphagnum bog, a habitat otherwise rare in London, patches of heather and a number of rare mosses and lichen.

Once the woodlands supported what was supposed to be the finest concert of nightingales in London. The nightingales have gone, but a very wide range of visiting and breeding bird species remain, making this an exciting area for birdwatchers. Hobby can be seen over the open areas or hawking for dragonflies above the meres, skylarks sing high over the heathland, green woodpeckers forage around the nests of yellow meadow ants, and the trees support some of our less common woodland birds like lesser spotted woodpecker and the tree pipit. There are butterflies, too, and the oaks around Queensmere support a colony of the beautiful purple hairstreak. The adults, which vary greatly in number from year to year, spend much of their time in the upper canopy of the trees. They can therefore be quite difficult to see, but closer examination often reveals the caterpillars. These brownish, woodlouse-shaped creatures live inside a silk web spun around the base of a clump of leaves. They can be found in June by feeling the bases of leaf clumps until you come across one which is spongy to the touch. Perhaps the most surprising creature reported from the common, however, is the sugar glider. In 2006 and 2007, wildlife message boards buzzed with stories of a small colony of this Australian marsupial – a sort of flying opossum – living on the common. Some claimed they had been around since at least 2000. If they are here – and the reports were met with considerable scepticism – they are, like the ring-necked parakeets and the grey squirrel, another example of escaped pets establishing themselves in the wild.

Wimbledon Common and Putney Heath were originally part of the Manor of Mortlake, and as such were granted by Edward the Confessor to the See of Canterbury. The ensuing centuries saw many changes of ownership, the owners including several figures of national renown: Thomas Cromwell, whose father was said to have been a butcher in Putney, but who rose to become first minister to Henry VIII; Queen Henrietta Maria, wife of the ill-fated Charles I; and the Roundhead General Lambert, who retired here when he felt he had been slighted by the Protector. In 1744 it was bequeathed, together with Wandsworth Common, to John Spencer, and with this began the modern story of the struggle with the Spencer family to preserve the common.

For generations past the commoners of Wimbledon had cut furze and pollarded oaks for fuel, grazed cattle, gathered wild foods, and dug for gravel, turf and loam. These rights were restricted to certain parts of the year. At Michaelmas, in September, the Parish Beadle went around with a bell to 'cry the common open' and on Lady Day, in the following April, he 'cried it shut'. For the rest of the year the Lord of the Manor had exclusive use.

There were regular disputes of course and these were regulated by the Manor Court, which met three or four times every year and consisted of all the Lord's tenants, presided over by his steward. Rolls for the Wimbledon Manor Court still exist from as far back as 1461, but although the court survived into the days of the Spencers it had long ceased to be an effective regulatory body. Encroachments had become numerous, as had other depredations, such as 'persons shooting night soil or other filth onto the common'. But in 1812 it was the Lord of the Manor himself who broke custom and rule by cutting down all the pollarded oaks and selling them off for timber. In 1864 matters came to a head when the then Earl Spencer came up with a plan to sell off 300 acres of common, using the proceeds to enclose the remaining 700 acres. There was not much the Manor Court could do. By this time it only had nine members left, and by one means or another the Earl was able to secure their compliance. The proposal then went forward as a Private Bill to Parliament in 1865.

At this stage Earl Spencer found he had a second group to reckon with. The passage of years had brought the development of the urban fringes to the edges of Wimbledon Common, and the new middle classes who had settled there did not hesitate to make their voices heard. In 1865 they set up a Wimbledon Common Committee, electing Henry Peek as their chair. A House of Commons committee came out against the Bill on its second reading, but by this time the Wimbledon Common Committee had already taken the case to law. They initiated proceedings in Chancery concerning the dilapidated state of the common, and these dragged on until April 1870, when Spencer decided to reach an out of court settlement. Ownership of the commons passed to a board of trustees, and Spencer received an annuity equal to his average earnings from the common over the last ten years. The continued upkeep of the common was to be paid for from the proceeds of a rate levied on all properties with a rateable value over £35 within ¾ mile of the Common. The system was incorporated into an Act of Parliament in 1871. The trustees purchased Earl Spencer's annuity from him in 1967 and the rest of the scheme survives to this day.

Our route across the common begins at its southern edge, passing the grand houses of Camp View, with their exuberant decoration of seraphs, nymphs, trumpets and cornucopia. Running from here and up through the heart of the common, the long, straight Windmill Road leads to one of the common's most attractive features. A black cone of slatted wood sits atop a low octagonal brick building and supports the white, revolving, body of the Wimbledon Windmill. With its white sails to the front and its fantail wheel projecting outwards and upwards to the rear, it resembles a white dove perched on a black branch. It is an elegant building, beautifully restored. The 'old Surrey working woman', as John Betjeman described it, now looks positively adolescent.

In 1817 Charles March of Roehampton petitioned for the enclosure of ¼ acre of the common for the erection of a mill. This was granted 'upon this special condition that he shall erect and keep up a public Corn Mill, for the advantage and convenience of the neighbourhood'. The first miller was Thomas Dann, who was required to combine his work as miller with the office of constable, by using his vantage point in the mill to keep watch for thieves and robbers – and for that other scourge of the Common, the duellist.

Wimbledon Common had been a favoured place for duelling since at least 1652, when Lord Chandos is recorded as having killed a Colonel Compton. It was here, too, that Castlereagh and Canning, the Duke of York and Lieutenant Colonel Lennox, and other famous names duelled out their differences and shot out their slights. On one famous occasion in 1798, William Pitt met William Tierney, MP for Southwark; the two gentlemen measured out the required twelve paces, raised their pistols and fired, but both being totally ignorant in the use of firearms, they missed. They fired again, and missed again. Perhaps it was deliberate – 'Honour' had been satisfied. But there is one other little detail of this story to interest us. The duel was fought by a little hillock on the north east side of the common. It is known to this day as Jerry's Hill, after Jerry Abershaw, a famous highwayman whose body hung here from a gibbet. It was in the shadow of his still dangling corpse that Pitt and Tierney fought out their duel. Of Jerry Abershaw we shall be hearing more on our route to Kew.

The last recorded duel on the common took place in 1840, between Lord Cardigan and Captain Tuckett, and was witnessed from his tower by Thomas Dann. Since the practice was now illegal Thomas reported the incident. Cardigan was brought to trial the following year in the House of Lords, and though clearly guilty was acquitted by a jury of his 'peers' at the end of the first day. The mill itself ended its working life in 1864 when Earl Spencer, as part of his plan to sell off this part of the common, persuaded the miller to leave so that he could take back the leasehold. The mill was taken over by the Conservators in 1871 and fell into a state of dilapidation. In 1976 it was restored and re-opened as a Windmill Museum.

Not far to the east of the windmill, Queensmere, one of the most pleasant of the Wimbledon pools, lies hidden in a wooded hollow. It is a pear shaped pool overhung with trees, the home of clumsy coot and early morning heron. In spring toads spawn here in their hundreds. In summer, sunlight filters down onto the surface of the water through the leaves of oak and beech. And in autumn, mist hangs below the trees, and the large leaves of the American Red Oak put on their spectacular display of colour. The pool was created in Victorian times by the damming of a stream running into a boggy clearing in the woods. As with many other London pools and springs, it was made possible by the junction of porous gravels with the impervious clay.

As we descend from here towards Kingston Vale and the lower, western sections of the common, we pass through what must be the most attractively located war memorial in London. Set within a copse of oak and surrounded by a high circular hedge, it has something of the feel of an ancient magic about it. It would be idyllic were it not for the roar of traffic from the Kingston bypass, but perhaps that too carries an echo of the dull thunder of distant guns. Dedicated to the memory of the local dead of the 'Great War', the grooved stone cross bears an unusual inscription: 'Nature provides the best monument. The perfecting of the work must be left to the gentle hand of time. But each returning spring will bring a fresh tribute to those whom it is desired to keep in everlasting remembrance.'

Finally we reach the Beverley Brook, the stream which has cut down through gravels into the clay and created the valley here. Running twelve miles from Sutton to join the Thames at Barn Elms, it is rather a sluggish river, its last seven miles all being less than 50 feet above sea level. It draws its name from the beavers which survived in Britain into Saxon times. The European beaver has now been experimentally reintroduced to Scotland. It may be too much to hope that we one day see them again on Wimbledon Common and the Beverley Brook.

Richmond Park

ROUTE:

- Cross the main road by the pedestrian crossing to reach the Robin Hood Gate into Richmond Park.
- Beyond the gate, take the gravel path that leads off almost immediately to the left and follows the park perimeter. The path runs pleasantly between trees before climbing to the top of Broomfield Hill.
- As you reach the brow of the hill, beside a bench, look for the car park on the right. Cross the grass to reach its near right hand corner and then follow the little path that runs along its right hand side.
- Cross the park road and continue straight ahead along the right hand side of the fenced copse then turn left along the back of the copse.
- On reaching cross paths at the far end of the copse turn right and follow the path across the grass and then downhill to reach the gate into Isabella Plantation.
- Inside the plantation and to the left of the gate is a small stream. Do not cross it but follow the path that runs on its right hand bank all the way through the plantation, to reach Pegs Pond at its far side.
- On reaching the pond cross the stream and follow round the pond perimeter briefly before forking left to reach a gate back into the main park.
- Cross the disabled parking area and follow its access track leading to a junction with a park road.
- Cross the road to take the small path immediately opposite. Keep left at the first fork, staying close to the perimeter of the oak plantation. The path follows the woodland perimeter and then winds through bracken and tussocky grass to reach a pond.
- Bear left around the top end of the pond, following a grassy path which crosses a broad track, passes a second small pond and then joins a horse ride, heading gradually uphill and parallel to the main park road.
- At the top of the hill, cross the road to the left and walk through the car park to reach Pembroke Lodge.
- Go through the gate and turn right in front of the buildings, continuing along the path where it forks left away from the tarmac roadway.
- Continue in front of the thatched cottage then bear right to follow the

path that leads to the top of King Henry's Mound.

- Descend King Henry's Mound on the far side then turn back left along the bottom. Take the first little turning on the right, leading through a gate onto open parkland on the hillside.
- Follow the broad grassy path running downhill and to the right, towards the children's playground visible below. At the bottom of the hill turn right to reach Petersham Gate.

FACILITIES: Toilets at Robin Hood Gate. Refreshment kiosk (summer months) at the car park on Broomfield Hill. Toilets, café and information point at Pembroke Lodge. Toilets by playground at Petersham Gate.

LOOKING AT WILDLIFE: Large herds of red and fallow deer. Beautiful old parkland trees, including oaks, wych elm, beech, sweet and horse chestnuts. This is the largest area of lowland acid grassland in London, and supports such typical plants as harebell and tormentil. A speciality on the muddy margins of pools is the rare and decreasing mudwort. There is a wide variety of parkland birds, including jackdaw, stock dove, green woodpecker, tree sparrow, treecreeper, meadow pipit, little owl and tawny owl, with nine species of bat, including the noctule. Insect specialities include stag beetle, the blacktailed skimmer dragonfly, the rare cardinal click beetle, a good variety of grassland butterflies and nests of yellow meadow ants on the hillside below Pembroke Lodge. Isabella Plantation has a collection of rhododendrons, azaleas and camellias and beautiful clumps of royal fern along the brook. It is a good place to see and hear tits, nuthatch and warblers. There is a collection of ornamental waterfowl on Peg's Pond, but also feral populations of mandarin duck and red crested pochard.

When Queen Caroline asked Horace Walpole what it would cost her to enclose the royal parks in central London, he is said to have replied, 'Your throne, madam'. Perhaps he had learnt from the folly of King Charles I and the consequences of his attempt, two hundred years earlier, to enclose the royal park at Richmond.

Shene Chase at Richmond had been a royal hunting ground since before the time of Henry VIII. Charles I hit upon the idea of enclosing it – and not just the Chase but an equally large area around it belonging to local landowners. The landowners resisted, but when many of them refused to sell, the King began work anyway, building a perimeter fence which denied them access to half their own land. It was a rank injustice, and from a king whose incompetence, vanity and folly were already leading to a dangerous dissatisfaction amongst the people. The news soon spread and, as the Earl of Clarendon said in his *History of the Rebellion*, 'It increased the murmur and noise of the people who were not concerned as well as of them who were; and it was too near London not to be the common discourse.'

Despite opposition from his own advisers, the king had completed the enclosure by 1637. This was just one in the long line of actions that, in 1649, was to cost him his head. That original wall, 13 miles long, still encloses the

2,470 acres of Richmond Park today. Despite the fate of Charles, he was not the last of the monarchy to attempt to exclude the public. In 1747 George II appointed his youngest and favourite daughter Amelia to be Ranger of Richmond Park. Three years later she closed the park to everyone but personal friends and key-holders. The procedure for obtaining a key was made so difficult that few could achieve it. Even the Lord Chancellor, it was said, was refused a key. A public petition was ignored and a test case brought against the Deputy Ranger was dismissed. And there matters might have rested were it not for the direct action undertaken by John Lewis, a brewer of Richmond.

In 1755 Lewis waited outside the Sheen Gate until it was opened to admit a carriage. He followed it in and, claiming a public right of way, set out to walk across the park. He was intercepted by gatekeeper Martha Gray and ejected. He then brought a case, nominally against the gatekeeper but effectively against Princess Amelia herself. By one means or another the judiciary put off the case for three years but eventually, in 1758, it came to court. Lewis claimed a right of way granted to pedestrians by Charles I, a concession he had been forced into when enclosing the land in the first place. And on this the case was won. Amelia put up ladder stiles for public use but made sure that the rungs were so widely spaced that they were unusable. Lewis went back to court to challenge this and once more won his case.

Single-handed, John Lewis had taken on the daughter of the reigning monarch and won. In 1761 Amelia lost interest in what was no longer her private garden, resigned the Rangership and retired to Gunnersbury. Nonetheless she probably fared better than Lewis himself. The personal expenses he had incurred at law were compounded when the River Thames flooded his brewery and counting house at Petersham. He died in poverty in 1792, having lived his last years supported only by a small annuity raised from the residents at Richmond at the instigation of the local parson.

The oldest inhabitants of the Park today are the deer. They have been there since before enclosure, and one of the earliest of all the park records shows a payment of £100 made in 1637 to keepers Lodowick Carlile and Humfry Rogers for 'pease, tares and hay, for the red and fallow deer'. It is these two species which still graze the grass of Richmond, around 300 red deer and 350 fallow. Their numbers fluctuate from year to year, but hopefully not as much as they did in 1886-87, when rabies reduced the population by more than a hundred.

These open, tree-dotted grasslands, with grazing herds of deer slowly moving across them, make this the picture of traditional English parkland. There are over 200,000 trees here, including English elm, wych elm, beech, hornbeam, Spanish and horse chestnut. But it is the oaks which predominate, some of them pre-dating enclosure, and many more of them at least 200 years old. The large, old and often hollow trees – there are over 1,200 official 'veteran' trees in the park – attract nesting birds, including tree sparrows and green woodpeckers. According to Eric Simms, Richmond has more birds and small mammals than any other London park – including the not so welcome presence of more than 2,000 grey squirrels. Among the birds, there are reckoned to be over 100 visiting species, with 63 of them nesting. The flocks of wild turkeys kept in the park in the reign of George III have now gone, but there are still treecreepers, yellowhammers, pheasant, red-legged and common partridge, little owl, tawny owl and much more. In summer the skylarks are a highlight, having increased from three pairs in 1992 to twenty in 2010, whilst in winter there are the woodcock to look out for. They can be seen most often around dawn and dusk, flying on the fringes of the densest areas of woodland. But perhaps the last word should go to the jackdaws. W.H. Hudson says he was assured by a keeper that there were 'millions', adding that his informant was 'a very tall white-haired old man with aquiline features and dark fierce eyes and therefore must have known what he was talking about'.

Our route through the park begins at the Robin Hood Gate and proceeds up Broomfield Hill to reach the Isabella Plantation. The Plantation was originally natural woodland, which was transformed in 1951 by the then Park Superintendent, George Thomson. Now a little brook winds through a woodland garden to reach Peg's Pond at the far end. It is best seen in early spring for the blossom, or in late autumn for the leaf colour. The trees are under-planted with a great variety of rhododendrons, azaleas, camellias, magnolias and heathers, and with such beautiful specimen shrubs as the Pocket Handkerchief Tree and *rhododendron fictolacteum*, known as Nature's Weather Vane. It is good to be able to note that the gardeners have been commemorated here, in particular Wally Miller, one time Head Gardener. He has both an island named after him, Wally's Island in Peg's Pond, and his own rhododendron, the grandiosely but engagingly entitled *Rhododendron yakusimanum x glamour 'Wally Miller'*.

From the Plantation our route crosses coarse grassland to reach the little White Ash Pond and then on to Pembroke Lodge. This was originally, and more interestingly, known as Molecatcher's Cottage, but it was enlarged in 1788 by the architect Sir John Soane, and renamed when Eliza, Countess of Pembroke moved in. In 1847 it was granted by Queen Victoria to her Prime Minister, Lord John Russell, who died here in 1878. Just two years before that, the young Bertrand Russell was orphaned at the age of three and moved here under the care of his grandparents. He was to remain here until completing his degree at Cambridge in 1894. During these childhood years, he later wrote, he 'grew accustomed to wide horizons and an unimpeded view of the sunset'.

Today a privately run café and conference centre, Pembroke Lodge continues to command views from the top of Richmond Hill. It could well be one of the 'reasons to be cheerful' that Ian Dury sang about. Dury was a regular visitor with his children, and has his own commemorative bench in the rather undeveloped 'poets corner' at the end of the arched laburnum walkway. The bench was designed to be operated by solar power and to play selections from eight of his most famous songs. He would probably be amused by the fact that, like most such 'interactive' features, it has long since ceased to work.

The undoubted high point of this high place, however, is King Henry's Mound. This was originally a barrow of some sort and, when excavated in 1835, was found to contain a considerable concentration of ashes. Originally higher, and with a more pronounced domed crown, it would have constituted a dramatic feature on the skyline, and provided a convenient vantage point for the various kings who engaged in deer hunting in the royal park. This is undoubtedly the origin of the various apocryphal stories of Henry VIII waiting here to receive the news that Ann Boleyn's head had been successfully sundered from her body. Today from the Mound there are incomparable views across the Thames Valley and out to Berkshire and beyond. From here, on a clear day, it is possible to make out Ham House, Hampton Hill, Strawberry Hill, Marble Hill, Twickenham, Eel Pie island and as far west as Runnymede and Windsor Castle. Such is the quality of the view that it would be very easy to descend from the Mound and miss altogether its real treasure, lying in the other direction entirely and disguised by a screen of tall hollies. Look through the circle in the metal structure between them, however, and you are looking through 'the vista', one of the finest views in London. Through a gap in the leaves the eye travels down a long avenue of parkland trees and across the ten intervening miles to reach a perfectly framed St Paul's Cathedral. On a good day it seems to shimmer, and to hang dreamlike in thin air. With the surrounding clutter of twentieth-century buildings virtually invisible, it is like looking through time as well as through space, to the St Paul's of a lost eighteenth-century pastoral setting. It is since this time, at least, that the vista has been a formal and defined feature of the park, and the inspiration for it may have come from the famous Piranesi keyhole in the Villa Malta in Rome, through which the dome of St Peter's Basilica can be seen along an avenue of clipped cypresses. But here, the disciple has outstripped the master. For its sheer length and for its landscape importance, 'the vista' is unsurpassed in Europe.

Petersham and the Riverside

ROUTE:

- Leave the park through the Petersham Gate and cross the road to reach the footpath immediately opposite. The path curves round left beside the churchyard to reach a gravelly lane.
- Turn right along the lane and then continue straight ahead where the lane bears left, to follow a path running between hedges across the fields.
- Continue ahead where the path enters the open meadow, and on the far side continue through a small park (Buccleugh Gardens) to reach the riverside towpath at the far end.
- Follow the towpath along the riverside to reach, and pass beneath, Richmond Bridge.
- Continue beyond the bridge to reach the cobbled Water Lane, which runs down to the riverside from the right.
- Turn up Water Lane, and at its end turn left onto George Street and immediately left again onto King Street.
- Take the alleyway on the right, Paved Court, leading up to Richmond Green.

To join Walk 9:

At the end of the alleyway turn left along the south side of the green until you reach the old palace gatehouse on the left.

To complete this walk:

At the end of the alleyway continue straight ahead along the side of the green to reach the little Brewers Lane on the right.

Follow Brewers Lane to rejoin George Street and turn left to reach Richmond Town Centre and the station.

FACILITIES: Pubs opposite Petersham Gate and at the end of Water Lane. Cafés and restaurants along the riverside. Pubs, cafés and toilets in Richmond town centre.

LOOKING AT WILDLIFE: A fine collection of yews in Petersham Churchyard. Cormorant and wildfowl on the river, including feral Egyptian geese which breed here alongside the abundant Canada geese. The 'Riverside Plane', one of the Great Trees of London and the tallest plane in the capital, stands next to the Groucho Grill, on the towpath approach to Richmond Bridge. The riverside flora includes large stands of purple loosestrife and of marsh ragwort.

The church of St Peter, which may well have given its name to Petersham, is a beautiful example of an eighteenth-century country church. Inside it is lined with box pews, whilst outside the rather jumbled appearance arising from its various extensions, fails to obliterate a certain obstinate stateliness. It is low, as befits a marshland site; red-brick, with a small castelled tower topped by a tapering belfry. There is a multiplicity of shaped yews in the churchyard, which also holds the grave of George Vancouver, the 'discoverer' of Vancouver Island. The whole site retains a riverside atmosphere, even though you can't quite see the river from here. Together with the adjacent Petersham Meadows, where sheep still graze a waterside field with a view of white villas on the far bank, the view is almost Arcadian. Buccleugh Gardens were once the grounds of one of these riverside villas, Buccleugh House. Nothing now remains of it but a brick shelter, and the tunnel that led from the house to more gardens on the other side of Petersham Road.

Beyond here we join the Thames towpath, passing the 'Richmond River Plane'. Looking up from the base of this, the tallest plane in London, it seems to have the size and spread of a tropical timber tree. Its drooping manner seems far from melancholic, more a form of relaxed confidence that comes with its old age. Its backdrop is Richmond Bridge, one of the best of the Thames bridges. It has distinctively pointed arches and a facing of Purbeck stone ageing into a variety of tones from fawn to grey. For four hundred years, from the reign of Edward III onwards, there was a ferry crossing here, and it was not until 1773 that an Act of Parliament permitted the building of a bridge. Under the Act, a body of 90 Commissioners was set up to oversee the project, and among these were several prominent inhabitants of Richmond, including David Garrick, Horace Walpole and Capability Brown. The bridge was completed in 1777 and remained a toll bridge until 1859, passing into public ownership only as late as 1931. But by this time, according to a letter to the *Evening Standard*, it had become, 'probably the most dangerous of all the bridges which span the Thames'. Huge increases in traffic created a dangerous congestion and threatened the very structure. 'The effect of a shower', wrote the same correspondent 'is terrific. Not only do the heavy lumbering land craft skid about ... but the roadway is churned into a mass of oily mud which is flung over the clothes of the pedestrians by the heavy wheels of the traffic. There is no escape.'

The problem was how to widen the bridge without destroying its beautiful proportions, the debate continuing until 1939, when part of the solution was to reface the widened span with the original Purbeck stone. Today the undersides of the arches give evidence of this successful ploy; the lighter colour of the added section being almost the only visual clue of the work that has taken place.

No doubt the wealth and influence of many of the inhabitants of Richmond helped to secure the respectful treatment of the bridge. But the attempt to retain the character of the area has led to some strange consequences elsewhere. Immediately beyond the bridge we come to a series of formal stepped terraces, lined with gravel paths and leading up to an amazing assemblage of seemingly Georgian buildings. Most are in red brick, others in stucco. There are elegant windows and balustraded porches and a facade of towers, domes, belvederes and decorated urns. A central arch leads up steps into Heron Square, with its not unattractive but positively chilly, and rather hybrid, assemblage of offices and homes.

The whole complex is not Georgian at all – it is the now famous Richmond Riverside Development, with its curious mix of completely new building and new facades on old structures. It was designed by Quinlan Terry, whose work is part of the reaction to modernism espoused by Prince Charles, a great admirer of the development. But as 'Piloti' pointed out in *Private Eye*:

few ever noticed that behind the neo-Georgian facades there were abominations like reinforced concrete construction, or that the gratuitous arched tops of Georgian windows exposed dropped ceilings and service ducts. For all that matters is to lard buildings with lots of details copied from Palladio and Bramante.

Getting home

Richmond Station: London Overground, Underground (District Line), Network Rail (Waterloo).

Buses: (from the station or New Road) 65, 190, 371, 391, 419, 490, 493, H22, H37, R68, R70

■ WALK 9: RICHMOND TO KEW BRIDGE

Getting started

From Richmond Station (London Overground, Underground (District Line), Network Rail (Waterloo) **and buses** (65, 190, 371, 391, 419, 490, 493, H22, H37, R68, R70 to Richmond Station):

The walk starts from the station exit

From Walk 8:

From the Green, turn left through the old palace gatehouse.

Sheen and the Green

ROUTE:

- From Richmond Station take the pedestrian crossing to the left of the station entrance. Cross the road and enter the alleyway just a few yards to the right of the pedestrian crossing, under Oriel House.
- At the end of the alleyway turn left onto Parkshot and Little Green.
- On reaching the first small green on the right, take the path that runs diagonally across it.
- Continue across the small road (Portland Terrace) and continue ahead on the path that runs diagonally across the main green.
- The far side of the Green is reached beside a post box and opposite the old palace gatehouse. Go through the gatehouse and cross the yard to the right to reach the entrance to a path marked by two white bollards in the far corner.
- Follow the path and at its end turn left onto Old Palace Lane to reach the riverside.
- A brief diversion to the left will reveal the Asgill House Copper Beech; the main route continues to the right, following the Thames towpath beneath the railway bridge.

FACILITIES: Pubs, café and toilets in Richmond Town Centre. Pub on Old Palace Lane.

It is as the result of a royal whim that this area came to be called Richmond. At first it was Sheen, or Shene, site of a Franciscan friary and of one of the most important of England's royal palaces. It was Henry I who first built here, in 1125, and it was to remain a royal residence for over 500 years. As a plaque on Old Palace Lane puts it, Edward III, Henry VII and Elizabeth I all died here – making it sound something like the regal equivalent of an elephant's graveyard. But, stretching from Richmond Green to the riverside, what more attractive place could there be to come to die.

RICHMOND AND THE RIVER
RICHMOND TO KEW BRIDGE ~ 9

FINISH

To 'ALONG the BRENT VALLEY' →

Kew Bridge

RIVER BRENT
GRAND UNION CANAL

KEW PALACE

KEW GARDENS

SYON PARK

SYON HOUSE

RIVER THAMES

TRANSPORT ~ Finish
KEW BRIDGE
BUSES

King's Observatory

OLD DEER PARK

TOWPATH

START

Richmond

TWICKENHAM ROAD

RICHMOND

RICHMOND GREEN

RICHMOND LOCK

RICHMOND BRIDGE

N
W · E
S

TRANSPORT ~ Start
RICHMOND
BUSES

From 'WIMBLEDON to RICHMOND'

©SCRIY 2012

154

It is with Henry VII, founder of the new Tudor dynasty, that the palace is particularly associated. He rebuilt it after an earlier fire and came to love it so much that he renamed it Richmond after his earldom in Yorkshire. And thus he gave the area its name. The palace lasted until the years of the Commonwealth, and most of it was demolished in 1660 after the restoration. It is still, however, the arms of Henry VII that remain engraved on the surviving gatehouse.

From the site of a royal residence, Richmond was to become, in the twentieth century, a popular destination for day trip by river or by rail. The railway station, where our walk begins, was rebuilt in 1937 to a design of John R. Scott, the grandson of George Gilbert Scott, who features so regularly along *The Green London Way*. One of the popular destinations would have been the Richmond Theatre, opposite Little Green. This was built in 1899 by Frank Matcham, the first and greatest of Britain's theatre architects, who designed over 200 theatres across the country. It had a rather peculiar origin, however, having started as the Cephalic Snuff Warehouse, where patrons buying snuff would be treated to a performance at the same time.

Little Green itself was given to the town by Charles II for use as a bowling green, whilst, just beyond it, the main Richmond Green is said to have been a jousting green for the palace. It is one of the largest village greens in the country and, according to Pevsner, 'one of the most beautiful urban greens surviving anywhere in England'. Today the equally competitive sport of cricket has replaced the jousting, but this game has itself been associated with the green since 1730 when Middlesex and Surrey played the first recorded game on the site. For the record, Surrey won.

Whilst Harold Wilson, twice Britain's Labour prime minister between 1964 and 1976, lived on the north side of the green, the finest range of buildings runs along its south side. They include the 1724 Maids of Honour Row, a red brick three-storey terrace fronted by fine magnolias. The walls bear a collection of old fire insurance plaques, and through the windows you can catch site of the fireplaces themselves, with their ornate plasterwork surrounds. At the end of the row, beside the castellated Tudor gatehouse, an old umbrella pine spreads over the courtyard wall. This is another of the designated 'Great Trees of London', though its commemorative plaque is strangely absent. A beautifully shaped tree, named from its 'upside down' foliage, it is, in fact, one of two 'Great Trees' on this stretch of the walk.

The gatehouse still bears the coat of arms of Henry VII, who loved this palace best, but Elizabeth I loved it too, and it was to a room in the Wardrobe, the building on the left beyond the gatehouse, that she came to die. With the execution of Robert Devereux, the Earl of Essex and the last of her favourites, for plotting against her in 1601, she had lost much of her will to live. Several of her closest companions had recently died and, now nearly seventy, she was suffering from blood poisoning caused by the lead in the white ointment she habitually wore. Though ill, she refused, with her characteristic stubbornness, to rest in bed and was eventually persuaded to lie down on cushions that her ladies-in-waiting had spread across the floor. Here she lay in silence for four days before, too weak to argue any more, she was finally transferred to a bed.

Only then did she fall into a deep sleep, and with her courtiers and Counsellors – and the Archbishop of Canterbury – around her, died on 24 March 1603.

The Wardrobe, with its warm red brick and its rows of spangled chimneys, was a single building until divided into three in 1957. It originally housed the soft furnishings of the Palace when they were not in use, including, no doubt, the rich tapestries of kings and heroes for which the palace was famous. It is also said to have housed chests containing 2,000 of Elizabeth's dresses. Beyond this Great Court, the Middle Gate once led deeper into the palace complex. Demolished in 1702 to make way for private residences, some echo of it survives in the name – Trumpeters House, derived from the trumpeting figures that once flanked the old gateway.

Crossing the courtyard to the right, beside its unnecessarily fenced lawns, we reach Old Palace Lane, with its lovely whitewashed cottages, its holly hock gardens and its inviting pub. At the end of the lane, and fronting the river, stands Asgill House, a 1760 Palladian villa built on the site of the palace brew house. Its glowing honey coloured stone is reminiscent of Cotswold buildings, but its beautifully symmetrical appearance conceals the oddity of its octangular inner rooms. It is named after Sir Charles Asgill, a banker and one time Lord Mayor of London, for whom it was built, and the Asgill House Copper Beech was planted around 1813 to celebrate the birth of a grandson. It can be seen by detouring to the far side of the house – a very serious tree in its maturity, large and magnificently domed but with a sombre purple foliage.

Along the river to Kew

ROUTE:

- Follow the towpath under the railway bridge and continue along it for approximately three miles to reach Kew Bridge.
- On reaching Kew Bridge turn right alongside the base of the bridge to reach the steps. Climb the steps and turn left to cross the bridge.

To join Walk 10:

On reaching the far side of the Bridge turn left down the steps to reach The Hollows.

To complete this walk:

Cross the pedestrian crossing at the end of the bridge and turn right to reach Kew Bridge Station.

FACILITIES: Pub and café close to Kew Bridge Station.

LOOKING AT WILDLIFE: The river provides a rich variety of wildlife, including grey wagtail, a variety of gull species, cormorant, mute swan, great crested and little grebe, teal, gadwall and other wildfowl. Herons are plentiful and their nests can be seen in the trees on the island opposite the Kew Gardens car park. On the other side of the towpath, the ditches between path and the Old Deer Park are particularly interesting, and support tits, linnets and other finches. Kingfishers can also be occasionally seen here. Between them, these habitats support an interesting range of plants, including alexanders, tansy, cuckooflower, purple loosestrife, marsh ragwort and other marshland species. Trees include large old black poplars, white poplars, alders, oaks and willows.

Our route along the riverside begins beneath two bridges – the cast-iron girders of the Richmond Railway Bridge followed by the concrete drabness of the Twickenham Bridge, built in 1933 as part of major road developments in west London. The bridge is a suitably ugly monument to the motor car, but would have been uglier still had Maxwell Ayrton's original design – which included two fortress-like towers with flanking walls at each end of the bridge – been allowed to proceed. These towers were only removed from the design after a concerted campaign by the public, the Fine Arts Commission and the *Daily Telegraph*. There is another river crossing not much further along the tow-path, this one a footbridge. It runs across the top of the Richmond Lock, the very last of the locks as one travels downstream along the Thames. It is an interesting structure in green and yellow painted cast iron, with stone piers and alcoves.

In the second half of the nineteenth century there were numerous complaints to the Thames Conservators concerning the increasing quantities of mud being deposited along the river banks. This was blocking the navigation as well as creating offensive smells, and it was a particular headache, perhaps literally, to the operators of ferries and passenger steamers. As one witness put it at an enquiry in 1873, 'you may stand on Richmond Bridge and see the scum coming up from London and ... sometimes it seems thick enough to walk upon'.

In 1871 an engineers' report stated that the abstraction of water by the metropolitan water companies was reducing the river's flow by up to 110,000,000 gallons a day, and that increasing amounts of raw sewage were being discharged into this reduced flow. The quantity of local sewage was compounded by that from the rest of the city which, after the removal of the old London Bridge, was daily washed back upstream by the tide. The engineers came out against a proposed weir on the grounds of the great amount of 'excrementitious material' that would become impounded. Their own suggestion was that a deeper channel should be dredged.

This did not satisfy the complainants. They appointed their own engineer, and it was his proposal for a combined lock and weir that finally won the day. But not quite soon enough. Thames river steamers were designed to be able to float in a mere sixteen inches of water. Nonetheless on Monday 25 August 1873, every steamer between Richmond and Teddington went aground. They were forced to discharge their passengers into small boats in mid-channel and the steamers remained stuck on the bare and stinking mud from 10am to 10pm. 'The silvery Thames', said the 1873 report, 'was unserviceable for traffic, whether of pleasure or commerce ... it threatens to become a noisome dried-up ditch during the most enjoyable period of the summer months'. The lock and weir was completed in the next few years and the footbridge above it opened in 1894.

If the silting here was largely due to sewage, the silting further on along the river, where it gently curves northwards, is of a more natural kind. It has led to the creation of the long low island where the bend in the river coincides with the emergence, on the opposite bank, of the River Crane. In fact the island has constantly changed its shape. A map of 1635 shows four separate islands on this spot, and these have gradually reduced in number over the years to the single ten-acre island remaining today. This is the Isleworth Ait, sharing the 'ait' part of its name with many of the Thames islands. This old word for island also occurs in other forms – in 'eyot' and in the word endings -ey and -ea in place names such as Bermondsey, Hackney and Swansea – evidence that, at one time at least, an island existed in these places.

All along this stretch of the river we have been walking alongside the Old Deer Park, a large flat expanse of grassland disappointingly devoid of deer of any age. The main point of interest remaining is the distant prospect of the Kew Observatory, looking like a stumpy white lighthouse amidst a sea of green. The Deer Park was part of the grounds of George III's palace, and it was he who ordered the building of the Observatory. Designed by William Chambers, it was completed for the express purpose of observing the transit of Venus across the sun in 1769. The two plain obelisks in the park close to the towpath are, despite their resemblance to funerary monuments, attached to the Observatory. They were set up during the building process in order to adjust the transit instruments. Later the Observatory had its own full-time staff of astronomers, and became the centre for the setting of national mean time, a responsibility which later passed to Greenwich. Today it serves as a weather station.

One of the porters at the Observatory in its earlier days was John Little, who was often the sole attendant on George III during his walks in the grounds. On the night of 23 June 1795 this 'quiet, gentlemanly person' left the Observatory, walked across the park and entered the house of two elderly friends to whom he was in debt. There he beat them to death with a large stone. He could have got away and left no clues as to his identity, but, as he himself later said, having completed the crime he found it completely impossible to quit the building. He was arrested in the house, brought to trial and sentenced to death. In August of that year he was taken by cart from the gaol to Kennington Common, there to be hung. In the same cart, on his way to meet the same fate, was the famous highwayman, Jerry Abershaw, whose name we have already encountered on Wimbledon Common.

As we reach the end of the Deer Park, much of it now covered by a golf course, the vista of Syon Park opens up on the opposite bank. It is dominated in the centre by Syon House and is still part of the estate of the Duke of Northumberland. The name is a corruption of Zion, for the site once held the 'Monastery of the Holy Saviour and St Brigid of Zion', founded by Henry V in 1415. The grounds owe their present appearance to the landscaping by Capability Brown who, from the evidence of *The Green London Way* alone, either had some equally capable assistants or was an extremely busy man. Among his plantings were the famous swamp cypresses which can still be seen clearly from our side of the river.

Syon House has seen several unhappy occupants, chief amongst them the unfortunate Lady Jane Grey. During the reign of young Edward VI, the Duke of Northumberland had become one of the most powerful figures in the

Council of Regency which governed the country. When it became clear that Edward was dying and that Northumberland would be unable to maintain his position under Mary, the heir to the throne, he prepared a coup d'etat. He married his son to Lady Jane Grey, a granddaughter of Henry VII, and, here at Syon House, bestowed upon her the crown of England. But the country rallied to Mary and even Northumberland's own men refused to fight for him. Jane's reign lasted exactly twelve days and this reluctant queen, the innocent victim of ambitious men, died on the block. A later Earl of Northumberland had the house restored in the 1640s by Inigo Jones. Despite this it remains a rather bland building, topped with a large lion which makes it rather reminiscent of the old Waterloo Station.

From way back along the towpath we have been catching incongruous glimpses of a Japanese pagoda. It is our first introduction to Kew Gardens and to the many stories which surround this site. Kew has particular associations with the Hanoverians, the German family imported to sit on the English throne in 1715. In the 1720s George II and Queen Caroline were living in Richmond Lodge, the grounds of which included the Old Deer Park. Their eldest son, Frederick, Prince of Wales, lived in the old Kew Palace. The two estates were separated by Love Lane, but between the two halves of the family there was no love lost at all. Frederick led a scandalous life and was hated by his very rigid and strictly orthodox parents. His mother once told Lord Hervey, 'My dear first-born is the greatest ass and the greatest liar and the greatest canaille and the greatest beast in the whole world, and ... I heartily wish him out of it.' She was to have her way. Frederick died in 1751 before he could inherit the throne. 'Here lies Fred', wrote the satirists, 'Who was alive and is dead'. They then went on to berate the entire family, ending with the couplet, 'Had it been the whole generation, much better for the nation'.

It was Fred's widow, Augusta, who started the Botanic Gardens, laying out nine acres of the estate, complete with two dozen exotic ornamental structures designed by William Chambers. These included an orangery, a ruined arch, the House of Confucius, the Temple of the Sun, the Temple of Aeolus, the Temple of Belladonna, the Alhambra and a Mosque. Of the buildings which still survive, the pagoda is the most noticeable. It is an octagonal structure rising to ten storeys and 163 feet in height. It represents the rage for chinoiserie that was just then sweeping Europe.

The eldest son of Frederic and Augusta came to the throne as George III. He inherited Richmond Lodge on the death of George II and the Kew estate on the death of his mother. The two properties were then joined, and Sir Joseph Banks became the unofficial director of the grounds. Banks had sailed with Cook on *The Endeavour* and had collected plants from many countries in the course of his extensive travels. During the reign of George III he, and the many other collectors he sent out, introduced 7,000 new species of plant to Britain. Banks himself had tried to bring back a 'noble savage' to crown his collection, 'to keep as curiousity as well as my neighbours do lions and tigers'. His candidate for this post, perhaps mercifully, died in Batavia en route to England.

George and his queen, Charlotte, went on to have thirteen children and to outgrow the Kew Palace in which they were now living. Their answer was to buy the house 'next door' and to use it as an extension – largely as a nursery for the children. It is this building, the 'Dutch House', which we see over the wall as we come towards the end of the gardens. It had been built in 1631 for a merchant of Dutch origin and is an attractive building of red brick laid in Flemish bond, which was just then becoming fashionable in English building.

From 1788 George III began to show increasing signs of madness, suffering from a condition now recognised as porphyria. In 1802 he was moved into the Dutch House. Here, he lived out the years in virtual confinement under the constant supervision and unpleasant ministrations of the two Doctors Willis. It is more than probable that their ministrations were actually making him worse, for he was being regularly dosed with antimony. Antimony contains significant traces of arsenic, and arsenic is a trigger for porphyria. Thus they were constantly aggravating his condition until in 1811 his 'insanity' became permanent. It was not until his death in 1820 that his ordeal finally came to an end.

Unlike the king, and despite some difficult early years, Kew Gardens was to go from strength to strength. Today its 300 acres constitute one of the most beautiful botanic gardens in the world. But more than this they also house a famous School of Horticulture, important research laboratories, a library of more than 120,000 volumes and a herbarium, with more than 5 million specimens of plant from all over the world. Perhaps most importantly, it is now home to the Millennium Seed Bank, the largest plant conservation project in the world. Working with partners in 50 countries, the collection has 'banked' seeds from 10 per cent of the entire world flora. Their target is 25 per cent by 2020.

Getting home

Kew Bridge Station: (Waterloo)

Buses: (from Kew Bridge or Chiswick High Street) 65, 237, 267, 391, 440, H91

8. Along the Brent Valley

FROM BRENTFORD TO GREENFORD

On the west side of London the River Brent and its tributaries cut a valley running down from the low hills of south Hertfordshire to a junction with the Thames opposite Kew. This is a gentler river than its east London equivalent, the Lea – a more amicable flow in a smaller valley, characterised by meadows rather than marshland. Despite urbanisation it remains a pleasant, meandering and surprisingly rural walk.

Brentford and Greenford stand at either end of our route up the valley. They both derive their names from river crossings, but apart from this they have little in common. Greenford represents the higher reaches of the river, with a rural history surviving into the twentieth century. Here was a small hamlet surrounded by the hayfields which once characterised much of Middlesex. Urbanisation arrived here rather later than in the southern suburbs, and as a result of the motor car as much as of the railways. The building of major arterial roads between London and the west brought industry to the urban fringes, and the houses followed. The fields disappeared and the hamlet in the meadows became an amorphous and industrialised suburb, its configuration some thing of a mystery, even to its own inhabitants.

Brentford, on the other hand, was always an important town. The significance of its location, at the point where the Thames, the Brent and the Bath road all meet, is reflected in the fact that two major battles have been fought here. One was an engagement between Edmund Ironside and the Danes, the other a battle of the Civil War. Brentford has a history as a lively, and often notorious, market town, later seeing the early arrival of the industrial revolution with gas works and distilleries, soap works, docks and wharves, and the slum streets of Troy Town. It is also a town of great radical credentials, of John Wilkes, John Horne Tooke and the infamous business of the Middlesex elections.

Between 'urban' Brentford and 'rural' Greenford we have walks which take in not just a river, but the Grand Junction Canal and its narrow-boats, the Great Western viaduct and its bats, a beautiful church disowned by its architect, and a 'lunatic' asylum which occupies one of the most progressive places in the history of British psychiatry.

This chapter covers 9 miles from Kew Bridge to Greenford Station. It can be taken as two separate walks.

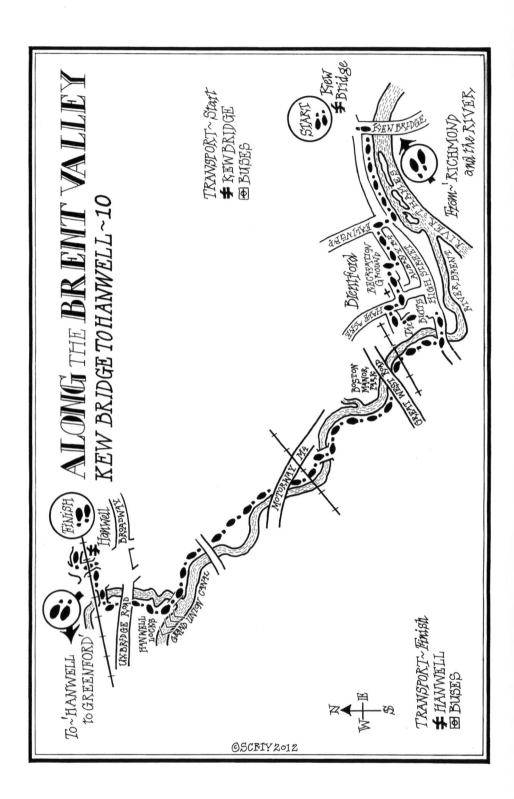

ALONG THE BRENT VALLEY
KEW BRIDGE TO HANWELL ~ 10

TRANSPORT~ Start
KEW BRIDGE
BUSES

START

Kew Bridge

KEW BRIDGE

RIVER THAMES

From~ RICHMOND
and the RIVER

RIVER BRENT

EALING RD

Brentford

RECREATION
GROUND

ALBERT RD

HIGH STREET

HALF ACRE

The Butts

GREAT WEST ROAD

BOSTON
MANOR
PARK

MOTORWAY M4

To~ HANWELL
to GREENFORD

FINISH

Hanwell

BROADWAY

UXBRIDGE ROAD

HANWELL
LOCKS

GRAND UNION CANAL

N
W——E
S

TRANSPORT~ Finish
HANWELL
BUSES

©SCRTY 2012

WALK 10: Kew Bridge to Hanwell (5 miles).

WALK 11: Hanwell to Greenford (4 miles).

▦ WALK 10: KEW BRIDGE TO HANWELL

Getting started

From Kew Bridge Station:

From the station turn right and cross at the pedestrian crossing to reach Kew Bridge.

Take the road (The Hollows) that runs along the immediate right hand side of the bridge down to the riverside.

From buses (65, 237, 267, 391, 440, H91):

Alight at Kew Bridge Station

From the station turn right and cross at the pedestrian crossing to reach Kew Bridge.

Take the road (the Hollows) that runs along the immediate right hand side of the bridge down to the riverside.

From Walk 9:

Cross Kew Bridge from the south bank. Take the steps on the left leading down to The Hollows.

Turn left to reach the riverside.

Gas Works and Withy Beds

ROUTE:

- Keep to the riverside as far as you can before briefly joining the main road opposite the Musical Museum.
- Turn left on the road then almost immediately left again to enter Waterside Park.
- Follow the riverside through the Park and then behind the Watermans Arts Centre. Continue as far as you can until eventually joining a stepped alley back onto the main road.

FACILITIES: Pub and café at Kew Bridge. Tea room at the Musical Museum. Pub on High Street, close to the riverside path. Café and Bar at the Watermans Art Centre. The Musical Museum is open daily except Mondays from 11am to 5.30 pm (entrance fee). The Steam Museum is open daily except Mondays from 11am to 4pm (entrance fee).

LOOKING AT WILDLIFE: There are interesting riverside and wasteland wild flowers along the riverside walk. The islands support willows and poplars, and the large nests of herons can be seen in the trees. As well as heron along the riverside there are a variety of gulls, cormorant, wagtails, great crested grebe, waterfowl and occasional waders at low tide.

The elegant Kew Bridge, 366 feet of Cornwall and Aberdine granite surmounted by the arms of Middlesex and Surrey, was opened on 20 May 1903. Its three arches form flattened ellipses, and the piers between them, with pointed fronts like the prows of ships, penetrate eighteen foot into the London clay beneath the river bed.

The demolition of the old Kew Bridge, 'at once so picturesque and so fraught with memories', was regarded by many artistic people as 'little less than a local calamity', according to E. Beresford Chancellor writing in 1903. The *Daily Mail's* reporter shared the same view:

> Could the old bridge tell only a little of the meetings it saw! The lovers who met and kissed there; the sweethearts who sighed and said their fond goodbyes ... The tranquil twilight time when youth and maid first understood; the silent star time, when heart spoke to heart as never before; the moonlight time, when the tender gleams of reverie played with the old man's thoughts till he brushed aside a tear; the mysterious midnight time when night's lamp had gone behind a cloud and the lily-stars looked down on grief and guilt and darkness ... Life is always cheating us; our hopes are dashed and our dreams come to nothing.

So wrote Charles Cutting on the opening of the new bridge. Like the traffic, the journalism goes much faster today.

Before 1757, when the first bridge was built, the crossing was made by ferry. The ferry service was established in 1659 by Robert Tunstall, who also oper-ated lime-kilns alongside the river. It is perhaps the kilns which gave the name of The Hollows to this first stretch of riverside we follow. Though new develop-ments are changing the atmosphere, there are still neat house-boats lining the water's edge, each with its own little fenced patch of privacy.

Occasionally, looking landwards through the more and the less ugly post-modern blocks, we catch glimpses of one of west London's finest landmarks. Although the main buildings of the Kew Bridge Pumping Station are ungainly and inelegant, this matters little next to the wonderfully tapering tower, 235 foot of yellow brick cut across with stone courses in red and beige. With its shallow recesses, running the height of each face, its octagonal lantern and its crowning wind vein, it rates alongside Abbey Mills Pumping Station and Stoke Newington Waterworks as one of the loveliest examples of Victorian industrial architecture.

The station was built in 1837 by the Grand Junction Water Works Company as their third attempt to establish a pollution-free source of drinking water for west London. The tower was added in 1867, and houses two systems of vertical pipes through which the water was pumped by Cornish beam engines to give it sufficient head before entering the mains. The beam engines survive here in what is now the Steam Museum, home to an extensive collection of large steam pumping engines.

The waterworks were just part of the concentration of industry which came to the Brentford riverside. Waterside Park, opened in 1984, now occupies the site of one of the oldest gasworks in the world, covering 8 acres of land and ¼ mile of river frontage. It was established in 1824 specifically to light the turnpike road from Kensington to Hounslow. Within a few years the gasworks were taken over by the Brentford Gas Company, under the chairmanship of Felix Booth. By 1926, it had grown to serve 124,000 customers across 130 square miles of London. At this stage it was taken over again, this time by the ambitious Gas, Light and Coke Company, whose story we encounter in Beckton. Like the Beckton plant, it closed in 1964, made redundant by the advent of North Sea gas.

Felix Booth also happened to be the owner of the breweries and malt houses next door. This even larger site covered 11 acres, including the area now occupied by the Watermans Arts Centre. Together the Gas Company and the Royal Brewery constituted two of the largest industrial units in early nineteenth-century Britain. The main building of the Brewery was a huge granary with a double purpose. On one level it stored grain to serve a distillery that produced a million gallons of the famous gin a year, while on the floor below stood a bullock house, fattening 300 beasts at a time for the London market.

Booth's proudest year was 1829, when William IV came to the brewery to discuss the arrangements for a Polar expedition which Booth was financing. Booth contributed £17,000 to the voyage of Sir John Ross, and in due course received both a baronetcy and a place in the atlas, when a newly discovered peninsular was given the name Boothia Felix in his honour. Meanwhile, opposite what was now the Royal Brewery, High Street was lined with atrocious slum dwellings occupied by poorly paid labourers from Booth's two plants. Behind these, in an area known as Troy Town, many more were packed into one of the most overcrowded slum areas in London.

Today both the slums and the works are gone. The sole survivor from the period is the low white stone church with stumpy octagonal tower, glimpsed across High Street and the park wall. Though built in the shadow of the gas works in 1867, it looks as if it belonged in fields on the edge of the Essex marshes. Next door, in an older whitewashed building, is the Church School. This was founded in 1768 by Sarah Trimmer, as the inscription says, 'for religious instruction and industry sponsored by annual subscriptions and benefactors and the produce of the children's work'. The church was closed in 1959 and became the site of one of London's more eccentric museums. Here Frank Holland, looking for a home for his collection of automatic pianos, founded the Musical Museum in 1963. Today it has moved to a brand new three-storey site just along the road, and it now includes a 230 seat concert hall with a 'Mighty Wurlitzer' rising, in the traditional manner, from beneath the stage.

The two larger islands just off-shore from the park are Brentford Aits, separated by a gap once known as Hog's Hole. Waterfowl paddle in the shallow water, heron stand on the tidally revealed mud, and cormorant perch in the island trees. The willows and poplars form a lovely grouping of contrasting shapes, but from the 1300s to the eighteenth century it was osier willows which were cultivated here. However, with the industrial and residential growth of Brentford the many market gardens began to disappear, as did the demand for baskets which had maintained the trade in osiers for 400 years.

Lots Ait, a third and slightly higher island, can be seen alongside the Arts Centre. From 1881 to 1965 the Thames and General Lighterage Company had boat building yards along the riverside here, and these were enlarged by slipways on the Ait itself in 1926. The dilapidated and slightly mysterious buildings still dominate the island. In the 1980s the Ait was purchased by the Speyhawk Company, which proposed to develop it as an exclusive residential village. The proposals were rejected after a public enquiry in which the London Wildlife Trust played an important part. Part of the opposition case was the presence here of a breeding colony of rare snails. The two-lipped door snail, *clausilia biplicata*, is rare enough to feature in the *Red Data Books* of threatened species and is found in only five other locations in Britain. One of these is just across the river, beside the Public Records Office in Kew, where it has been found to subsist on dog faeces. The only puzzle is this: if the creature can feed on dog mess, why is it not common throughout the capital?

Troy Town

ROUTE:

- From the top of the alleyway, cross the main road (High Street) and go straight ahead up the major road opposite (Ealing Road).Take the first turning on the left (Albany Road).
- Continue on Albany Road until reaching the recreation ground on the right. Follow the alleyway that runs between the recreation ground and the houses to reach the park entrance.
- Turn left through the park following the avenue of limes through to the far side.
- Exit from the park onto St Paul's Road and continue straight ahead to reach Half Acre.

FACILITIES: Cafés on Ealing Road and Albany Road. There is a lunchtime café in St Paul's church open weekdays 12 to 1.30pm.

LOOKING AT WILDLIFE: Beautiful tall limes in the recreation ground.

Brentford, it is refreshing to be able to say, was unbeloved of poets. James Thomson called it 'a town of mud', John Gay a 'tedious town ... For dirty streets and white-legged chickens known'. In *Oliver Twist*, Dickens describes Brentford as 'in the prime of its muddiness', with the mire so thick that it was often up to the axle boxes of the coaches.

For several million years the River Brent has carried down to Brentford masses of brick earth, the fertile loam which lines the lower valleys of many of the Thames tributaries. As the Thames makes its sharp curve to the south, it cuts into the brick earth creating an area which was good for market gardening but less so for transport. In any rainy spell the main road through Brentford became saturated and was churned by the passage of vehicles into a thick mud. In 1754 *Gentleman's Magazine* described High Street as 'the worst public road in Europe'.

But, paradoxically, it was transport which helped make of Brentford the prime market and manufacturing town of Middlesex. High Street carried the major road from London to Bath, and at the Brent crossing it reached its first staging post. In 1800, 83 stage coaches a day were passing through the town. In that same year the Grand Junction Canal was completed, linking the Thames through Brentford Lock with the entire canal network to Oxford and the Midlands. The 'great fruit garden north of the Thames' was turning into an industrial town, with a population of labourers employed in soap and varnish factories, saw mills, flour mills, tile and pottery works, breweries and distilleries. By the middle of the century the town was afflicted with a combination of heavy traffic, malodorous factories, slum dwellings, polluted air and a polluted river. It was said that no town in the country had more poverty relative to its size. By 1873 it was described in the *Brentford Advertiser* as 'the filthiest place in England'.

From Ealing Road, through the backstreets to Half Acre, we cross the site of the worst of all Brentford's slum areas, Troy Town, its name drawn from a Cornish expression describing a labyrinth of disorderly streets. It was here that Booth's workers, and many more, lived in back-to-back terraces and dilapidated weatherboard cottages – dwellings with high rents, low states of repair and no sanitation whatsoever.

The clearance of Troy Town began in 1910, but it was not until 1958 that the last of the derelict cottages was demolished. Before this, however, the wealthier inhabitants of the town had already made their own contribution to urban improvement. In 1887, to mark Queen Victoria's Jubilee, they raised a public subscription to open a recreation ground on the edge of Troy Town, complete with a domed drinking fountain and an inscribed commemorative 'needle'.

The simple square recreation ground is surprisingly atmospheric, largely due to the avenues of tall limes which bisect it, and the alignment of this central avenue with the roads at either end. Look to the north from the park and you see a simple but attractive terrace of red-brick housing. Look to the south and you see an inchoate mess of post-war planning, the development with which the planners replaced Troy Town. It looks suspiciously as if the architects who designed the site never got round to visiting it.

St Pauls Road, beyond the Recreation Ground, has some attractive old church school buildings on the left and St Pauls Church itself on the right. The church was built in 1868 to serve the growing population of the town and is a typical white ragstone Victorian church with a particularly high steeple. It has recently undergone a comprehensive modernisation, with the chancel turned into a chapel, an extension built out to the north and the main body of the church turned into a community space. Despite one or two jarring notes, it is, overall, a successful adaptation of a church to meet the needs of the twenty-first century. And it is worth timing your visit to coincide with the lunchtime café, for inside it does have one unique feature. In the late 1800s John Zoffany, who lived in Kew, painted a picture of 'The Last Supper' and presented it to St Anne's on Kew Green. St Anne's turned the gift down. Their objection was that the faces of the apostles had been modelled on local fishermen – a particularly surprising objection since a fair proportion of the disciples had been fishermen themselves. The painting was eventually brought to St Paul's, on the edge of old Troy Town, where it should probably have been all the time. And here it still hangs, in the chancel, those proletarian disciples gathered around Jesus, whilst Judas gets up to leave and two servant boys, one white and one black, crouch in front.

From the Butts to the Bells

ROUTE:

- From St Pauls Road turn right onto Half Acre and then left onto The Butts. On reaching the square, cross it diagonally to the far right hand corner to enter Market Place.
- Follow Market Place to the main road (High Street) and turn right to cross the bridge over the River Brent.

FACILITIES: Pubs and cafés on Market Place and High Street.

LOOKING AT WILDLIFE: On the right hand side on the approach to Brentford Bridge a small marshy area contains sea buckthorn and sallow.

In 1760 John Horne Tooke became incumbent of the third and oldest of Brentford's churches. He had wanted to be a lawyer but entered the church to please his father, and was of that eccentric order of clergymen who believed that the social welfare of his parishioners was as important as their spiritual health.

Accordingly he took up the study of medicine in order to help those members of his congregation too poor to afford a doctor. In 1767, during a visit to Paris, he met the radical politician John Wilkes. It was an encounter that was to change the course of both men's lives and to have some interesting consequences for Brentford.

Wilkes had gone to Paris in avoidance of British 'justice'. In 1762, whilst MP for Aylesbury, he had started a magazine, the *North Briton*, virulently critical of the corrupt condition of British politics. His particular targets were Lord Bute, the Prime Minister, and the Whig circle that surrounded and supported George III. In the famous issue number 45, Wilkes attacked the king's speech at the opening of parliament, showing that in it the king had countenanced a lie by Bute. Bute resigned but Wilkes was imprisoned in the Tower for sedition. The charge could not stand: Wilkes was protected by privilege and the Lord Chief Justice was forced into the ignominy of ordering his release. Wilkes sued the government for illegal arrest and won – and the government in response dug up another charge against him. On the basis of another contribution to the magazine, this time a poem, he was expelled from the House and charged with 'obscene libel'. A trip to Paris became expedient and he was found guilty in his absence.

During their meeting in Paris, Horne Tooke persuaded Wilkes to contest the constituency of Middlesex, which held its hustings in Brentford. On election day the roads to the town were packed with excited crowds of Wilksites. No-one was allowed to pass unless they displayed about their body the famous number 45. Cries of 'Wilkes and Liberty' rang out all over Brentford as the announcement was made that Wilkes had been elected, beating his nearest rival by a margin of six to one. Parliament immediately declared the election void. But the Middlesex voters remained undaunted. They continued to elect Wilkes in three consecutive contests until Parliament finally allowed him to take his seat in 1774. He went on to become a Lord Mayor of London and a Chamberlain of the City, retiring from politics at the age of 73. He remained all his life a champion of press freedom.

Wilkes's influence on Tooke, even though they later fell out, was far-reaching. Tooke intensified his interest in social reform and resigned his place at St. Lawrence's in 1773 to resume his legal studies. He campaigned against Enclosure Acts and in favour of parliamentary reform. In 1775 he organised a subscription for 'our beloved American fellow subjects who had preferred death to slavery' and 'were for that reason only murdered by the King's troops'. For this he was fined £200 and imprisoned for a year. He maintained a flow of radical writing throughout his life. Along with Thomas Paine, he was a founding member of the Corresponding Society, the first working-class political organisation in the country. In 1794 he was put on trial for treason, along with other members of the Society, but was triumphantly acquitted.

John Horne Tooke died in 1812. He had wanted to be buried in his own garden in Windmill Lane, Hanwell and to this end had inscribed his own memorial stone to 'John Horn Tooke, late proprietor and now occupier of this spot. Content and grateful'. He was buried instead in St Mary's Church, Ealing.

This section of our route brings together Tooke, Wilkes and the Middlesex elections. It also takes us through the most attractive parts of present-day Brentford. The Butts is a wobbly, dipping and irregular square, its attractiveness only marred by the demands of modern and out-of-character car parking. The surrounding houses are almost all pre-1720, large, luxurious but unfussy dwellings in Queen Anne red brick, and with beautifully proportioned and regularly arranged windows, contrasting with the irregularly ridged tiled rooves. On the dipping west side of the square is a much later but equally characterful building. This is the 1904 Boatmen's Institute, now a private house but originally a London City Mission serving the boat people who plied the adjacent canal. The narrow-boat families, constantly on the move, living in the cramped conditions of their tiny cabins, working longer hours for less pay as competition from the railways intensified, were some of the country's poorest workers. Here in one building they were provided by the Mission with a school, a church, and a maternity hospital.

The Butts was originally an archery range. It was also the main site for public festivals and local celebrations. When development began in the 1690s, it soon became a select residential area, and this was a source of friction, for the boisterous annual Brentford fairs, and the even more boisterous Middlesex elections, took place here or in the adjacent Market Place. The elections for Knights of the Shire, and subsequently for the MP for Middlesex, were always a very bawdy affair, even before the Wilkes years. They are described in contemporary accounts as 'riotous', 'disorderly', 'tumultuous' and 'drunken'. In 1768 for example, Sir William Proctor, one of Wilkes' opponents, included in his election expenses the sum of £1090 for drinks and food consumed by his supporters and for damage done by them to public houses.

Meanwhile Market Place had its own unfettered outpourings in the annual six-day fair. The Market itself had outgrown High Street and moved here in 1560. Traders could avoid the greater congestion and sharper competition of the City and make use of riverside meadows for storing their goods or fattening their cattle. As the Bath Road and the river were only fifty yards apart it was an ideal spot for the transfer of loads, and the whole town became known as 'Market Brentford'. It was not only buying and selling which took place here. Market days also saw the sentencing of offenders to a public flogging or the pillory. When Market House was pulled down, its site, appropriately enough, became the Magistrates Court. The market itself was abolished in 1933 and the Brentford Fairs died with it.

Back on High Road we pass, on the left, the pale body of St Lawrence's Church, looking sad and wan behind a line of lime and horse chestnut. There has been a church here since at least the twelfth century, but the present building dates from the incumbency of John Horne Tooke himself. It was while the church was closed for rebuilding – in yellow stock brick with a white ragstone tower – that Tooke took the opportunity to visit Paris, and hence his meeting with Wilkes.

The church was closed again in 1961, this time for good. In 1979 it was leased to the St Lawrence Brentford Trust, with aim of turning it into a 'Brent Dock Theatre and Community Centre'. Sadly this has come to nothing, and the overgrown grounds have grown dank with evergreen oak and elder. The fading church building continues to look out upon the river and on the Six Bells pub, named after the now silent peel of St Lawrence.

From Brentford Lock to Hanwell Locks

ROUTE:

- After crossing the bridge turn right onto the riverside. Do not cross the gauging lock but continue on the left bank through the old Brentford Depot site and the new housing.
- Continue to follow the towpath which runs under the Great West Road and shortly afterwards curves round to run briefly parallel to the M4 Motorway. Shortly after this the towpath changes bank across a 'roving' footbridge. Cross the bridge and continue along the towpath on the opposite bank.
- Beyond Osterley Lock the towpath crosses a weir. Immediately beyond this the path forks. Leave the towpath to take the broad gravel path winding uphill and ahead.

- Keep left at all junctions, remaining roughly parallel to the canal. Follow the path, returning to the towpath just before the next road bridge.
- Continue along the towpath to reach Hanwell Locks.

FACILITIES: There is a real ale pub on Green Lanes, just before the Hanwell Locks.

LOOKING AT WILDLIFE: There is an interesting flora all along the towpath, including wasteland, hedgerow and waterside species. Arrow-head grows in the water of the Brentford Depot and just beyond it a large clump of Duke of Argyll's tea tree is growing on the towpath. Clitheroe's Island has more than a hundred species of wild flowers, including purple loosestrife, gypsywort, parsley water dropwort, water pepper, meadowsweet, giant hogweed and two species of balsam. There is a fragment of relic oak wood alongside Osterley Lock, with a ground flora including red campion, common cow wheat and goldilocks. Birds to look out for include the commoner waterfowl, Canada goose, shoveller, heron, grey and yellow wagtail and the kingfisher. Elthorne Waterside, where we leave the towpath for a while, has a variety of habitats, including hay meadows, hedgerows, ditches, ponds and woodland, and attracts green woodpecker, goldcrest and linnet, as well as foxes and weasel.

The River Brent rises in Hertfordshire as the Dollis Brook. It is joined at Neasden by the Silk Stream and flows on as the Brent. It formed, at one time, the boundary between the two great kingdoms of the East and West Saxons, and Offa himself held a Council on the banks of the river in Brentford in 780. Later a new kingdom was carved out between these two and gave its name to the county of Middlesex. That too is now extinct – a county and an Anglo-Saxon people surviving only in the name of a cricket club and a postal district.

The last three miles of the Brent today have been canalised to form the lowest section of the Grand Union Canal, running into Brentford Dock and the Thames. The canal, originally called the Grand Junction Canal, was launched at a meeting in Birmingham in 1792. The purpose was to build a canal from Brentford to Braunston in Northamptonshire, thus shortening the water route between London and Birmingham by 60 miles.

The section from Brentford to Uxbridge was the first part of the canal to be completed and was opened in 1794. The company charged for use of the canal according to load – half penny per ton per mile – and as we turn onto the canal from High Street we pass the Gauging Lock at the entrance to the Brentford Depot where the charges would have been reckoned. In its day the Brentford Depot was a major freight terminal, trade on the canal building up until in the early 1900s it was used by over 20,000 narrow boats a year. Thereafter began the sad story of the waterways decline, with over half the network lost and a great national asset largely neglected. Until, that is, their development potential was realised. Now we have lengths of bland new waterside homes with little sense of locality. That is certainly the case here, where the once bustling depot is now lined with dull yellow blocks with glass penthouse apartments and projecting metal balconies that look like empty hanging baskets. A few of the empty warehouses still survive at the far end, projecting in a mysterious resounding space of still water and corrugated iron.

From the depot site we follow the canal for nearly three miles to Hanwell, passing first under the railway and then under the Great West Road – the two routes which between them finally put an end to the importance of the Old Bath Road through Brentford. The Great West Road was specifically built to ease this congested highway and, having been talked about for over a hundred years, was finally opened in 1925. The section we pass became known as the 'Golden Mile', and was lined with large and stylish factories such as Firestone, Gillette and Pyrene. They were built in the modernist and art deco styles of the 1920s and 1930s, criticised at the time but campaigned for as treasures today – particularly after the Firestone building was hurriedly demolished by developers in 1980 to avoid the effects of a preservation order. Today they have been added to by the likes of the Glaxo Smith Kline headquarters, a large anonymous building, its black glass seemingly designed to give as little away as possible and to protect its corporate secrets.

Beyond Boston Manor Park, on the opposite bank, we come to Clitheroe's Lock, where the natural river and the navigable cut flow round either side of Clitheroe's Island. The island, which can be reached by crossing the lock, is a good place to look for wildlife. It has 22 species of tree and shrub, more than a hundred of wild flowers and 29 species of bird. The apex of the island, where the canal rejoins the natural river, forms a little marsh with flag iris and reed mace and the graceful hanging heads of pendulous sedge. There are two invasive plants which crop up here – and often elsewhere along the towpath. For a tough plant, Himalayan Balsam has its pink flowers hanging on remarkably slender threads. They are called Policeman's Helmets, but most closely resemble something worn by the Keystone cops or an earlier generation of firemen. Giant hogweed is an even tougher plant, which came to us from the Caucasus via Kew; so perhaps this canal side was one of the first places where it took hold in this country.

The survival of all this wildlife is made more remarkable by the huge, ugly and aggressive intrusion of the M4. It strides on raised piers like an insensitive giant across what would otherwise be a beautiful stretch of riverside, cutting off canal from meadow and polluting a whole area, not just visually but with its noise, a continuous, dull thunder. It is a constant reminder of a society which values going places above being there.

Shortly after passing Osterley Lock we leave the towpath for a while to cross the 'Elthorne Wetlands'. The path here looks rather over-engineered – as though it were being prepared for a troupe of the household cavalry – but it leads us through a patchwork of habitats, including scrub and secondary woodland and meadow land. It used to be a landfill site but has now been landscaped with both wildlife areas and sculpture trails. It provides an interesting variation in the riverside route before we return to the towpath at Trumpers Way and the final stretch up to Hanwell.

Fitzroy Walk and the Hanwell Asylum

ROUTE:

- At Hanwell Locks the river and the canal separate. Between the first two locks in the Hanwell flight, take the signposted path off to the right, to follow the river along Fitzherbert Walk.
- Continue along the riverside to reach and pass below Hanwell Bridge.
- NOTE: The path below the bridge can be flooded at times, in which case walk up to, and cross, the road and rejoin the path on the other side.
- Continue ahead along the riverside and across the meadow to reach the viaduct.
- Turn right across the footbridge below the viaduct

To join Walk 12:

On crossing the footbridge, turn left beneath the viaduct and alongside the river.

To complete this walk:

On crossing the footbridge, turn right again on the trodden path through the woods, keeping parallel to the green fence to reach a style.

Cross the stile and turn left up a broad tarmac path beside a small park to reach a road (Station Road).

For trains, turn left under the bridge then bear right along Golden Manor. Take the first turning on the right (Campbell Road) to reach Hanwell Station.

For buses, turn right down Station Road to reach Hanwell Broadway

FACILITIES: Pub at Hanwell Bridge. Pubs, café and shops in Hanwell.

LOOKING AT WILDLIFE: The interesting riverside flora continues. Feral mandarin duck and kingfishers both breed around Hanwell.

Just below Hanwell, river and canal part company. As it swings off to the west the Grand Union Canal leaves the Brent valley behind, climbing fifty-three feet through a flight of six locks. It takes a narrow boat approximately 1½ hours to negotiate this one third of a mile of waterway, a process which looses tens of thousands of gallons of water into the downstream canal. The Hanwell Locks were built between 1793 and 1796 and are today a scheduled Ancient Monument.

From the Hanwell Locks to Hanwell Bridge we follow Fitzherbert Walk, named after the founder of the Brent River and Canal Society. For most of its length this path follows the boundary of the new St Bernard's Hospital – and the old Hanwell Asylum. Built in 1830, largely by French prisoners of war, the asylum dates from a time when the 'insane' were regarded as something sub-human, when conditions were squalid and degrading, and when regimes were based on whipping, intimidation and physical restraint. But from this tradition Hanwell stands aside. From the day it opened, with 600 patients, on 16 May 1831, it was at the forefront of radical change and daring experimentation. It occupies a special place in the history of psychiatric medicine.

The first medical superintendent was William Ellis, with his wife as matron. They regarded the hospital as a community or family and held the startling view that 'there are but few … who, if a particle of mind be left, are not to be won by affectionate attention'. Ellis was largely self-taught and was highly influenced by the doctrine of phrenology, but he also championed two great causes in psychiatric nursing: that of proper training and pay for mental nurses – who had previously played more the role of prison warders-and of gainful employment and training for patients. For this the Hanwell site was ideal. It occupied 44 acres and within them developed its own bakery, brewery and farm, where patients grew most of the hospital's supply of vegetables. By 1837, 454 of the 612 patients at Hanwell were engaged in daily work.

Sadly, Ellis only lasted one more year, resigning after a row with his management committee, but he was replaced by another remarkable man. Ellis had already abolished physical punishment at Hanwell. Now, within four months of taking up post at the largest asylum in the country, and with no previous experience of asylum management, Dr John Connolly abolished every form of personal restraint, including straitjackets, shackles and coercion chairs. It was Connolly's belief that there was no strong and definable boundary between sanity and insanity, and this led him to develop the concept of community outreach and a mental health service that would treat many of its patients in their own homes. He propounded these and other ideas in a series of lectures which became hugely popular and highly influential. He died in 1866, described by Sir James Crichton-Brown as 'a Wilberforce who devoted his life to the abolition of slavery of a particularly grievous kind'.

The Hanwell Asylum was renamed St Bernard's Hospital in 1937. In 1980 the large new Ealing district hospital was built on what used to be the asylum's staff playing fields. Thus, in the year of its 150th anniversary, the old Hanwell Asylum became the new St Bernard's Annexe, housed in concrete buildings that resemble the worst of Soviet housing blocks.

Getting home:

Hanwell Station: Paddington

Buses: (from Hanwell Broadway) 92, 195, 207, 282, 427, 607

■ WALK 11: HANWELL TO GREENFORD

Getting started

From Hanwell Station (from Paddington):

From the station turn left into Campbell Road then left again into Golden Manor at the end.

Continue under the railway bridge and turn immediately right onto the footpath. After about a hundred yards take the style on the right and follow the path down through the woods and parallel to the green fence to reach the river.

Turn right under the viaduct.

From Buses (92, 195, 207, 282, 427, 607):

Alight on Hanwell Broadway

From the Broadway head up Station Road. Just before the road goes under a railway bridge take the footpath on the left. After about a hundred yards take the style on the right and follow the path down through the woods and parallel to the green fence to reach the river.

Turn right under the viaduct.

From Walk 10:

On crossing the footbridge turn left beneath the viaduct and alongside the river.

From Hanwell to Greenford Bridge

ROUTE:

- Bear left at the first junction of paths beyond the viaduct to continue along the riverside and parallel to the viaduct.
- Continue to follow the path when it curves around to the right, ignoring the signposted steps on the left, and continuing ahead to reach the Millennium Maze.
- From the Maze take the path leading uphill passed the children's playground and animal enclosures. Pass the lodge and continue on the path curving right to reach the lychgate beside the church.
- Go through the lychgate and turn immediately left down the path beside the church to reach the river bridge.
- Cross the bridge and turn immediately right alongside the river bank.
- At the first fork, take the left hand path, keeping straight ahead on the trodden path that follows a hedgerow cutting across the golf course.
- After passing through a small coppice, branch right to reach a footbridge. Cross it and turn immediately left across the grass, now following the river on its opposite bank.
- Keep to the left, following the paths that run closest to the river bank and ignoring branches to the right.
- Continue along the path which eventually runs alongside a sports pitch, to reach the road beside Greenford Bridge.

ALONG THE BRENT VALLEY
HANWELL TO GREENFORD ~ 11

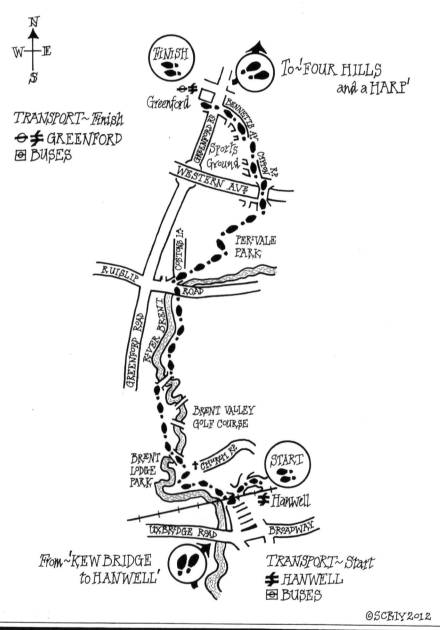

N W E S

FINISH

Greenford

To 'FOUR HILLS and a HARP'

TRANSPORT~ Finish
GREENFORD
BUSES

Sports Ground

BENNETTS AV

CATTON RD

WESTERN AVE

GREENFORD RD

PERIVALE PARK

COSTONS LA

RUISLIP ROAD

GREENFORD ROAD

RIVER BRENT

BRENT VALLEY GOLF COURSE

BRENT LODGE PARK

CHURCH RD

START

Hanwell

UXBRIDGE ROAD

BROADWAY

From ~'KEW BRIDGE to HANWELL'

TRANSPORT~ Start
HANWELL
BUSES

©SCRIY 2012

FACILITIES: Brent Lodge Park has toilets and a café and a small free zoo.

LOOKING AT WILDLIFE: Heron and kingfisher are sometimes seen along the riverside. Waterside and wasteland plants include giant hogweed, angelica, pepperwort and goats rue, and a lovely avenue of pollarded willow. Brent Lodge Park has a large collection of birds and animals, including sacred ibis, egrets, marmosets and mara. The old hedgerows on the golf course are worth examining for hedgerow shrubs, flowers and small birds, including warblers, and there are green woodpeckers on the open grassland.

North of Hanwell Bridge the river flows peacefully across Brent Meadow. Here, where blackthorn hedges line the riverside, it is possible to relive the time described by nineteenth-century novelist Bulwer-Lytton, who walked with his sweetheart 'on the green banks that shade Brent's humble flood'. But such pleasures were not to last too long.

In 1897 the engineer E. Bailey Denton was commissioned to survey the reaches of the now polluted Brent. His report describes the upper river as 'merely an open sewer'. Between Hanwell and Ealing all the fish had long since been killed, and 'even the water rats had fallen victims to the foulness of the water'. Further up, 'black lumps of sewage were floating down stream and on all sides gases were building up from its bed'. The smell in general 'was such as to make my companion and myself ill'.

Denton blamed the local sewage works, and the local councils proceeded to blame each other. Eventually the matter of 'the unfortunate valley of the Brent' was raised in Parliament, and an Act passed to deal with the sewage problem. It is a different form of pollution which has to be dealt with today – industrial effluent and road run-off, their concentrations intensified by the amount of water drawn off at the Welsh Harp Reservoir.

The river runs through 4½ miles of Ealing, its banks and surrounding parklands forming a continuous ribbon of land which varies in width from 200 yards to half a mile. Over 170,000 people live within a mile of this strip, and it was to provide for them that the founder members of the Brent River and Canal Society conceived the development of a linear waterside park. The existing dereliction should be cleared away, hundreds of forest trees planted, all-weather paths established, and all improvements based on the existing landscape. The organisation began its work in 1974, enrolling 600 members within its first year. By 1976 it had convinced the Ealing council of its case, and thereafter the two bodies began a close co-operation that has given rise to the Brent River Park and several miles of the best in city walking. The planners of the Brent River Park showed from the beginning the sense that was so conspicuously lacking in the early days of the Lea Valley Regional Park – the awareness that a landscape is a resource of its own not just an open space for the development of 'leisure facilities'. Their philosophy was summed up by landscape architect Brian Green in an early report for the Society:

Many landscape architects in the past have designed from a basis of being arbiters of leisure and recreation facilities. Provide the people with that which is eminently designable ... and assume that dog owners will find somewhere else to walk their pets, the courting couples will find somewhere else to be alone, the pensioner somewhere else to study the runners in the 2.30 at Newmarket ... I would prefer to leave alone entirely and land to continue to give the pleasure it already does than to design for the sake of designing.

Bulwer-Lytton would surely have approved.

The elegant eight-arch span of the Wharncliffe Viaduct (named after Lord Wharncliffe, who chaired the Lords Committee that passed the Great Western Railway Bill) was built in 1835 by Isombard Kingdom Brunel to carry the Great Western Railway across 300 yards of the Brent Valley. At 65 feet high, it was the first of his large-scale designs to be constructed, and, in stark contrast to the motorway flyover on the previous walk, enhances rather than denigrates the landscape. Beneath the motorway all is dark and dead; beneath the viaduct the high brick spans let light into an attractive glade on a picturesque curve of the river, where bird-song and butterflies enliven the bushes. The huge brick piers are hollow and there are plans to further enhance the wildlife by developing them as bat roosts.

Beyond the viaduct we follow the edge of Church Fields, where the distant and incongruous calling of peacocks leads us into the Brent Lodge Park. Brent Lodge was once one of the largest houses in the area but was demolished in 1932. Only the stable block still stands and is today an environmental centre. The private gardens have become an exceedingly pleasant park, with a small zoo continuing one of the proudest of old-fashioned municipal traditions.

St Mary's, the parish church of Hanwell, stands at the top of the park. It is a large, dark and imposing building with a flint frontage, like an East Anglian church, and a tall octagonal tower topped with a tapering spire. It is undeniably a church of the Victorian middle classes and was erected for them by George Gilbert Scott in 1841. Scott, whose work we have met often on our route round London, designed this as one of a batch of six intended to revolutionise concepts of church architecture. He was later to turn against his own work, describing all six as 'a mass of horrors'. His original church had no chancel and this was added in 1898, only to be damaged by a serious fire in 1912.

The attractive white pebble-dash Rectory Cottage opposite the church was built by the Reverend George Glasse. Glasse was a man of high connections and considerable wealth, who extended his domains by acquiring the adjacent Brent Lodge. Perhaps in so doing he ran beyond his means for in 1802 he was in trouble for defaulting on a sum of money belonging to a charity of which he was treasurer. And money problems led to his death, but in a rather peculiar way. According to an account in *Gentleman's Magazine* in 1809, he took a coach from Hanwell to an inn in Bishopsgate. On alighting from the coach he somehow left behind him a large sum of money which, for some unspecified reason, he was carrying. Thereafter began frantic attempts to recover it, but to no immediate avail. A few hours later the honest driver returned, having discovered the money in his coach. He was too late. The Reverend Glasse had already taken his own life in desperation.

A little path beside the church leads us down to Boles Meadow and the Boles Bridge. Here we cross a golf course along the line of ancient hedgerows, where hawthorn, blackthorn and hazel arch right across the path and insulate us from the surrounding golf-green monotony. And then, along the last section of route before Greenford Bridge, we follow a shallow and placid river which winds its way around little gravel beaches lined with pollarded willows. The sense of seclusion is increased by the high banks above the path, another result of the landscaping of earlier landfill tipping. Here the lilac coloured flowers of goats rue grow among a profusion of white pepperwort, whilst above, on a flat plateau of Ealing's landscaped garbage, and indifferent to its unsavoury origins, skylark, pheasant and partridge have all bred in recent years.

Unfortunately, however, Ealing's garbage continues to despoil this otherwise beautiful route in another way. On the far bank of the river is a Waste Transfer Station, whose rubbish – especially the ubiquitous plastic bag – continues to blow beyond its fences, clinging to the trees and floating in the river between heron, coot and gulls. It is something of an irony that an amount of litter that would not be tolerated on a local street is allowed to pollute an area all around the facility responsible for disposing of it.

Perivale Park and Greenford

ROUTE:

- Leave the riverside and turn left to cross Greenford Bridge.
- On the far side bear immediately right across the grass into Costons Lane and after a short distance take the broad tarmac path on the right into Perivale Park.
- The path crosses a small brook and then curves left to reach a road entrance. Do not leave the park here but continue to the right alongside the playing fields.
- At the far end of the pitches fork left to reach Western Avenue and cross this major road by the footbridge.
- From the footbridge turn left then almost immediately right into Cayton Road, almost directly opposite the Perivale Park exit point.
- At the end, join the footpath which runs around the perimeter of the playing fields, ignoring the first exit on the right.
- Where the tarmac path ends, exit onto Bennetts Avenue and follow it as far as Greenford Road.

To join Walk 12:

Turn right onto Greenford Road. Walk under the railway bridge and then cross Rockware Avenue immediately beyond it.

To complete this walk:

Cross Greenford Road and continue straight ahead down Uneeda Drive.

Turn right at the end to reach Greenford Station.

FACILITIES: Pubs and cafés around Greenford Station.

LOOKING AT WILDLIFE: The recent efforts to diversify Perivale Park have led to an improvement in its birdlife, including thrushes and woodpeckers, with redwing in winter.

In one of the old mills along the course of the Brent, a seventeenth-century miller had the misfortune to be crushed between his mill stones. Since his ghost continued to haunt the building, no one else was prepared to take up residence there except an elderly miser. No doubt its frightening reputation and consequent isolation were exactly what he was looking for. But after a time, the miser too went missing. The only local person brave enough to enter the cursed mill to look for him was a young foundling by the name of Simon Coston. Coston stumbled across not only the old man's body but also his gold. Making a quick and surreptitious exit, he fled with it to Flanders. Thirty years later and now a respectably married man, Coston returned to the area of his childhood and bought himself an estate. His early trick, the first step on his ladder to material success, remained a secret until after his death.

Sadly, this local legend is almost entirely untrue. Simon Coston did live on an estate here, but all we know about him was that he was rich, had six children and died in 1665. He left his name behind however, both in Costons Lane and in the little tributary of the Brent that we cross in Perivale Park, Costons Brook.

Perivale was the smallest of the parishes which later went to make up the Borough of Ealing, and the park is on the site of one of its largest hayfields. It was a regular venue for local sports and recreation, and, perhaps to preserve this use, Ealing Town Council purchased it from the ubiquitous Ecclesiastical Commissioners when it came up for building development in 1934. But it soon lost the charm of a hayfield, and for many years remained a dull flat expanse of playing field and golf course grass, populated by strutting crows. More recently efforts have been made to improve its ecological value, with some areas planted and others left uncut so that today thrushes and green woodpeckers can be seen feeding in the grass, while great spotted woodpeckers call from the older oak trees.

Western Avenue was built in 1921 to replace the previous London to Oxford highway. Its original redeeming feature – cycle tracks – has long since been removed. This major road was one of three arterial roads built in the area in the space of only ten years. Suddenly the small parish of Greenford, surrounded by pasture and arable land to the south, and woodland to the north, was one large industrial development site. Among the firms establishing themselves was Hoover, with a factory building so famous that it merits mention in an Elvis Costello song, and the now disappeared Rockware Glassworks, which gave its name to Rockware Avenue. After the factories came the houses, but with no distinct pattern, centre or community. As a columnist in the *Middlesex County Times* wrote on 30 November 1935, 'I am now able to announce that we have discovered Greenford. Even the Greenford folk don't know where it is. Everybody one meets is a stranger'.

Getting home:

Greenford Station: Underground (Central line), Network Rail (Paddington)
Buses: (from the station or Rockware Avenue) 92, 105, 305, E6

9. Four Hills and a Harp

FROM GREENFORD TO BRENT CROSS

The suburbs of north west London are Middlesex become Metroland. In 1862 the Metropolitan railway company opened the first underground railway in the world, running from Paddington to Farringdon Street. It was an 'insult to common sense' said *The Times*, to suggest that people would ever accept the idea of being driven 'amid palpable darkness through the foul subsoil of London'. *The Times* was wrong, and so successful was the company that by 1884 the lines had been extended out to Harrow. It was the railway company itself which dubbed the area Metroland, as the hills and hayfields of Middlesex disappeared under the urban development which was now made possible.

From the midst of an otherwise undistinguished expanse, four hills rise up like islands above the proverbial sea of housing. Each one of them preserves, in its own way, something of the character of the lost county of Middlesex, and our route reaches all four 'summits' before bringing us back to the valley of the Brent. Horsenden Hill, with Perivale Wood below it and Horsenden Wood on its flank, retains the most rugged air of the three, and Horsenden Lane runs around it as though it were still a country backwater. Harrow-on-the-Hill stands a short distance further north, displaying the distinctive profile of twin spires arising from the clustered trees. The village itself is brooding rather than beautiful, and has become over time more an extension of the school than a village in its own right. But the climb up Harrow Hill is well worth while, and the visit poses some fascinating questions, not least among them that of how an altruistic charitable foundation could become one of the most privileged and patrician institutions in the world. Finally, we reach the Fryent Way Country Park, with Barn Hill and Gotford Hill on either side of the dividing main road. The park offers at one and the same time a fascinating episode from our national history, a living nature reserve, and a landscape more like old Middlesex than anything else we are likely to see.

Barn Hill survives because local authorities of the early twentieth century were able to purchase and preserve land for a variety of purposes. Though the earlier struggles of commoners feature again in this chapter, a common theme is that of beautiful open spaces surviving only because of the actions of district or County Councils. Their foresight permanently altered the shape of our city, provided a network of green spaces and a vital resource for all who live here. It is a particularly relevant point today, when both the powers and the budgets of

FOUR HILLS AND A HARP

GREENFORD TO SOUTH KENTON ~ 12

N
W — E
S

HARROW SCHOOL

FOOTBALL

LANE

Harrow on the Hill

HARROW SCHOOL PLAYING FIELDS

WATFORD ROAD

DUCKERS POOL

NORTH WICK PARK

NORVAL RD

To 'SOUTH KENTON to BRENT CROSS'

South Kenton

FINISH

NATHANS

ROXETH HILL

SUDBURY HILL

GREEN LA.

SOUTH VALE

Sudbury Hill Harrow

Sudbury Hill

TRANSPORT ~ Finish
⊖ ✦ SOUTH KENTON
▣ BUSES

WHITTON AVE.

HORSENDEN LA. NORTH

HORSENDEN WOODS

HORSENDEN HILL

GREENFORD ROAD

GRAND UNION CANAL

START

Greenford
⊖ ✦

BENNETTS AV.

PERIVALE WOODS

TRANSPORT ~ Start
⊖ ✦ GREENFORD
▣ BUSES

From ~ 'ALONG THE BRENT VALLEY'

©SCRIY 2012

London councils are continuously curtailed and when the likelihood of intervention to preserve an open space is increasingly unlikely. This too will have a permanent impact upon the shape of London.

This chapter covers 12 miles from Greenford to Brent Cross. It can be taken as two separate walks.

WALK 12: Greenford to South Kenton (6 miles)

WALK 13: South Kenton to Brent Cross (6 miles)

■ WALK 12: GREENFORD TO SOUTH KENTON

Getting started:

From Greenford Station (Underground (Central line), Network Rail (Paddington)) **and Buses** (92, 105, 305, E6 to Greenford Station or on Rockware Avenue):

From the station turn left under the railway bridge then right into Rockware Avenue.

Where Rockware Avenue crosses Greenford Road, cross to the diagonally opposite corner of the road junction.

From Walk 11:

Follow Greenford Road under the railway bridge and across Rockware Avenue.

Over Horsenden Hill

ROUTE:

- At the grassy area at the junction of Greenford Road and the continuation of Rockware Avenue, take the left hand path running parallel to Greenford Road.
- Follow the path beneath a subway then continue as it curves to the right and eventually reaches the canal beside a footbridge.
- Do not cross the bridge but turn right along the canal towpath, following it for approximately ¾ mile to reach a road bridge.
- Go beneath the bridge to find the steps up to it on its far side, then cross over the bridge.
- Beyond the bridge turn immediately right through the iron farm gates, and a few yards along the drive take the path on the right that drops down to run parallel to the canal.
- At the end of the children's playground, the path curves left to reach a car park. Cross the car park and continue straight ahead towards the group of buildings.

- Go up the steps to the right of the old farm house and continue through a courtyard to the path beyond.
- Follow the path gently uphill, ignoring a first crosspaths, to turn left at a T-junction. Follow this path to go through a gate, and immediately beyond it turn right, following the path as it runs parallel to fenced woodland and across a hummocky meadow.
- At the first crosspaths turn right to cross a stile into the woods.
- Follow the winding path as it works its way uphill through the woodland. It rises through several flights of wooden steps, bears left at a small glade onto a length of boardwalk and continues up more steps to the summit.
- On reaching the grassy summit plateau, continue ahead to the concrete trig point. Carry on straight ahead to reach a cross path close to a bench, and turn right on a broad grassy track to leave the plateau.
- After a few yards fork left but as the path enters the woodland, keep to the right hand path, heading downhill into Horsenden Wood.
- At the bottom of the bank join a track which comes in from your left. Turn right along it towards houses.
- After a few yards take the path on the left that runs through the wood parallel to the backs of houses.
- At the end of the wood, where a road (Whitton Drive) comes in from the right, turn left along the main tarmac path running through trees and eventually reaching the road (Horsenden Hill North).

FACILITIES: Pubs and cafés at Greenford Station. Toilets at the old farm house on Horsenden Hill. Ballot Box pub on Horsenden Lane North.

LOOKING AT WILDLIFE: There is abundant wildlife throughout this stretch of the walk. There is a pond and wetland on the Greenford Nature Reserve, with a viewing point and an artificial sand martin nest bank. Beyond this there are waterside species along the canal, relics of ancient oak woodland at Perivale and Horsenden Woods, and meadow species on the slopes of Horsenden Hill. Specialities to look out for include the spectacular early summer display of bluebells in Perivale Wood, dyers greenweed on Horsenden Hill, and the large yellow meadow ants' nests on the hillsides. Highland Cattle now graze some of the meadows between August and October to preserve both the ant hills and the scarce plants. Fifty-six bird species have been recorded breeding on and around Horsenden Hill, and the top of the hill is a good place for watching migration, especially in late autumn. The 27 species of butterfly recorded here include white-letter hairstreak, marbled white, and small populations of ringlet and brown argus. The area is also a stronghold for the stag beetle, which can most easily be seen at dusk between June and August, when it flies in search of food and of a mate. Slow worm is common here, and both smooth and great crested newts occur in the ponds.

In 1805 the canal builders completed the long main line of the Grand Junction Canal, carrying trade from the manufacturing towns of the Midlands down towards the Thames at Brentford. Even before the main canal was finished, however, work had taken place on a branch that would link this main line directly into the Paddington Basin and Central London. The 'Paddington arm', winding its way around the base of Horsenden Hill, immediately became a busy trade route, carrying not only numerous cargoes but also several passenger services, including the six-hour packet boat journey from Paddington to Uxbridge. Thomas Homer was one of the operators on this route, and it was he who dreamt up the idea of a further addition to the canal network: from Paddington it would run all the way around the city to join the Thames and the new docks at Limehouse. Thomas Homer's scheme was adopted by the Regents Canal Company, and Homer himself rose to become its Treasurer. His success was short-lived. In 1815, before the new canal was even completed, an anonymous letter revealed that he had been embezzling company funds. He fled to Belgium, then to Scotland, where he was overtaken and brought back to London. Homer's career ended with a much longer boat trip when the poor man was sentenced to seven years' transportation.

Middlesex was a traditional hay growing region, and by the 1840s a single parish such as Greenford was producing over 1,000 tons a year. Much of this was carried into London on the narrow boats, whence they returned with loads of 'mack', a fertiliser for the hay fields comprised of domestic rubbish, butcher's offal and manure. Though no longer treated with mack, the fields on the far side of the canal are today part of the Horsenden Hill Open Space, and for sound conservation reasons are being returned to traditional methods of management. Hay making has come back to this corner of Middlesex on the banks of the Paddington canal.

Another fragment of the earlier landscape survives on the towpath side of the canal, where it passes alongside the length of the Perivale Wood. This remnant of the Great Forest of Middlesex is a rich oak and hazel woodland, and one of the most important nature reserves in London. It survived the felling of the rest of the forest because of the efforts of the Selbourne Society, founded in 1885 to celebrate the work of Reverend Gilbert White, whose detailed observations of his parish in Hampshire were published in the classic *Natural History of Selbourne*. In 1920, the bicentenary of Gilbert White's birth, the Brent Valley branch of the Selbourne Society completed the purchase of these 27 acres of woodland. Just as the wood here is all that remains of the greater forest, so the Brent Branch is all that remains of a once national society. It continues to manage this site, which in 1957 was declared a Site of Special Scientific Interest. So far recorded here are 22 different types of butterfly, 350 species of wildflower and fern, 17 of mammal and 115 species of bird. The reserve is most famous for its spectacular spring display of bluebells, and it is only on special days at this time of year that it is open to the general public.

Above the canal, Horsenden Hill rises to 276 feet, the heart of a 236-acre open space preserved for conservation and wildlife by the London Borough of Ealing. The hill draws its name from the Old English horsa's dun, or horse's down. Stories linking it with the saxon chief Horsa are fanciful, but it has been in occupation for over 7,000 years, and traces of an Iron Age fort can still be seen near the summit. And that was not the last of its defensive uses, for in World War Two it also became the site of an anti-aircraft battery.

Our route up the hill follows the flank of Home Mead. The meadow is rich in wild flowers, particularly in high summer, and this is the place to look for dyers greenweed, a speciality of Horsenden. This yellow flowered and slightly shrubby member of the pea family is unusual in London, but appears to be thriving here. Both its English name and its scientific name, *genista tinctoria*, give a clue to its traditional usage. A yellow dye extracted from the plant was mixed with the blue from woad to produce a standard green dye. In Gloucestershire at one time women known as 'wood-waxers' were paid 1s 6d a hundredweight for collecting the plant from the wild, where it was torn up by the roots. Today it is too uncommon to be picked by anybody.

The ten-acre Horsenden Wood on the far flank of the hill is another remnant of the Middlesex forest. Primarily of oak and hornbeam, it lacks the rich ground flora of the Perivale Wood. The trees were managed for coppice until 1810 when a local farmer began to clear it for crops. If he had not gone nearly bankrupt in the process, this piece of woodland would have disappeared along with all the others.

Between the hills

ROUTE:

- Turn right on Horsenden Lane and follow the road (which later becomes Melville Avenue), passing a number of side roads to reach the junction with the main road (Whitton Avenue East).
- Go straight across the main road and into Rosehill Gardens. At the end of Rosehill Gardens turn left along the path that runs along the edge of Ridding Lane Open Space, crossing the end of Ridding Lane itself and continuing straight ahead, parallel to the railway line, to reach Greenford Road.
- Turn right through Sudbury, passing first Sudbury Hill Station and then Sudbury Hill and Harrow Station and, immediately beyond this second station, turn left onto South Vale.
- Where South Vale curves sharply to the left, take the public bridleway (Green Lanes) on the right, signposted to Sudbury Hill.
- Continue to the end of the bridleway, ignoring a branch to the left, and at the end cross the end of South Hill Avenue to join the main road (Sudbury Hill) and follow it uphill.
- Where Sudbury Hill begins to descend again, fork right to follow London Road into Harrow-on-the-Hill.

FACILITIES: Cafés and restaurants in Sudbury.

LOOKING AT WILDLIFE: Mature oak trees and relic hedgerows on Ridding Lane Open Space. Alongside Green Lanes there are clumps of winter heliotrope and several species of fungi.

Ancient tracks and modern railways both follow the trough of lower ground between the Horsenden and Harrow Hills. The path leading us on to Horsenden

Lane was originally one of the ancient forest trackways, while the path through Rosehill Gardens follows the tube lines which played such an important part in the later development of the area. Even here there are reminders of much earlier times in the mature but isolated oaks which have survived the felling of the forest all around them, and in the hedgerow relics of earlier field boundaries.

The tube line here is not the Metropolitan but the Piccadilly, which was extended to Sudbury Hill in 1931. The station was built by Charles Holden, in what was then regarded as a new architectural style. It is, says Pevsner, 'an outstanding example of how satisfactory, purely by careful detailing and good proportions, such unpretentious buildings can be'.

The name of Sudbury is first recorded in 1273, and refers to the burgh or dwellings to the south, presumably of the Harrow Hill. Green Lanes is, as its name suggests, another of the ancient trackways, and is shown clearly on Rocque's map of 1745. Now it is a pleasant backwater between playing fields and back gardens; then it was part of the main north-south route from Harrow to London.

The higher we get up the hill, the larger and lovelier and more prosperous the properties become. Julian House, Kennet House, and other villas surviving from before suburbanisation, display a range of styles, with bays and beam-ends, cottage extensions, mock-tudor timbering and stained-glass windows. We are walking here over what was Roxeth Common until an Act of 1803 permitted enclosure of all the wastes and commons of Harrow. This Act was opposed by an association of the smaller proprietors in the area, over a hundred of whom got together to put forward a petition. Their entreaties were ignored and the enclosure was completed in 1817, at the beginning of what was to be one of the greatest periods of hardship and depression in English agricultural history. In accordance with the Biblical precept, 'him that hath, to him shall be given', the largest shares went to the largest landowners. Lord Northwick, to whom we shall return later, added 71 acres to his existing 1,187 in the area and Harrow School took over an additional eight. While local farmers were going bankrupt, these were turned into cricket pitches for the schoolboys.

Over Harrow-on-the-Hill ...

ROUTE:

- Follow London Road onto High Street and through Harrow-on-the-Hill.
- Continue onto Peterborough Road. As it begins to descend beyond the main school buildings, look for Football Lane, signposted as a public footpath, on the right.

FACILITIES: Cafés and restaurants in Harrow-on-the-Hill, one of them ironically called the Old Etonian.

The 130-metre Harrow-on-the-Hill rises from the Harrow weald, visible for miles around as a tree-clad mound topped with two steeples and flanked by open fields. It is a welcome sight, like land appearing above the choppy waves of ridge after ridge of suburban rooftop. Its height helped save it from development and also provided a strange footnote to its history. The end of the world has always been at hand and sixteenth-century astrologers gave the official date as 1 February 1524, when a great flood would destroy all London. This led the local rector, Cuthbert Tunstall, to build himself a fortress atop the hill in which to sit out the deluge. It was demolished early in the twentieth century.

Harrow School has played its part in preserving the hill from suburban development, but at the same time its own growth has destroyed the village. Harrow School has no distinctive campus and has simply multiplied over the centuries like the amoeba, engulfing bit by bit the existing village. 'The school', says Pevsner, 'has sucked so much of the life blood out of the town that we can now only with difficulty reconstruct the pre-school or even pre-Victorian appearance of Harrow-on-the-Hill.' As the school spread, other residents and their local shops were driven away. Mostly they went down to the bottom of the hill to form the new settlement of Greenhills; and now, as Dennis Bridgeman wrote in 1978, 'Harrow-on-the Hill stands to the majority of Harrow residents as Kanchanjunga does to the natives of Darjeeling – they don't go up it.'

The story of the school begins in 1572, when local landowner John Lyon obtained a charter from Elizabeth I, 'for the perpetual education, training and instruction of boys and youths of said parish (of Harrow)'. The first buildings were completed in 1615, and the original classroom, known as the fourth form room, still exists. The charter sets a number of very strict conditions for the conduct of school life, but on the question of discipline is remarkably enlightened for its day. 'The schoolmaster', says Lyon, 'shall use no kind of correction save only with a rod moderately'.

It is clear from the charter that the school is expressly established for the education of local children, and Lyon's bequest also pays for the teaching of 30 poor children from the parish. Yet from this beginning the school was to become one of the most privileged and patrician establishments in the world. According to Don Walter in his *Book of Harrow-on-the Hill*, there are three main reasons for this amazing transformation. In his original school statutes, Lyon allows for the schoolmaster to take in as many additional paying students as could properly be taught and housed. Since he also allowed the schoolmaster to set whatever fees he liked for these students, it is not surprising that they soon became the main focus of attention. Within a short period of time the 'Foreigners' were outnumbering the 'Foundationers'.

Lyon also stipulated that from the second form on, Latin should be the language of all the students – in the playground as well as the classroom. The Roxeth farmer and the Harrow butcher may not have thought this an entirely relevant education for their sons.

The rival Eton school, meanwhile, had developed a strong High Tory and High Church allegiance, and this provided the final factor. Harrow became the natural alternative for nobility of the Whig persuasion. In 1810 local people appealed to the Court of Chancery that the Foundation was for local use and ought to be adapted to meet local needs, but they were unsuccessful, and by 1867 the *Harrow Gazette* was complaining that 'aristocratic invaders like the vandals of old have by sheer force of numbers taken possession and overrun the Hill and excluded the aborigines from their cherished and time-honoured school'.

Our route over the hill follows London Road, passing West Acre on the left. It is a daunting red brick construction, with rows and rows of symmetrical windows and a forest of chimneys. It is one of the school boarding houses, and looks like something out of *Tom Brown's Schooldays*. Local history does not seem to record what started the fire which gutted it in 1908, simply that it was rebuilt that same year. The Harrow-on-the-Hill Fire Brigade at that time was still dependent on horse power, and the keeper of the Kings Head Hotel, just a little further along the road, was paid an annual retainer to have horses ready for the Brigade's use. With this they guaranteed to be able to turn out their equipment in just 1½ minutes. It was little help in the case of West Acre.

Sadly, the Kings Head Hotel is now closed, but the building survives on one side of the tiny triangular green, where the large metal sign frame still stands, without a sign and now resembling something more like a gibbet. The Park, further along the High Street on the right, was built in 1803 as a second home for Lord Northwick, one of the main beneficiaries of the enclosures of the same year. In 1831 this too became a school boarding house. Beyond it we come to the central school buildings, which stand around the junction of Church Hill and High Street. On the left, at the beginning of Church Hill, is the building known as Old Schools. Though set about with later additions, this was the original school building, and it contains the unchanged Fourth Form Room, focus in its time for two 'school rebellions'. The fiercer of these broke out in 1805, when the post of headmaster became vacant. The serving Assistant Master, Reverend Mark Drury, was passed over by the school governors in favour of an outsider, Dr George Butler. The school favoured Drury, and the hostilities which broke out were headed by the schoolboy Byron. For perhaps the only time, the mottoes of 'Liberty' and 'Revolution' were hung in the Fourth Form Room, while outside the main road was blockaded and all communication between Harrow and London stopped for several days. According to one account, a trail of gunpowder was laid into the Head Master's House. Nonetheless it was Butler, not Drury, who got the job.

The School War Memorial and the Master's Room stand at the apex of Church Hill and High Street, while on the opposite side of High Street are two buildings which do more than any other to justify Pevsner's description of Harrow School's 'hearty and confident gloom'. Both buildings were the work of George Gilbert Scott. The school chapel was built in the 1850s when the school outgrew the use of the Parish church. Though its spire has helped create the profile of the hill, it was in fact a later addition, put up in 1865 in memory of Billy Oxenham, pupil and master at Harrow for fifty years – an odd thought since Billy himself had always opposed the idea of a steeple.

The Vaughan Library next to it was built in 1861-63 and was opened by

Prime Minister Lord Palmerston. This too was an odd choice. During the mid-century, debate raged intensely around the respective merits of classical and gothic styles of architecture. Palmerston was a passionate classicist and his dislike of Scott's work was public knowledge. He had previously and personally turned down Scott's design for the Foreign Office, a design which Scott recycled at St Pancras Station. It must have been galling for Palmerston to turn out for the Harrow opening, and after the ceremony he left abruptly, declining to stay for the customary meal.

Finally, as we follow High Street into Peterborough Road, we walk beneath the shadow of Speech Room, built by William Burges in 1874-77. Its situation here, on the slope of the hill, necessitated deep excavations and the shifting of huge amounts of rock and soil. With its small cupola and a balcony supported on a massive stone bracket, it is in a style labelled 'Venetian Gothic'. It was very unpopular when first built, and not surprisingly, for the effect is severe and foreboding. For a while its impact was softened beyond measure by a vigorous growth of ivy, a striking example of nature excelling, or at least improving, art – but that, too, has now been removed.

The Ducker Pool and Northwick Park

ROUTE:

- From Peterborough Road turn right onto Football Lane.
- At the bottom of the lane a footpath signpost points half left. There is no visible path and part of the route has been improperly blocked by a tennis court. Head first to the left hand corner of the tennis court.
- Ignore all diversion signs, unless absolutely necessary, and head out diagonally half left across the pitches, heading towards a dip where a line of young trees comes in from your right and marks the course of the brook. By following this direct route you will be helping to keep the proper footpath open.
- On joining the brook, turn left alongside it, eventually reaching a style onto the main road.
- Cross the main road and pick up the Ducker footpath immediately opposite.
- The path curves around the back of the fenced Ducker Pool and then runs alongside the hospital perimeter.
- Continue between the pitch and putt course and the hospital perimeter until crossing a brook to enter the park.
- Turn right along the tarmac path. On reaching the park entrance, stay within the park, turning left over the grass along the backs of houses.
- Before the rail embankment turn right onto Nathans Road.

To join Walk 14 or to complete this walk:

Follow the subway on the left leading to South Kenton Station.

FACILITIES: Pub at South Kenton.

LOOKING AT WILDLIFE: The playing fields are chiefly interesting for the hedgerows, and for the scattering of stags-horn oaks. These support some interesting bird species, including whitethroat, linnet, stock dove and tree sparrow. Redwing and fieldfare, and sometimes snipe and redshank, visit the fields in winter and there are occasional passage migrants. The hedgerows on the Northwick Park golf course are also interesting. Plants to look out for here include the native bluebell and stone parsley.

The 360 acres of open space which now flank the eastern slopes of Harrow-on-the-Hill were once damp meadowlands of the thick London clay, producing both a rich hay crop and an abundance of wild flowers. Here was found the beautiful and now rare snake's-head fritillary, with its strange chequer-pattern head. Part of the site, over to the east, remains the Harrow School Farm, producing enough dairy produce to supply the school and local restaurateurs, but the rest has been drained and levelled for rugby pitches and golf courses. The wild flowers are gone, but some of the hedgerows survive, with blackthorn, hawthorn, field maple, elm, ash and wild roses, often with nesting whitethroat and linnet. Above them here and there rises the tall and stark form of a stags head oak, sheltering the nests of kestrels, tawny owls and perhaps even a pair of sparrowhawks.

In wet winters the area resumes something of its original form when water floods the playing fields with broad shallow puddles. Then the fieldfare and mistle thrush, the crow and rook, are joined by the redshank and snipe that once waded and fed amongst the wet winter grasses. The small stream which drains the fields runs alongside our route towards Watford Road and here is the last place where a few of the interesting wild flowers remain – meadow sweet and water mint, yellow flag and gipsy-wort and other plants typical of the rural stream-side.

Beyond the main road this little stream fills the Ducker Pool, which was once the Harrow School bathing pool, but is now semi-derelict. Newts instead of schoolboys swim in the water, while bats roost in the mature trees round about. Until recently these trees were also home to one of London's last rookeries. As the city spread outwards London's rooks had further and further to fly to reach feeding grounds and one by one the rookeries were abandoned. Here in Harrow eleven nests remained up to 1987 but these and the trees suffered badly in the great October storm. Only three pairs returned the following year and no young were reported. Given the continued growth of the city, they are unlikely ever to return.

Skirting the walled Ducker Pool, the footpath runs through pleasant mixed woodland, planted in 1907, before reaching a pitch and putt course and then Northwick Park. An attempt by the golf course owners to divert this path was eventually overturned, but its massive pylons and netting still incongruously dominate the landscape.

'How nature has exalted Harrow-on-the-Hill,' wrote John Norden in 1593:

… from whence in the time of harvest, a man may behold the fields round about, so sweetly to address themselves to the siccle and sith, with such comfortable abundance of all kinds of graine, that the husbandman which waiteth for the fruits of his labour, cannot but clap his hands for joy, to see the vale so to laugh and sing.

But the prospect from the hill was a very different one by the beginning of the nineteenth century.

When the 1803 Act of Enclosure was put into effect in 1817, Lord Northwick, already the largest landowner in the district, increased his holding substantially. Northwick, as we have seen, had built himself a house in Harrow, but despite this he remained an absentee landlord, living at his country mansion in Worcestershire, and administering his Harrow estates through a bailiff. The effect of the enclosures compounded what was already an atrocious situation for agricultural labourers, who were paid wages below subsistence levels. Now they had also lost their common lands, through which they had supplemented their incomes by grazing their own cow or collecting fuel.

After the Napoleonic wars a depression set in, with grain prices plummeting and sheep remaining unsold in the markets. In 1828 heavy rain left the wheat mildewed and the sheep unhealthy, and destroyed seven-eighths of the Middlesex hay crop. The labourers would no longer accept their pitiable wages and began to riot. On farm after farm haystacks were set ablaze, and the declared culprit was always the same 'Captain Swing', a mysterious Robin Hood-style hero who appeared all over the country wreaking vengeance on landowners. Indeed he wrote a letter to Lord Northwick threatening retaliation for the wrong he had inflicted on labouring men.

The tenant farmers also suffered in the depression. The situation on the Northwick estate became so bad that the bailiff Quilton, not usually loathe to enforce his master's commands, was forced to ask for rent reductions for the tenants. Northwick was unbending. Either the farmers paid up or the farmers were out – and so was Quilton. In Roxeth, Farmer Samuel Greenhill hung himself in despair. In the south east the terrible conditions led to rioting throughout the area. The government's response was repression – 450 men were transported and 9 were sentenced to death. Today we have the ultimate irony – a public park named after a man who oppressed his tenants, on the land which he obtained by stealing the people's commons.

Getting home

South Kenton Station: London Overground, Underground (Bakerloo line)
Buses (from Windermere Avenue, just beyond the station): 223

■ WALK 13: SOUTH KENTON TO BRENT CROSS

Getting started

From South Kenton Station (London Overground, Underground (Bakerloo line)):
From the station platforms turn right through the subway and pass the Windermere pub to reach Windermere Avenue.

From buses (223):
Alight at South Kenton Station on Windermere Avenue
The walk starts where Windermere Grove meets Windermere Avenue.

From Walk 12:
Continue through the subway and pass the Windermere pub to meet Windermere Grove.

Uxendon Farm and the Babington Plot

ROUTE:

- Coming from the direction of the station, turn right down Windermere Avenue and take the first left onto Allonby Gardens. At the end find the footpath that leads through to the next road (Montpelier Rise).
- Turn right on Montpelier Rise then, after a few yards, left into Preston Park. Head straight across the park to reach College Road.
- Turn right on College Road and take the first left into Glendale Gardens.
- At the end of the road turn left into Longfield Avenue, then right into Grasmere Avenue, to reach Preston Road.
- Turn left up Preston Road. Cross the road at the crossing outside the station and continue ahead, taking the first right into Uxendon Crescent.
- Turn right at the end, onto The Avenue, and immediately beyond the railway bridge bear left, past the grassed area, briefly into West Hill then left again into Uxendon Hill.

FACILITIES: Cafés on Preston Road.

LOOKING AT WILDLIFE: There are interesting trees in Preston Park, including magnolias, robinias, birches and pines.

When the Wealdstone Brook, now a concrete encrusted and litter-strewn channel, was still a living and soft-banked stream, it ran through the dense Forest of Middlesex, linking the isolated settlements that had grown up along its length. Of these settlements, Coena's homestead was eventually to become Kenton, while the Priest's farm survives in the name of Preston. Slightly south of them both, the Wixans, a Saxon tribe who also gave their name to Uxbridge,

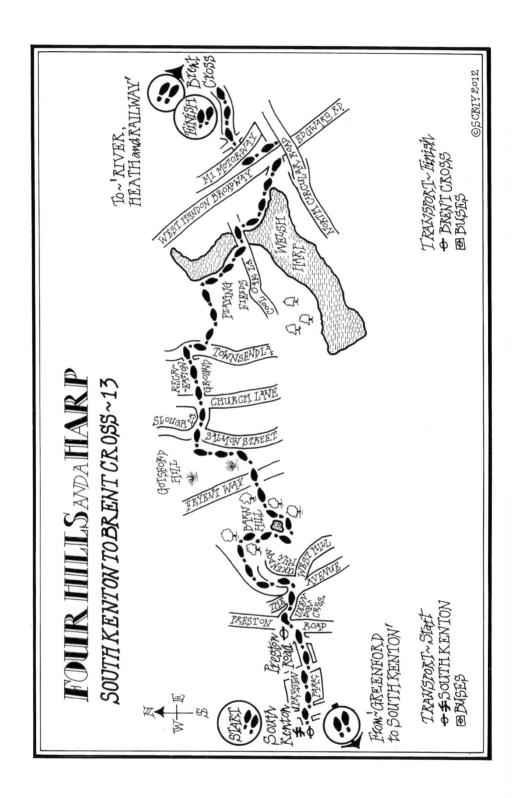

FOUR HILLS AND A HARP

SOUTH KENTON TO BRENT CROSS ~ 13

©SCRIV 2012

194

founded a settlement which survived for centuries as Uxendon Farm. It remains today only in street names; Uxendon Crescent and Uxendon Hill stand on either side of the modern channel of the Brook. Yet Uxendon in its time played a small but dramatic part in one of the most compelling stories in our national history.

By 1585, Mary Queen of Scots had been in luxurious imprisonment in England for seventeen years. As a focus for the Catholic opposition she was a potential threat to Queen Elizabeth, who for year after year was unable to decide whether to release her or to put her to death. Execution was the course favoured by Elizabeth's Chief Secretary, Lord Walsingham, who knew that for years Mary had been involved in secret and smuggled correspondence with foreign powers and enemies of the state. He decided to secure evidence against Mary, and in December 1585 she was moved to a tighter and more secure confinement at Chartley in south Derbyshire. There she began to smuggle letters in and out of the castle using beer barrels. She did not know that the system had been set up for her by Walsingham and that every word she wrote or received was first intercepted, read and copied. It was in the course of this correspondence that she became involved in the Babington plot.

Anthony Babington was a young Catholic noble, still only 25 years old when he was elected to lead the group pledged to Elizabeth's overthrow. The conspirators would assassinate the Queen and release Mary, thus signalling a general rising of the English Catholics, supported by an invasion from Spain. It was a crude, unrealistic and insubstantial plot. But Mary went along with it, and smuggled out a note on 17 July 1586, giving her support.

It was everything that Walsingham needed, and more. In August he moved against the conspirators. Babington got wind of developments and fled. He made for the thickest part of St John's Wood, where he hid himself for a time, cutting off his hair and staining his skin with walnut juice. It is at this stage that Uxendon Farm enters the story. It was in the hands of the Bellamy family, and Jerome Bellamy was a recent convert to Catholicism. Regarding it, therefore, as a safe house, Babington left the wood and headed towards Harrow. Despite the danger, Bellamy took him in. But no doubt Walsingham's spies already knew everything. They arrived at Uxendon Farm late in August, searched it, and took Babington away. With him they took

Bellamy. On 20 September, Anthony Babington was tied to a hurdle and dragged across London. At St Giles Fields he was hung, drawn and quartered in an execution so prolonged and barbarous that Elizabeth ordered that the rest of the conspirators should be merely hung. A few days later Jerome Bellamy was executed alongside them. On 4 February 1587, Mary Stuart herself went to her death at Fotheringay.

Over Barn Hill

ROUTE:

- Follow Uxendon Hill. Where it curves more sharply to the right look for an unmade track on the left which runs between houses number 79 and 81.

- Ignore the path that runs sharply right along the backs of houses and continue instead along the broad path running through woodland parallel to the tube lines.
- When the path reaches a meadow continue straight ahead across the grass until meeting a cross path originating from a footbridge on your left. Turn right along this path heading towards the woodland.
- Keep straight ahead through the woodland, ignoring cross paths and heading for the top of the hill and the pond.
- Walk to the right around the pond to reach the triangulation point. Follow the broad grassy drive to your left, down to a line of pencil-shaped Lombardy poplars, opposite the ending of a road (Barn Hill).
- Beside the poplars, take a path on the left heading into trees. Follow this to the first cross-paths and turn right to walk downhill along an attractive avenue lined with more Lombardy poplars.
- Follow this path all the way until it passes through a gap in the hedgerow to meet the main road (Fryent Way).
- Cross the road and go through the gap in the hedgerow on the opposite side. Continue straight ahead across the field, alongside another hedgerow on your right, until you reach a cross paths beside a bench and a sign post, where another hedgerow joins you from the left.
- In the meadow immediately beyond this hedgerow, take the path that runs half left, diagonally across the field, towards a single oak tree standing in a gap in the far hedgerow, where several paths can be seen to converge.
- Beyond this gap, continue on the right hand path towards another gap.
- Continue through this and turn immediately left to cross a small plank bridge. Of the paths that radiate in front of you, take the central one, running straight ahead across the open field towards another hedgerow, beyond which is the summit of the hill.
- Passing through the gap in the hedgerow on the far side of this field you may want to detour briefly to the left to reach the summit of Gotford Hill. To continue on the main route, follow the hedgerow that curves round to the right for about thirty yards, passing a bench and coming to a gap beside a tall tree.
- Go right, through the gap into a small field, and follow the path to its diametrically opposite corner. Turn left here, along the main path beside a fenced paddock, to reach an exit from the country park leading shortly onto a road.
- At the exit, cross the road in front of you and follow Slough Lane immediately opposite. At the end of Slough Lane go straight across the main road (Church Lane) and into the recreation ground.
- Go straight across the recreation ground to the exit immediately opposite and on the far side. Continue straight ahead along Elthorne Way, passing the end of Carter Close, to reach Townsend Lane at a T-junction opposite a children's playground on another open space.

FACILITIES: Pub on Church Road.

LOOKING AT WILDLIFE: The woodland of Barn Hill is rich in both birds and butterflies. Look in the glades for interesting plant species such as betony, devil's bit scabious and the adder's tongue fern. There are patches of native bluebell, whilst in the meadow areas there is an abundance of both vetch and grass species. Other plants to look out for include greater burnet, salsify, pepper saxifrage, sneezewort, stone parsley and the rare narrow-leaved bitter vetch. The ancient hedgerow relics also support a great diversity of wildlife. The Fryent Way Country Park is a good site for bats, and supports common and soprano pipistrelles, as well as the noctule bat, which is declining elsewhere in London.

It was not until the 1930s that Uxendon Farm followed its erstwhile owner into extinction. It was then that railway lines, orderly streets and neat ranks of semi-detached housing began to cover its fields and pastures. One corner of the former farmlands survives, Barn Hill, now part of the wider expanses of the Fryent Way Country Park. The 252 acres of the park include regenerating woodland, traditional meadow and no less than 15 ponds, many of them old farm ponds of the sort that have almost disappeared from our countryside. It is home to seventy species of bird, twenty-two of butterfly and five of dragonfly, and it exists because of the purchasing policies of local authorities in the 1920s and 1930s, policies that government constraints have made impossible today.

From the open meadows beside the Jubilee rail line, lush with grasses and aglow with buttercups, we climb through some of the fifty acres of woodland that flank the hill. Here there are oak, ash and hornbeam, with scrub between, and the healthy sign of young saplings regenerating the woodland. Speckled wood butterflies fly along the path edges and from the trees comes the repetitive two-note song of the chiff-chaff.

At the top of the hill we come, incongruously, upon a clearing around a pond. A few anglers sit amongst reeds and yellow flag iris, in a studied silence broken only by the raucous and incongruous calls of ring necked parakeets. That sound aside, it could be a scene from an eighteenth-century painting, and perhaps it is as deliberately composed. It was probably the work of landscape architect Humphrey Repton, who was employed here in 1792-93 by Richard Page, the owner of the large Wembley Park estate which once spread from here as far south as the present Wembley Stadium.

It is the stadium which dominates the view from the top of the hill, and which seems to fill much of the horizon. Its signature feature is the soaring 440-foot high steel arch, supporting the largest single span roof structure in the world. Set against the rather uniform bulk of the rest of the building, however, and from the top of the hill, it looks rather stringy. Lacking the interesting lines of something like the Arsenal's Emirates Stadium, it remains disturbingly reminiscent of the half open mouth of a giant clam – or perhaps of a coal bucket with a half raised handle. It is, nonetheless, the headquarters of English football, with a seating capacity of 90,000 – and since it has a retractable roof, it can claim to have the largest roof-covered seating capacity in the world. It was completed in 2007, replacing the old Wembley Stadium with its famous 'twin towers' which stood on the same site. The construction, however, was marred by controversy, being completed four years late at an eventual cost of around £1 billion and amid a welter of litigation between the various contractors and sub-contractors involved. In one court case, the cost of the photocopying alone was said to exceed £1 million. Even after its opening, the controversies continued, with the pitch being subject to constant criticism by national and club managers – with England and Chelsea captain John Terry describing it, at the 2010 cup final, as the worst pitch he'd played on all season. It was eventually re-laid a total of eleven times.

The stadium's hosting of both the men's and the women's football finals in the 2012 Olympics continues an interesting tradition, for the previous Wembley Stadium was the main site for the 1948 Olympics. This was the Games where Fanny Blankers-Koen of the Netherlands, known as 'the flying housewife', took four gold medals and became the first woman to hold the Victrix Ludorum. It was also the first Olympics after the war years and, set against a background of financial difficulties and rationing, became known as the 'austerity Olympics', with every event held in an already existing facility. Perhaps there is an important lesson there for the future.

From the top of Barn Hill we descend through open woods and meadows to reach Fryent Way, on the far side of which we climb to Gotford Hill, the final of our four 'summits'. This eastern area of the country park has large expanses of meadow, and constitutes a view almost unique in London – that of flower-rich fields surrounded by suburban housing. It represents, according to the old London Ecology Unit, 'a microcosm of the lost countryside of Middlesex'. The area was purchased by the County Council in 1938 and then leased to a local farmer, who turned it to arable use, thus destroying much of the hedgerow in the process. Since its reversion to pasture, and to traditional forms of management, the wild flowers have made a remarkable recovery, spreading inwards from the unploughed field margins. As well as the great variety of vetches – common vetch, meadow vetchling, smooth tare, hairy tare and many more – there are several unusual species, such as stone parsley, with its petrol-scented foliage, and narrow-leaved bitter cress, previously believed to be extinct in Middlesex.

The surviving hedgerows have been the subject of intensive study by Lesley Williams. His work reveals that the line of the hedges is much the same as that shown in maps of 1597, while some of them can be dated as far back as the 1300s. It is one of the happiest consequences of the purchase of land by the then Wembley and Middlesex Councils that they thereby preserved in existence corners of our countryside with 700 years of continuous history.

Welsh Harp and West Hendon

ROUTE:

- Cross the road to the playground and walk around it to the right. Head for the road you can see joining the open space on the far side of the grass.
- On reaching the road, do not leave the open space here but turn right to walk alongside the wooden garden fence.

- At the end of the fence turn left through the gap in the hedgerow, then turn right to continue alongside the hedgerow on its opposite side.
- At the end of this first small field, another line of trees and shrubs comes in from the left. On passing this, turn immediately left to follow along their far side.
- Where the hedgerow ends, turning sharp left at a field corner, continue straight ahead across the grass, with pitches on your left and scattered groups of shrubs off to your right.
- Head for a tall, pencil-thin poplar tree ahead of you, with a tarmac path crossing in front of it. The path curves away to the left with a small dead end of tarmac coming off on the right.
- Walk across the short tarmac stub, and continue through the gap between the corner of the bowling green on your left and a large oak tree on your right, into a small field.
- Head diagonally across this field to reach, in its far right hand corner, a path dipping down into woodland.
- Follow this path as it winds in and out of woodland, running roughly parallel to an arm of the lake on your left.
- Ignore turnings to right and left, keeping to the main path until it dips down on the left to reach the waterside and passes a hide. Continue on this path until it eventually reaches Cool Oak Lane beside a bridge.
- Turn left to cross the bridge (which has a pedestrian control button) and, a few yards beyond it, take the footpath on the right that runs between the boat club car park and the backs of houses, and winds round to regain the water's edge.
- Continue along the path between the backs of houses and the lake, passing a number of access paths to (locked) hides on the right.
- The path becomes less distinct and more overgrown in places, but continue along it until passing a stretch of old iron railing on your left, with dense reed beds on your right. You then come to a fork in the paths with a distinct left turn between a fragment of the fence and a wooded earthen bank.
- Turn left here then immediately right on to the path that runs along the bottom of the earthen bank.
- The path becomes less distinct but continue to follow it along the bottom of the bank until you cross a weedy area and a bank, to emerge on the road beside a bus stop.

LOOKING AT WILDLIFE: Brent Reservoir is primarily famous for its water birds. It has breeding colonies of common tern and great crested grebes, and large numbers of little grebe, gadwall, teal, shoveller, pochard and other duck, especially in winter. Little egret are increasing in number, reed warblers sing in the reed beds, and kingfisher, water rail and snipe all turn up here. Away from the waterside there are stock doves, and buzzards are becoming more regular visitors. The site is, however, also very good for butterflies, and the marbled white, first seen here in 1999, has now established a colony. Alongside the more common butterflies, the white-letter hairstreak, the common blue and the ringlet all occur. There is also a good range of wild flower species, both in the meadows, with species such as pig nut, and in the woodland areas, where wild garlic, or ransoms, can be found.

In 1835 the Brent River was dammed at its confluence with the Silk Stream in order to provide a source of water for the nearby Grand Union Canal. The result was a large artificial lake, submerging the old boundary of Hendon, Kingsbury and Willesden and known officially as the Brent Reservoir. More commonly, and more attractively, it is called the Welsh Harp. This would be an accurate allusion to the shape of the reservoir, but the name actually derives from an old alehouse which once stood on the Edgware Road. The presence of a lake at the back of the pub worked wonders for its popularity, and from 1860 to 1910 the Welsh Harp was the place to be. It was a venue for concerts, horse races, boxing matches, pigeon and duck shooting and ice skating, and it figures in at least four different Victorian music hall songs.

The Welsh Harp remains an important centre for recreation, though today the birds are watched rather than shot and it is sailors rather than skaters who take to the water. Though sailing and bird-watching are not always compatible, the reservoir has managed to accommodate them both, and the area today boasts over 150 species of bird. It hosts some of the best documented bird life in Britain. In winter the duck population includes gadwall, teal, and sometimes smew, while in summer tufted duck, pochard, Canada geese and shoveller all breed here. But most famous among them is the great crested grebe, which has here probably the largest breeding colony in the country.

In 1860 this beautiful and fascinating bird had been hunted almost to extinction. Its soft white breast plumage had become fashionable in the trimmings of clothes and hats, leading to a wholesale massacre. In reaction to this, a small group of women formed themselves in 1889 into 'The Fur, Fin and Feather Folk' and pledged 'to refrain from wearing the feathers of any birds not killed for the purpose of food'. Both the grebes and the Feather Folk rapidly increased in numbers. By the end of its first year the group had a membership of over 5,000, and in 1904 it was remodelled as the Royal Society for the Protection of Birds. In this way the plight of the great crested grebe was to lead to the establishment of what is now the largest conservation society in Great Britain.

Our route around the waterside takes us to the eastern end of the reservoir and a rich area of reed beds. In the 1960s, road building and the construction of the Brent Cross shopping centre pushed silt and slurry into the River Brent, which then built up a shallow estuary at the point where it flows into the reservoir. This was soon colonized by reeds, providing an excellent habitat for birds. It may be the best thing to have come out of Brent Cross. Small crustacea and insects feed on the silt beds and provide food for the diving ducks, while large numbers of small fish are food for the grebes. Here too, several rafts have been moored to encourage the nesting of common tern. These muddy, and sometimes flooded, fringes, are not the most conventionally beautiful, but they are the richest in bird life, with the path winding through secretive and little-used paths, beneath pollarded willows and alongside the shallow reedy water where teal feed alongside floating parking cones.

Brent Cross

ROUTE:

- On emerging onto the road, turn right, crossing the end of Priestley Way and then the river. Then take the crossing on the left which runs under the flyover.
- On the far side of the crossing, turn left alongside the motorway to take the first turning on the right (Brent Park Road).
- Follow Brent Park Road under the railway and motorway bridges and then continue beyond them into Layfield Road.
- Follow Layfield Road to its end where a yellow gate leads into the Brent Cross car park. Continue on the path across the bottom of the car park then straight ahead along a covered walkway to reach an entrance to the shopping centre.

To join walk 14:

Turn right to follow the outside perimeter of the shopping centre, leading round to the Brent Cross bus station.

Beyond the bus station, continue along the perimeter of the shopping centre. At its far end, climb a set of steps on the left and continue along the far end of the centre to reach a department store entrance.

Turn right here to follow a covered walkway across the car park to reach the road and, a few yards to the left, a zebra crossing.

Cross here and turn left to reach the entrance to an underpass.

Go through the underpass to reach and cross a road at its far end, continuing on a short stretch of path between a road and a hedge to reach a large roundabout.

Go round the roundabout to the left, crossing Prince Charles Drive and Renters Avenue to take the third turning (Shirehall Lane) that runs beneath the railway arch.

Follow Shirehall Lane to reach a gate into Hendon Park on the left.

To complete this walk:

For buses:

Turn right to follow the outside perimeter of the shopping centre, leading round to the Brent Cross bus station.

For Underground:

Turn right to follow the outside perimeter of the shopping centre, leading round to the Brent Cross bus station.

Beyond the bus station, continue along the perimeter of the shopping centre. At its far end, climb a set of steps on the left and continue along the far end of the centre to reach a department store entrance.

Turn right here to follow a covered walkway across the car park to reach the road and, a few yards to the left, a zebra crossing.

Cross here and turn left to reach the entrance to an underpass.

Go through the underpass to reach and cross a road at its far end, continuing on a short stretch of path between a road and a hedge to reach a large roundabout.

Go right around the roundabout, crossing the entrance to Brent Cross Gardens to follow the path that slopes down beside the next, ramped road (Cooper Road), then turns left beneath it.

Follow a short stretch of the River Brent to the left, to pass beneath the railway bridge and reach a footbridge over the main road.

Cross the footbridge and from the bottom of the ramp turn right along the main road, then right into Heathfield Gardens.

An alleyway on the right leads from Heathfield Gardens into the station.

NOTE: This entrance is closed on Sundays, when you will need to continue ahead to Highfield Avenue and turn right to reach the main station entrance.

FACILITIES: Toilets and cafés at Brent Cross.

From the wooded tip of a lake, busy with birds and the rustling of poplar leaves in the breeze, we emerge to finish our walk in a sort of post-industrial apocalypse. It is wasteland and warehouses, fly-tipping and flyovers, the ceaseless aggressive noise of countless cars. There in the centre of it all, suitably sandwiched between three major trunk roads, is a mega-store complex, where the air is conditioned, the light is artificial and even the sun is out of bounds. It is Brent Cross, consumerism made concrete, billed by its designers as 'the housewife's dream'.

Brent Cross should hold a horrible fascination for us, for it was the model of what was to come. Here, where consumerism meets the motor car, was one of Britain's first purpose-built 'out-of-town' shopping complexes. The idea came from America, home of the car culture, in the 1950s. The preference of English town planners had previously been for the regeneration of existing town centres, but in 1959 the Hammerson Group began looking for a development site in London. With the help of the London Borough of Barnet they identified 52 strategically placed acres of semi-dereliction, the site of old chemical works and a disused greyhound stadium. Work began in 1972, and four years and £30 million later, the Brent Cross Shopping Centre was opened to a fanfare of publicity.

It is a great two-storey bunker of a building, looking as you approach it along Layfield Road, like an old generation nuclear power station. Inside, its 610 feet of marbled malls contain 82 shops, and converge on a domed fountain court. It is an environment completely insulated from the outside world, with piped music, pumped air and a complete absence of natural light. It has thereby managed to create an almost contradictory combination of sterility and shabbiness.

The location was carefully chosen to put it within easy driving distance of a potential 1,250,000 customers and, to attract them, it was provided with 5,217 car parking spaces. This emphasis on the motor car does more than maximise the market; it also has a role in determining the sort of shoppers that come here. As a 1982 GLC report commented, 'Brent Cross caters for the car-mobile sections of the community but at the same time lies outside the choice framework of the not inconsiderable proportion who do not enjoy motorised personal mobility.' It self-selects, in other words, the more prosperous consumers.

So successful was the model that it was soon sweeping the country and, as inner city shopping streets declined, so they too became colonised by the new wave of entirely enclosed shopping malls. And with these the individual identity of the British town began to disappear. Stand inside Brent Cross or any other of these uniformly anonymous centres and you could be anywhere from Exeter to Aberdeen.

Getting home:

Brent Cross Station: Northern line.

Buses: (from Brent Cross Bus Station) 102, 112, 142, 143, 182, 186, 210, 232, 266, 324, 326, C11

10. River, Heath and Railway

FROM BRENT CROSS TO FINSBURY PARK

Hendon, Hampstead and Haringey are three very different parts of north London, linked in this chapter by riverside and railway walks. From Hendon to Hampstead much of our route is along the upper reaches of the River Brent and its tributary the Mutton Brook which drains the northern slopes of Hampstead Heath. On either side of the heath, on 'twin peaks' of gravel atop the London clay, stand Hampstead and Highgate, most famous and most fashionable of London suburbs and the focal point of this chapter. Beyond them run a string of woodlands, remnants of the once great Forest of Middlesex, leading us eventually to the Parkland Walk, a semi-rural ribbon formed from an abandoned railway and one of the most attractive sections of *The Green London Way*.

This route demonstrates the importance of green corridors in an urban area, and of the rich diversity of wildlife habitat they can provide. In this section of the walk these corridors link a number of outstanding open spaces, but also some interesting urban areas which serve as illustrations of different aspects of London's development. We begin at Brent Cross, that hideous shopping bunker that helped pave the way for similar 'out-of-town' shopping developments across the country. These developments come from a school of town planning which holds that civilisation stems from the motorcar, and which has wreaked havoc upon our cities. The broad tree-lined streets of Hampstead Garden Suburb, by contrast, seem relatively car free. Here is town planning of a very different order, a worthy experiment in social engineering which nonetheless failed in its intention to bring all social classes together. The Garden Suburb is a totally planned environment, and its undeniably beautiful homes set around a Central Square have almost the air of a museum piece, of something preserved behind glass.

Hampstead proper has a very different atmosphere, with all the vigour that comes from a largely unplanned growth. Its explosive period of development came with the opening of its first medicinal wells in the early eighteenth century. Since then it seems to repeat a strange cycle consisting of select fashionability followed by popular growth resulting in decline. This is happening in Hampstead again today. Next to it, Highgate, is its rival in both fashion and residential desirability. Beyond these, the Parkland Walk takes us through the once-select southern suburbs of Haringey – Crouch End, Stapleton Hall and Stroud Green. These developed with the growth of the City, and with the steam boom and the building boom which went hand in hand, covering the fields with the roomy villas of the Victorian professional classes.

RIVER, HEATH AND RAILWAY
BRENT CROSS TO HAMPSTEAD ~ 14

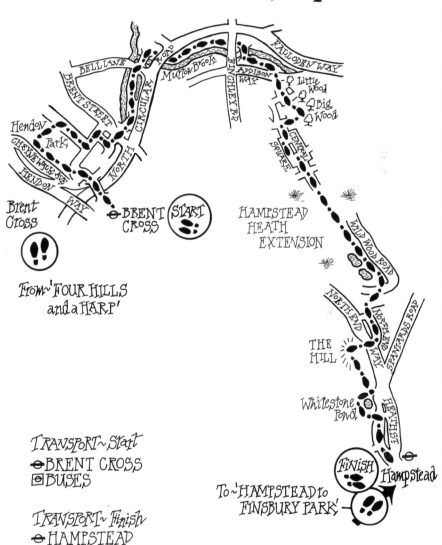

BELL LANE

BRENT STREET

BRENT CIRCULAR ROAD

MUTTON BROOK

FINCHLEY RD

ADDISON WAY

FALLODEN WAY

Little Wood

Big Wood

CENTRAL SQUARE

Hendon Park

CHEYNE WALK AVE

HENDON WAY

NORTH

Brent Cross

BRENT CROSS

START

HAMPSTEAD HEATH EXTENSION

WILD WOOD ROAD

NORTH END

NORTH END WAY

SPANIARDS ROAD

THE HILL

Whitestone Pond

HEATH ST

From~'FOUR HILLS and a HARP'

FINISH

Hampstead

To ~'HAMPSTEAD to FINSBURY PARK'

TRANSPORT ~ Start
BRENT CROSS
BUSES

TRANSPORT ~ Finish
HAMPSTEAD
BUSES

©SCRIY 2012

Urban developments and surviving green spaces – from the Brent bunker to the sandy slopes of the heath – are integral parts of the walks in this chapter. Together they represent something of the complex tapestry of London and of different models for its development. In this respect they also present us with a challenge to consider the future of London, and the kind of city in which we would like to live.

This chapter covers 12½ miles from Brent Cross to Finsbury Park. It can be taken as two shorter walks:

WALK 14: Brent Cross to Hampstead (5½ miles)

WALK 15: Hampstead to Finsbury Park (7 miles)

■ WALK 14: BRENT CROSS to HAMPSTEAD

Getting started

From Brent Cross Station: (Northern line)

From the top of the escalators take the exit to the left signposted to Heathfield Gardens. Turn left on reaching Heathfield Gardens to reach the North Circular Road.

NOTE: This exit is closed on Sundays. Leave by main exit and turn left and left again to reach Heathfield Gardens.

At the bottom of Heathfield Gardens, take the footbridge over main road. On the far side, turn left from the bottom of the ramp, along the North Circular Road and heading away from the complex of flyovers.

After a few yards turn left into Shirehall Park and follow it as it curves left to reach a T-junction.

Cross the road in front of you (Shirehall Lane) to find the entrance to Hendon Park on your left.

From Brent Cross Bus Station (102, 112, 142, 143, 182, 186, 210, 232, 266, 324, 326, C11):

With your back to the shopping centre, turn left to follow its perimeter. On reaching the corner of the building, climb a set of steps on the left and continue along the far end of the centre to reach a department store entrance.

Turn right here to follow a covered walkway across the car park to reach the road and, a few yards to the left, a zebra crossing.

Cross here and turn left to reach the entrance to an underpass.

Go through the underpass to reach and cross a road at its far end, continuing on a short stretch of path between a road and a hedge to reach a large roundabout.

Go round the roundabout to the left, crossing Prince Charles Drive and

Renters Avenue to take the third turning (Shirehall Lane) that runs beneath the railway arch.

Follow Shirehall Lane to reach a gate into Hendon Park on the right.

From Walk 13:

From Shirehall Lane take the gate into Hendon Park on the left.

From Brent Cross to Brent Street

ROUTE:

- On entering the park follow the path straight ahead and parallel to the railway line, continuing straight ahead at the first crosspaths which comes in from a footbridge on your left.
- Take the next path on your right between the Millennium Wood and a children's playground and follow it through to the far side of the park.
- Leave the park through the alleyway beside the memorial fountain and turn right onto the road (Park View Gardens).
- Turn left at the bottom of Park View Gardens into Shirehall Lane.
- Take the third turning on the right (Shirehall Park) opposite the red brick cottages, then turn left onto the link road leading to the main road (Brent Street).

FACILITIES: Toilets and café in Hendon Park.

LOOKING AT WILDLIFE: The Millennium Wood in Hendon Park will be an increasingly valuable habitat as it matures. The park also contains one of the largest *Acer palmatum*, a Japanese maple, in London and is a good place to see pipistrelle bats.

From Brent Cross eastwards the area we are walking across would once have been part of Renters Farm. It existed here from at least the fourteenth century and is still celebrated in the name of Renters Avenue, just to the east of the park. Hendon Park, on a site known as Steps Fields, remained part of the farm until turned into a park by what was then Hendon Council in 1903. It still carries something of its original Edwardian atmosphere, a certain staid respectability that would have been considerably disturbed by the happenings of Sunday 21 July 1940. In what must have been the park's biggest ever event, the local Ministry of Information Committee organised a 'Rout the Rumour Rally', intended to build morale and reinforce the message that gossip and rumour prejudiced the national war effort. The organisers had hoped to get Duff Cooper as the principal speaker, Minister for Information and previously the leading critic of Neville Chamberlain's appeasement policy. Instead they got Harold Nicolson, Duff's junior at the Ministry. Nicholson was sacked by Churchill later the same year and is perhaps better known now as a member of the Bloomsbury set, and husband of the writer and garden designer Vita Sackville-

West. His contribution to the event was no doubt leavened by the impressive array of stars which were also on the bill – Renée Houston, Will Fyffe, Flotsam and Jetsam, Jack Hawkins and Jack Warner, later to be better known as Dixon of Dock Green; all of whom had given their time free of charge. They were not, however, greeted with universal approbation. Since it had been held on a Sunday the local clergy sent letters of complaint that the rally had profaned the Sabbath with 'entertainment'. The accusation was vigorously refuted by the Committee Chairman in letters to the local press. 'Yes,' he agreed 'we are going to have flags and marching and stirring music by the Band of the Grenadier Guards, and why not?'

The park has a few other reminders of those war-time years. There is a Holocaust Memorial Garden and the current café is housed in an old bomb shelter which, in deference to the area's large Jewish population, declares itself 'the only kosher park café in the country'. One of the most recent additions to the park is the Children's Millennium Wood, planted by local schoolchildren. Its mix of tree species, including wild cherries, oaks and beeches, under planted with primroses and other spring flowers, will provide an increasingly valuable habitat as they mature and fully justify the designation of the park, and its adjacent railway embankments, as a local nature reserve.

The parish of Hendon which covered this area was one of the largest in Middlesex, and just on its fringes stood the hamlet of Brent Street. Among the genteel villas for which it was renowned was Shire Hall, giving its name to Shirehall Lane. The Hall was demolished in 1920, but at the end of the street there still exists a small but attractive group of eighteenth and early nineteenth century houses, two of them with their old Sun Insurance fire marks. The white-painted Penfold House, previously known as Albert Cottage, was built in 1713, and is said to have been a lodge for drovers. Behind it the attractive Load of Hay pub survived until 2004, when permission was somehow granted for its demolition. Gone with it is Salisbury Place, site of the original pen fold where the animals would have been kept overnight, leaving Penfold House as the only surviving reminder of the days when Brent Street was a drove road, and cattle and sheep were herded down here towards the end of their long journey into the London markets.

Brent Park and Mutton Brook

ROUTE:

- Cross the main road and turn right. A few yards down find the entrance to a path on the left, just before the River Brent bridge and leading down to the riverside close to two pepper pot turrets beside a weir.
- Follow the path between houses and the river, cross a small footbridge and turn left to continue parallel to the riverside.
- On reaching Decoy Pond, turn left and follows the path as it runs between the pond and the river.
- Leave the park through the gate beyond the pond and turn left on the

road (Bell Lane). Just before the bridge, take the path on the right which continues along the riverside.

- Cross the little footbridge and then take the right fork which follows a tributary stream (Mutton Brook). The path soon runs through a subway under the North Circular Road.
- Continue on the path alongside Mutton Brook to reach Finchley Road.
- Cross Finchley Road and continue alongside the brook. Follow the path that runs across the footbridge and continue, now following the opposite bank of the brook.
- Ignore the exit onto a road on the right and continue alongside the brook for as far as you can. The path eventually turns between houses to emerge onto Addison Way.

LOOKING AT WILDLIFE: Woodland flora in Brent Park includes cow parsley, red campion, wild garlic and Jack-by-the-hedge. There are some interesting trees, including coast redwood, Monterey cyprus and blue atlas cedar. Green woodpeckers occur on the meadows around Mutton Brook, and there are occasional patches of marsh marigold.

From Brent Street we follow linear parks along the upper reaches of the River Brent and its tributary, the Mutton Brook. Brent Park is a long, wooded dell: shady, rather seedy and with an air of down-at-heel gentility. Close to the park entrance a little, litter-strewn weir spans the river, and standing on either side are circular and sadly dilapidated pepper-pot towers. They are remnants of the old villas of Brent Street, and of the villa gardens which have given their atmosphere to the park today. But there are older associations too. The Manor of Hendon belonged originally to the Abbots of Westminster, who some time between 1319 and 1326 built themselves a Manor House here. To serve their kitchens they dammed the Brent to form fish ponds, and in later years these were turned into a duck decoy, which survives as the quiet, tree-lined pond half-way along the length of Brent Park.

Duck decoys were an elaborate method of trapping wildfowl for food. Artificial funnel-shaped channels were dug from an existing water course, gradually narrowing into 'pipes' covered with osier and reed and ending in a net. The wild birds would be attracted by tame duck, or driven by specially trained little dogs known as pipers; once inside the narrowing channel the birds would fly onwards until trapped. The construction of an effective decoy was a considerable skill, and only 200 of them are known from the whole of the British Isles, the majority in the Norfolk Broads. The existence of Decoy Pond in Brent Park is therefore something of an archaeological rarity, though, sadly, its brown and over-shaded waters support few duck today.

At the end of Brent Park, the attractively balustraded Mutton Bridge carries Bell Lane over the river, and a short distance beyond here the Brent splits into two. The larger stream is the Dollis Brook which flows down from Hertfordshire, while our path follows the Mutton Brook, which drains from the northern slopes of Hampstead Heath. Brookside Walk occupies 25 acres of what used to be Fox Hole Wood and was acquired by Barnet Council in 1930. Though most of the woodland is gone, it could still be an attractive waterside walk through undulating meadows fringed with hedgerows, were it not for two features. One is the constant drone of traffic from the nearby North Circular Road, which has recently been further widened; the other is the state of the water.

In March 1990 local residents, who had long been alarmed at the state of the Mutton Brook, paid for an independent analysis of its water. The resulting report concluded that it was highly polluted and constituted a health hazard, particularly to children. Barnet Council, who were presented with the report, claimed to have spent over £50,000 looking for the source of the problem without being able to isolate its cause. The 'solution' instead was to line the walk with warning signs, thus giving the Brookside Walk the distinction of a being a green strip running between a highly polluting road and a highly polluted river. Though now fading, the red signs, reminding you to stay out of the water, remain there today.

Hampstead Garden Suburb

ROUTE:

- Turn left along Addison Way, passing Erskine Hill, to find the path on the right next to number 76 and leading into Little Wood.
- Keep straight ahead on the main path through the wood to join Denman Drive North on the far side. Follow the Drive ahead to reach the path into Big Wood.
- Follow the main path ahead through Big Wood, and at the first tarmac crosspaths turn right. Follow the path gently uphill and at the top of the slope bear right at the T-junction to exit onto Temple Fortune Hill.
- Continue along Temple Fortune Hill and turn left at the first crossroads into Erskine Hill, following it to reach the Free Church at one end of Central Square.
- Follow the road round to the right and take the steps onto the pedestrian route across the square and under the ornamental lantern. At the end of the square follow the road to the left around the far side of St Jude's church.
- Take the first right into Heathgate. Follow it across Mead Way to reach the steps leading onto the Hampstead Heath Extension.

LOOKING AT WILDLIFE: Big and Little Woods are relic oak woodland. They support snowdrops in early spring followed by patches of wild bluebell. Plants worth looking for include the wild service tree, guelder rose, yellow archangel and lily-of-the-valley. There is a variety of woodland birds, including woodpecker species, nuthatch, tawny owl, tits and warblers.

On Christmas Eve 1884, the Whitechapel settlement of Toynbee Hall first opened its doors. Founded by Canon Samuel Barnett, its aim was to bring relief to the East End poor, and in particular to offer them the advantages of a liberal education. Early 'settlers' here included William Beveridge, R.H. Tawney and Clement Attlee, and the work of the Hall was to give rise to both the Worker's Educational Association and the Whitechapel Art Gallery. The Youth Hostels Association had its first office here, and it was here too that the idea for the Hampstead Garden Suburb was born.

It was part of settlement thinking that the working classes would benefit by mixing with those of a more privileged background who, through education and example, would attempt to share their advantages. For Henrietta Barnett, the Canon's wife, this did not go far enough. Her dream was to create a place where people of all walks of life could live alongside each other, in quality housing and in pleasant surrounds. When the Eton College estate put onto the market its property near Golders Green, she decided that her moment had come.

Wyldes Farm had been owned by the college since 1449. It was situated to the north of Hampstead, and the expected extension of the Northern line meant that it would soon be within easy commuting distance of Central London. Henrietta bought the estate in 1905, and two years later work began on the Hampstead Garden Suburb. The planners for the scheme were Raymond Unwin and Barry Parker, who had been involved in the first Garden City experiment at Letchworth. The guiding principles were laid down by Mrs Barnett and the committee she had established. There were directives on the density of housing, the materials to be used, the width of the streets and the planting of trees. The roads were to be on a variety of lines – neither all straight nor all winding – and to respect the existing contours. The focal point, to be placed at the highest part of the suburb, was the Central Square. In keeping with Mrs Barnett's vision and values, it was to contain two churches and an Educational Institute, to be designed by Edward Lutyens.

The most intriguing question concerning the Garden Suburb is how something intended as a social leveller can have become so exclusively the territory of the upper middle classes. To walk through the tree-lined avenues today is to feel like a trespasser within a private and very inward-looking domain. 'Sanctuary!', wrote Philip Davies in the *Evening Standard* in February 1991, 'that's why I live here'; and such is the contrast between the cherry-tree charm of these streets and the nearby noisy fringes of the North Circular that it does seem something like an isolated island of calm. Much of the explanation for the changing social composition of the suburb lies in its original design. The plans included housing for a variety of income brackets, but the different groups were segregated from the start. Smaller flats for artisans were concentrated in the north of the suburb, middle-class homes were located in the west, and the choicest, richest villas were sited in the south, overlooking the heath. Soon, rising rents and house prices were to force out the manual workers altogether. Moreover the plans for the suburb had deliberately relegated all shops, pubs, cafés and cinemas to the unreformed fringes, and public transport was almost non-existent. For all but the wealthy and the totally mobile, it was an impossible place to live. In the history of English town planning, Hampstead Garden Suburb was of enormous importance, its influence spreading across the country and out to Holland, Germany and America. But as a social experiment it has failed.

Our route across the suburb takes us through two remnants of the ancient Middlesex oak forest which the planners wisely incorporated into their designs. Completely surrounded by housing, the two woods are quiet, private places. Little Wood has an oak canopy underset with hornbeam and field maple. The 18-acre Big Wood has a few hornbeams but a greater variety of other shrubs and trees, including hawthorn, hazel, crab apple and the wild service tree. In both woods, chiff-chaff, willow warbler and blackcap can be heard in early summer when the wild bluebells bloom across the woodland floor. The London Borough of Barnet has reintroduced hazel coppicing to Big Wood and this practice should eventually increase both plant and bird diversity.

From Big Wood, Erskine Hill leads us into Lutyen's Central Square. Here the Free Church and the Anglican Church stand at opposite ends of the neat lawns. With their dark red brick and their huge roofs swooping down almost to the ground, they seem to be turned in on themselves, brooding perhaps about the quietness of the square. The Free Church is domed and has a rather Byzantine feel, while the Anglican Church – named St Jude's after Canon Barnett's parish in Whitechapel – has a fine steeple arising from an open tower and is a landmark for many miles around.

From the south side of the square, Heathgate leads us along an attractive paved piazza onto the Heath. The solid line of houses along the edge of the Hampstead Heath Extension is known, revealingly, as the Great Wall. It stands like a defensive barrier to protect the suburb against the rest of the world with its confusing diversity and its perplexing and perpetual change.

North Hampstead and The Hill

ROUTE:

- From the end of Heathgate walk across the grass, ahead and to the left, to reach the bridge over a little brook by a gap in the line of trees.
- Walk ahead across the next long field, keeping the curving hedgerow on your left and heading towards the broad gap you can see in the line of trees at the far end of the field.
- Go through the gap and bear left on the path that curves behind the changing rooms and then curves right, running gently uphill beside a line of large oaks.
- Continue on this main track, passing ponds to your left.
- Towards the end of the ponds, and beside a stone fountain, the main path curves right. Leave it here to continue straight ahead on a grassier path that eventually crosses a small bank to reach the road.
- Cross the road to find a path on the opposite side between two posts. Follow this for just a few yards to reach a crosspaths close to a stone culvert. Turn right here.
- The small, trodden path runs through woods, parallel to the road, then continues as an unmade road running along the backs of houses.
- The road curves left to join North End Avenue. Continue along the

Avenue as it goes over a crossroad. A short distance beyond this you reach a metal barrier, beyond which the road reverts to track. Continue on this uphill through an avenue of trees.

- At the top of the slope the track curves round to the right to reach the road opposite a large red-brick mansion.
- Turn right on the road and almost immediately left again onto Inverforth Close.
- Follow the broad path signposted to the Hill Garden to reach the entrance gate on the left.
- Turn right inside the garden and keep to the right on a path that loops around the bottom of the fenced park until reaching the bottom of a long and imposing flight of steps.
- Climb the steps as far as you can, to reach the top of the loggia, with fine views across London.
- Follow the pillared arcade until it reaches a T-junction at the back of the Leverhulme Mansion and turn right to continue along it.
- At the end of the pergola descend the spiral staircase and at the bottom take the door on your right along a short stretch of path leading to a gate back into the open woodland.
- Turn right out of the gate and after a few yards reach a junction with a broad track. Turn left along it until you reach a fork with a flight of steps leading uphill on your left.
- Follow the steps to reach the summit beside a flagstaff. Walk ahead across the summit keeping Whitestone Pond on your immediate left.
- As you follow round the top of the pond, ignore the first turning on your right and take the second (Hampstead Grove), through a gravelled pedestrian area with benches, signposted to Fenton House.
- Follow Hampstead Grove straight ahead, ignoring side turnings and passing Fenton House. Carry on down Holly Hill to emerge onto Heath Street.

To join Walk 15 or to complete this walk:

Cross Heath Street to reach Hampstead Underground Station.

FACILITIES: Pubs and cafés in Hampstead town centre.

LOOKING AT WILDLIFE: The grassland of the Heath Extension supports sorrel and stitchwort, with foxgloves along the hedgerows. The ponds have a particularly rich flora, with common reed and bulrush and a variety of other flowering plants, including ragged robin. Sandy Heath and West Heath are good places to look for redpoll and siskin on birch trees in winter. Beside the path leading up to the Hill Garden there is a large patch of ling, one of the restored areas of heather on the heath. Rabbits can be seen grazing in The Hill at dusk and the pond here is a good place to see newts.

In the hundred years since the first 220 acres of Hampstead Heath passed into public ownership, this beautiful urban open space has expanded to occupy

800 acres. This is the result of a positive policy of acquisition, which is almost impossible under local authority financing today. It has added to the Heath not just extent, but also diversity, and has given it some of its most characterful corners: The Hill, Pitt's Garden, Wildwood and many more. Among these later additions is the prosaically named Hampstead Heath Extension, the gift of Henrietta Barnett and part of her original Wyldes Farm purchase. It forms a protruding tongue of land running up through the neat housing of Golders Green to end at the Great Wall, and bears the unmistakeable imprint of an earlier agricultural landscape. The open expanses of the fields are made more interesting by hedgerow boundaries, remnants of woodland and by the string of little ponds along the brook. Growing here are white water lilies, blue forget-me-nots, yellow spearworts, and the greater willow-herb, with its blossom a soft pink and cream. Here too is the lovely ragged robin, with its red and tattered-looking flowers, a typical plant of damp meadows but unusual in London.

From the Extension we cross a corner of Sandy Heath and follow a pleasant tree-lined avenue before curving through a corner of heath known as Pitts Garden. It was to a house on this site that William Pitt the Elder moved in 1767 after a serious mental collapse which forced him to resign as Prime Minister. Here at Hampstead he locked himself in a room, communicating with no-one and receiving his meals through a hatch in the wall. In 1778, having emerged from his retirement, Pitt was in the House of Lords, delivering an impassioned harangue against the war with America. At the end of the speech he fainted in his seat and was carried back home to die. The large house was demolished after bomb damage in World War Two and its garden was added to the Heath in 1954.

From Pitt's Garden we cross North End Road to reach The Hill Garden, one of the most beautiful and most secluded parks in London. In 1776 the actress Mrs Lessingham caused a riot by building herself Heath Lodge on the common land of Hampstead. In 1906 this house was bought by the soap magnate William Lever, who already owned the adjacent property known as The Hill. Lever demolished Heath Lodge and linked the two gardens with a system of elevated walkways, stone terraces and gazebos. The two gardens were separated only by a public right of way which Lever spanned with an ornamental arch. He wanted to go even further and eliminate the footpath, but in this he was strongly opposed by the Hampstead Heath Protection Society and the matter was still in dispute when he died in 1925.

The site is now divided again. The old house and its immediate grounds belong to the Manor House Hospital, while, on the other side of the footpath, The Hill Garden was purchased for the public in 1963. Here a well-managed and shrub-lined formal garden forms a striking contrast with the wildness of the West Heath beyond. Rabbit-grazed lawns slope steeply upwards to a formal pond and, above it, the raised walkways and pergolas give a wonderful view out over London. The terraces deteriorated badly over the years but have been beautifully restored by the Corporation of London. They form one of the most romantic settings along *The Green London Way*.

Across West Heath we reach the summit of Hampstead Heath, marked by the flagstaff beside Whitestone Pond. The Victorians adapted an earlier dew pond here and fitted it with ramps, so that a thirsty horse which had pulled a heavy carriage up the hill could walk straight in at one end and out at the other. At 443 feet above sea level this is the highest point in Central London. ''Tis so near Heaven', said Daniel Defoe in his 1724 *Tour through the Whole Island of Great Britain*, 'that I dare not say it can be a proper Situation for any but a race of mountaineers, whose lungs had been used to a rarify'd air'. The adjacent housing development, 'The Summit', has attempted to capitalise on this setting but instead has created something that looks like a modern Alcatraz, complete with perimeter wall and guard towers.

The covered reservoir at the top end of Hampstead Grove was built in 1856 and is now the site of the Hampstead Scientific Society's Observatory. This was previously the Hampstead village green, and the parliamentary elections for Middlesex were held here until they moved to Brentford in 1700 (see Chapter 8). It was in this same year that Admiral's House was built, just a short distance off Hampstead Grove to the right. In 1791 it was occupied by a naval officer called Fountain North, who amended the flat roof to look like the quarter-deck of a ship. He is said to have moved several cannons here and to have fired them off on celebratory occasions. For walkers of *The Green London Way* it is of interest as the one-time home of the architect George Gilbert Scott, whose work has featured repeatedly on our route around London.

Further down Hampstead Grove is Fenton House, built in 1693 and therefore probably the oldest surviving house in Hampstead. It was built by Joshua Gee, a silk trader, but gets its name from Philip Fenton, a Riga merchant who purchased it in 1793. Fenton played a leading part in 1829 in the opposition to the Lord of the Manor's plans to build on the Heath. In 1952 the house was bequeathed to the National Trust, and today it houses a collection of early keyboard musical instruments. From Fenton House, Hampstead Grove descends into Holly Hill and makes its narrow way down past the Holly Bush Inn and a row of artisan's cottages, to reach the very heart of the village. At the cross-roads of Hampstead High Street and Heath Street stands the Hampstead Underground Station and the end of our walk. In Hampstead even the tube station has to be remarkable: at 220 feet it has the deepest tunnel in the whole of London.

Getting home

Hampstead Station: Northern Line

Buses (from Heath Street or Hampstead High Street) 46, 268, 603:

▨ WALK 15: HAMPSTEAD TO FINSBURY PARK

Getting started

From Hampstead Underground Station:

Turn left from the station exit.

From Buses: (46, 268, 603)

Alight at Hampstead Underground Station

From the station exit at the junction of Heath Street and Hampstead High Street, head down Hampstead High Street.

From Walk 14:

On crossing Heath Street continue ahead down Hampstead High Street, passing the Underground Station.

Hampstead Village

ROUTE:

- From the Underground Station, head down Hampstead High Street. After a short distance turn into Flask Walk on the left.
- Follow Flask Walk as it broadens into a road and then continue ahead into Well Walk. Follow Well Walk straight ahead to its end opposite the open heath.

FACILITIES: Cafés, restaurants and pubs throughout Hampstead. There is a café at Burgh House (closed Monday and Tuesday), which is also the home of the Hampstead Museum (Wednesday, Thursday, Friday and Sunday).

More words have been written about Hampstead than about any other part of London. It is probably also true that more words have been written in Hampstead than in any other part of London. According to a local joke, Hampstead book shops put on special promotions for books 'Not written by local author'. Hampstead is extremely beautiful, atrociously rich and highly fashionable, but this has not always been the case. Until the end of the seventeenth century it was a small village surrounded by wild heathland and inhabited by pig farmers and washerwomen. Then came the development of its chalybeate wells, and the fortunes of the village became, largely, the fortunes of its medicinal spa.

In 1698 the Honourable Susannah Noel, acting on behalf of her 13 year old son, the Earl of Gainsborough, Lord of the Manor of Hampstead, granted six acres of land on the edge of the heath for the benefit of the poor. The land contained springs which were high in iron content and had an unpleasant, bitter taste that qualified them as a cure for almost anything. A charitable Wells Trust was established to exploit the springs and began to bottle the water for sale to the apothecaries of London. Then, in 1701, the Trust appointed John Duffield

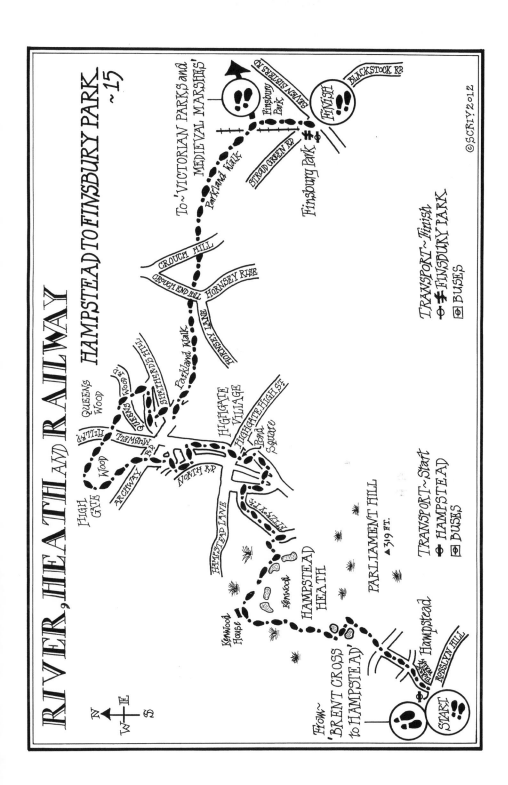

RIVER, HEATH AND RAILWAY

HAMPSTEAD TO FINSBURY PARK ~15

To ~'VICTORIAN PARKS and MEDIEVAL MARSHES'

Parkland Walk

SEVEN SISTERS RD

Finsbury Park

BLACKSTOCK RD

FINISH

STROUD GREEN RD

Finsbury Park

CROUCH HILL

CROUCH END HILL

HORNSEY RISE

HORNSEY LANE

Parkland Walk

QUEENS WOOD

SHEPHERD'S HILL

QUEENS WOOD RD.

MUSWELL RD.

HIGHGATE VILLAGE

HIGHGATE HIGH ST.

HIGH GATE WOOD

ARCHWAY

NORTH RD.

Pond Square

HAMPSTEAD LANE

THE BISHOPS

Kenwood House

Kenwood

Kenwood

HAMPSTEAD HEATH

PARLIAMENT HILL
▲319 FT.

From ~
'BRENT CROSS to HAMPSTEAD'

Hampstead

ROSSLYN HILL

START

TRANSPORT ~ Finish
⊖ ≢ FINSBURY PARK
⊞ BUSES

TRANSPORT ~ Start
⊖ HAMPSTEAD
⊞ BUSES

N
W—E
S

©SCRIY 2012

to manage the site. Duffield was an entrepreneur with ambitious intentions, and he built the famous 'Long Room', where visitors could take the waters and then recuperate to music, dancing, cards or other entertainments. The growth of Hampstead as a fashionable spa had begun. By 1720 it had risen, wrote Daniel Defoe, 'from a Country Village to a City'.

This growth had unforeseen results. With an increasing range of attractions, including a race-course, bowling greens, tea houses and alehouses, and with its closeness to London, Hampstead began to attract more and more day trippers. It was no longer select and, according to some, it had become downright disreputable. The rich and fashionable ceased to arrive, the wells were closed and John Duffield went bankrupt. In the 1730s the spa was relaunched, with a brand new Long Room, but history repeated itself and after a period of success this too fell into disfavour and decline. Perhaps this whole cycle is repeating itself. Having developed as the fashionable home of the liberal literati, Hampstead is again becoming a victim of its own popularity. The Sunday streets are packed with trippers, boutiques have burgeoned, and restaurants have opened shoulder to shoulder. The smell of cooking permeates the whole of Hampstead, and its South End has become more like Southend.

The history of the Hampstead wells can be retraced in the course of our walk. Flask Walk draws its name from the days when water was bottled at the Flask Tavern and sold for 3d a bottle. The Walk today opens up into a very pleasant lane with a narrow green and with houses in a wide variety of styles. At the end of the Walk are the 1888 buildings of the Wells and Campden Baths and Wash Houses, one of the charitable products of the Wells Trust, now converted into a private house. At the junction with Well Walk, Burgh House can be seen off to the left, a tidy Queen Anne building erected in 1703 and occupied at one time by the physician to the wells. The house was purchased by the Hampstead Borough Council in 1946 and opened as a community centre, but the fabric was so badly neglected that by 1963 Camden Council was considering demolishing it. Saved by a public campaign, the building is now administered by its own Trust and run as a museum and exhibition centre.

Wells House, the Council estate in front of Burgh House, occupies the site of the second Long Room, which was demolished after bomb damage in World War Two. The flats were designed to harmonise with Burgh House and for this they won a RIBA Bronze Medal. The first Long Room stood on the site of Gainsborough Gardens just off Well Walk, and it is here that we come across the original chalybeate spring with its memorial to Susannah Noel:

> Drink traveller and with strength renewed
> Let a kind thought be given
> To her who has thy thirst subdued
> Then render thanks to heaven.

The green copper stains beneath this reveal the location of a later sign which, until very recently, stated baldly 'Unfit for drinking'.

Across the heath

ROUTE:

- From Well Walk cross the main road and follow the broad tarmac path straight ahead alongside the block of flats (The Pryors).
- The path, a pleasant avenue of limes, dips down to cross a brook and then rises to meet a crosspaths beside a commemorative stone to the 1987 storm.
- Turn left and follow the path which crosses The Viaduct, high above the lake. About twenty yards beyond The Viaduct take the path on the right leading to Bird Bridge.
- Cross the bridge and carry on ahead and uphill to reach a T junction at the top of the slope. Turn left and follow the path as it curves round right to reach the gate into Ken Wood.
- Turn left inside the wood and follow the path which soon runs between fences.
- As the path begins to descend it reaches a fork. Take the left hand path running downhill beside another memorial plaque.
- Ignore the first turning on the left to reach a T-junction at the bottom of the hill. Turn left here to cross the bridge over the tip of the lake.
- Beyond the bridge, walk half right across the grass aiming for the left end of Kenwood House and the flight of steps you can see on the embankment below it.
- At the top of the steps turn right along the broad path that runs in front of the house.
- NOTE: It is worth a detour to go through the door at the end of the main range and down the steps to visit the Bath House.
- Continue along the main path as it curves round to the right. Ignore the first gate on your left to exit through the Millfield Gate, closer to the lake.
- Turn right along the tarmac path leading downhill past the spring and alongside Stock Pond.
- At the end of Stock Pond there is a junction of paths beside a metal barrier. Turn left to climb the grassy and often muddy bank.
- Walk straight ahead across the field until you reach a path going off to the right and up a few steps, just before the allotments. Follow this through a gate onto the lane.

FACILITIES: Cafés and toilets in the Coach House block at Kenwood House.

LOOKING AT WILDLIFE: Hampstead Heath is a very good venue for bird watching and supports a large number of species. On our route water rail can sometimes be seen in winter from The Viaduct and it is worth taking bird food to put out on the balustrades of Bird Bridge, where tits and nuthatches can be watched at close quarters. Stock dove, kestrel and woodpeckers breed in Kenwood, which is now the closest site to central London for jackdaws. The oaks in the wood also support a good population of the purple hairstreak butterfly, which can most easily be seen in the early evening. There is a varied flora on the heath but it has to be looked for in areas less trodden by visitors. Plants include sorrel, lady's bedstraw and even the occasional broad-leaved helleborine. Heather is now also being restored to selected parts of the Heath. There is a rich collection of fungi in the autumn, including fly agaric around birch trees. The Heath is an excellent site for bats and supports common and soprano pipistrelles, noctule, and Natterer's bats, as well as Daubenton's bat, which can often be seen above Stock Pond on summer evenings.

If **Hampstead is the most written about** place in London, then the heath has the most documented flora. It seems impossible to be a plant in Hampstead and not be listed. As long ago as the sixteenth century London's apothecaries were coming here to gather herbs for their medicines, among them John Gerard, who walked here regularly from his home in Holborn. Gerard's famous *Herbal* was published in 1597 and is still available today.

Early in the next century, botanist Thomas Johnson explored the heath, recording all the plants he found and producing the first known local Flora in Britain. Floras of Hampstead have been compiled from that day to this, and reading them illustrates some of the depredations the heath has suffered: progressive loss of habitats to building, digging, in-filling, sand-pits, brick works, and the sheer pressure of tens of thousands of visitors a year. Though the heath has grown to encompass a much larger area, it has lost its original character as an acid heathland, rich in heathers. The last remnants of this once extensive plant were thought to have been destroyed by the tipping of blitz rubble after World War Two, until a single surviving plant was discovered in the 1980s. The Hampstead Heath Conservation Team, which for some while protected the plant in a 'secret' location, has now had considerable success in creating new areas of heather heathland.

Of all the threats to the heath over the past few hundred years none has been as persistent or as damaging as the wilful obstinacy of a single person, Sir Thomas Maryon Wilson, who became Lord of the Manor of Hampstead in 1821. His estates also included the Manor of Charlton and in this connection we have already met the family in Chapter 3. In 1826 Parliament approved a new turnpike, the Finchley Road, which crossed the heath and thereby increased its value for development, and in 1829 Maryon Wilson introduced a Bill to Parliament which would give him the power to lease off plots to builders. With this, a forty year battle had begun.

Maryon Wilson's Bill was greeted by a storm of public opposition and was withdrawn before its second reading. But Wilson was a stubborn and uncompromising man, made furious by any attempt to restrict what he saw as his absolute right of ownership. Over the following years he was to introduce no less than fifteen different parliamentary bills in pursuit of his aim to profit from the heath. His last Bill was narrowly defeated in 1866, but nevertheless he began to build, provocatively choosing the summit of the heath as the site of his estate office. He was challenged by Samuel Gurney Hoare, a wealthy local Quaker who had led much of the public struggle against him. Assisted by Octavia Hill and the Commons Preservation Society, Hoare began legal proceedings against Wilson, who, embittered and embattled to the last, died before the case could come to court.

The new Lord of the Manor was his brother Sir John Maryon Wilson, who took a very different attitude and sold his rights to the Heath to the Metropolitan Board of Works. The purchase was ratified by Parliament, and in 1871 Hampstead Heath became a public open space. Since then a succession of purchases has added Parliament Hill, Kenwood, Golders Hill Park and numerous other smaller parcels of land. Today the whole complex is run by the City of London, which successfully bid for control of the Heath on the abolition of the Greater London Council.

From Well Walk our route follows Boundary Path and an atmospheric avenue of lime trees planted by the London County Council in 1905. After crossing a brook, the source in fact of the River Fleet, we come to an inscribed stone commemorating the replanting of the avenue after the great storm of October 1987. It bears the name of the London Residuary Body, the body set up to dispose of the assets of the Greater London Council after its abolition by Margaret Thatcher. It seems ironic that such a purely temporary body should now have its own permanent marker. We turn left from here onto a path which marks another remnant, one of Thomas Maryon Wilson's many attempts at building. In 1844 he planned the grand estate of East Park and began work on a road which would run through the middle of the development. A swampy valley was dammed to form an ornamental pond and the road taken across the top of this on a viaduct. But Wilson forgot to allow for the softness of the underlying soils and the foundations of the viaduct repeatedly collapsed. By the time the viaduct was finished he had run out of funds to continue with the scheme and the isolated bridge became known as Wilson's Folly.

Kenwood, with its house, gardens and woodlands, constitutes its own separate sanctuary within the confines of the Heath. The mature woodlands, unfortunately under planted with rhododendrons, provide a sense of seclusion hard to come by on other parts of the busy heath. The broad paths wind beneath a canopy of oak, sweet chestnut and holly and are maze-like in their complexity. Here and there are tree stumps used as regular bird feeding stations, where tits, and even nuthatches, have become so tame that they will take food from the hand. And from the woods the formal lawns slope up from ornamental ponds towards a perfectly sited mansion.

Kenwood House was built in 1616 but was extensively remodelled in 1724 under the ownership of William Murray, first Earl of Mansfield. Mansfield was a judge, a liberal man for his day, who had reversed the conviction of John Wilkes for seditious libel (see Chapter 8). He played a major role in the reform of English commercial law and developed the modern concept of copyright. He was also a staunch opponent of slavery, and alongside his own daughter brought up the illegitimate daughter of his nephew, Captain John Lindsay, and 'Belle', an enslaved African woman. The painter Zoffany, whose work we also encountered in St Paul's, Brentford, painted a striking portrait of Dido Mansfield Belle and her cousin Elizabeth which is still owned by the family and hangs at Scone Palace in Scotland. It was Mansfield who had the Kenwood grounds landscaped and then called in the famous Robert Adam to remodel the house.

Adam created a cool, white and perfectly proportioned mansion – perhaps too cool a building. The adjacent servant's quarters and coach house block, with their more interesting shapes and purple-brown brick, make it seem almost bland.

In 1914 the sixth Earl of Mansfield attempted to sell off the Kenwood estate for building. The Kenwood Preservation Appeal raised money to purchase as much of the land as it could, but by 1925 had run out of funds. The LCC intervened to buy the rest of the grounds and that same year businessman Edward Cecil Guinness, first Earl of Iveagh, bought the house. He had it refurbished to contain his collection of paintings, including works by Rembrandt, Vermeer, Gainsborough, Van Dyck and Turner. When he died, only two years later, the house with all its contents was bequeathed to the public.

Highgate Village

ROUTE:

- Follow the lane until it joins Fitzroy Park at the end of a row of cottages. Turn left here to climb up the lane until it emerges onto The Grove.
- Turn right here until level with the end of the fenced reservoir on the opposite side of the road. Cross here and go down the short stretch of road and cross a second road to reach the Flask public house on the right.
- Walk round the front of the pub and then to the left along South Grove, taking the raised pavement on the opposite side in front of The Old Hall.
- Reaching the gravel covered Pond Square on your left, cross back over the road and walk across the square to where you see a small road leading out of it on the far side, up towards the mock Tudor Gatehouse pub.
- Just before this road, find a small flight of steps between houses on the right. Climb these and turn right to reach a zebra crossing.
- Cross the main road and enter Southwood Lane ahead and to your left.
- Follow Southwood Lane then take the first turning on the left (Castle Yard).
- At the end of Castle Yard turn right along North Road. Pass Park Walk and Hillcrest to turn right into Park House Passage.
- Exit the passage to continue straight ahead on The Park, then take the second turning on the left (Bishops Road)
- On reaching the main road (Archway Road) turn left briefly to reach the controlled crossing. Cross the road then walk back right to reach the gate into Highgate Wood.

FACILITIES: Toilets and cafés in Pond Square. Cafés and pubs in Highgate.

From Fitzroy Park on the edge of Cohen's Fields we are in Highgate. Highgate and Hampstead constitute the twin peaks of North London, with Highgate just

16 feet, and a couple of degrees on the social scale, lower than Hampstead. Fitzroy Park, on the southerly slopes of the Hampstead-Highgate ridge, was built on the site of Sherricks Hole Farm. Today it has a number of millionaire mansions, and if this is not apparent in the architecture it can certainly be seen in the security devices which surround them. Highfields Grove in particular resembles not so much a home as an open prison, its red-brick blocks protected by perimeter fence and electric gates.

From Fitzroy Park we follow The Grove, regarded as Highgate's most elegant street. The oldest houses, dating from the 1680s, are towards the end and in one of them (number 3) the poet Samuel Taylor Coleridge lived for nine years. He is just one of a posse of poets we will be meeting in Highgate. Both Hampstead and Highgate have a Flask public house, and both are associated with spas. The mellow brick front and the cobbled courtyard of the Highgate version date from 1767, whilst its rambling interior is composed of numerous nooks and crannies, and enticing snugs and alcoves. Beyond here, down South Grove, we reach the centre of this urban village, clustered, as it is, around Pond Square.

The area was once part of the Hornsey estate of the Bishops of London, and it was around one of the gates into Bishop's Park that the first little community developed. The gate, later to become a toll gate on the main road north, gave its name to both Highgate and to the Gatehouse pub. The village was made up largely of estate workers, but there was also a hermit, living where the chapel of Highgate School now stands, who was responsible for maintaining Highgate Hill – the main road running up from Islington. The digging of gravel for this purpose caused the formation of the ponds, which gave Pond Square its name, though, becoming stagnant, they were filled in again in 1864 – leading to the anomaly today of a Pond Square that is both waterless and triangular. Neither are these the least of its peculiarities, for Pond Square also has the rare distinction of being haunted by a headless chicken.

Sir Francis Bacon was a writer, philosopher and politician, who rose eventually to the position of Attorney General under James I. By 1621, however, his political career had ended in disgrace when he pleaded guilty, for reasons that have never been properly explained, to 23 separate counts of corruption. He retired to concentrate on one of his other key areas of interest – science, an area in which he is generally credited with having invented the empirical method. It was in pursuit of one of his experiments that he was to meet his fate. Journeying to Highgate one snowy day with his friend Dr Winterbourne, the King's physician, he is said to have been seized by the idea of using the snow to preserve meat – the idea, in other words, of refrigeration. Resolving to experiment with this as soon as possible, he got down from his coach, purchased a chicken from a house at the bottom of Highgate Hill and proceeded to stuff it with snow with his bare hands. As a result of this he seems to have been taken ill remarkably quickly, and was taken to the house of his friend the Earl of Arundel on South Grove, the site now occupied by Old Hall and St Michael's Church. Here his illness turned to pneumonia, compounded apparently by him being put into a bed with damp sheets, and here, on 9 April 1626, he died. Strangely, it is not Sir Francis but the chicken that haunts the vicinity, with 'frequent reports' of a half-plucked fowl appearing from nowhere and running round Pond Square in frenzied circles – a sort of phantom progenitor of the refrigerator.

After leaving the Square – and crossing Highgate High Street at the top of Highgate Hill – we pass the buildings of Highgate School, in unmistakeable public school style. The school was founded in 1565 as a foundation for the poor of the parish, as well as a fee-paying school, but its main buildings date from the nineteenth century. Wrought-iron gates lead onto a drive, at the end of which stairs rise on either side of an entrance topped with a wall-mounted sundial. The adjacent chapel is in a warm red brick pierced by a rose window. Above rises a slender spire and a clock tower topped with a pyramidal roof. T.S. Eliot was a master here for a while and Gerard Manley Hopkins was a pupil, as was John Betjeman, who recalls being tormented for his foreign-sounding name. Betjeman also lived locally – on Highgate's West Hill – and refers to Highgate no less than eight times in his poetry including a reference to:

> Hot silence where the older mansions hide
> On Highgate Hill's thick elm-encrusted side
> And Pancras, Hornsey, Islington divide.

Yet another poet is commemorated on North Road, which we reach by walking down Castle Yard – rather disappointingly named after a pub which once stood here and not after a castle. Off to our left is a lovely terrace where, behind long leafy front gardens, cottages in soft, worn brick or in wooden Essex weatherboarding, jostle with homes in a grander Palladian style. Here, in Byron Cottage, A.E Houseman lived and wrote his most famous work, *A Shropshire Lad*. Close by, at number 92, a plaque records a stay that Dickens made in 1832, though Dickens seems to have stayed at an inordinate number of houses in north London. Further along North Road our route passes Park Walk, which marks the southern boundary of what was, from 1885 to 1940, the House of Mercy. This was a High Church reformatory for prostitutes where, within the confines of a high surrounding wall, the women practised needlework or embroidered trousseaus for the bountiful – and no doubt literary – ladies of Highgate.

The Highgate woodlands

ROUTE:

- Enter Highgate Wood through the Archway Gate and take the first turning on the left, passing the toilet block and the children's playground.
- Keep to the left to continue along a bench-lined path around the perimeter of the cricket pitch.
- At the far corner of the cricket field, close to the practice nets, the path re-enters the woodland, sloping gently upwards and parallel to the wooden perimeter fence. Ignore the first fork to the right, continuing ahead and crossing a small valley to reach Bridge Gate.
- Turn right here, back into the woodland, to reach a crossing of paths

beside a granite water fountain. Continue straight ahead on an earthen path.

- Just beyond the keepers cottage, as you approach another exit gate, bear right and shortly after, left, following paths that run parallel to the woodland perimeter and the road beyond, until you drop down to the next exit gate (New Gate).
- Cross the main road (Muswell Hill Road) to enter Queen's Wood immediately opposite.
- Take the path almost immediately right, opposite the café and signposted to Wood Vale.
- The path runs downhill, passing a pond, to reach a crossing at the bottom. Turn left here following the sign to Frog Pond.
- Continue past the pond until you reach an exit at the far side of the woods. Ignore the exit to turn right, then keep to the left hand path running uphill and parallel to the backs of houses.
- Ignore the first exit onto the road on your left and continue a few more yards to reach the road, with more woodland on the opposite side. Cross here and join the tarmac path opposite.
- The path dips down then rises steeply, passing between houses to reach a road (Priory Gardens).

FACILITIES: Cafés in both Highgate Wood and Queens Wood. Toilets in Highgate Wood. Information point and display in Highgate Wood.

LOOKING AT WILDLIFE: Both Highgate and Queens Wood have a good selection of bird species, including nuthatch, treecreeper, blackcap and greater and lesser spotted woodpeckers – and there has been suspected breeding of hobbies in Highgate Wood in recent years. Highgate Wood has special bird feeding stations as well as a 'Big Brother' camera point next to the toilet block. The edges of the meadow area are also a good place to look for bats towards dusk. Special areas have been created in Highgate Wood to re-establish the native bluebell, but the better display of ground flora is to be found in Queens Wood. Here, there is a good collection of ferns, including lady fern and hard fern, both unusual in inner London, and large swathes of wood anemone in spring. Also to be found are smaller patches of wood sorrel, the woodland buttercup goldilocks and the parasitic common cow-wheat. Several new ponds have been created in the wood, including the conversion of an old abandoned paddling pool, in order to attract amphibians.

Despite the vicissitudes of its history, and the impacts of the changing regimes to which it has been subject, Highgate remains a deeply atmospheric woodland. It has undergone nearly 2,000 years of more or less continuous management, and walking its heavily shaded paths you can still feel the resonance of its past – as part of the once Great Forest of Middlesex, as a fragment of the Bishop of London's hunting estate, as Brew House Wood, as Gravel Pit Wood and, most recently, as the Corporation of London's Highgate Wood. Across most of these centuries it was maintained in the same traditional way as 'coppice with standards', that is, with periodically coppiced hornbeams growing among the taller, straighter oaks.

The hornbeam would have been cut on cycles varying from seven to twenty years, and its primary use was for fuel, both for firewood and for charcoal. In 1962 a Roman pottery site was discovered in the wood and later excavations revealed as many as ten kilns, alongside working platforms and pits for the puddling and storage of clay. The 'Highgate ware' produced here was distinctive, characterised by its very dark colour and its decoration with lines of raised dots. Part of the original attraction of the site would have been the presence of the hornbeam, supplying the charcoal for the kilns, and evidence has been found that between AD50 and 170, the site was vacated and re-occupied at periods of approximately twenty years – coinciding, that is, with the normal cycle of coppicing.

This highly sustainable approach to woodland management was to survive into the nineteenth century. It was then, however, that the woodlands began to deteriorate. In 1813 gravel pits were dug in the woods to provide the surfacing for the new Archway Road, and from 1842 coppicing came to a virtual halt when the site was leased by the Earl of Mansfield – who we previously met as the owner of Kenwood House – and who seems to have treated the site with a form of benign neglect. Worse was to follow, however, when the Earl's lease ended in 1884. It reverted to the Church Commissioners, who promptly announced their intention of developing 1,000 acres across the area for housing. The fight against this proposal was led by a local politician, Henry Reader Williams, and seems to have taken place largely in the pages of *The Times*. The upshot, however, was that the wood was purchased by the Corporation of London in 1886, whilst down in Crouch End the central clock tower was built in honour of Williams' efforts.

Purchases by the Corporation of London have preserved for us surprisingly large tracts of public land. They include Epping Forest, Burnham Beeches, and several of the Surrey heathlands, as well as the much more recent acquisition of Hampstead Heath. Much of this expenditure was directed at providing open spaces for the rapidly growing and densely packed population of inner London – showing an awareness of the importance of open space to human wellbeing that is sometimes sadly lacking today. But the idea of providing recreational sites for Londoners was soon to be seen in an approach to management which filled the woods with a superfluity of tarmac paths and benches as well as children's playgrounds and a nine-acre cricket pitch. This 'parkification' of a wild woodland site also included a massive 'tidying up' and the clearance of all scrub and undergrowth. The process was described ironically by local resident and poet A.E. Houseman:

> So thickly was it overgrown … that if you stood in the centre, you could not see the linen of the inhabitants of Archway Road hanging in their back gardens. Nor could you see the advertisement for Jiggins ale on the public house at the south corner of the wood. Therefore the … Corporation … cut down the intervening brushwood and now when we stand in the centre we can divide our attention between Jiggins ale and our neighbours' washing. Scarlet flannel petticoats are much worn in Archway Road and if anyone

desires to feast his eyes on these very bright and picturesque objects, so seldom seen in the streets, let him repair to the centre of the wood.

The revelation of scarlet petticoats was only one of the unintended consequences of this approach to management. The greater numbers of people now able to access all parts of the site led to heavy trampling, whilst, simultaneously, the cessation of coppicing was contributing to a denser canopy. The woodland understorey completely disappeared and the wood took on a barren appearance, contrasting sharply with the more exuberant Queen's Wood across the road. Natural regeneration also ceased, leading to a population of uniformly ageing trees, whilst many of the wood's 1,400 oaks went into serious decline, with compaction of soil around the roots considered the most likely cause. By the end of the twentieth century, however, a quiet revolution was taking place in ideas of open space management, with Highgate Wood playing its part in the adoption of more sustainable and ecological approaches. Coppicing of specified areas was resumed as early as 1977, whilst other parts of the wood were fenced off on a rotational basis to encourage regeneration. Efforts were also being made to re-establish traditional woodland plants, including areas of native bluebell, and from the eight surviving mature Wild Service trees – the typical indicators of ancient woodland- new cuttings were being planted.

The manifest benefits of these 'new' approaches can be seen on our route around the wood. From the ornamental Archway gate, with its decoration of woodland animals, we follow the perimeter of the cricket pitch. Though the pitch was a more recent imposition, the clearing itself, as indicated by old maps, has been here for several hundred years. In colonies around its edges several species of mining bee can be found, each with its associated species of parasitic cuckoo bee, whilst in the middle of the field dead patches in the grass in dry weather reveal the anchorage points of a barrage balloon sited here in World War Two. Re-entering the woodland again, we cross a small valley and a seasonal stream bed – one of the feeders of the River Brent – before reaching one of the most interesting features of the wood. Here is the easiest place to make out the rather mysterious earthwork that runs through the site, originally two parallel earthen banks, although only one is now clearly visible. Since the trees have grown up on it, it must predate the woodland and must at the very least, therefore, predate the Roman occupation of the site. Early maps also show that it once extended far beyond the current Highgate woodlands, though what it was for, no-one is certain.

Crossing areas where attempts are being made to re-establish the native bluebell, we reach the granite drinking fountain, the 'gift of a few friends' in 1888. It is inscribed with lines by Coleridge:

> Drink pilgrim here
> Here rest
> And if thy heart be innocent
> Here too shalt thou refresh thy spirit
> Listening to some gentle sound
> Of passing gale
> Or hum of murmuring bees.

The spirit today is more likely to be responding to the gentle sound of buggy-pushing Highgate nannies, and the murmur of distant traffic.

Passing the 1868 mock Tudor keeper's lodge – the work of architect Maurice Jones, who also created the old Billingsgate and Leadenhall markets – we finally drop down to the New Gate on Muswell Hill Road. Immediately opposite is the gate into Queens Wood and the two entrances facing each other across the highway tell their own story of the comparative wealth – and perhaps of gravitas – of the City of London and an ordinary London borough. Whilst the Corporation's wood has an attractive cast iron gateway and a solid and shapely wooden signboard, the Haringey owned woodland opposite has an insignificant gate overshadowed by a brash and ugly metal signboard. Nor is this the only difference between the two adjacent woodlands. Cost constraints have also had their benefits, and Queens Wood has escaped much of the obsessive over-management that was inflicted on Highgate. It has, as a consequence, always been the ecologically richer of the two and, perhaps, the more attractive. It ranks, in fact, as one of the finest areas of woodland in central London, best seen in spring when the white blooms of wood sorrel overhang the edges of the little brooks and the dark and rather sinister leaves of the cuckoo pint begin to unfurl. Then too, great drifts of lesser celandine and wood anemone come into flower under catkin-draped oak trees where the squirrels have built their dreys. Since 2008 there has been a concerted attempt to reintroduce coppicing to the wood – with the exciting result that in the most heavily shaded areas the total number of plant species has increased from 39 to 188, in just three years.

When the Church Commissioners sold Highgate Wood to the Corporation of London, they hung on to this adjacent portion of woodland, intending to sell it as a series of plots to the builders then developing the North London suburbs. A spirited public campaign managed to raise a quarter of the asking price and the local authorities contributed the rest. The wood was opened to the public in 1898, and in commemoration of Queen Victoria's Jubilee the name Queen's Wood replaced its earlier name of Church Bottom Wood. In the same year it was described by the great Victorian naturalist W.H. Hudson as 'the wildest and most picturesque spot in North London'. Demonstrating his own concern about the dangers of 'over-municipalisation' he went on to express his earnest hope that:

> the landscape gardener will not be called in to prepare this place for the reception of the public – the improver on nature whose conventional mind is only concerned with a fine show of fashionable blooms, whose highest standard is the pretty, cloying artificiality of Kew Gardens.

The Parkland Walk

ROUTE:

- Turn right along Priory Gardens until you reach a path on the left hand side between numbers 63 and 65.
- Follow the path to reach Shepherd's Hill and turn right here to reach the major road junction immediately ahead.

- Turn left at the junction and after a few yards turn left again into Holmesdale Road. Follow the road to reach the entrance gate to the Parkland Walk on your left.
- Turn right and follow the Parkland Walk for approximately 2¼ miles.
- At the end of the Parkland Walk turn left onto a footbridge that crosses the railway into Finsbury Park.

To join Walk 16:

Continue on the path running straight ahead.

To complete this walk:

Turn right at the end of the bridge, following the path between the tennis courts and the railway.

Fork right at the bottom of the slope to exit onto Stroud Green Road, opposite Finsbury Park Station.

FACILITIES: Cafés and bar on Archway Road. Café in Finsbury Park. Cafés and pubs near Finsbury Park Station.

LOOKING AT WILDLIFE: The Parkland Walk encompasses a variety of habitats, including grassland, woodland, cuttings and embankments, stands of bracken and copses of birch. Despite the heavy use, some woodland flowers hang on – or have been replanted – including primroses, wood anemones, dogs mercury and increasing amounts of ransoms. This is a good place to go bat watching, especially towards the western end, where the disused tunnel serves as a roost and a hibernaculum. Seven species have been seen here. There is also a good variety of birds, including warblers, green woodpeckers and the occasional tawny owl, with redpoll and goldcrests in winter.

The final part of our route provides over two miles of uninterrupted off-road walking. The Parkland Walk, a linear stretch of open space and the 'longest nature reserve in London', was originally a railway, part of the route from Finsbury Park to Edgware. Opened in 1867 it carried extensive passenger traffic and had its own spur line to serve Alexandra Palace, the 'People's Palace', just to the north. However, demand for the line declined: the last passenger train ran in 1954 and the last freight train ten years later. For a time the line found a use as part of the underground network, and was used for the transfer of Northern Line rolling stock from Drayton Park to Highgate, but by 1970 it had become completely redundant. The tracks were removed and this long strip of land, fast being recolonised by shrub and tree, passed into the ownership of Haringey Council.

The Council's first thought was to build houses along as many stretches of the route as possible. Public opposition to this eventually led to an enquiry, and the protesters won the day. The Council was later to embrace the conservation cause with enthusiasm, establishing the Parkland Walk and even a short-lived Field Studies Centre in one of the old station houses. But this was not the last threat to this lovely urban walkway. Early in 1990, over a thousand people gathered at Haringey Town Hall to support the 'Save the Parkland Walk Campaign' in its struggle against Department of Transport proposals to run a six lane arterial road along the walk, with the additional demolition of at least three hundred flanking houses. These proposals, too, were defeated and for the time being the Parkland Walk remains a much loved and much used treasure for this part of London.

Though it is over forty years since the last trains ran here, some remnants of its railway origins survive, and you can still make out the location of the stations. The platforms of the one-time Crouch Hill Station form an interesting feature of the walk and, beside the bridge over Stapleton Hall Road, stands the handsome white station house of what was the Stapleton Hall Station. Here, too, you have the slightly odd sensation of seeing three layers of transport passing one above the other.

Today the Parkland Walk is a popular for cycling, walking and dog walking, though this popularity has brought its own problems. The route is a good example of the degradation that is inflicted on a site by an excess of defecating dogs, whose manure adds nitrogen and phosphates to the soil, encouraging the course growth of nettle, bramble, dock and couch grass at the expense of a wider range of more specialist species. Thus a number of plants have been lost to the site over recent years, including the attractive and delicate hare's-foot clover. But a number of specialities hang on, with the wild clematis or traveller's joy being of particular interest. The clematis is a plant of lighter and preferably limey soils, and is therefore not common on the heavy London clay. But here the free-draining railway embankments have provided it with a suitable habitat, and it scrambles over shrubs along the route, its white 'beards' looking in winter like a coating of hoar frost against the dark bark of the trees. Elsewhere the chive-like leaves of the wild onion are common along the grassy path edges. You will look in vain, however, for their wine-red flowers, as this plant generally reproduces without them, producing bundles of fertile bulbils at the top of the stem which drop off and grow independently. Its alternative name of crow garlic indicates its 'worthlessness' compared with the cultivated onion, garlic or leek – it is a garlic only fit for crows.

More unusual are the tree mallows which have been growing on one stretch of the Parkland Walk since at least 2004. Found near the Blythwood Road gate, just beyond the Crouch Hill cutting, this is a tall, woody mallow the size of a garden hollyhock. It is almost exclusively a plant of the seaside, growing at the base of cliffs or on rough ground beside beaches, and is strangely out of place here in inner London. Perhaps the best ecological site of all, however, is the small south facing meadow on the steep embankment slopes beyond the Crouch Hill Bridge, just before you reach the Blythwood gate. This area of acid grassland, an unusual feature for the area, supports heathland plants such as mouse-ear hawkweed and sheep's sorrel as well as colonies of small skipper butterflies. Here too there are nests of several species of mining bee, which dig burrows for themselves in bare patches in the soft sandy soil – and, unfortunately for them, for their parasites as well. Both cuckoo bees and robber flies search out these burrows and lay their own eggs in them, their grubs eventually devouring the living larvae of the bees. Some of the species found here are rare enough to feature in the national *Red Data Book*, but the most notable species is an ant. *Formica funicularia* is a large, dark brown mining ant that was recently rediscovered on the site – but it has an interesting precedent. Horace St John Kelly Donisthorpe, who died in 1951, was regarded as the foremost myrmecologist (or student of ants) of his day. It is not surprising that an element of eccentricity went alongside such a degree of specialism and he was known both for an over-enthusiastic naming of species that he claimed were 'new' and for his lavish parties – so lavish, in fact, that they dissipated his family fortune. His most important work was *British Ants: Their Life Histories and Classification*, published in 1915. It contains a description of a colony of the same ant in this location, found by a Mr. E.A. Butler. It is entirely possible, therefore, that the funicularia ants living here today are the direct descendants of a colony that has survived for over 100 years.

Getting home

Finsbury Park Station: Network Rail (Kings Cross), Underground (Victoria and Piccadilly lines)

Buses: (from Station Place/Seven Sisters Road) 4, 19, 29, 106, 153, 236, 253, 254, 259; (from Bus Station) 210, W3, W7

11. Victorian Parks and Medieval Marshes

FROM FINSBURY PARK TO VICTORIA PARK

Everything meets at Finsbury Park. The boundaries of Hackney, Haringey and Islington coagulate somewhere around that choked traffic interchange where trunk roads, bus routes, tube and rail lines all come together. Only the meeting of many cultures, of Asian stores, North African cafés, Chinese supermarkets and West Indian restaurants, gives these fume-laden streets their colour. Cultures meet here, too, in another way, making this a transition along the long circular route of the Green London Way: it is at Finsbury Park that the leafier outer suburbs meet Inner London; at Finsbury Park we quit Hampstead for Hackney, and with Hackney we enter the East End.

While Hampstead and Highgate, Muswell Hill and Alexandra Palace occupy the healthier heights along the clay ridge that curves around North London, the poorer communities were concentrated down in the damp and marshy valley of the Lea, and further east along the banks of the estuarine Thames. This section of our route takes us from one corner of Hackney to the other, from Stoke Newington down to Cambridge Heath and the edges of Globe Town and Bow, across the borough which has long been amongst the very poorest in Great Britain. Yet this is a route which is rich in both variety of feature and in open spaces; it takes in bird-rich reservoirs, an 'abandoned' cemetery, the main street of one of London's villages, four nature reserves, a mediaeval marsh and a canal. And it owes its wealth of open spaces to three other features – the Victorian parks, the New River and the Lea.

The River Lea provides the backbone of these two walks. It was the Lea too which shaped the marshes, though it was the struggles of local people which preserved them. The Walthamstow Marsh is today one of the most significant and unusual natural history sites in London. It has a strange and brooding beauty, a beauty which is unconventional, particularly in winter, with its flat, brown and wind-blown reed-lands set in a landscape of pylons, railways, tower blocks and industry. This is typical of much of *The Green London Way*; it should never be approached as an urban substitute for the countryside, but with openness towards its own strange and singular character.

It is the Lea valley that also provides the route for the New River. It is neither new nor a river but a seventeenth-century waterway designed to deliver a supply of fresh drinking water to London. It is also a remarkable feat of early

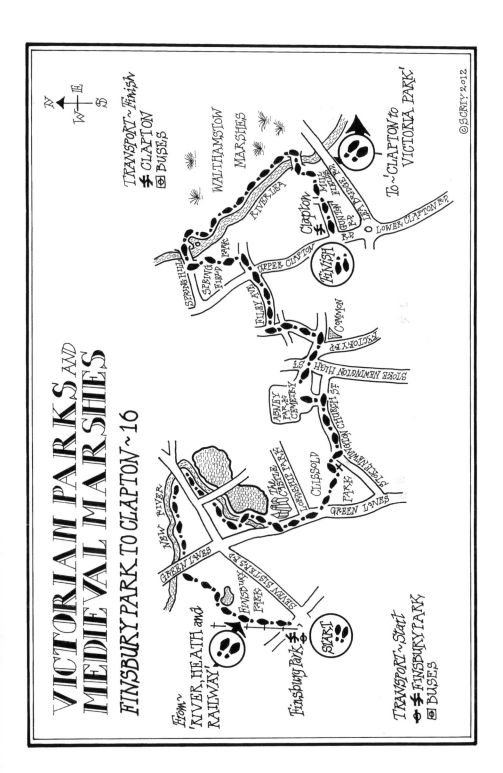

VICTORIAN PARKS AND MEDIEVAL MARSHES

FINSBURY PARK TO CLAPTON ~ 16

TRANSPORT ~ Finish
CLAPTON
BUSES

WALTHAMSTOW MARSHES

RIVER LEA

SPRING HILL

SPRING FIELD PARK

UPPER CLAPTON

FILBY AVE.

Clapton

GUNTON RD.

MILL FIELD RD.

LEA BRIDGE RD.

FINISH

LOWER CLAPTON RD.

To ~ CLAPTON to VICTORIA PARK'

© SCRIV 2012

STORE NEWINGTON HIGH ST.

COMMON

FACTORY RD.

ST.

ABNEY PARK CEMETERY

STOKE NEWINGTON CHURCH ST.

STOKE NEWINGTON

CLISSOLD PARK

LORDSHIP PARK

OLD THE CASTLE

GREEN LANES

NEW RIVER

GREEN LANES

SEVEN SISTERS RD.

FINSBURY PARK

From ~ 'RIVER, HEATH and RAILWAY'

Finsbury Park

START

TRANSPORT ~ Start
FINSBURY PARK
BUSES

233

engineering, clinging close to the side of the valley to follow the 100 foot contour along the whole of its 32 mile journey. Until recently this was a closed and secretive riverside but the growth in urban walking has seen a change in attitude, and now that the route is accessible we follow it along its final stretches, and alongside the two large reservoirs where the river now ends.

Finally, a long string of Victorian parks also shapes this section – Finsbury Park, Clissold Park, Springfield Park and Victoria Park. Few people today recognise the significance of these parks in the social history of London in general, and of the East End in particular. They arose from a concern for the well-being of working people at a time when almost intolerable living conditions were combined with a rapid loss of existing open spaces as London spilt outwards. Their existence is a tribute to vigorous public campaigning by wealthy philanthropists, social reformers, the new middle classes and the London poor. These nineteenth century campaigns have been echoed in the struggles of recent years to retain the remaining open spaces of Hackney – Abney Park, the New River, Stoke Newington Reservoirs, and the Walthamstow Marshes have all been threatened and defended, including a battle against road proposals that would have despoiled the whole southern reach of the Lea valley. In our route across this area, and sometimes in the most striking surrounds, we find both social history and natural history combined.

This chapter covers 11¼ miles from Finsbury Park to Cambridge Heath Road in Hackney. It can be treated as two separate walks:

WALK 16: From Finsbury Park to Clapton (6½ miles).

WALK 17: From Clapton to Victoria Park and Cambridge Heath (5 miles).

■ WALK 16: FINSBURY PARK TO CLAPTON

Getting started

From buses (210, W3, W7):

Walk through the station underpass to reach Station Place.

From Station Place turn left to cross the main road (Stroud Green Road) to find the large entrance into Finsbury Park.

From Finsbury Park Station (Network Rail (Kings Cross), Underground (Victoria and Piccadilly lines) **and buses** (4, 19, 29, 106, 153, 236, 253, 254, 259):

From the main forecourt of Finsbury Park Station (Station Place) turn left to cross the main road (Stroud Green Road) to find the large entrance into Finsbury Park.

On entering the park take the first fork to the left and continue ahead, parallel to the railway and passing behind the tennis courts.

On reaching a T junction, with the railway footbridge on your left, follow the tarmac path to your right.

From Walk 15:

After crossing the footbridge at the end of the Parkland Walk, keep straight ahead into Finsbury Park.

Finsbury Park

ROUTE:

- Continue ahead to cross the park road, then take the first fork to the left. Pass the café and the toilet block to reach the edge of the lake.
- Continue ahead following the lake perimeter, curving to the right between the lake and the running track and sports area.
- On reaching a T-junction at the tip of the lake and just beyond the sports pavilion, turn left.
- Follow the perimeter fence of the sports area, pass a wooden shelter, and at the next junction after this take the middle path of three, curving away from the sports area and sloping down through trees.
- Cross another park road to reach a gate onto the main road (Green Lanes).
- Cross the road and walk to the left for a few yards to find the entrance to the New River Walk on your right.

FACILITIES: Café and toilets in Finsbury Park.

LOOKING AT WILDLIFE: The area between the path and the railway embankment has been allowed to grow wild and supports an interesting range of wild flowers, including oxeye daisy, teasel, lady's bedstraw, common toadflax, yellow vetch, broom and everlasting pea. There are chiffchaff and blackcap in the park trees and, as well as the large numbers of Canada geese, there are often herons on the lake.

Hornsey Wood, set on the south-facing slopes above London, was once the most southerly outpost of the great Forest of Middlesex. Its swathe of tangled woodlands and sunnier clearings provided a convenient site for Londoners with a score to settle, and became the frequent haunt of duellists. It is this tradition which is commemorated today in the mosaic design of crossed pistols on the platforms of the Finsbury Park Underground Station. At the highest point of the road that cut through these woods stood the Hornsey Wood Tavern, a little roadside inn fronted by three widespread oaks. For many years, according to Hone's 1826 *Everyday Book*, it was run by Mrs Lloyd and Mrs Collins, two 'ancient women and large in size', who would sit on a bench slung between two of the oaks, drinking beer and chatting with the customers. Having lived and worked and drunk together, they died within a few months of each other.

When the craze for tea-drinking arrived, the oak trees were cut down, the tavern enlarged into a tea-house and an ornamental lake dug alongside it. Hornsey Wood became one of the most popular venues in London for angling and pigeon shooting, and for taking tea and promenading in the gardens. But by the early nineteenth century the tea craze was past, the gardens were in disrepair and most of the old woodland had been felled. It was this despoiled site that was chosen for the new Finsbury Park.

The nineteenth century saw London's expansion from a comprehensible city into an illimitable urban sprawl. As the population exploded, the City's surrounding villages were swallowed up in its uncontrollable growth. During this period the population of the inner London borough of Finsbury reached half a million, and the borough's fields and gathering grounds disappeared under a sea of housing. Finsbury people became so concerned that in 1850 they convened a meeting to press for the creation of a new public open space on the City outskirts. The campaign thus launched led in 1857 to the Finsbury Park Act, the very first legislation enabling the creation of a public park in London, although it was not until 1869 that the park was opened.

The park is not especially rich in wildlife, but there is at least one bird for which it has provided a significant sanctuary: writing in 1898 W.H. Hudson, that best of writers on London's wildlife, describes the song thrush as common here, even though it was rare in the rest of London:

Even in December and January, on a dull, cold afternoon with a grey smoky mist obscuring everything, a concert of thrushes may be heard in this park with more voices in it than could be heard anywhere in the country ... What makes this all the more remarkable is the noisiness of the neighbourhood ... Here, more than anywhere in London, you are reminded of Milton's description of the jarring and discordant grating sounds at the opening of hell's gates: and one would imagine that in such an atmosphere the birds would become crazed.

The New River

ROUTE:

- Follow the riverside path for approximately half a mile to emerge onto a main road (Seven Sisters Road).
- Cross the road (there is a controlled pedestrian crossing a short distance to the left) to rejoin the riverside walk on the far side.
- Continue on the path as it crosses a lane then curves round to the right to run alongside the first reservoir (East Reservoir).
- Beyond East Reservoir the path emerges onto another road (Lordship Road). Go straight across the road and continue alongside the right hand side of the river, initially through the landscaping of a housing development.
- The path continues alongside the New River and West Reservoir.

Eventually the river parts company from the reservoir; shortly after this, cross a footbridge on the left to reach the 'castle' site.

- Turn right on a short stretch of road alongside the castle to reach the main road (Green Lanes).

FACILITIES: Café at the West Reservoir Centre

LOOKING AT WILDLIFE: Common tern can sometimes be seen patrolling up and down the New River, which also supports dragonflies such as the emperor dragonfly and the azure damselfly. 'Wasteland' wild flowers such as common poppy grow alongside the path, as does wood horsetail, and there are long feathery strands of fennel pondweed within the river itself. Alongside the reservoirs there are stands of meadow cranesbill, meadow sweet and purple loosestrife. The East Reservoir, in particular, supports a variety of duck and gull species, as well as little and great crested grebe, and there are regular visiting rarities, especially in winter. Reed warbler can be heard singing in the reed beds. Peregrine falcons are sometimes seen on the 'castle' building.

By the beginning of the seventeenth century London's population was swelling, with more than 300,000 people living in the crowded city. Their water supply came from an army of water carriers, drawing water from the Thames or from local springs, and carrying it about the streets in loaded buckets or inflated pigs' bladders slung from a yoke across the shoulders. These sources were becoming increasingly contaminated and the need to find new ones was becoming urgent. In response to this a special Act of Parliament was passed in 1607, empowering Sir Hugh Myddleton to construct a 'New River', bringing drinking water into London from springs in Hertfordshire.

Myddleton was a City goldsmith and the king's jeweller. He was also the MP for Denbigh and a member of the Merchant Adventurers – a sort of early form of venture capitalism. Despite all this weight behind it, the project faced numerous obstacles and came close to total collapse. It was saved only by the intervention of the king. James I had watched the works progressing from his palace in Theobald's Park and had developed a personal interest in the project. He therefore agreed to provide half the cost of the work in return for half the profits.

This was work on a grand scale: 200 labourers at any one time, digging and puddling the long channel and providing it with over 200 bridges. The distance from the Chadwell spring to the City of London is 20 miles but the river took nearly 39 miles to get there, following long loops in order to cling to the 100 foot contour. In fact, in all those miles the river drops only 18 feet. Since a simple plummet was the only measuring device then available, this was an engineering triumph. It was completed when the works reached their final destination at the New River Head in Islington in 1613.

For four hundred years the New River has remained one of the important water supplies for London. Although truncated after World War Two and now terminating at the Stoke Newington Reservoirs, it still supplies 48 million gallons a day – some 8 per cent of London's massive consumption. For many of those years it has also remained closely fenced and gated, a long ribbon of inaccessible and almost invisible waterway. It is a mark of the growth of interest in urban walking in general – and the campaigning of the New River Action Group in particular – that in 2003 it was finally opened to the public as the 28-mile New River Path. It is a stretch of this path that we follow from Green Lanes, with a view to the north of pleasant rows of workman's cottages, and above them in the distance the hilltop silhouette of Alexandra Palace. Occupying the same high ridge as Hampstead and Highgate, Alexander Palace represents an ill fated attempt to create a north London equivalent to the Crystal Palace, blighted by fires, and never quite successful in its attempts at regeneration. Off to the south, however, the views are very different, and represent part of the massive redevelopment sweeping across north and east London, fuelled by the London Olympics and by the rediscovery of waterside – however small it might be – as an asset. Here the new buildings are interspersed with the old red brick blocks of what was itself the pioneering development of its day, the Woodberry Down estate.

The London Labour administration of 1934 came to power pledged to the radical reform of the capital's housing, and to relocating the city's huge and overcrowded 'slum' population. Sixty-four acres of large and ageing Victorian villas were chosen for one of the first schemes – against the opposition of local residents, the Conservative-controlled local council and the local press, which dubbed it a '£1,000,000 Slum Dwellers' Paradise'. Plans for the estate were delayed by a public enquiry, a High Court challenge, and finally by the outbreak of World War Two. But by the end of the war 90 per cent of all Stoke Newington's housing had suffered damage, while the borough's population was growing by 150 a month; and the 1945 elections saw Labour win every seat in the borough and elect its first ever Mayor. It was in this new climate that the development began.

It was to be a showpiece estate, with 6,500 people living in nearly 1,800 homes. There were to be a wide range of community facilities, including the first purpose-built Health Centre and comprehensive school in the country. 'We felt like King and Queen', said Olga Adams, one of the first tenants to move in – who had previously shared one room in Finsbury with her husband and two children. It was a brave attempt, but was eventually to suffer the same problems as all attempts at social engineering on such a grand scale. By 1990 the school was gone, the older flats were crumbling from the rumblings of the Victoria Line beneath, and two of the newer blocks – part of the 1960s wave of system building – had already been demolished.

Beyond the busy Seven Sisters Road our second section of path leads past a yellow brick gauging house which spans the river, and alongside the Stoke Newington Reservoirs. By the early nineteenth century the supply of water from the New River was no longer adequate and in 1833 the New River Company built two large holding reservoirs, the oldest of their kind in the world. By this time however cholera epidemics had become a recurring feature of London life, sweeping the capital every few years. By mid-century a clear link had been established between cholera and the state of the water supply and the Metropolitan Water Act made the filtration of water compulsory. Alongside the reservoirs, therefore, the New River Company constructed a number of filter beds, now disappeared beneath housing on the far side of Green Lanes. To pump the water through them it also commissioned a new pumping station from William Chadwell Mylne, whose father had been a surveyor to the New River Company, and whose family connection was so strong that he had even been named after one of the river's sources. To meet local objections, and disguise the station's real functions, Mylne adopted the style of a mediaeval Scottish castle. Completed in 1856, its 'keep' housed 6 steam engines and 18 boilers, whilst the main tower concealed the chimney, with fly wheels set in each of the buttresses. Used today as a climbing centre, it remains a splendidly eccentric building with each of its three towers a completely different shape, and the company logo on its walls in such tangled lettering as to be indecipherable.

Clissold Park and Church Street

ROUTE:

- Turn left along the main road, passing the castle and crossing Manor Park to reach a gate into Clissold Park.
- A few yards into the park, take the path on the left that runs around the left hand side of the lake.
- Follow the path where it runs between the two ponds and continue ahead along an avenue of trees with the children's play hut on the left.
- On reaching Clissold House, walk to the right around the front of the house and immediately beyond it turn left between the house and the gardens.
- Continue ahead and slightly to the left to reach the back of Old St Mary's church. Immediately beyond the church take the gate on the right leading into the churchyard.
- Follow the path through the churchyard to emerge onto Stoke Newington Church Street.
- Turn left to follow the main road for about ¼ mile through Stoke Newington until reaching a gate into Abney Park Cemetery on the left.

FACILITIES: Café and pubs on Green Lanes between the castle and the park. Toilets and café in Clissold Park. A wide choice of cafés, pubs and wine bars in Stoke Newington Church Street.

LOOKING AT WILDLIFE: Clissold Park has a wild fowl collection, deer paddocks, aviaries and a butterfly tunnel. There is also an interesting collection of exotic tree species, including dawn redwood, ginkgo, holm oak, manna ash, Judas tree, mulberry, black walnut and yellow-leaved ash. Wild duck, including pochard, sometimes visit the lower lakes in winter. On Church Street, outside the Town Hall, there is a fine row of the yellow-flowered *Koelreuteria* trees, also known as the Pride of India.

At the end of the eighteenth century Stoke Newington, on its higher seat above the City and the Lea, was developing as a country retreat for wealthy Londoners. It proved particularly attractive to merchant bankers, and among those who moved here was Jonathon Hoare, building himself 'Paradise House', a large yellow-brick home with a six-pillared portico. By 1811 the leasehold on the house had passed into the hands of another banker, William Crawshay, who paid a yearly rental for it of '£109 and a fat turkey'. Mr Crawshay and his family attended the nearby parish church of St Mary's and it was there that his daughter Elizabeth fell in love with a young curate, Augustus Clissold. The two began a discreet romance, which infuriated old Mr Crawshay. He took drastic measures to keep the young couple apart: after forbidding their meetings he raised the height of all the walls around his 54-acre estate and, when that seemed to have failed, he threatened to shoot anyone caught delivering messages between them. Despite, or perhaps because of, all the obstacles, Elizabeth and Augustus remained constant and were finally able to marry after Crawshay's death. They also inherited the family home and Clissold House is now named after them. In 1886 the house and its grounds went on the market, due to be sold off as building plots. After a public outcry, a newly formed Preservation Society began a campaign to save the site, and after raising much of the money itself, the Society persuaded the London County Council and the local vestries to buy the estate. It was opened to the public as Clissold Park in 1899.

It must have been a fascinating place in those days, for two quite separate 'rivers' ran through it, one natural, the other artificial. Traces of them both can still be seen. The Hackney Brook rises in Islington and runs into the River Lea at Hackney Wick, but it has become one of the 'lost' rivers of London, now running in concrete casing underground. The two ponds in the slight depression where we enter Clissold Park are one of its few remaining traces and were dug out from the river to provide bricks during the building of Paradise House. At the top of the hill, the long curving pond in the deer enclosure is a remnant of the New River, which now terminates at the Stoke Newington Reservoirs, but before the Second World War continued from here down through Islington to the New River Head near the Angel. Apart from the ponds and one or two other remnants, these last few miles of its course were then filled in.

The path which leads us through the graveyard of Old St Mary Church is short but has an appropriately gothic quality: dank, gloomy and overgrown. The low red church has ancient origins but underwent a restoration in 1583, a date which can be seen carved above the south doorway. As Stoke Newington rose in both size and status it was decided to build a new and larger Parish church, and this alone has saved Old St Mary's from the excesses of a further, Victorian, renovation. The new St Mary's was built in 1858 and the two now face each other across Church Street, symbolic of the transition of Stoke Newington from rural village to middle-class suburb. The new church is grey and stark and less appealing. Its architect was George Gilbert Scott, several of whose buildings are along the route of *The Green London Way*. In the new church the worldly wealth, rather than spiritual yearning, of his clients is reflected in the 254-foot spire, in its day the highest church steeple in London.

Stoke Newington Church Street leads us through the heart of the old village.

It is a jumble of a street where fine old houses rub shoulders with ugly post-war development. Following years of dilapidation Stoke Newington became one of the centres of inner city gentrification, as the professional classes recolonised and new wine bars were opened to serve them. Stoke Newington was once a borough in its own right and the first building we pass on the left is its old Town Hall. Its real curiosity is the camouflage paint with which it was coated in World War II. Though fading, it is still visible, as though the buildings were camouflaged as a zebra. Further along, opposite the public library, is Bridge House, a Queen Anne house constructed in 1714 for the four Bridge sisters and one of the oldest and finest buildings on the street. Beyond this, on the same side of the street, is Defoe Road and it was in a house near here that Daniel Defoe wrote *Robinson Crusoe* in 1719. His is not the only famous name connected with Stoke Newington. Edgar Allen Poe was educated here whilst Leigh Hunt, the poet, John Howard, the prison reformer, and Isaac Watts, the hymn writer, all lived here. There are also many who took up a far more permanent residence after death, for not far along on the left hand side is the gate into Abney Park, one of London's great Victorian cemeteries.

Abney Park and Stoke Newington Common

ROUTE:

- Enter the cemetery, following a small paved path to reach the main path, and turn left.
- Follow this broad route ahead ignoring side paths until, shortly after passing Frank Bostock's lion memorial, you come to a major crossing of paths with the chapel buildings visible to your right.
- Turn right to reach and pass the chapel and then continue straight ahead to reach the main gates.
- From the gates cross the main road to follow Northwold Road opposite and slightly to the right.
- Walk down Northwold Road, crossing the railway and following the side of Stoke Newington Common, to take the second turning on the left (Kyverdale Road).
- Follow Kyverdale Road across Cazenove Road and then turn right into Filey Avenue.
- At the end of Filey Avenue cross the main road (Upper Clapton Road) and take Springfield, almost opposite and to the left. A short distance down Springfield, take the gate into Springfield Park on the left.

FACILITIES: Disabled toilet and information centre on Stoke Newington High Street at the cemetery entrance.

LOOKING AT WILDLIFE: Abney Park Cemetery has secondary woodland with exotic species surviving from the original planting. These include Bhutan pine, hybrid oaks, service tree of Fontainbleu, Monterey cypress and stone pine. There are more than 30 species of breeding bird, with many more, including goldcrest, occurring as visitors. There is a good selection of butterflies, including large numbers of speckled wood.

Among the great villas erected in Stoke Newington, two were particularly imposing. One of these was Abney House, built by Thomas Gunton in 1714 and subsequently occupied by Sir Thomas and Lady Abney. Thomas Abney was another banker, later to become a founder of the Bank of England and a Lord Mayor of London. The Abneys were host to many house guests, and among them was Isaac Watts, who arrived in 1714 for a 'few weeks' recuperation after a nervous breakdown. He stayed for 35 years. Watts composed many of his best-known hymns here, including 'O God our help in ages past', and is commemorated by a statue in the cemetery.

There is a mound in the north east corner of the present park, now marked with a plaque, where Watts is supposed to have sat whilst composing. This mound has another famous association: according to local tradition Oliver Cromwell was buried beneath it. At the time of his official funeral at Westminster Abbey it was already feared that Cromwell's tomb might be subject to future violation, and a substitute body was therefore interred at the Abbey while the genuine item was said to have been brought here for safe-keeping. But why to Stoke Newington? The connection is with the other great house in Church Street.

While Abney House occupied the site now marked by the entrance to the cemetery, immediately next to it, on the site of the present Fire Station, was Fleetwood House. This was built in 1662 for Charles Fleetwood, previously Commander-in-Chief of the Commonwealth armies. His wife, Bridget, was Oliver Cromwell's eldest daughter. This gave rise not only to the story about the burial but also to a long running connection between Stoke Newington and religious dissenters. Two centuries later, when the estates of Fleetwood House and Abney House were amalgamated to form the Abney Park Cemetery, it was specifically planned as a burial ground for nonconformists. Among the most famous of these was William Booth, founder of the Salvation Army, whose grave, together with those of a number of other early Salvationists, can be seen shortly after we enter the cemetery grounds.

Abney Park Cemetery was designed by William Hosking, Professor of Architecture at Kings College, London. The centrepiece was to be the neo-Gothic chapel, and to satisfy the needs of a variety of nonconformists the usual cruciform shape was eschewed for the Greek cross – a cross with four equal arms. This effect, however, was rather undone by the subsequent addition of a large carriage porch at the southern end. The park opened in May 1840, and within fifteen years 14,000 burials had taken place here. To the Victorians a cemetery was not just a reminder of human mortality, it was a place for a pleasant promenade, a picnic or a family outing, and Abney Park was certainly laid out with this in mind. It was landscaped by Loddiges and described as 'one of the most complete arboretums in the neighbourhood of London'. Over 2,500 trees were added to those preserved from the original estates, and 1,029 roses were planted. But this proud place was soon to fall into decay. The early popularity of the cemetery ensured that it was soon full and the proprietors, in an attempt to maintain their revenue, went on packing the bodies into whatever space they could find – taking up paths, reducing the verges and filling the gaps between graves. By the twentieth century little maintenance was being done and the park was running wild. Death had ceased to be profitable, and by the 1970s the cemetery company was bankrupt. It was then that the Save Abney Park Cemetery Committee was formed to preserve the site, and at the instigation of this group it was eventually purchased by Hackney Council for the nominal sum of £1.

The delightfully overgrown Abney Park of today is an island of secondary woodland in an intensely urban area. Thick growths of sycamore, birch and ash cover much of the ground, concealing here and there the more mature trees of the original planting. Horsetail is abundant, woundwort and red campion flower along the woodland edges, and Canterbury bells, asparagus and asters spread out from the graves on which they were planted. Breeding birds include stock dove, kestrel, tawny owl, blackcap, spotted flycatcher, coal tit and bullfinch. More surprising than any of these, perhaps, is the mallard. As many as twenty pairs a year have bred here, and on fledging the young ducklings have to be walked the half mile or so to the nearest park lake. In summer visiting whitethroat and great spotted woodpecker increase the variety of birds, while, in winter, linnet, redpoll and goldcrest might all be seen feeding here. In 1883 James Braithwaite French wrote a book entitled *Walks in Abney Park*. 'Death', he mused, 'is but a contrivance for gaining more life.' That statement must be even truer for the cemetery today.

The main gates to Abney Park are formed by four solemn white Egyptian pylons decorated with lotus flowers, leaf motifs and the winged orbs emblematic of eternal life. On either side are flanking temples – once stonemason's workshops – bearing hieroglyphic legends which translate as 'The gates of the abode of the mortal part of man'. From these gates our route crosses the Stamford Hill road – its name derived from a stoney ford over the Hackney Brook – and continues alongside Stoke Newington Common. This genuine remnant of ancient commoners' rights is today a drab and uninviting affair, gouged by the railway and enlivened only by the lines of mature plane trees. Once nightingales sung here, today they would hardly be heard above the traffic.

The main housing development around the Common took place in the late 1870s. It was during this time that Mr Worthington-Smith, a 'local antiquarian', noted in the sides of foundation trenches a thin band containing numerous sharp flint fragments. His discovery turned out to be one of the most important early Palaeolithic sites in the country, a buried land surface where 200,000 years ago men and women had lived and worked at what must have been a regular hand axe industry. Two to three hundred of these small flint tools were discovered here, as well as innumerable flint flakes from the workings. The surface extended from the cemetery in the west, across the common and as far as Upper Clapton Road in the east. Our route along Kyverdale Road and Filey Avenue runs across the very centre of it, an area where a long-standing population of Hassidic Jews now share the streets with more recently arrived Muslims. These streets bring us to the gate of Springfield Park and, from here, to the marshes.

Walthamstow Marshes

ROUTE:

- On entering the park follow the path as it curves left towards the White House. Immediately beyond the house take the central path of three leading to two beech trees beside a flight of steps.
- Do not descend the steps but turn left following the path that runs along the brow of the wooded hill. The path eventually curves right to run alongside the park perimeter and reach a gate.
- Do not leave by this gate but continue ahead across the grass and parallel to the road to reach the gate in the bottom left hand corner of the park.
- Leave through the gate and take the footbridge over the river.
- Continue ahead following the perimeter fence of the marina.
- Cross a small bridge over a channel and then turn right through a set of black gates. Immediately beyond them take the path on the left leading into Horse Shoe Thicket. Keep to the right within the thicket, passing two ponds to exit again beside the river.
- Turn left to follow the riverside. Continue beyond the railway arches until reaching a distinct rise in level. Shortly beyond this, look for a footbridge crossing the river on the right.
- Cross the river and turn left following the river which curves to the right.

To join walk 17:

Continue along the riverside towpath.

To complete this walk:

Where the river curves back again to the left, two paths run off to the right beside a sculpted cast iron tree. Take the left hand path, crossing the grass to reach the left hand perimeter of the housing. Follow the path as it runs up between the housing and the fields until it reaches a road (Casimir Road).

Turn left on the road then immediately right up Gunton Road to reach Upper Clapton Road.

Turn right on Lower Clapton Road for buses and BR station.

FACILITIES: Toilets and café in the White House, Springfield Park. Café beside the river at the bottom of Springfield Hill.

LOOKING AT WILDLIFE: Springfield Park is a Local Nature Reserve with a good selection of bird species, including tawny owl. It is also a good place to see bats at dusk including both species of pipistrelle and noctule. The park is also geologically important, situated on the spring line between the London clay and the Hackney terrace gravels, and is a regional geological site. Walthamstow Marsh, with its thickets, its reed beds and its waterside marshes, is one of the most important wildlife sites in inner London. Its many plant specialities include the rare creeping marshwort, found around the grazed edges of ditches. It has a breeding colony of Essex skipper butterflies and a good variety of dragonflies. Together with the neighbouring reservoirs it is a particularly important area for birds. Heron and cormorant are frequent, terns appear around Horseshoe Point in summer, short eared owls have occasionally roosted in Horse Shoe Thicket and reed buntings, sedge and reed warblers can all be seen or heard in the reed beds.

'Fresh air,' said Mr Cornwall, when he performed the opening of Springfield Park in 1905, 'will help to change the habits of the people and to keep them out of the public houses'. This worthy aim was not entirely realised. It was however typical of the intentions of many of the Victorian reformers, for whom public parks were as important for the moral as for the physical well-being of the labouring classes. Certainly Springfield Park was built on an 'uplifting' site, with its panoramic view of the Lea Valley and the marshes; but it is a view more fascinating than beautiful: wide expanses of tall grasses and reed-beds alongside the waterways, yet dominated by railways, electricity pylons and the tower blocks of Leyton. The top of the slope with its extensive view and little spring must have made it an attractive site for a settlement. The Romans thought so, and two of their stone coffins were unearthed here in the nineteenth century. The existing house, built from locally extracted brick earth, is Georgian and was part of a 32-acre estate stretching down to the river at Horseshoe Point. This estate, together with its 'White House', was put up for sale in 1902 and purchased at a cost of £40,000 by the LCC and the local boroughs. The 16-hectare park on the site was designed by J.B Sexby, one time head of London parks, whose 1905 book on the capital's municipal parks has been quoted several times along the route of *The Green London Way*.

The steep slopes of the park lead us down to the riverside, and beyond that to the flat expanse of the Walthamstow Marsh. That even this extent of it has survived is something of a marvel. Once the wetlands and the water meadows would have stretched for miles along the bottom of the broad valley of the Lea, but Tottenham Marsh, Leyton Marsh, Hackney Marsh, and many more, have disappeared beneath infilling and football pitches, reservoirs, housing and formal 'leisure' facilities. But here, at the heart of it all, is 88 acres of ancient lammas land which have enjoyed an uninterrupted continuity since the middle ages. The antiquity of the marshes is demonstrated by the plants themselves. One of the commonest sedges here is the hybrid *Carex x subgracilis*. This hybrid is infertile, which means that the large stands on the marsh must have spread themselves vegetatively over hundreds of years from a single accidental clone. This site is therefore unique – yet it would not have survived without the efforts of the Save the Marshes Campaign.

In 1979 the Lea Valley Regional Park Authority declared its intention to extract gravel from the marsh and turn it into a marina for motorized water sports. The Save the Marshes Campaign led and won the fight against this proposal. Again in 1982, when British Rail proposed to tip 8,000 tons of ballast onto part of the marsh, it was the Campaign which led the protest. It is only in more recent years that the various statutory authorities have caught up with local people and come to regard an ancient marsh as something worth preserving. In 1984 formal notification of the marsh as a Site of Special Scientific

Interest was commenced and by 1985 the Lea Valley Regional Park Authority was proposing to manage the area as a nature reserve. The Save the Marshes Campaign was able to transform itself from an ad hoc campaign into a permanent 'Walthamstow Marsh Society'.

The marsh consists of a succession of habitats from open water to dry grassland. Much of the area is covered with reed, sedge and marshland grasses. In spring and summer there are great swathes of colour from the purple-blue Russian comfrey, the white and frothy meadow sweet, the upright poles of yellow flag iris and the delicately drooping pink and cream blooms of great willow herb. In autumn they are supplanted by the rich brown seed-heads of the docks and the dark blue ranks of Michaelmas daisy. These are the dominant plants, but there are many more to be found among them; water figwort, ragged robin, soapwort, orange balsam, purple loosestrife, wild angelica, even the little adder's tongue fern, another indicator of antiquity. It is the docks which have most excited the specialists, for among the many species to be found here there have arisen some very unusual hybrids. One of these, a cross between Greek dock and broad-leaved dock, has been named *Rumex x lousleyi* in honour of the botanist Ted Lousley, a leading light of the London Natural History Society who died in 1975. The plant on the marsh is one of only two specimens known anywhere in the world. It is an example of evolution proceeding in our own time.

A diversity of plant life gives rise to a diversity of insect life. During the campaign to save the marshes, Harry Britain identified 800 species, though there must be many more. He also calculated that the total population of bees and wasps alone outnumbered the human inhabitants of Hackney by three to one. Among the seventeen species of butterfly breeding here, the Essex skipper is of special note. It was only discovered in this country in 1888, probably due to its great similarity to the small skipper, from which it differs only in having a small dot on the underside of its antennae. It is on the extreme northern edge of its world range in Britain and the breeding population on the marsh is probably the closest colony to central London.

There are specialities among the birds as well. The reservoirs to the north of the marsh have one of the largest heronries in the country, and at almost any time of day, but particularly at dawn and dusk, these birds can be seen flying overhead like lumbering pterodactyls. The list of birds to have bred on the reservoir and marsh include little grebe, cuckoo, skylark, sand martin, stonechat, reed warbler, sedge warbler, whitethroat, spotted flycatcher, yellow wagtail, reed bunting and linnet. It is a unique experience to stand in a reed-bed under the shadow of a railway embankment and hear, on a spring day, the busy chirruping of a hidden reed warbler, while overhead a skylark, framed by pylons, looses its unending stream of notes as though in the heart of the country.

Our route over the marsh takes us from Coppermill Bridge around the back of the Springfield Marina where, at dusk, pipistrelle bats come out to feed. The marina was created in the early 1970s by enlarging the old bend in the river at Horseshoe Point. The extracted silt was dumped on the adjacent marsh and has given rise to Horse Shoe Thicket, a dense growth of sallow supporting a large population of finches, tits and warblers. The section of the marsh down to the railway is known as Inner Marsh. On the far side of the arches a plaque explains that A.V. Roe built a little triplane here in 1909 and made history by staging the first all-British powered flight. His plane can still be seen in the Science Museum at South Kensington. From here the route continues across Outer Marsh until we reach a sudden rise marked by a line of tall trees. This rise marks the old boundary between Walthamstow and Leyton; and also between their contrasting treatment of the marshlands. Behind us is a scene of rich and ever-changing natural complexity. Ahead of us is Leyton Marsh, a marsh in name only, infilled with rubble after the blitz and turned into playing fields. Its drab expanse attracting nothing but Sunday footballers and seagulls.

Getting home

Clapton Station: Liverpool Street

Buses: (from Clapton Station) 106, 253, 254, 393

WALK 17: CLAPTON TO VICTORIA PARK

Getting started

From Clapton Station (Overground) **and buses** (106, 253, 254, 393 to Clapton Station)

From the exit to Clapton Station turn left then immediately left again into Gunton Road. At the bottom of Gunton Road turn left and after a few yards turn right along the path that runs between the housing and the fields.

On reaching the riverside path turn right.

From Walk 16:

Continue along the riverside path from the end of Walk 16.

From Millfields to the Filter Beds

ROUTE:

- Follow the riverside path under Lea Bridge Road. Shortly beyond this it crosses a footbridge onto the opposite bank and reaches the entrance to the Middlesex Filter Beds Nature Reserve.
- Go through the entrance gate and after a few yards turn right at a T junction, following the central concrete causeway through the middle of the beds.
- At the end of the causeway turn right along the track leading to a gate out of the reserve.

VICTORIAN PARKS AND MEDIEVAL MARSHES

CLAPTON TO VICTORIA PARK ~17~

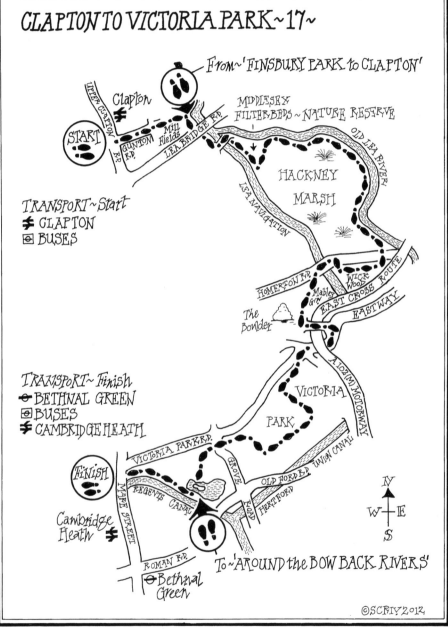

From ~ 'FINSBURY PARK to CLAPTON'

Clapton

Upper Clapton Rd.

START

Gunton Rd.

Mill Fields

Lea Bridge Rd.

MIDDLESEX FILTERBEDS ~ NATURE RESERVE

OLD LEA RIVER

HACKNEY MARSH

LEA NAVIGATION

TRANSPORT ~ Start
- ⚡ CLAPTON
- ⊡ BUSES

HOMERTON RD.

Mabley Grn

WICK WOODS

EAST CROSS ROUTE

EASTWAY

The Boulder

TRANSPORT ~ Finish
- ⊕ BETHNAL GREEN
- ⊡ BUSES
- ⚡ CAMBRIDGE HEATH

A102(M) MOTORWAY

VICTORIA PARK

FINISH

VICTORIA PARK RD.

MARE STREET

REGENTS CANAL

GROVE ROAD

OLD FORD RD.

UNION CANAL

HERTFORD

Cambridge Heath ⚡

ROMAN RD.

⊕ Bethnal Green

To ~ 'AROUND the BOW BACK RIVERS'

N W E S

©SCRIV 2012

248

FACILITIES: Prince of Wales pub on Lea Bridge Road. The Middlesex Filter Bed Nature Reserve is open daily from 8.30am.

LOOKING AT WILDLIFE: There are 'brownfield' wild flowers on the uncut strip alongside the towpath, including common poppy, opium poppy, hoary cabbage, weld and comfrey, with patches of pond water crowfoot in the river itself. The canal side walls, especially the locks and bridges, support a number of ferns, including common polypody. The Middlesex Filter Beds demonstrate a succession of ponds, reed-beds and willow scrub, with a variety of water and waterside plants, including great willow herb, marsh dock, water dock, celery leaved crowfoot, water plantain, bulrush and reed mace. Both the Filter Beds and the Old Lea are good for birds; look out for heron, kingfisher, little grebe and a variety of wintering wild fowl, with gadwall a speciality. There are also reed and sedge warblers, reed bunting and occasional snipe on the Filter Bed site. Giant hogweed grows along stretches of the Old Lea despite attempts to eradicate it.

In the year 527 the Saxon leader Erchewin rebelled against Octa, his king, and went off to form a kingdom of his own with its capital at London. Determined to suppress this rebellion Octa sailed here from Rochester with a force of 15,000 men. He planned to leave his boats on the Lea and march south on London. Erchewin forestalled him and arrived here to cut short the advance. The Battle of Hackney was fought beside the river, on the unlikely site of the Millfields. Octa was seriously wounded in a struggle, which cost the lives of thousands of his followers. It was the 'Londoners' who were victorious. The river became the boundary between the two Saxon kingdoms, and later of the two English counties derived from them – Essex and Middlesex.

The Millfields owe their name to a later, more peaceful time. In the eighteenth century there were huge mills here, grinding out 300 quarters of corn a week. The story of the corn mills also ends in calamity, however, for in 1791 an immense fire consumed the whole mills, including 30,000 quarters of wheat and flour, in less than two hours. The fields were also the site of extensive diggings, for they yielded the valuable brick-earth, a soil deposit frequent across East London, formed by a combination of glacial and river action. Until the 1830s this was mixed with road sweepings and other refuse to make the characteristic London brick.

Beyond the Lea Bridge Road the river splits in two. Off to the left, beyond the weir, is the Old Lea, whilst to the right is the 'Hackney Cut', a navigable channel dug in 1770. We cross it on the Curtain Gate footbridge, and soon reach one of the most attractive sites along the lower Lea Valley, the abandoned Middlesex Filter Beds. This northern section of the Hackney Marsh was bought by the East London Waterworks Company in 1829. Just twenty years later came one of London's worst cholera outbreaks, killing 14,000 East Enders. It was in response to this that the company built the six Middlesex filter beds, a number which had grown to 25 by 1852, with an additional complex across the river. When last in use, this succession of concrete tanks must have presented a somewhat bleak prospect, but after their closure in 1969 the old tanks filled with silt and were colonised by plants that provided an almost textbook illustration of fen evolution. Just about every stage in the progression from pond through reed-bed and willow scrub to eventual woodland is now evident here. Many of the plants – water plantain, water crowfoot, almond-leaved willow – must have come in on the feet of visiting wildfowl. Increasing numbers of duck visit in winter and in early summer there is a frantic chattering chorus from the warblers in the reed beds. This is a closer, more private site than the open marshes, and has a real sense of seclusion, despite the factories and tower blocks a few hundred yards away across the river. One of its most distinctive occupants is the Edible Frog. This is one of three closely related frogs that can now be found in this country, notoriously difficult to distinguish, and all more or less green in colour. There is some evidence that the Pool Frog is a native; the Edible Frog and the Marsh Frog are most definitely not. The Edible Frog spends almost all of its time in water and will drop beneath the surface at the slightest sign of a predator. There is a significant population around this part of the Lea Valley, though numbers fluctuate with the harshness of the winter. Should you be thinking of culling a few for culinary purposes however you should probably be aware that domestically reared 'grenouilles de parc' are considered by gourmets to be much superior to the wild caught 'grenouilles de peche'.

Hackney Marshes and Wick Woods

ROUTE:

- From the Nature Reserve exit turn sharp left, ignoring the cycle paths to follow a grassy path alongside the Nature Reserve perimeter and signposted to the Waterworks Nature Reserve.
- Follow the path as it curves round to the right to run alongside the river. Do not cross the footbridge on the right but continue ahead on the tarmac path that continues along the right hand side of the river.
- NOTE: It is also possible to follow a parallel, trodden earthen path that runs closer to the river, though this may be overgrown in places.
- After approximately ¾ mile you pass a footbridge onto East Marsh on your left (White House Bridge). About 50 yards beyond this, take the gravel path on the right that leads to a car park at the back of the Hackney Marshes Centre. Walk through the car park to reach the main road (Homerton Road).
- Cross the road to find an entrance ramp into Wick Woods opposite. Turn immediately right in the woods to follow the path that runs through the woodland perimeter, parallel to the road.
- Where the main path curves away to the left, shortly before reaching the river, keep to the right to reach steps up to the road just before the river bridge. Turn left across the bridge.

LOOKING AT WILDLIFE: The uncut meadows on the edges of the Hackney Marsh support an interesting and attractive range of wild flowers including wild carrot, vetches, weld, goatsbeard, musk mallow and knapweed, and this in turn supports a good population of grasshoppers and of grassland butterflies. The river supports a range of wildfowl, especially in winter, including duck species, common sandpiper, little grebe and the occasional kingfisher. Wick Woods supports a range of woodland birds, with the more common species supplemented by the occasional woodcock and snipe. Muntjac have also been seen here, but the most obvious feature of interest is the surviving line of rare native black poplars alongside Homerton Road.

Hackney Marsh is a virtual island between the two channels of the Lea. On the eastern side runs the canalised channel of the Hackney Cut, dug in 1776 to provide flood relief and shorten the Lea Navigation. The River Lea has been in regular commercial navigation since at least 1220. Even before this, in the ninth century, channels were dug by King Alfred, as a defensive measure. In 895 the Danes had sailed up here to attack the town of Ware in Hertfordshire. The citizens of London turned out to oppose them en route but were driven off with heavy losses. King Alfred then ordered the digging of drainage channels at various places along the river, including here at Hackney, which reduced the water level in the Lea. This stranded the Danes up-river, where, without their precious boats, they were attacked and defeated.

The drainage channels would have had the additional effect of lowering the water table on the marshes, thus rendering them usable as hay meadows. The Hackney Marsh, like much of the rest of the area, became lammas lands. From the lammas festival in August, through to the next April, the landowner had exclusive right to the hay harvest, but for the rest of the year the marsh was open to common grazing. These various rights were supervised and protected by 'marsh drivers' who were elected annually by the court of the manor. But gradually the area became more and more popular as a playground for the East End, one bull-baiting contest in 1791 being watched by as many as 3,000 people. They were catered for by the White House Inn, on the south east corner of the marsh, which also provided a well stocked fishery and was described in the 1850s as 'a delightful resort for holiday folk'. By the end of the nineteenth century, however, the marsh drivers were coming into conflict with participants in a newer sport – football. Largely as a result of pressure from mission halls and other places which organised teams, the London County Council bought the 350 acres of Hackney Marsh in 1893, the site eventually providing over 120 football and cricket pitches.

At their peak, there were 120 pitches here and the view out across them was one of bleak and wind-swept tedium. This has been somewhat relieved in recent years by the planting of more trees and the creation of uncut meadow edges, but nonetheless it is still fairly surprising to find along one side of this sporting plateau, a riverside walk of considerable attraction. Unlike the straight and stiff-banked channel of the navigation, the Old Lea meanders under overhanging trees, its earth banks the home of waterside plants, moorhens and even a kingfisher or two. In winter the duck fly in, in numbers which increase with the harshness of conditions, common sandpiper fly low over the water and small parties of little grebe circle and dive, seeming to spend as much time under the river as on top of it. This has also been something of a battleground with the giant hogweed, which still survives but not in the quantity of a few years ago. This monster of a plant can reach up to twelve foot high, with flat white flower heads up to three foot across. It advances up the river valley like an invading army, which perhaps is what it is. Having arrived here from the Caucasus, the plant is rapidly spreading across southern and eastern England.

On the far side of the Homerton Road, Wick Field was once part of this area of pitches. After a period of uncertainty, of occupation by travellers and threats of development, it was planted as 'community woodland' between 1996 and 2000. Perhaps it is fortunate that this happened before the Olympic bid was finalised, for this site would otherwise almost certainly have become part of the massive development of the Olympic fringes, which can be seen in the form of the gaudy but otherwise undistinguished high rise blocks thrown up in indecent haste further along the Homerton Road. Though used as a rubbish dump in the late nineteenth century, this site escaped the fate of so many of the surrounding marshes, which became the infill site for the dumping of post-war bomb rubble. It remains, therefore, at a lower level than the adjacent Hackney Marsh, and a damper site, ideal for the 18 native black poplars that were planted here in 1894. This is the rarest of our native trees but was once the archetypical tree of the English marshland, distinguishable from the much commoner hybrid black poplar by its knobbly shape. Many of the trees were destroyed by the building of the A12 East Cross Route across part of the site in the 1990s – the noise of which now provides a new form of pollution to the marshes – but a fine line of them still survives along the line of the Homerton Road.

Victoria Park

ROUTE:

- Cross the bridge to reach Mabley Green on your left. Pass the first area of fenced pitches then set off diagonally across the Green towards the monumental boulder in the centre.
- Beyond the boulder, continue diagonally to reach a junction of tarmac paths in the far corner.
- Follow the slope up to the footbridge that crosses the main road onto Red Path.
- At the end of Red Path turn right along the road (Eastway).
- Follow the road round to the right under railway and motorway bridges to reach the pedestrian crossing which leads across the road to one of the gates into Victoria Park.
- Enter the park and continue ahead, bearing bear right in front of the lodge to follow the large drive through the park.
- Remain on the drive until you reach a crossroads with the Queens Gate and a pub on the right. Ignore the main left turn here to take the smaller tarmac path on the left, just a few yards beyond it.
- Where another small path comes in from the left, continue ahead to pass the bowling green.

- Turn right at the next junction to follow a larger avenue which passes the Old English Garden and then runs between East Lake and the new playground.
- About 50 yards beyond the lake take the path on the right, heading directly towards the Burdett-Coutts memorial fountain.
- At the fountain, take the path on the left that curves right to rejoin the main park avenue close to the ornamental Royal Gate.
- Leave through the gate and cross Grove Road to enter the western section of the park.
- Ignore the left turn at the first major fork and continue ahead to take a smaller path approximately 20 yards further along on the left.
- Follow the path to reach the wooden shelter. At the shelter, ignore the path to the right to take the central path that follows the lake perimeter.
- Continue ahead to reach the path on the left that runs across a bridge onto the island. Continue across the island and then across a second bridge to join a main park avenue.
- Turn left along the avenue for just a few yards then right to reach Rose Gate onto the canal towpath.

To join Walk 18:

From Rose Gate turn left along the towpath.

To complete this walk:

From Rose Gate turn right along the towpath and continue as far as the next road bridge.

Walk up the steps on the right to join Cambridge Heath Road and Mare Street.

There are buses along Cambridge Heath Road. Cambridge Heath Station is just under ¼ mile down Cambridge Heath Road to the left. Bethnal Green underground station is approximately ¾ mile in the same direction.

FACILITIES: Pub beside Queen Gate. Pub and cafés on Grove Road between the two sections of park. Cafés, restaurant and toilets in Victoria Park.

LOOKING AT WILDLIFE: 'Fairy rings' on Mabley Green. Victoria Park has several lakes and a collection of wildfowl. There is a variety of native and introduced trees, including hornbeam, cockspur thorn, turkey oak, Indian bean tree, ginkgo, strawberry tree and mulberry. There is skullcap, gypsywort and woundwort along the canal edges, with fennel, viper's bugloss and wild carrot among plants, possibly sown, alongside the towpath.

A large slab of quarried Cornish granite forms a rather incongruous feature at the heart of Mabley Green. It was installed, under the unsurprising name of 'Boulder', by artist John Frankland in 2008, and is one of a pair, with a second in Shoreditch Park. It has been taken seriously by the climbing community, who have already listed 23 climbs up its various faces. From the Green, Red Path runs alongside what was once the Hackney Wick Coal and Goods Depot and onto Eastway, from where it is just a short distance to one of London's grandest parks.

Victoria Park was built as a direct response to the squalid, overcrowded conditions of Bethnal Green and the East End. In 1839 a 'sanitary reformer' by the name of William Farr pointed out that fresh air and exercise provided by a park would 'probably diminish deaths by several thousand and add years to the lives of the entire population'. He further noted that 'epidemics which arise in the East End do not stay there, they travel to the West End and prove fatal in the wide streets and squares'. This was no doubt the clinching argument. In the following year a committee was set up under the local MP, and began to organise a petition which eventually attracted 30,000 signatures. It was presented to Queen Victoria and it was her interest in the project which ensured its original designation as a royal park. It was laid out by James Pennethorne in the Romantic style and planted with over 10,000 trees and shrubs.

The site used for the park was Bonners Fields, named after an infamous Bishop of London, noted for burning protestant heretics during the reign of Mary I. These fields had long been a gathering ground for workers' rallies and radical demonstrations, and this tradition was carried over into the new park. In 1848 the last great Chartist rally was scheduled to gather nearby, and the park was turned by the authorities into an armed encampment for the occasion. Stationed within the gates were 1,600 foot police – 500 of them armed with cutlasses – 100 mounted police and 500 recalled police reservists. Just to make up the numbers a cavalry detachment from the 1st Life Guards was stationed on the opposite bank of the canal.

In subsequent years the radicals regained the park for themselves. The militant suffragettes gathered here, as did striking dockers, and, in the late 1970s, the Anti-Nazi League. One group which didn't make it was Oswald Mosley's Blackshirts, who tried to march to the Park but were halted by barricades along the way. The area known as the Forum – or locally as the Forem and Agin 'em – became a second speaker's corner. Speakers here included Bernard Shaw, William Morris, Tom Mann and Ben Tillett. The Forum, sadly, ran out of steam round about 1939.

The lake was added to the park in 1846, the work being carried out free by the East London Waterworks Company, using old brick-earth pits. The completed lake was stocked with wildfowl by the Ornithological Society on condition that a Victoria Park branch was set up. The branch recruited local members, charged dues and organised lectures and 'bird observations', generally surprising respectable folk that the working classes were capable of such pursuits. W.H. Hudson complains that the park was too heavily used – 20,000 visitors on Good Friday 1845 for example – to admit of much interesting bird life, but these lakes have been the scene of at least one milestone in ornithological history. The tufted duck, such a common sight now on our park ponds and urban canals, has reached high numbers only in the course of this century. When a pair raised a brood here in 1912 it was one of the very first breeding records for the whole of London.

The most striking architectural feature in the Park is the Victoria Fountain. In 1862 the Baroness Angela Georgina Burdett-Coutts, the richest woman in

England, took it upon herself to remedy the shortage of drinking water for the masses that thronged the park. The Baroness was a philanthropist and friend of Dickens, a woman with a very independent turn of mind and a special interest in the East End; her acts of charity could be fulsome and sometimes even foolhardy. The Victoria Fountain is on her usual grand scale. Over fifty feet high, it is built of red Aberdeen granite, in what Pevsner calls a 'Gothic-cum-Moorish' style. The drinking cups were originally of bronze, silver-plated on the inside and bearing outside the motto 'Temperance is a bridle of gold'. The whole thing cost her nearly £7,000 and makes an extravagant memorial to an extravagant but generous woman. Its original cost, however, has been rather dwarfed by the £12 million revamp to the park in 2011. This included the restoration of not just the Fountain but of several other elements of the original Pennethorne design – including the Old English Garden, the bright red Chinese pagoda on its island in the West Lake, and the bridges that we follow across it – one of them finally bearing his name.

Getting home

Bethnal Green Underground Station: Central Line

Cambridge Heath Station: Liverpool Street

Buses: (from Cambridge Heath Road) 26, 48, 55, 106, 254, 388

12. Around the Bow Back Rivers

FISH ISLAND, PUDDING MILL AND THE GREENWAY

From Hackney to Stratford we are crossing the valley of the River Lea. Here, just a few miles from its confluence with the Thames, the river fans out into a complicated network of channels criss-crossing this broad, shallow valley. It was the site of the inhospitable Stratford marshes, an almost impenetrable barrier between London and the Essex hinterland. For centuries the Old Ford remained the only way across it, until, Queen Maude, said in some stories to have taken a tumble herself into the muddy waters, built the twelfth-century causeway that was later to become the Stratford High Street.

Throughout the twentieth century the semi-drained marsh became a sort of industrial edgeland, a site of depots, waste plots, warehouses, small works and an increasingly toxic soil. Still, for those who knew it, it hid its own exciting secrets: anarchic allotment sites, reed-beds in the shadow of railways, sandpipers flying over muddy tidal channels, skylarks singing above rusting gas holders and the largely undiscovered architectural treasures of Three Mills and the 'cathedral of sewage'. On our route through all these sites we see illustrations of the attitudes towards such marginal lands stretching over several hundred years – and at least three examples of the grand improvement project. The Regents Canal, where we begin this walk, was, in the eyes of its champion John Nash, not so much a commercial venture as an adjunct to his remodelling of London from Piccadilly to Marylebone – a remodelling which has bequeathed us today the Regency splendour of Regents Park, Portland Street and Regents Street. More altruistic in intent was Bazalgette's great sewage disposal system, dealing with one of the most intractable problems of the nineteenth century, a huge Victorian public works programme created to carry London's effluent through miles of embanked sewer encircling the city. Its bequest was not just a major improvement in the sanitation of the City – and a six mile walking route – but a significant impact on the architecture of London, most especially the great Victoria Embankment of central London.

But the most recent, and by far the most visible, of these projects is the 2012 London Olympic Park, and our route along the Greenway runs right through the heart of it. Occupying over 500 acres and stretching for nearly two miles, it was built to host 23,000 athletes from 205 nations and an estimated 9 million visitors during the brief period of the games. An additional building, the size of several aircraft hangars, was built to house a further 20,000 people from the media. The legacy is the Queen Elizabeth Park, and the spreading multi-storey

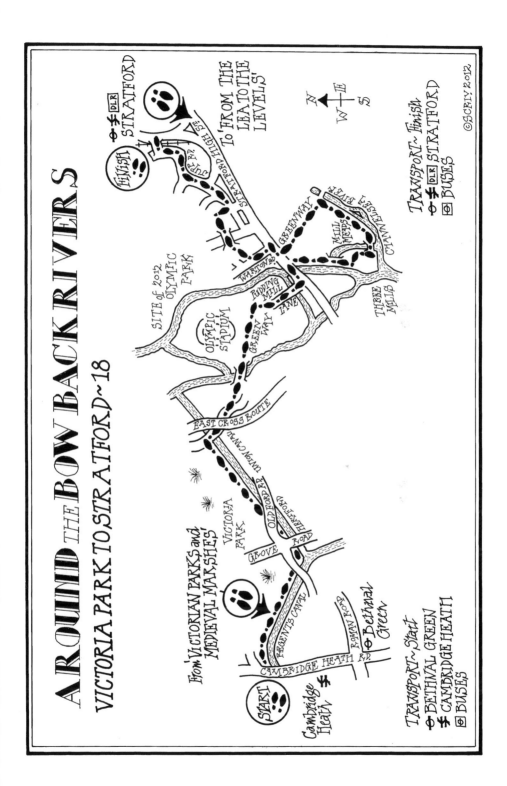

AROUND THE BOW BACK RIVERS
VICTORIA PARK TO STRATFORD ~ 18

'From VICTORIAN PARKS and MEDIEVAL MARSHES'

FINISH

STRATFORD

To 'FROM THE LEA TO THE LEVELS'

SITE of 2012 OLYMPIC PARK

OLYMPIC STADIUM

STRATFORD HIGH St

OLD FORD RD

WARTON RD

RIPPLING MILL

GREEN WAY LANE

GREENWAY

MILL MEADS

THREE MILLS

CHANNELSEA RIVER

EAST CROSS ROUTE

UNION CANAL

VICTORIA PARK

GROVE ROAD

HERTFORD

REGENTS CANAL

ROMAN ROAD

Bethnal Green

CAMBRIDGE HEATH RD

START

Cambridge Heath

TRANSPORT ~ Start
- Ⓣ BETHNAL GREEN
- ☰ CAMBRIDGE HEATH
- ▣ BUSES

TRANSPORT ~ Finish
- Ⓣ ☰ DLR STRATFORD
- ▣ BUSES

N
W E
S

©SCRIV 2012

city that has shot up on its fringes. Perhaps this latest of the grand projects has finally tamed the unruly Lea and its tidal marshlands. But the new site provides its own cautionary tale. The massive ArcelorMittal Orbit, largest artwork in the country, a massive steel tower designed to provide an eye-catching centrepiece to the Olympic Park, was inspired, according to its designer, by the story of the Tower of Babel. And Babel is a story of the dangers of human arrogance, and of the damming results of building too fast and too high.

This chapter covers a single walk of 4 ½ miles stretching from Cambridge Heath Road in Hackney to Stratford Station.

◼ WALK 18: FROM VICTORIA PARK TO STRATFORD

Getting started

From Bethnal Green Underground Station (Central Line):

Take the exit signposted for Cambridge Heath Road (East side) and continue up the road passing the church and the Museum of Childhood on the right.

After approximately ¾ mile, cross the canal bridge just beyond Vyner Street and turn right on to the towpath.

From Cambridge Heath Station (Overground):

From the station exit turn left to cross Hackney Road and continue in the same direction up Cambridge Heath Road for approximately ¼ mile to join the canal on the right hand side just after Vyner Street.

From Buses (26, 48, 55, 106, 254, 388):

Alight on Cambridge Heath Road near the canal bridge, close to the junction with Victoria Park Road

Join the towpath on the opposite side to Andrew's Road, heading towards Victoria Park.

From Walk 17:

Leave Victoria Gate through Rose Gate and turn left along the towpath.

The Regents Canal and the Hertford Union

ROUTE:

- Follow the towpath along the Regents Canal which soon runs alongside Victoria Park. The towpath reaches a hump back bridge at a junction of canals. Take the canal path running off to the left (Hertford Union), which soon rejoins the perimeter of Victoria Park.
- Just after the second lock, and before the towpath passes below the motorway, turn left off the canal up a ramp leading onto the road (Wick Lane).

LOOKING AT WILDLIFE: There is a rich flora along the tow-paths. Lesser skullcap, gypsywort and woundwort grow out of the sides of the canal whilst on the other side of the towpath can be found plants such as fennel, viper's bugloss and wild carrot. These stretches of the canal are also well known for occasionally turning up rare 'alien' species.

FACILITIES: Canal side pub at the towpath exit onto Wick Lane.

In 1803 Thomas Homer, 'a local gentleman', took over the operation of a packet boat service along a branch of the Grand Junction Canal – now known as the Grand Union. The branch, which ran from Uxbridge into Paddington, had turned Paddington into a thriving inland port, and this gave Homer the idea of creating an extension that ran all the way around London to meet the Thames beside the Isle of Dogs – a canal equivalent of the North Circular. It would take trade further into London, avoid the tortuous turns of the tidal river, and link up with the major programme of dock building then going on in East London. The man in charge of that programme, himself a canal engineer, was John Rennie, and it was to Rennie that Homer first pitched his idea. Rennie did indeed come up with a scheme, but it ran too close to central London, thus making the cost of land purchase prohibitive. The persistent Homer did not give up but approached instead the prominent and flamboyant architect and dandy, John 'Beau' Nash. Nash took up the project with relish, delivering between 1812 and 1820 the 8½ mile canal from Paddington to the Regents Canal Dock in Limehouse, where it joins the River Thames.

The Canal's backers were optimistic about its commercial prospects – indeed it was built with double locks along its length in anticipation of particularly high levels of trade. It is probable, however, that this is not primarily what motivated John Nash. He was at that time engaged in a grand project for the complete redesign of a large portion of London. This was an early example of 'regeneration': a master plan backed by the Prince Regent, stretching from Piccadilly as far as Marylebone and on to Primrose Hill, the creation of a city that would rival Napoleon's Paris. Here was housing and parkland for the wealthy – elegant town houses surmounted by statuary, on gracefully curving crescents surrounded by areas of landscaped garden or grassland. And for Nash the canal was the perfect complement, boats gliding by on a waterway through parkland, 'a grand and novel feature in the metropolis'.

Here, towards the eastern end of the canal, there is an extra twist to this story where the Regents Canal meets Victoria Park. Whilst the canal was the work of John Nash, Victoria Park was designed by James Pennethorne – his protégé and adoptive son. Since Nash was rumoured to be 'medically unfit for marriage', it had caused some surprise among court circles when he announced his intention of marrying Mary Ann Bradley, a coal merchant's daughter. Their marriage was punctuated by six strange interludes, during which Mary disappeared from society for a while. Each time she reappeared with a child, which, she said, had been 'given' to her by a poor 'Mrs Pennethorne'. This steady growth in the Nash family was matched by only one thing – John's wealth and status within the court of his friend and patron, the Prince Regent. The Prince was notorious for his immorality and had a house close to Nash's country retreat on the Isle of Wight. This naturally led to a certain amount of unpatriotic speculation about the real origins of the Pennethorne children. By 1820 the Prince Regent had become King George IV and in that year one of the most scandalous manifestations of such speculation was a cartoon showing the half-dressed king embracing Nash's wife whilst uttering the words 'I have great pleasure in visiting this part of my dominions'.

Nash's success was to both rise and fall with that of his patron. During his most productive years he was to name a street, a park and a canal after the Regent. But when King George IV died in 1830 Nash's career was virtually at an end. Here, however, where Nash's Regents Canal meets Pennethorne's Victoria Park, all the characters in this little drama are brought together again.

The hump-backed bridge along the towpath marks a junction. The main canal heads on south through Mile End and Stepney, whilst our route lies to the left, eastwards along the 'Hertford Union'. The early years of the Regents were so successful that in 1830 Sir George Duckett had the idea of launching a private venture that would link the traffic on the Regents Canal to that on the River Lea. His expectations of quick profits were to be disappointed, however, and within a few years he was forced to ask the Regents Canal Company to take the canal off his hands. The Hertford Union – or Duckett's Cut as it is commonly known – joins the two waterways at their closest point, running in a straight line for over a mile between Victoria Park and the rows of warehouses that once supplied timber to East End craftsmen.

There has been an increasing awareness in recent years of the wildlife value of this East London canal network. Despite its murky appearance there are fresh-water sponges on the wooden piles of the locks, swan mussels in the muddy bottoms of the cuts, and wandering snails and fresh-water winkles clinging to the concrete piles of the towpath. These provide food for tufted duck and pochard, and in winter grey wagtail are regular visitors all along the waterways. But it is for their flora that the canals have become best known.

The Regents, the Lea and the Hertford Union provide an urban habitat for the sorts of plants which one would much more readily associate with a quiet pastoral stream: gypsywort, soapwort, hemlock water dropwort, angelica, skullcap and comfrey. In addition there are national rarities and a number of colonising, invading 'aliens'. One of these is a tropical grass, *Paspalum paspalodes*, which is found in only one other place in Britain. Another is an American bur-marigold, *Bidens connata*, which while rare elsewhere has spread all the way along the canal-side from Southall to Bow. The water-borne seeds are clearly washed along until they lodge and take root in crevices in the concrete bank; a practical demonstration of the way in which the canal system provides arteries for the spread of wildlife.

The Olympic Embankment

ROUTE:

- From the top of the canal side ramp, turn left and follow the road beneath the motorway.
- Beyond the motorway bridge, continue ahead along Wick Lane to find the entrance to the Greenway on the left.
- Follow the Greenway over the River Lea and through the Olympic park site.
- Immediately beyond the Olympic site, take the path on the right that slopes down and then passes under the railway to reach Pudding Mill DLR station.

FACILITIES: Cafe and toilets at the 'view tube'.

LOOKING AT WILDLIFE: There is a strange combination of plant species along this length of the Greenway. Plants from neglected planting schemes, such as rosa rugosa, mix with deliberately sown 'wild' flowers including cornflower, sainfoin, viper's bugloss, ox-eye daisy, musk mallow and teasel. Amongst these, and gradually reasserting themselves, are the true self-sown wild flowers of a brownfield site such as goat's rue, common and purple toadflax, white and yellow melilot, lucerne, tansy and everlasting pea. The real speciality here, however, and which has persisted since before the area's redevelopment, is the dwarf elder or danewort, elsewhere a scarce plant in London.

The short stretch of Wick Lane that we follow beyond the canal flanks Fish Island. This is not, in fact, an island but a small area of streets tucked away in an angle where the Hertford Union meets the Lea Navigation – and deriving its name from the fact that many of its streets are named after fish. At the bottom end of Fish Island we encounter the beginning of the Greenway, a pathway that leads through the heart of the Olympic site, and which we also follow in Walk 1. Despite its bucolic name, the embankment we are now standing on carries 100 million gallons of sewage a day, the biggest sewage flow of anywhere in the UK. The embankment and the sewage pipe beneath it were part of another of the grand public realm projects that changed the face of London, whose story is told more fully in Chapter 1. As well as the major works along our walk, the scheme also contributed a defining change to the architecture of central London, with the creation of the Thames embankment.

The Greenway runs along the embankment of the Northern Outfall Sewer, and from here we get our best view of the most recent of our three 'grand projects', the Olympic park site. Set here on what was once Stratford Marsh, it covers 500 acres and stretches for nearly two miles. To the south is the area used for the athletes' warm-up; to the north an assemblage of nine sporting centres, arenas and stadia, some temporary and some permanent, set about the divergent channels of the estuarine Lea. Closest to our route is the main stadium, site of the athletics events as well as the opening and closing ceremonies.

It was designed for a capacity of 80,000 during the Games themselves, thereafter reducing to a more manageable 25,000, its upper layers having been removed, and its final form resembling a fairly unpretentious sunken soup-bowl. Further to the right, the building with the curved roof is the Velodrome, known locally as the Pringle, with, next to it, the Water Polo and the Aquatics Centres. Said to be based on the shape of the wave, it looks like another, junior, pringle.

The combined cost of these sites, together with all the rest of the Olympics expenses, was put at £9.3 billion, three times the original estimate, and something of a bread and circuses approach to the simultaneous recession. It is interesting to compare this with the two previous London Olympics. The first, held in 1908, was originally scheduled to take place in Rome but was transferred to the UK after the eruption of Vesuvius. The second, in 1948, took place shortly after the Second World War and became known as the 'Austerity Games'. In both cases the emphasis was on economy and on the use of facilities already in existence. In the 1948 games, athletes were housed in barracks at Vauxhall and Roehampton, and were even expected to bring their own towels. Perhaps this is the model for a truly sustainable and international Olympics – one that can be based in countries other than the world's few richest nations.

It is, however, the final two structures, off to our left, that stand as icons of the modern Olympic movement and its commercial values. The giant red structure, with a resemblance to a helter-skelter after an earthquake, was designed by Anish Kapoor after London Mayor Boris Johnson had decided that the Olympic site needed 'something extra'. Kapoor originally named it Orbit, but it is now officially known as the ArcelorMittal Orbit – after the steel company owned by its chief sponsor Lakshmi Mittal. The country's largest piece of public art is therefore officially named after the country's richest man. Further away beyond this structure is the great bulk of the Westfield Shopping Centre, described in more detail in Chapter 1.

From Pudding Mill to Three Mills

ROUTE:

- From the front of Pudding Mill Lane Station follow the road that runs straight ahead (Pudding Mill Lane).
- Follow the road until it crosses a river channel and on the far side of the bridge take the footpath following the riverside to the left.
- At the lock gates, just after a junction of channels, climb the flight of steps onto Blaker Road.
- Turn right down Blaker Road and follow it the few yards to the main road (High Street).
- Detour to the left to find the crossing over High Street then back to the right to rejoin the path along the riverside.
- Continue along the path, crossing over another channel and continuing past a park (Three Mills Green).
- Shortly after passing a memorial, the path reaches a junction with a

bridge on the right and a small road running off to the left. It is worth a short detour straight ahead to visit Three Mills but to continue the main walk turn left here.

LOOKING AT WILDLIFE: There is a variety of plant life along both the riverside and the footpath. The river here is, however, no longer tidal, and has lost much of its wildlife as a consequence. There are large carp to be seen in the channel, but these and other introduced species have displaced the original fish population. There are a variety of sown meadow plants in Three Mills Park.

Across Stratford marsh, and not much more than two miles from its confluence with the Thames, the River Lea ramifies into a confusion of tidal channels. They fan out over the broad flat valley which once carried masses of melt-water south from the retreating glaciers of the ice age. City Mill River, Pudding Mill River, Three Mills River, Waterworks River, Channelsea River, Abbey Creek and Prescott Channel together constitute the Bow Back Rivers, finally re-unifying at Bromley-by-Bow to wind a tortuous last half mile into the Thames. It has been the struggle of centuries to control and direct this unruly water.

Pudding Mill was one of the many mills built along these stretches, and operated from medieval times through to the nineteenth century. Not only is the mill now gone, but the channel which operated it, running between Pudding Mill Lane and Marshgate Lane, has also disappeared, though a fragment of its retaining concrete wall can still be made out on the left of Pudding Mill Lane. We soon join another channel, however, along which we reach the City Mill Lock, once a junction between the navigable channels and the tidal Lea. Its isolated lock cottage, on the opposite bank, stood for many years in splendid dilapidation, half-hidden behind encroaching foliage. Despite its surroundings of industrial dereliction it was a site reminiscent of secret childhood fantasies. Today the site has been opened up and the cottage restored, serving as a police command centre during the Olympics.

Crossing Stratford High Street – once the route of Queen Maud's causeway across the area's flat marshlands – we follow the footpath known as 'Short Wall', which continues to follow the river. Alongside the recently revamped Three Mills Park we reach a moving monument to Godfrey Maule Nicholson, George Elliott and Robert Underhill. These three men died whilst successively trying to rescue a fourth man, Thomas Pickett, who had descended into a well and been 'overcome by foul air'. They were all workers at a local distillery to which the well was attached and which occupied the large building ahead of us, Nicholson's Gin Distillery – part of a company founded in the 1730s during the London gin craze. Nicholson was also responsible for an early version of the kind of sponsorship deal so evident in the nearby Olympic Park. After the Company Chairman had funded the MCC's purchase of the Lords Cricket Ground in 1864, as well as the construction of a pavilion there, the club changed its colours to red and yellow – the corporate colour scheme of the gin company. The building today has become the Three Mills Studios, the largest working TV and film studio in the country, where artists such as Robby Williams and Amy Winehouse have recorded.

The studios form part of the wider Three Mills complex, which contains the only mills in the area which have survived to the present day – though there are actually two of them, not three. Mills have stood on the site for at least nine hundred years, for in 1134 they are recorded as having been endowed to the newly founded Abbey of Stratford Langthorne (see chapter 1). The concentration of tidal mills in the valley led to many disputes, as various millers attempted to capture a head of water for their own wheels. The illicit practices of damming or digging new cuts would either reduce the flow for other mills or raise water levels to such a height as to block the wheel altogether. To settle these disputes a 'Court of Sewers' was established, which enforced a legal depth of 4½ feet for the millers' channels. The mills ground corn for the local bakeries until 1734, when a new trade was established. In that year Peter Lefeuvre agreed with others to become 'co-partners, joint traders and dealers together in the several arts, trades or mysteries of meal men, corn factors, millers and distillers'. From that time on the mills ground corn to serve the distilleries.

Daniel Bisson was one of the partners in this enterprise, and built the present House Mill in 1776. We approach it from behind, passing a yard overgrown with the pink-flowered Himalayan balsam. It once housed as many as four mill wheels and twelve millstones. Milling continued here up to 1941, but the site suffered heavy bomb damage, including the complete destruction of the attractive Miller's House. Following the war the site remained neglected for many years, and one of the best-kept secrets in London, but has now been beautifully restored by River Lea Tidal Mills Trust. Clock Mill, facing it across the flagstone way, stands beside two broad channels of the Lea, where mute swans swim under the old sack hoists and a causeway carries the towpath down to Bow Locks and the Limehouse Cut. Clock Mill dates from 1817, though the handsome, octagonal clock-tower is older, and may well have survived from an earlier weather-boarded mill. With its handsome oast-house drying towers it is appropriate perhaps that it was saved by a brewery, for the mill was restored in 1970s when it became, for a time, offices for Bass Charrington.

Around Mill Meads

ROUTE:

- Turn left on the small road just beyond the memorial (or right if you are returning from a detour to the Three Mills site) and follow the road alongside the black railings to reach a pedestrian gate at the end.
- Go through the gate to reach the riverside beside the Three Mills Lock.
- Turn right beside the river to reach and cross the footbridge. From the footbridge follow the path, overgrown in places, that runs alongside the channel, keeping to the right and closest to the river at any junctions.
- The path eventually climbs up to join the Greenway. Turn left and follow the Greenway embankment to reach Stratford High Street.
- Cross the main road and turn right.

- Take the first turning on the left (Warton Road) and after approximately a hundred yards take the path on the right (Friendship Way).
- Follow the path between the flats and a school to reach and cross Carpenters Road.
- From the bottom of the ramp on the far side of the footbridge, take the path on the right leading through the estate.
- The path leads on to a stub of road and then on to a T junction. Turn left here on Jupp Road West which soon becomes Jupp Road and leads to a footbridge over the railway.

To join Walk 1 or to complete this walk:

Cross over the railway and turn left to reach Stratford Station and bus station.

LOOKING AT WILDLIFE: A variety of birds can be seen from time to time on the still tidal channel, including heron, grey wagtail and common sandpiper. Here too there are reed beds and marshland plant species mixing with the introduced Himalayan balsam along the muddy margins. The path is lined with willows and poplars and there are some interesting patches of butcher's broom. The Greenway embankment contains the same strange mix of natural and sown plant species as the previous stretch, including St John's wort, lucerne and sainfoin.

The route from Three Mills along the side of the studios brings us back to the river. We are now beside the Prescott Channel and the massive Three Mills Lock. This was built to replace the earlier and much smaller Prescott Lock, and to allow for the passage of 350 ton barges, delivering material for the Olympic construction site. It also formed the key part of the barrage impounding the waters of the upstream Lea. There are eight kilometres of waterway across the Olympic site and until recently these were tidal. In order to provide a more conventionally attractive site, and to create both residential moorings and desirable riverside properties, they are now maintained by the barrage at permanent high-tide level. The Olympic developers changed much about the Lea, removing masses of debris – including 3 tons of tyres, 40 motorbikes and 120 shopping trolleys – and creating new wetland sites. They also, however, succumbed to the nation-wide trend of destroying estuarine sites, and in so doing of damaging vital ecosystems, whilst increasing the long-term risk of flooding and pollution. Tidally revealed mud is one of the richest of habitats, and its destruction entails the loss of a myriad of invertebrate species as well as the birds that depend on them. It remains to be seen whether fish returning up the river to spawn, such as the shoals of bream that were once seen here, will be able to use the fish ladders provided in the Lock. The fact is, however, that the warmer temperatures of the impounded upstream waters has already led to their place being taken by large introduced fish such as common and mirror carp.

After crossing the Prescott Channel – over a strikingly high footbridge – we are following the 'Long Wall', an ancient footpath that runs between the

Channelsea River and the site of Mill Meads. Here, below the barrage, the muddy banks of the tidal riverside support stands of yellow flag iris, Himalayan balsam and great hairy willow herb. Common sandpiper can be seen flying along the channel in the autumn migration period and herons feed at low tide. All this is framed by a landscape of pylons, gas works and tube lines on the further shore. The seven nineteenth-century gas holders once formed part of the old Bromley-by-Bow gasworks, but the site has a peculiar history. Here in 1817 the East India Company built a factory for the production of the first military rockets, the invention of William Congreve, designed for use by the British army in India. From 1813 there were two regular Rocket Troops in the British army supplied with Congreve's weapons and they even played a minor part in the Battle of Waterloo. Here, from the East End, came the very beginnings of rocket technology, a technology which just over a hundred years later was to send the V1s and V2s back again in far more deadly fashion.

On this side of the river, Mill Meads once formed the rich waterside meadows of the Stratford Langthorne Abbey. For many years they remained a large and rather eccentric open space, where trail-bikers defeated every attempt to deny them access but somehow failed to deter the wealth of wildlife there, which included strangely urban pheasants alongside skylarks, yellowhammers and brambling. Today this has given way to a new generation of sewage works. Bazalgette built his initial system when the population of London was still only 2.5 million – and he had the foresight to build it for a population of 4 million. But with the population now exceeding twice that number, his network has become inadequate. To relieve the overstretched system – and the increasing problem of sewage spillage into the Thames – the Lee Tunnel has been dug from here, running for four miles from the Abbey Mills works to sewage treatment works at Beckton. It follows the route of the old sewer embankment but runs deep below it, as much as 75 metres in places, and thus constitutes the deepest tunnel in London. An even bigger project will be the planned London Tideway Tunnel, a fourteen mile system to run from here along the line of the Limehouse Cut and then the River Thames, as far as Richmond and Ealing. Its exact route – and the siting of its various ventilation shafts – remains highly contentious.

Looking across these works you are able to compare two generations of public service buildings. In the foreground is the modern, onion shaped pumping station, built in 1997 in gaudy silver. Behind it is the Victorian version, the magnificent and original Abbey Mills Sewage Pumping Station. It is one of the most remarkable buildings in London (though somewhat obscured at the time of writing by the razor wire that surrounds the tunnel construction site and makes it look like a high security prison). Though it is known locally as 'the cathedral of sewage', the name is misleading, for, with its dome, coloured bricks, fancy tile-work, dressed stone, piers and columns and carved capitals, it has more the atmosphere of one of the great mosques of Istanbul. It even had minarets once, but these outlying two-hundred-foot octagonal chimneys were demolished in World War Two, when it was feared they were serving as landmarks for enemy bombers. All this – and the famous interior iron work – was built to Joseph Bazalgette's design between 1865 and 1868, its job to pump the sewage down the Outfall Sewer to Beckton.

Along the Greenway, with the high chimneys of the cottages provided for gas workers visible on our right, we reach the final few streets into Stratford, a once industrial centre turned sudden high rise city on the back of the Olympic development. It is not to everyone's taste. In his book *Ghost Milk*, Iain Sinclair describes it as 'a haemorrhaging road crash' of an area and goes on to assert that:

> the urban landscape of boroughs anywhere within the dust cloud of the Olympic Park has been devastated with a beat-the-clock impatience unrivalled in London since the beginning of the railway age. Every civic decency, every sentimental attachment, is swept aside for that primary strategic objective, the big bang of the starter's pistol.

This is not, of course, the first indignity to be heaped on Stratford, with its earlier concentration of 'noxious' industries that were banned from within the City of London, while the route which we follow along Walton Road was once known as 'stink bomb alley'. But nothing can have been so rapid or so striking as this recent transformation. On the eve of the Olympics, as the Qatari-owned property development, where even a bedsit costs half a million, was anticipating its influx of young professionals, the surrounding streets bore stickers in their windows proclaiming, hopelessly enough, 'Save Our Estate'. Perhaps the final symbolic indignity was the routing of Olympic Marathon – originally planned to run through the East End, but then moved to the more photogenic West End, to finish in Hyde Park instead of the usual grand culmination in the main Olympic Stadium.

Getting home

Stratford Station: Network Rail (Liverpool Street), Underground (Central line, Jubilee line), DLR, London Overground.

Stratford Bus Station: 25, 69, 86, 97, 104, 108, 158, 238, 241, 257, 262, 276, 308, 339, 425, 473

Index